Please Note:

This book is a tract – a rather elaborate Christian tract.
A testimony of praise and thanksgiving to God for saying:
"Be a medical missionary" to an eleven-year-old farm boy.
Responding to that call is my life's story
presented here as an autobiography.

Every thought and action for ninety years
has been molded by these four words.
You are invited to thumb through and glance at some
pictures that may prompt a perusal of the script.

For me, recording this deeply personalized account is
presently the only way I know of being able to share the
impact of God's love on my life. I sincerely want to share
the message of salvation through Jesus Christ.

The "Basis for My Faith" is found in Chapter 92.

BE A MEDICAL MISSIONARY

By

Lowell A. Gess, B.D., M.D.

Copyright © 2012 by Dr. Andrew Gess.
All rights reserved. No part of this book may be reproduced in any form or by any electronic or mechanical means, including information storage and retrieval systems, without permission in writing from Dr. Andrew Gess, except by a reviewer who may quote brief passages in a review.

First Edition
First Printing: 2012
ISBN # 978-0-615-52651-5

Graphic/layout design and pre-press production:
Spectrum Marketing Services, Alexandria, MN

Books may be purchased for $15 (plus $5 for shipping and handling) from:

Dr. Lowell Gess
111 15th Avenue East
Alexandria, MN 56308
lowellgess@gmail.com or gessla@charter.net
320-762-1888 or 320-815-6855

Dedication

To Ruth

(written in 2002)

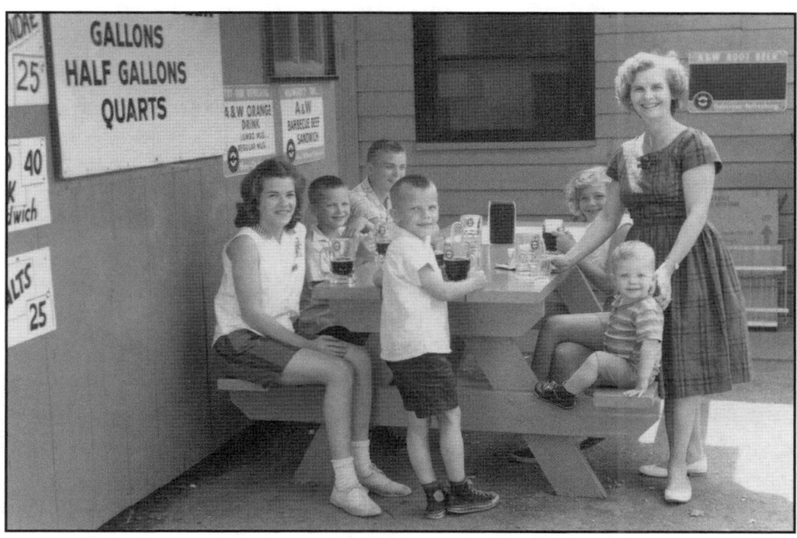

My dearest, please hear me while there is yet life and breath. I thank God that out of all the people in the world we found each other and that we had the privilege of growing in our love, which has gotten better and sweeter with the passing years. I love you more today than ever before.

Besides being the love of my heart, in all your winsome ways, you have been an ideal mother as well as wife. You were willing to leave the country of your birth to share your and my calling of a healing ministry in the name of Jesus Christ. It has been such a joy to bring people new physical sight and spiritual insight into the love of God through our work from day to day.

Our children could have had no more wonderful a mother than you. You were there for them from their earliest years when they reached out their hands and hearts. They knew security and understanding.

It may have taken a little longer to do the baking with all those little "helping" hands, but you were not only fashioning a cake, you were helping to mold precious lives.

As the Lord continued to open new doors to us, you simply bundled the family together and we took off for Africa where we were to spend the best part of our lives. You always made do, whether it was as teacher to our children or the making of clothes or sifting little visitors out of the flour.

You were a nurse administrator par excellence with an uncanny intuition in understanding the character of staff applicants.

Above all, you made things happen ... a true helpmate!

Never once did I hear you complain that I wasn't doing my best to make provision for you – even when our annual income was less than $3,000 for a family of six. We were immensely rich spiritually.

For all these blessings I am deeply grateful. You have blessed me in a way I never thought possible.

We look to the Lord for His continued leadership and grace in the days that He yet allows us together, for we hold to the promise that we are *"...Heirs together of the grace of life."* 1 Peter 3:7

I am happy that it was possible to give this tribute while you were still able to appreciate and comprehend it. You need to know of my deep love for you as well as for our children. You have exemplified the commendation of Jesus. You have done *"what you could."* Mark 14:8

God uniquely created you. Your husband, children, grandchildren, and all your friends and patients thank God for your wonderful and long life.

Ruth, you and I have enjoyed recalling past memories and experiences, and yet we are encouraged by the apostle Paul, *"We are forgetting those things which are behind, and reaching forth unto those things which are before, (we) press toward the mark for the prize of the high calling of God in Christ Jesus."* Phillipians 3:13-14

It is still our firm conviction that we face a humanity too precious to neglect.

We know a remedy for the ills of the world that is too wonderful to withhold.

We have a Christ who is too glorious to hide.

We have an adventure that is too thrilling to miss.

Foreword

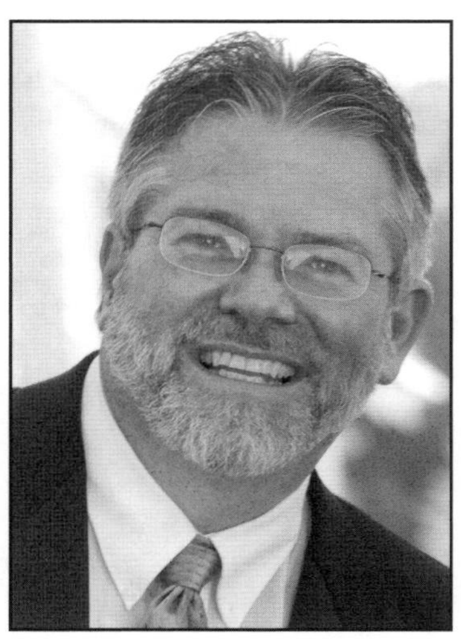

My dad is a good storyteller. When I was in first grade I shared a room with a number of other missionary kids at the boarding school we attended. Occasionally, when parents came to visit, one would volunteer to tuck us in and tell a story. Dad was always a favorite. I remember the squeals of delight whenever "Uncle Lowell" volunteered to regale us with a tale.

But when I first approached my dad with the idea of writing a book, it was not primarily because he was a good storyteller; it was because he had such interesting – and important – stories to tell. We, his family, had heard most of his stories (and many of us, in fact, had lived them with him). But these stories needed to be told and shared with others. This he did in his first book, *Mine Eyes Have Seen the Glory.*

Later, as my dad began to reflect and marvel at the growth and spread of the gospel, particularly in Africa and specifically within the denomination that he had served in, he felt that story also needed to be told. He documented this in his second book, *Glorious Witnesses for Africa.*

This book, however, is more personal. Not only does my dad share some of the missionary experiences that cover more than a half-century of service to medical missions, but he also shares more of the personal stories of his life. These stories provide the backdrop of the unfolding drama of his life's work.

My dad grew up in a time (and rural culture) that is fascinating and – though common to them – is extremely unique to us in many ways. For one, life in the U.S. and in Minnesota was quite provincial. Not many in his community travelled or even dreamed of travelling to overseas locations, let alone the African continent. That is why it is so noteworthy when my dad talks about his "call" to medical missions. However, as interesting as reading his upbringing is (and as helpful that upbringing might have been to his success as a missionary doctor), it is simply the backdrop for another important message. The important message is that God calls some of the most common people (with common upbringings) to the most extraordinary tasks. This is reflected in his life and it is reflected in the lives of most of the heroic Biblical figures. God calls ordinary people to extraordinary things if we are willing to yield to His will.

In the telling of his life, my dad refers to various turning points. He describes these as the pivots upon which his life turned and which most contributed to the story that he lived. Certainly the most important, as he would say, was his conversion experience as a boy and subsequent call to serve the Lord as a medical missionary. It is clear that his life would have been different if he had not yielded to God's specific call to medical missions. But to Dad, it would have been a life of disobedience, so strong and so clear was his sense of leading from the Lord. The good news, however, is that he did yield, he did obey, he did serve – and that has made all the difference.

Please enjoy reading this story about a man (my dad) and a woman (my mom) who came from humble beginnings but who – because of their yieldedness to God – made a huge impact on the lives of tens of thousands of people in Africa and around the world.

Dr. Andrew Gess
Arden Hills, MN

Foreword

Presently I am ninety-four years "young." Lowell is four years my junior. I have known him since he was born. His father and my mother were brother and sister. We lived on farms at the opposite ends of a section. If one were to follow the sides of a right triangle (Pythagoras' Theorem), it was two miles to visit each other. Travelling by the hypotenuse, it was less than a mile and a half. Our families visited each other at least once a week. My father cut Lowell's hair until he was ready for high school. Lowell's favorite dish was my mother's chicken fricassee.

In spring and summer we played softball. Later in life Lowell was to make a mark for himself as a fastball pitcher. We began skating at about the time we learned how to walk. In winter, hockey was the main interest. In college, Lowell played against Mariucci, the outstanding University of Minnesota hockey player after whom the arena is named.

After serving in the navy during World War II, I went into the business world, ending up as a John Deere vice president. Lowell attended seminary and medical school in preparation for medical missions. We lost contact for a while, being on separate continents. However, in recent years we often have telephone conversations. When Jean Anne, my wife, died several years ago, I had to learn how to cook. When Lowell's wife, Ruth, became incapacitated four years ago, I had the pleasure of helping him learn how to cook acceptable meals. This is significant, as Lowell had never before prepared a meal in his entire life.

We love each other and have been blessed with long and enjoyable lives.

Frederick (Bud) Heitke
Minneapolis, MN

Acknowledgements

This memoir, *Be a Medical Missionary*, would not have been attempted or brought to completion had it not been for the friendship and help of Ms. Amy Krammes. I thank God for her literary, organizational, grammatical, editing and spiritual skills. She received raw material and then fashioned a finished product. It has been a privilege to be associated with her.

It was wonderful to receive the encouragement and help of our youngest son, Andrew. I tried to follow his advice. I was thrilled with the pictures that he made available for the cover as well as for the text.

It was kind of my cousin, Frederick Heitke, to be willing to be identified with me in our growing up together.

Appreciation is given to Sheryl Waldhauser who spent many hours transcribing from a tape recorder to the computer the material of this autobiography.

From Spectrum Printing, Sue Thoen has been especially cooperative and supportive throughout the vagaries of the three different books that she has overseen. Becky Wangsness has provided her design and layout expertise to both this book and *Glorious Witnesses for Africa*, for which I am very grateful.

I still remember the encouragement that Ruth gave even when she was greatly weakened and already being cared for in the Diamond Willow Nursing Home.

I thank my children for their enthusiasm and participation in helping me complete this book.

Finally, I thank God for the presence and awareness of the Holy Spirit that prompted a deep sense of gratitude for the step-by-step directions for an extended life. However, humble, I was allowed to speak and work for my Lord and Savior, Jesus Christ. It was a great joy to assist the blind to see as well as being able to share the Gospel for new creations.

> *"If anyone is in Christ, he is a new creation, the old has gone, the new has come!" II Corinthians 5:17*

Editor's Note

Amy Krammes and her daughter, Lillie.

Lowell entered my life just over a year ago. His youngest son and daughter-in-law, Andrew and Carrie, had invited my daughter and me up to their Lake Miltona cabin just a few miles north of Alexandria for the 4th of July weekend. Carrie and Andrew had been friends of mine for nearly a decade and had told stories of Lowell volunteering on the mission field well into his eighties, but I had never met him in person.

I was charmed. He was so gracious, inquiring after my family and profession. Andrew piped up and said I was a freelance writer and editor. Lowell quickly asked, "Perhaps you could help me with my book?" Initially I demurred, as editing a book seemed daunting, a task I didn't feel equipped to attempt.

A few months later, I had lunch with Carrie who said that Lowell was still very interested in my help. I was between projects at the time – and Lowell's story intrigued me – so I took on the assignment. Called *Glorious Witnesses for Africa*, the book chronicles the explosive growth of the Christian Church in Sub-Saharan Africa told through the eyes of missionaries who witnessed it in person and were personal friends of Lowell.

Within a few weeks of publication, Lowell asked if I would help him with his autobiography – *Be a Medical Missionary* – the third book in his writing series. I happily said, "yes," as it had been such a delight to work with him and he had grown so dear to me.

I have been both humbled and blessed to be on this journey with him – and I wouldn't be writing this small narrative if he hadn't insisted that I, too, "have a word." My job, through both books, has been to take what Lowell has sent and give it a little more order and shape, clean up a few things here and there, and provide a suggestion or two. (There may be a few things I missed, and for those I am truly sorry.) My hope and prayer through it all has been to do justice in presenting Lowell's life and work – and most of all, to underscore how good and faithful God is and has been. All glory and honor to Him!

Amy L. Krammes
Minneapolis, MN

Table of Contents

Part III: A World to Serve

Part IV: Ruth

Part V: Our Children

Part VI: Favorite Stories

Preface

"Daddy, tell us a story about when you were a boy."

There was a time when our six children were interested in my childhood. The stories I told over and over were mostly about my dog, Sport. He was my constant companion on the farm. When he was put-down because he was a suspected sheep-killer, my nine-year-old heart was devastated. Tears would flow almost every time I repeated the tale.

The boys liked the stories about gopher hunting, first with snares and later with an eleven dollar bolt action .22 rifle, which is the only gun I still possess having given away eleven other rifles and shotguns to my three older sons. (Andrew declared he was not a hunter, so I gave him a .32 revolver that had been my father's.)

The girls preferred other happenings, like my riding on the running board that supported the battery for my dad's car, or trying to drive the car when I was so young that I lacked the strength to control it and ran into the grain binder.

Other experiences followed. This memoir attempts to recall some of them. It remains to be seen if, as adults with children of their own, they have any interest in them as I tell them now in my ninetieth year.

I am calling this a memoir, which is a report or record of events based on the writer's highly personal observation and first-hand knowledge presented as an autobiographical account – and hopefully done so in a scholarly and appropriate manner.

When young, our children didn't know much of Ruth's and my background. Yet, I feel as my time on earth grows to a close, the events need to be told. I feel compelled to record the happenings that were part of God's plan for our lives, happenings too big to be ignored.

To Ruth's and my knowledge, our six children never verbally questioned why they were subjected to life on a foreign soil. From an early age and on up to young adulthood they were submerged in Africa. They were living at a time in a place when the Christian Church was experiencing a momentous growth in Sub-Saharan Africa.

In the following pages, there is an accounting of my active ministry and the chronicling of my journey of faith from the very earliest years. Thirty years were involved in preparing for a medical missionary career. Eighteen years were spent in an active medical missionary practice as missionaries commissioned by the United Methodist Church. During the thirty-four years that followed, we volunteered in Africa and other countries.

Originally *Be a Medical Missionary* was to be entitled *The Bible, a Softball, and an IOL*, as these items shaped my life in an unusual way.

The Bible. The first two songs I memorized and sang as a child were "Jesus Loves Me" and "The B-I-B-L-E":

> The B-I-B-L-E is just the Book for me;
> I stand alone on the Word of God,
> The B-I-B-L-E.

The Bible was part of my life. Through the years it has been my guide. The Bible was read daily in my home when I was growing up and I memorized verses and passages. In fact, my father was on his third reading through the entire Bible at the time of his death (admitting to skipping some of the "begats").

I cherished the Bible my Sunday School at the Salem Evangelical Church in Paynesville, Minnesota, gave to me. Students in every grade of my one-room school read the Bible. We had Bible clubs in high school at Calvary Evangelical Church. In college, we had a Bible study in the visitor's quarters of the dormitory. It was the central theme of study during seminary training at the Evangelical Theological Seminary in Naperville, Illinois, from 1942 to 1945. At medical school, I was part of an impressive Bible study group. In Nigeria, I was nicknamed "The doctor with the Bible."

I was always eager to gain new insight and understand the meaning of scripture passages. This involved supplying my library with different translations. At the present time, I have forty Bibles, sixteen New Testaments, one Hausa Bible and one Creole New Testament.

Through the years, we repeatedly read through *Hurlbut's Story of the Bible* to our growing family. Our oldest son, Tim, heard it over and over again with the addition of each new sibling. In his Old Testament course at Westmar University in Le Mars, Iowa, he received an "A" without any additional studying.

The Bible was and is central to my life.

A Softball. Who would have known that when I accidentally learned how to throw a softball underhanded as swiftly as overhanded, unbelievable opportunities and experiences would open up to me? The following pages of this memoir will turn up this fact again and again.

An Intraocular Lens. The discovery in ophthalmology that a special type of plastic could replace a cataractous eye lens had another tremendous impact on my life. I was serving as a medical missionary in the underdeveloped third world when I learned about this procedure from friend Mr. Peter Choyce in England. He had been the resident assistant to Mr. Harold Ridley, the pioneer of intraocular lens implantation.

With fifteen sterile intraocular lenses in my suitcase on my return to Alexandria, Minnesota, in 1976, a program was launched that expanded into surrounding states and ultimately took me to fourteen countries of the world to teach others how the procedure was done.

Undergirded by prayer, more things are wrought than this world dreams. So it is my heart's prayer that my children, grandchildren and great-grandchildren will first and foremost profoundly know and accept Jesus Christ as their personal savior; second, that they will grow in their faith and knowledge of Him; and third, they will be inspired, as Ruth and I were, to "go into all the world and preach the gospel." Hopefully others, through the reading of these pages, will be inspired to do so also.

In His service,

Lowell A. Gess, B.D., M.D.
July 13, 2011

Part I: The Calling

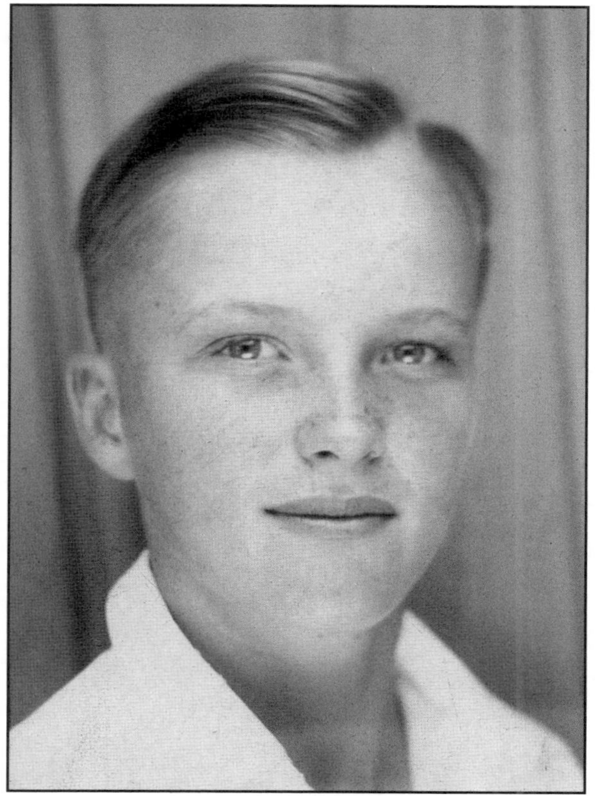

Lowell, age eleven, at the time of his calling.

Then I heard the voice of the Lord saying,
"Whom shall I send? And who will go for us?"
And I said, "Here am I. Send me!"
He said, "Go and tell the people. . . ."

–Isaiah 6:8-9a

Chapter One

"Be a Medical Missionary"

"Grandpa, does God talk to you?" This was a serious question, as it came from one of my grandchildren who was a philosophy major. "Did God tell you to be a medical missionary?" I answered, "It wasn't like what happened to Charlton Heston as Moses in *The Ten Commandments* when he encountered the burning bush. It was more like Abraham receiving the message 'Leave your country, your people and your father's household and go to the land I will show you.' (Genesis 12:1) While God did not tell Abraham which country it would be, in my 'burning bush' encounter I distinctly was made aware of Africa and becoming a medical missionary."

I had that encounter when I was eleven years old. Salem Evangelical Church (Evangelische Gemeinschaft), a church similar to Lorraine E. Pierce's description of evangelical churches in her excellent book *Marching Through Immanuel's Ground*, was having its annual fall evangelistic meetings. Prayer meetings were conducted to prepare for the services. I was enjoying the message from a dynamic pastor. My soul was at peace, as two years earlier I had stepped forward during an evangelistic service, knelt at the church altar and received forgiveness of sins and newness of life in Christ Jesus.

The message included Hannah's dedication of Samuel to the Lord, the calling of the apostles and the response of Paul to a lifetime of ministry. The pastor challenged: "What is God calling you to do? How are you going to live your life?" Under the spell and emotion of the moment there came an awareness of an inner message of "be a medical missionary." This was so strong that in submission I went forward and knelt at the communion rail and prayed, "Thy will be done." In the testimony period that followed I was asked about my coming forward. I simply answered that I was being "given direction for my life." That message, **"Be a medical missionary"** was so strong and strange that I decided to not confide in anyone – including parents and counselors. The more I thought about it, the less I wanted to acknowledge it. I simply would be in full time Christian service.

Yet, during the service, we had sung "I'll Go Where You Want Me To Go":

It may not be on the mountain height,
Or over the stormy sea;
It may not be at the battle's front
My Lord will have need of me;

But if by a still, small voice
He calls to paths that I do not know,
I'll answer, dear Lord, with my hand in Thine,
I'll go where you want me to go.

Perhaps today there are loving words
Which Jesus would have me speak;
There may be now, in the paths of sin,
Some wand'rer whom I should seek.
O Savior, if Thou wilt be my Guide,
Tho' dark and rugged the way,
My voice shall echo the message sweet,
I'll say what you want me to say.

There's surely somewhere a lowly place
In earth's harvest-fields so wide,
Where I may labor thro' life's short day
For Jesus, the Crucified.
So, trusting my all to Thy care,
I know Thou lovest me!
I'll do Thy will with a heart sincere,
I'll be what you want me to be.

Chorus:
I'll go where you want me to go, dear Lord,
O'er mountain, or plain, or sea;
I'll say what you want me to say, dear Lord,
I'll be what you want me to be.

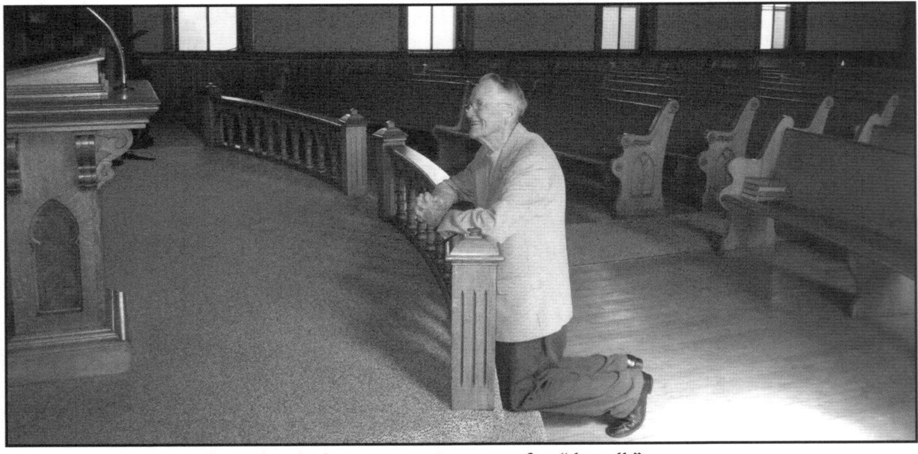

Kneeling at the same Salem Church altar seventy-nine years after "the call."

Incredible! Is it possible for an eleven year old to receive a "call" to medical missions in Africa – a Minnesota farm boy half a world away from that vast continent? Except for informatiaon I received in grade school, I knew nothing about Africa. However, I knew about missions. As Dean S. Gilliland stated in "My Pilgrimage in Mission" in 2000, "My denomination, the Evangelical Church, had a program for mission education at all levels. In 1948 this group became the Evangelical United Brethren (EUB) and later in 1968 merged with the Methodist Church to become the United Methodist Church. As a child, it was impossible not to know about missions." I, too, was fully aware of Livingston, Cary, Borden of Yale, Judson, Paul White and others. I had never seen or talked to a live African missionary, but the "cause of missions" was ever before me. Would anyone believe that God would speak to a boy whose only activities were cultivating corn and playing softball? I continued to keep " the call" to myself.

Unlike the Old Testament Samuel, I did not make further inquiry. I would not have said, "Speak, for your servant is listening" (I Samuel 3:10). Most assuredly I would not have said, "Here am I, send me" (Isaiah 6:8). Africa was far away. To my boyish mind it was dark and dangerous. I had no intention of leaving home and friends. I would not be a medical missionary.

It was to be another ten years before I would share with parents, Sunday school teachers, pastors, counselors and friends that I had received an unmistakable call to medical missions.

Lake Koronis Assembly Grounds had a tremendous impact upon my life. I was able to attend the LKAG summer meetings every year for the first twenty-one

The youth group from Calvary Evangelical Church at Koronis. I am second from right, front row. Standing behind me with a white shirt is Russell Praetorius, my best catcher. He became an outstanding preacher, following in the footsteps of his bishop father, E. W. Praetorius.

years of my life, having been carried to the first meeting as a babe in arms. My father, Arthur Gess, along with Pastor P. A. Long and Mr. William C. Miller, had the privilege of stepping-out the boundaries of the original assembly grounds. As a lad of fifteen, I walked down the straw covered aisle in Billy Graham-style to dedicate my life to Christian service. It was assumed that I was heading for the pastoral ministry. (It would be another eight years, however, before I actually had a meeting with Billy Graham.)

Purposefully, I avoided any subjects in college that related to medicine. One science course was required for graduation. I chose geology, the study of rocks, the farthest subject away from information relating to the human body and the pursuit of medicine. However, on the way to the Evangelical Theological Seminary to begin seminary training, I stopped at Lake Geneva in Wisconsin to rest. While sitting on the shore of that beautiful lake, I prayed. I came to realize that if I didn't honor the Lord in His calling, He might not be able to use me effectively in the pastoral ministry.

With this new commitment to prepare for medical missions, I was required to pick up physics, comparative anatomy, chemistry, and the other premedical requirements for medicine. I took these classes during my years at the Evangelical Theological Seminary in Naperville, Illinois, and two summer courses at Garrett Theological Seminary in Evanston, Illinois.

Upon completion of seminary and premedical work, I was accepted to the University of Illinois Medical School. World War II, however, drew so many pastors into the service that I agreed to fill a pastorate for two years in Minnesota. These were wonderful years. Ruth and I were married. We served the St. Cloud-Graham congregation as well as at the Mayer Evangelical Church. We even began our family. Unknown to me during this time, the medical school in Illinois was being overwhelmed with premedical applications from Illinois war veterans – and I was dropped from their queue.

After all the years of preparation I was finally ready to begin training as a medical missionary – and there was no place to go. It seemed that all returning veterans had decided to study medicine. My application to be one of eighty admissions to the Washington University School of Medicine in St. Louis, Missouri, was but one of more than 5,000!

Had I really been called to medical missions? Obviously, there was no place to begin. Some forty years later, Merlin Schendel, son of Pastor E. M. Schendel, told me something he had remembered from his childhood. His father prayed that Lowell Gess would be accepted into medical school to fulfill his calling. Applications were made to other medical schools but rejections came from all but one. I felt led to write to the dean of admissions at the remaining school, the Washington University School of Medicine (which was the fourth highest ranked medical school in the United States) to inquire of my status. It already was past mid-August 1946, and the new class was to begin in September. No word had been received as to acceptance or rejection. Within several days a letter of acceptance was received and medical training became a reality.

It was not until I was halfway through medical school that I learned from the dean the details of my acceptance. The mail that brought my letter of inquiry also brought a letter from a previously accepted student who decided not to attend. The dean simply handed my letter to his secretary, "Let this applicant have the opening." Providential? Perhaps the 4,920-plus remaining applicants didn't have prayer warriors interceding on their behalf.

After three years in Nigeria I was given the opportunity of taking a surgical residency to equip me for a new surgical program at the Hatfield-Archer Hospital at Rotifunk, Sierra Leone, West Africa. There we met a multitude of people needing surgery. Many among them were blind patients. Ultimately a three-year ophthalmology residency equipped me for a bona fide eye outreach in Sierra Leone. During the next forty-six year period, Ruth and I spent all or part of the year in Sierra Leone. In all, we crossed the Atlantic 182 times.

The foreseeable future is filled with plans for the continuing evangelical outreach through medicine and surgery at the Kissy UMC Eye Hospital, Freetown, Sierra Leone, as well as the Zing Eye Centre in Zing, Nigeria, and the Mutumbara Hospital in Zimbabwe.

I humbly thank God for His wonderful kindness and compassion. It is an immeasurable joy to minister to the blind and bless them with physical sight and spiritual insight into the love of God as revealed through Jesus Christ, our Lord.

God called Ruth and me, not to bestow on us greater honor, greater prestige or greater glory on this earth: God called us for a greater task and for a greater service. We served God by serving others. We were saved to serve.

"We preach not ourselves, but Christ Jesus the Lord; and ourselves your servants for Jesus' sake." II Corinthians 4:5

Chapter Two

Early Years

The photo my dad carried of my mother before they were married.

Born July 13, 1921, I grew up on an 80-acre dairy farm four miles north of Paynesville, Minnesota. We had a herd of thirty-three purebred Guernsey cows, each having her own name. The rich milk was bottled and hand delivered to clients in town. It was hard work. Even harder was the cleaning and sterilizing of the equipment, a job that fell to my mother. In retirement years, Dad almost wept when he reminisced of life on the farm and how hard Mother had worked, never with a word of complaint.

All dressed up to go into Paynesville four miles away.

My memories are nearly all happy ones. For me, the farm was a perfect playground with cats in the barn, piglets, lambs, new-born chicks, and my dog, Sport, who was a constant companion. Sport would accompany me when I had to go out at night to close the chicken coup. His death was perhaps the most traumatic episode in my life to that point. Some kind of animal was killing sheep on a neighboring farm and the farmer had shot Sport in retaliation. I had found Sport lying next to a fence after he had been shot. When the killing continued, it proved to my young heart that Sport had been innocent.

My sister, June, and I had a great friend in Sport.

I loved to ride with my father in his Model-T milk delivery truck. On one three-mile trip to a neighbor, he determined that I could not accompany him. Secretly, I positioned myself on the running board, held onto the battery box and made the trip without falling off when we rounded perilous corners. On arrival, he was too astonished to see me to think of a punishment.

I watched carefully how the car was started, engaged and driven. On one occasion I took a ride. Turning the steering wheel proved too much for my

Sitting on the Model-T's running board on which I sneaked a three-mile ride.

Mother had her hands full with June and me.

strength and I ran into a grain binder. My fear was not of my father, but my Uncle Arlie who owned half of the binder.

My farm work consisted of feeding silage to the cows. The Pine Tree milking machine was too cumbersome for me to handle. However, I was able, at an early age, to drive horses and cultivate corn for endless hours. We never owned a tractor, that new contraption some rich farmers were getting. We used horses and often they were obstinate. I knew the words that would bring them to life, words that I feared in later life might come out if I were given a general anesthetic. To date, I don't seem to have shocked anyone.

The strongest and liveliest of all our horses was Nellie. On the way home from the field one day I decided to hitch a ride and climbed on her back. Everything went well until we neared the barn that had an open, narrow and low side door. Sensing there was hay and oats inside, Nellie took off at a gallop – and I could not stop her. Nearing the door, I spread out prone on her back and miraculously was not knocked off while going through the door.

Nellie and I had our differences. While drawing the cultivator, she liked to reach down and nip the tops off the growing corn. This would compel me to use the whip and some choice words. On another occasion when I was feeding corn stalks to her and her teammate, Lady, she bit me on the shoulder. I had a thick coat on and was not injured. Nonetheless, a corn stalk was used for discipline. To her it must have seemed like being spanked with a wet noodle.

Salem Band about 1907. My father is the drummer standing next to the bass drum.

Nellie and Lady were Dad's favorites. He would use them to cut hay in the meadow. After the hay dried, it was raked into piles and loaded onto a hayrack. I always expected that some day the hayrack would tip over in the bogs with its high load, but it never did.

While haying in the meadow, there were times that I could slip away and enjoy wild strawberries that grew along the railroad tracks that cut through our meadow. Throughout my life I have never found strawberries that were equal to their taste.

During and early after a rain when farm work was not possible, I would hint to my father that we should go fishing. Rice and Koronis Lakes were great for pulling in lunkers. However, in all my early years, I can only remember once when he took my suggestion. There were always a million things to do around the farm come rain or shine.

My grandparents, Frank and Mary Gess. Seated is my great-grandfather, Knoble, from Switerzerland.

Donna the Guernsey. Every community had a "4-H" club. I was able to participate when my parents gave me a purebred Guernsey calf. From the day of her birth I spent time with her. I fed and trained her. She was a thing of beauty. I called her Donna. When I showed her at the Stearns County 4-H Fair, she was awarded a grand championship that rewarded me with a free trip to the Minnesota State Fair. Spending a week with all the other 4-Hers was a thrill.

Part of our herd of thirty-three purebred Guernsey cows.

On approaching the gate to the judging area, I was asked to present papers verifying the heifer to be of purebred stock. I had been unaware of this technicality. I thought that since all of my father's thirty-three Guernsey cows were purebred and this was one of the heifers, there should be no problem. They were adamant. "You have to present your credential papers to qualify for this main showing."

Donna and I returned to the cow barn. An official encouraged me to show her as a grade rather than a purebred and so after a delay of several hours, we again approached the judging area. Somehow Donna sensed the confusion and disarray and became so nervous that I couldn't present her in proper stances. We ended up twelfth out of a field of eighty-seven.

While disappointed, I bravely led my charge back toward the barn. On the way, someone commiserated with me about the registration mix up. For what was to come next I was not prepared. This person told me Danny Krueger's purebred heifer had won the Minnesota Grand Champion purebred Guernsey award. Danny's heifer was the runner-up to Donna at the Stearns County Fair! My world stopped – more like crashed! Silently, Donna and I went back to the stall. She lay down in the straw and I buried myself in it and sobbed.

Wearing Dad's uniform trying to learn drumming.

Thirteen-year-olds bounce back quickly. Within a few days I was to start Paynesville High School. The freshmen boys were set to play football against the seventh and eighth graders. In the tryouts I won the race. Consequently I was to be the ball carrier. Our uniforms were so awkward and heavy that I felt like David being weighed down by Saul's armor. In fact, on the field I could hardly get started with all the excess baggage. We suffered a humbling defeat to a younger team.

Electricity was not available in my early childhood. Kerosene lamps were omnipresent. For a really bright light, an Aladdin lamp with a mantle was used in most homes. Before the 1929 Depression, my father had money to buy a battery-operated radio. He stretched a speaker cord from the house to the barn. "Music for the cows produces more milk," he would say. One day in 1927 he excitedly ran from the barn to the house exclaiming: "He did it! He made it!" Lindberg had successfully crossed the Atlantic Ocean from the U.S. to France in his airplane. This news overshadowed "Jack Armstrong, the All-American Boy" which we listened to each day.

Grandpa Gess' steam engine and thrashing machine (in the background). Left to right: Arlie, Freda, Grandpa Frank, Arthur (on fence post), Grandma Mary, Alma.

Grandfather Gess owned a steam engine with a large flywheel that drove the grain separator with a crossed belt. He fired it with straw. I can remember tending the grain wagons into which the grain was dumped. One day I suffered an extensive cut on my right thumb. The men treated it by having a dog lick the wound. It healed. I carried a large scar for the rest of my life.

Whenever threshing was going on, the Salem pastor would always arrive, grab a fork and help feed bundles into the threshing machine. On his departure, he was given a sack or two of the grain to help feed his horses during the winter.

Floyd Arndt. Floyd Arndt lived on a neighboring farm. Being only a year and a half older, we were together a lot. On one occasion we earned money by clearing a mile of gravel road of its larger rocks. We used pitchforks with narrow tines. If the rocks slipped between the tines, they were allowed to remain on the road.

We loved to wrestle. Having an audience of thresher men made it all the more exciting. Once we rolled over a fresh "cow pie." Another evening after the hands had eaten and retired, Floyd and I slipped out to the steam engine. We wondered whether or not there was still steam power left in it. Floyd dared me to pull the whistle cord. IT BLEW! The next day the entire community was asking about the significance of the night whistle blowing. None ever learned how it happened (until now).

From right to left: Warren Reeck, Floyd Arndt, Norval Heitke, Bill Wagner, me.

Floyd and I would often go up to Ben Heitke's pasture where a ball diamond was laid out. It had been used by my father years earlier as well. Dad would tell of his exploits as a baseball pitcher and how Bill Heitke had his leg broken when a runner slid into him at second base. In my day, softball was the rage. It was organized at almost every social event. I loved it and would rather play than eat.

On one occasion when I had been playing softball for several hours, I received a telephone message delivered by Mrs. Ben Heitke. Mother had called asking me to return home. She was overwhelmed with the cleaning and sterilizing of the milking machine, bottles and other equipment. I stayed at the ball diamond. Much later when I returned home, I expressed surprise about her message, explaining that I had not received it. While I was doing all this talking and explaining, Mother was not facing me. When I glimpsed her face, I saw some tears coursing down her cheeks. Up until her death at 88, that was my last willful lie to her.

Chapter Three

The Great Depression

On Black Tuesday, October 29, 1929, the New York Stock Exchange crashed. In a frenzy, traders attempted to sell their stocks, but there was no one who would buy. The stocks became worthless. Fortunes were lost as well as some lives.

I was eight years old at the time of the stock market crash. My parents' savings was lost with the sudden bank closure. Being farmers, we had milk from the cows, eggs from the chickens, pork from the pigs, and popcorn for cereal. With cash in short supply, we had no buyers for our eggs and milk. Having money to buy flour, sugar and salt became our major problem. New clothes could not be bought; the old ones were mended and then re-mended again. Our only "new" clothes were castoffs from friends and relatives.

Our beautiful farmhouse – along with the barn and eighty acres – was sold in 1935 for $5,000.

To compound the Depression, a severe drought spread throughout mid-America turning it into a Dust Bowl. Each year, my father hopefully planted a crop, but for three years the grain binder wasn't used. The crops dried up. Our animals became thin. We were at the end of our rope. An auction was needed. Plans were made to dispose of all of our animals and equipment, as well as our buildings and land. Emotionally, my mother could not witness the auctioning off of our herd of cows. Our 80-acre farm – with its beautiful concrete blockhouse with hardwood floors, up-to-date barns and granary – saw the bidding stop at $5,000, take it or leave it. My parents had to take it, despite it being an extremely low sale price.

Plans were then made for a move to St. Paul, Minnesota, where my father's sister ran a merchandise store. She had come to know about a small grocery at Chatsworth and Rondo that was up for sale. On checking out the grocery store, with its living quarters above, the decision was made to invest in the grocery business. For three years, Mother and Father dutifully ran the business, but it was still the Depression and sales were few. My father took to selling vacuum cleaners just to make some extra cash.

Mother's relatives at Faribault.

Ultimately, after three years an opportunity was offered to move to Nerstrand, Minnesota, where my mother inherited a house from her deceased parents. The move to Nerstrand was one of great pleasure for both my mother and father because my father knew how to paint buildings. He was in demand – almost from the very first week in town – to paint houses and barns in the Nerstrand and Faribault area. Mother was a licensed teacher and one-room schoolhouses always were looking for teachers. Mother took on the teaching of all eight grades in one-room schoolhouses for the next fifteen years.

The three-year period in St. Paul was thoroughly enjoyed by June, my older sister, and me. We had the privilege of selecting ice cream and treats from the store. Also, the grocery store was located only two blocks from Central High School. We attended there and learned it had one of the nation's outstanding high school English departments.

During the summers I ran the icehouse that stood next to the grocery store. Large blocks of ice were delivered each morning, and then I would use an ice ax to cut the ice into appropriately sized blocks. With tongs, I would place these blocks on running boards or car bumpers. At other times I would deliver ice blocks to people's homes that had refrigerators that only used ice for cooling. It was while attending to the icehouse that I learned how to be a softball pitcher.

The St. Paul Softball League games were played under the lights at Central High School. Since the school was only two blocks away, I would watch Johnny Vollmer – the only pitcher known in the Twin Cities' area who used a snap ball delivery. Batters were awed by his speed. He was also an excellent hitter. His team rested safely at the top of the league.

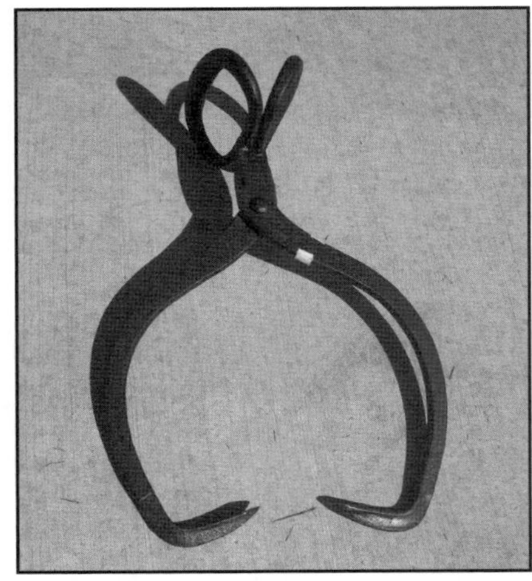

I used these ice tongs the three years I worked at the icehouse.

In between customers, I would throw a mushy softball against the back of my icehouse. I pretended to be Johnny Vollmer. One day, entirely by accident, all the right moves came together and the ball sped to the icehouse like a bullet. With repeated trials, I suddenly was able to duplicate that original serve.

At first, friends played catch with me but when I used the whirlwind snap delivery, they refused to play any more catch. I reinforced one area of the back wall of the icehouse and painted a target on it. Within a week or so, I was able to hit the intended areas.

God gave me the uncanny ability to fast pitch a softball, which opened up opportunities for leadership not only socially but spiritually as well.

Russ Praetorius was the captain of the Calvary Evangelical Church men's softball team. As a fourteen-year-old kid, I attended the church games but was not a member of the team. After one of the games, I asked Russ, who was the catcher, if he would catch a few for me.

At the next game, grown bearded men took to the field and a shy, retiring kid shuffled out to the pitcher's mound – akin to what Johnny Vollmer might have done some ten or fifteen years earlier. We won the game and ended up at the top of the league. I was off to a career in fastball pitching which was to change my entire life.

In the following years, I pitched in highly competitive leagues. When I was nearly thirty and in medical school, I was still in fairly good shape. When others learned I was an old softball pitcher, they persuaded me to join a team with a winning record and a first-rate catcher. We had a winning season and were in the final game for the championship when a base running fluke occurred that is too terrible to relive. We lost by that run but declared an emotional victory as we still considered our team the best.

As recently as the ninetieth reunion celebration of Koronis Ministries in August 2011, four different people recalled my pitching exploits during the Lake Koronis Assembly Ground meetings – first with the laymen in the early days and then with the ministers years later.

Chapter Four

The Early Years and Church

The Salem Evangelical Church and our grave markers.

Salem Evangelical Church stood on a natural rise of land. It was majestic with a tall steeple and a large bell that welcomed people to worship and tolled out the age of those who died. It was the center of our worship and social life. My name was on the cradle roll. It was there that I was baptized, converted and received my call to medical missions. My parents saw to it that I attended Sunday school, Vacation Bible School, Youth Fellowship and all the key social events in a German community surrounded by German Roman Catholics on the north and Scandinavian Lutherans on the south.

We would often walk the mile and a half to church in the summer. During the wintertime the Reuben Arndts, Floyd's parents, would pick us up with their horse drawn sled. We children would be buried under bear rugs. My only clear memory of those sleigh rides was the disciplining of the Arndts' dog to make him return home rather than accompany us to church.

On hot summer months when there was a lack of rain and the crops were in danger, prayer meetings were held, petitioning the Lord to send rain (only William Sack brought an umbrella).

June and I ready for Sunday School. People dressed their finest to go to church.

Salem Sunday school class. I am on the far left and my cousin Vernice Heitke is next to me.

My boyhood not only included the great Depression that began in 1929, but also a three-year drought in the early 1930s. Christmases were bleak. Gifts might include an orange and some peanuts in the shell. However, Dad's sister, Aunt Alma in St. Paul, always sent a Christmas parcel through the mail. My sister, June, and I carefully monitored the mail from the middle of December up until Christmas. Without fail, the box would arrive with a toy and new piece of clothing. What ecstasy!

We believed in Santa Claus who somehow always arrived at our farm while the family was at the Salem Christmas program, the most important event of the year. There would be plays and dramas with appropriate costuming. The most desired parts were always the wise men. Children would recite learned pieces or scripture. Once I failed to remember my lines and had to suffer the humiliation of being prompted. Years later when our firstborn, Tim, was given a piece to orate, we went over it with him a hundred times:

What can I give Jesus, small as I am?
If I were a shepherd, I'd give Him a lamb,
If I were a wise man, I'd do my part,
What can I give Him? I'll give Him my heart.

Tim's performance was perfect.

Some of the church services were in German. We children, however, spoke English as English was used in the schools. I can still remember the German songs, and especially the German prayers that often included our names. The church leaders felt responsible for all the children and would mildly discipline errant ones in the absence of their parents.

Summer Daily Vacation Bible Schools were memorable. The children were lined up and then marched into the church singing "Onward Christian Soldiers." The Bible memory work remained a blessing my entire life.

Evangelistic services were important annual happenings. A pastor from a sister church would be engaged. Visitations were made to the homes during the day. Spirited meetings with heavy praying were held in the evenings, usually for a week, ending on Sunday. Strong encouragement was given for every soul to have a spiritual birth date. Adults responded but so did the children. Cynics always wondered how children under the age of 10 could have a meaningful experience of confessing sins, receiving forgiveness, and then laying hold of a new spiritual life. The cleansing experience is clear in I John 1:9 "If we confess our sins, He is faithful and just to forgive us our sins and to cleanse us from all unrighteousness."

My conversion experience is remembered and very real to this very day eighty-one years later. I knew about Adam and Eve's rebellion. I was aware of my

My parents ready to go to church.

sins and shortcomings. I wanted salvation and was willing to repent. While the congregation was singing an invitation hymn like Billy Graham's "Just As I Am," or "All to Jesus I Surrender," "Why Not Now," "Jesus, I Come," "Almost Persuaded," "I Am Coming," or possibly "Only Trust Him," I made that difficult walk and knelt at the altar. I remember some tears were shed as I pled for forgiveness. I was suddenly aware of a lightness and joy, as if a great load had been lifted. I had not been counseled, as was usual. I simply stood up, feeling elated. On turning around, I found the smiling faces of Mother and Dad, and returned to them. I was born again. I had a spiritual rebirth. I had the assurance that all was right with God.

Salem Evangelical Church (later to be called Salem United Methodist Church) stands regally today. Curt and Carol Wegner, Rick Miller and others have been active in keeping it in repair for special events even though the congregation merged with the Paynesville United Methodist Church more than thirty years ago.

I can think of few places more hallowed to me than Salem and our church camp at Lake Koronis. The people and the congregation of Paynesville UMC supported Ruth and me in our medical mission work in Africa from 1952 until the present time. Especially touching was a gift in 2008 of $100 from Myrtle Hoeft on behalf of the Quilting Group as a final act before they disbanded. Three of their members were more than ninety years of age.

Chapter Five

Early Years and Education

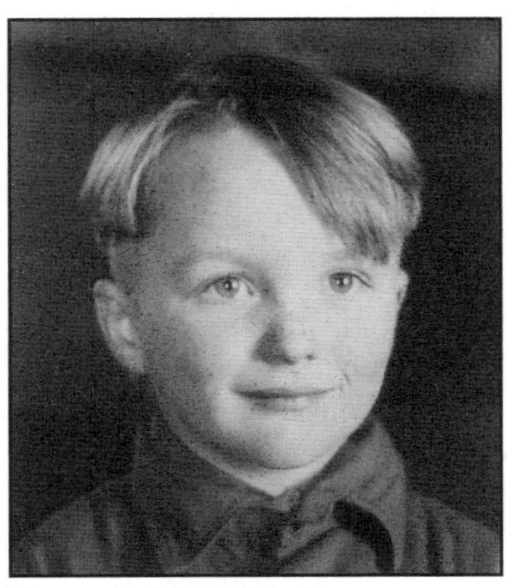
The popular haircut of the day.

My first seven years of schooling were in a one-room schoolhouse a mile and a quarter from home. Most times my sister and I walked unless it was too cold or the snow too deep. Sometimes Uncle Arlie gave us a ride when he picked up his daughter, Mae, whose walk was longer. We would alternately walk and run the distances between electric line polls. Vivid memories remain of the spring "rubber-ice" in the ditches. All too often it led to wet feet that made walking difficult and our reception at home less cordial. I do not remember becoming ill from these episodes, but at Christmastime each year I seemed to recover from an illness just in time to attend the church Christmas service.

Miss Teresa Breeze taught my first four school years. She was demanding, but most students rose to the challenge. In fact, Arlene Manz and I skipped the second year as we were reading at the third or fourth grade level since we had paid attention to what was being taught in the classes ahead of us. Being younger than my classmates in high school and college presented some problems in those maturing years. Twenty years later it was a thrill to recognize "Miss Breeze" in the Graham Evangelical Church congregation (the church I was pastoring) and learned she was married and had a son. We had a nostalgic visit.

In those early years, students helped the teacher get water from the well, coal from the outside shed, and clean the schoolroom each day. School programs were exciting events that drew not only parents, but people from the community as well. For one program three of us boys were taught how to play a mouth organ. I enjoyed playing it for many years.

One program stands out in my memory when I was in the second grade. It suddenly became very silent. Parents took hold of their children and hurried them into their cars and drove away. I did not understand what was happening until in the car I saw a burning cross across the road. The KKK had targeted the school because of a Catholic family that had moved in nearby, and their children attended our school.

The entire school on the merry-go-round.

Teacher Emeline Schmidt taught me to play the mouth organ when I was in the fourth grade of this one room rural school. I am in the back row, far right.

In early fall and late spring softball was the only sport of interest. On special occasions, schools would compete with one another. Our school won the tournaments. These memories run deep. Softball would continue to have a major impact on my life in the years to come.

If a striped gopher were spotted, the entire school would be energized. Buckets of water were poured down the hole, forcing the gopher out. There was no way he could escape the entire student body. There was a bounty of one penny on his tail. When not at school, I was able to capture gophers by snaring. I would place a slipknot of heavy fish line around the opening of the hole into which the gopher had hurdled. Lying down on the ground about eight feet from the hole, I waited patiently for about two or three minutes until the gopher's head popped up to give a "look around." Simply pulling on the line would secure the animal's fate.

Eventually I was able to save eleven dollars to purchase a new Remington single shot .22-caliber rifle. The demise of a gopher with a gun was a bit more humane but no more sure than with snaring.

Following grade school in Salem, I attended Paynesville High School during my freshmen year and participated in musical productions. At this point my parents sold the farm and moved to St. Paul where we attended Central High School. My junior high preparation was not adequate for coping with the Central High School English department's requirements. It was soon apparent that I would not be able to proceed with the class. The teachers decided that I was not of college-preparation caliber so steps were taken for me to be channeled into a course for manual skills. I was just one in the sophomore class of nearly 1,000 students who had to be ushered along.

When my parents learned that I was being directed down a commercial path, they realized I would not have college preparation. While Dad manned the grocery store, Mother accompanied me to visit Miss Cora Timm, my homeroom teacher and counselor, and ultimately arrived at Principal Marshall's office. The consensus again was that I would not be able to handle college training. However, they did offer an intelligence quotient test and an aptitude test that would later be called the SAT. The results surprised them. They agreed to allow me six weeks to prepare for readmission to the college preparatory group. Mother was a trained teacher, having taught school before her marriage. She literally went back to teaching when she tutored me. Along with the English teacher at Central High School, Mother put me through the paces. Finally the time came for me to join my peers.

From the first minimum requirement test to the last (which was taken three years later) the results were in the 95 to 100 percent range. On the basis of these scores, I was employed while a freshman at Macalester College to correct English papers for Professor McLean. My job was to note sentence structure, grammar and spelling. I was required to give a mark on each paper, but was never in a position to give a failing grade.

It was not until the 50th reunion of my class at Macalester College that I admitted to my classmates that I had been employed to correct their papers. I assured them that I never presumed to give a failing grade to any of my peers. That decision was left to the professor. After this confession, one of my classmates collared me later on during the reunion activities, and with a twinkle in his eye said, "Thanks for the 'A'."

High school buddies. From left: Carlyle Brand, myself, Alison Chermack and Charles Stevens.

The three years at Central High School were happy ones. My sister June, two years older than me, and I clerked at our parents' grocery store on Chatsworth and Rondo two blocks from school. Calvary Evangelical Church was a mile and a half away – the same distance that our farm had been from the Salem Evangelical Church. There was always some thing going on at church. Bicycles were important transportation vehicles. Many a time I was given a ride on someone else's bicycle and I would reciprocate as well.

Like today, the big moment in teenagers' lives was acquiring a driver's license. After receiving mine, I was eager to drive any one, any time, anywhere – even my sister to a meeting at church. June was a member of a sewing circle. St. Anthony Avenue had no stop signs from Lexington to Snelling. It was not brightly lit and one night my right foot became heavy on the accelerator. A flashing squad car brought us to a halt. I turned down the driver's window which moments later filled with a uniformed officer. In a detached and monotone voice he asked, "And where are you going in such a hurry?" June and I looked at each other. Suddenly I blurted out, "To church." "And what is happening at church to require such speeding?" Again, a pause before I answered, half under my breath, "A sewing class." The body in the window shifted. "Watch it – take it easy," he said as he retreated to his police car. He pulled out ahead of us. We followed slowly and cautiously. At Snelling he turned right; we turned left and began breathing again. At church no one could believe our story.

The youth at church formed a strong bond that carried over into school where we were together five days a week. All strove for good grades. Pranks and vandalism were not popular. Honesty was taken for granted. Help was available to the stranger. No hobo was refused food at our door. Much of my traveling as a teenager was by hitchhiking. The strongest drink available was a root beer – usually from an A&W restaurant. Only adult men smoked.

My time was engaged in a paper route and, during the summer, selling chunks of ice from the icehouse next to the grocery store. In the spring and summer, I played golf and softball, football in the fall, and basketball and hockey in the winter. The Hay's Office (a precursor to the current rating system) monitored the movies – many times shown as double features – which on the whole were presentable and had moral themes. Biographies were popular which included outstanding personalities such as Emile Zola, Dr. Louis Pasteur, Madame Marie Curie, Thomas Edison and past presidents. The streets were considered safe. Homes were not always locked. I knew of no one who had an air conditioner in their home. People lived together only if they were married.

Racism and bigotry, however, was very much present but not addressed otherwise by upstanding people and some churches. Individual piety and spiritual birthdays were considered the important events.

Significant events included seeing the famous Dionne quintuplets in a St. Paul Winter Carnival parade, hitting a homerun with the bases loaded, being elected "Chief Honor Camper" at Koronis Boys' Camp, and having the best and "ultimate" girlfriend change three times in three weeks – Vangie, Harriet, and Marietta – and then back again.

I have only good memories of high school days. We were protected and coddled, which lengthened our innocence. Kissing and other signs of affection were not on display. Having a walk with your girlfriend was a cherished and successful date. We lived life to the fullest.

Chapter Six

Living Above a Grocery Store

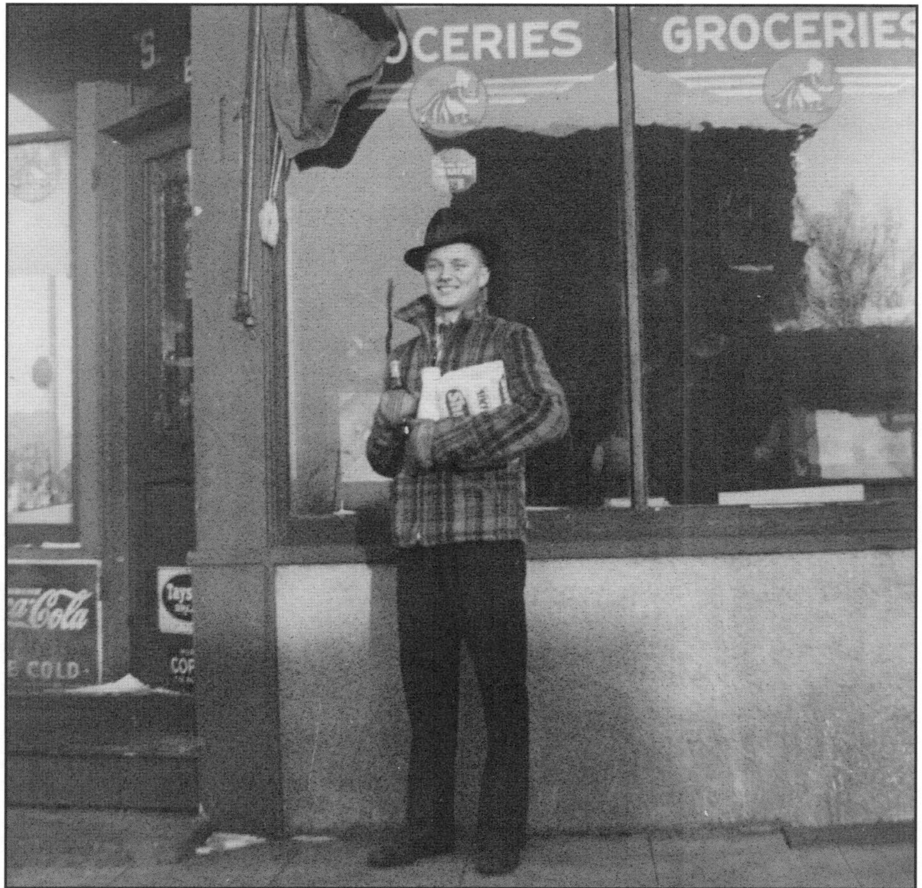

Delivering some groceries from our store.

Our life in St. Paul and in our new home above a grocery store (which was a very small building of 40 x 50 feet) was not like the elegant home we had enjoyed for all those years on our farm near Paynesville. And yet, in the Depression everybody was making do and we were successful in keeping body and soul together in our business as grocers. There weren't enough bedrooms for all of us, so I was given a cot in the stairway that led down to the grocery store. I can remember some nights there was a patter of little feet as our constant building dweller made his rounds. Despite three years of poison and traps, we were never successful in capturing the rat that had lived in the grocery store before we arrived and apparently was still there after we left.

In my teens I apparently showed signs of sleep apnea. My sister and mother told of some nights when they passed by my bed when I was sleeping, they noticed I wasn't breathing. Then after a great pause, I would suddenly breathe again. Yet, this never seemed to trouble me.

Without air conditioning, the building would become very hot. I remember one summer when the heat was so intolerable, we were forced to sleep outside and, like other people, headed for open parks. It was amazing to me as I look back that no one seemed to be afraid to be out in the parks at night. People were friendly. No one seemed to have much money because of the Depression. The fact that we were not aware of any danger spoke to the times. We lived in a mixed community of different ethnic peoples with about half white and half black. All the parents had rules for their children: they were to come in at night and honesty was assumed. It was almost like an undefiled Garden of Eden to be able to walk the streets at night – June as well as myself – without fear.

The streetcar that ran past our grocery store.

Since there was no television in those days, the local movie house was the main source of entertainment. A friend of mine and I would often take our bicycles and go to one of the local movie houses, and on occasion they even allowed us to bring our bicycles into the waiting area. One day, however, when I took my bicycle to Montgomery Ward to pick up some items for my mother, my bicycle was stolen. It was quite a shock to know that there were some dishonest people in the world. The story ended happily as several days later while driving down a street near our home, my father spotted the bicycle and sped up to it, the boy furiously peddling. He got out of the car, the boy ran, and my father was able to put the bicycle in the car's trunk. I had my precious bicycle back.

Summers were spent running the icehouse and the income it generated was greatly appreciated. Since the large ice blocks were not delivered until later in the morning, my work was mainly in the afternoons and early evenings. That allowed me to do things in the morning if I was not needed in the store. A favorite pastime was going to Como Park and playing golf with my friend, Wally Holm. We did this often. Another time Wally and I took an extended bicycle trip to Canon Falls all in a one day's time. Our goal was to visit his sister – who fed us a good meal – and then we returned again to St. Paul.

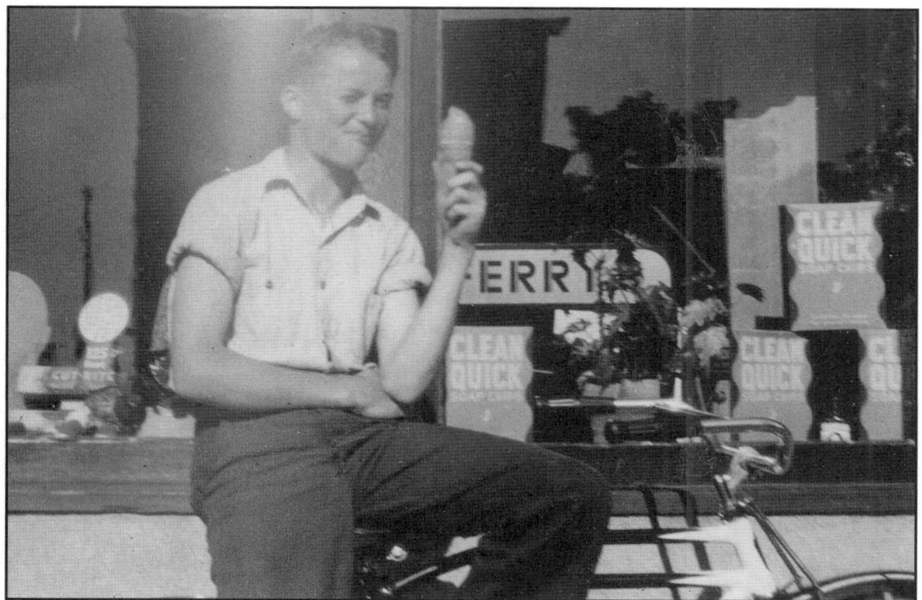

Sitting on my sturdy bicycle.

To this very day I have pleasant memories of those three years in St. Paul. I enjoyed helping with the grocery store and icehouse and having the privilege of attending Central High School with the excellent English department that prepared me for Macalester College. When my parents moved from St. Paul to Nerstrand, arrangements were made for me to stay with some friends. With my bicycle I was able to get to Macalester each day for the entire year. It would sometimes rain and be cold, but my faithful bicycle was my means of transportation. I was happy to be able to still be in St. Paul that additional year because, by now, I was pitching for several softball teams, playing hockey, and was on a basketball team that did some traveling. Of course, I did do some studying at college as well.

Chapter Seven

College

College frolicking with best friends (left to right): Beth Carlender, Roscoe Hoiosen, Joyce Molton, Harriet Anderson and Russell Sargent.

The transition to college was an easy one. I enrolled in Macalester College and roomed at the Bradley Kelloggs as my parents had sold the store January 12, 1939, and moved to Nerstrand, Minnesota. Many of the Central High School seniors continued their education at Macalester. In those days (1938-1942), Macalester held to its Presbyterian roots with many religious activities and events. Chapel was compulsory. It was my job to take roll of a section of my class – and I was not easily bribed to falsify an attendance. We had famous and outstanding speakers such as E. Stanley Jones, Dr. Walter Judd, Rosa Page Welsh and recent state governors. Prayer groups met in the dormitories. The King's English was used rather than the expletives used today.

Besides grading English papers for Professor McLean, I received a stipend for assisting Robert Elliot up and down stairs. There were no elevators at Macalester in those days. Bob had fallen from a tree in his childhood losing the use of his legs. He maneuvered well on braces and crutches as he had massive and strong shoulders. Another student and I would get under his arms and whisk him up and down the stairs. Twelve years later when he was an accomplished lawyer and I was a doctor on the way to Africa, he took care of the legal matters involved in selling our house. He and his wife, the former Betty Flad, remained close friends over the years. I had ardently admired Betty at Central High School and at Macalester College – along with Vangie, Faith, Marietta, Nancy, Eunice, Harriet and Beth.

An important event happened at Lake Koronis Assembly Grounds following my freshman year at Macalester and before arriving at North Central. Roger Allen was to speak to the Young Peoples' Union. When unable to attend the mid-June camp, Rev. Frank Spong asked if I would substitute for Roger and literally helped me with the speech. It was a success. Three days later I was elected the new president of the Young Peoples' Union. Ultimately this led to other state offices and finally to the presidency of the United Christian Youth Movement of the north-central area of the U.S. I was to be involved with this movement even during my seminary days. The fellowship with outstanding Christian young people and their youth leaders highlighted and immeasurably blessed my young life.

Dr. J. G. Heidinger, district superintendent of the Evangelical Church, had heard that speech at Koronis. He admitted a year later it gave him confidence that I could conduct the services at the New Trier Evangelical Church while still a college student preparing for the Christian ministry. With this appointment, I was able to finance room and board when I returned to Macalester. I rode a bus to Hampton where I was picked up by Mr. Charlie Wille and driven to the church. Prior to the service, I conducted Sunday school classes and catechism courses. I considered catechumens Darrel, Betty, and Joyce Ista, the brightest students in Minnesota. As late as 2009 and 2010, seventy-two years later, visits were still enjoyed with Joyce and her husband, Ivert.

More frolicking. Back row: Harold Berg, me, Ralph Rasmussen. Front row: Evangeline Praetorius on the left; my sister, June, on the right.

Although the college courses required more studying than in high school, I continued in basketball, softball, hockey and handball. I lettered in hockey at Macalester. A memorable game was played against the University of Minnesota. With the all-time star Mariucci playing for the U of M, we lost. Later the arena was named "The Mariucci Arena." Our Macalester playing coach was Ralph Colaizi. I had the thrill of defeating him in the handball championship my senior year. Two years earlier I had won the handball tournament at North Central College.

When my parents moved from St. Paul, plans were made for me to spend my sophomore year at St. Olaf College in Northfield, Minnesota, only eleven miles from Nerstrand. However, Dr. Eigenbrodt from North Central College in Naperville, Illinois, who had relatives in the Nerstrand-Faribault area helped me secure work in Naperville. So far away from home, I only spent one year there before returning to Macalester for my junior and senior years. Later on, I would again take courses at North Central College for three years while attending seminary. Their campuses were side by side.

During my sophomore year at North Central I was again employed to read and correct English papers of fellow students under the direction of Professor Wiley – yet another deep, dark secret kept from my peers. At one time I was spending four hours Saturday mornings correcting papers and then would serve tables at the Lindbloom Café from noon to 8:00 p.m. as well as working staggered hours during the week. Tips were especially important from the café, since I didn't receive any tips, peeling potatoes for two to three hours each day at a dormitory to pay for half of my board.

I enjoyed the collegiate and social life. I dated four charming ladies, but all ended up marrying other future ministers. At the end of 1939, when the New Trier Evangelical Church appointment was finalized, I was required to take courses for a preacher's license such as History of the Evangelical Church, which I successfully passed even while taking a full college course and working so many hours. I have such fond memories of my landlady who would provide buns and milk during late hours of studying. She was always warning me to get more sleep and not succumb to tuberculosis that her family had experienced.

Commencement that year had Dr. Daniel Poling addressing the graduates. It was with disbelief I learned two years later that on February 3, 1943, his son Clark was one of the four immortal chaplains who died following the torpedoing of the U.S.A.T. Dorchester. After ministering to the wounded and dying, these chaplains of different faiths gave their lifebelts to soldiers, linked their arms together and went down with 672 others. Only 230 survived. For their heroic action, a posthumous Special Medal for Heroism was conferred on them.

While at North Central College, I heard Dr. Ira McBride speak on his missionary work at Bambur, Nigeria, Africa. The visit with him brought back the memory of my call to medical missions. I remained adamant, however, in avoiding any pre-medical courses.

New Trier Evangelical Church.

June 2, 1940, was to be my first service at New Trier Evangelical Church. The congregation I met numbered two, Mr. and Mrs. Ed Willie. Rev. Georgius, the previous pastor, had not been there the two preceding weeks. The people had not been informed about my arrival. On June 9, I gave my first sermon, "God's Smile on Children," to a waiting congregation of thirty, the active number of this rural church. It is almost incomprehensible to believe that I was to serve New Trier for two years during my last two college years at Macalester. Many hours were spent in sermon preparation and quarterly conference meetings – hours that "could" have been used for college course preparation – but that, plus the athletic activities, still didn't prevent securing a Bachelor of Arts degree on June 8, 1942.

Supply pastor for the New Trier Evangelical Church, 1940-1942.

Dan Ruge, center, with Wilma Vandersall Macke on his right.

An important event during the summer of 1940 was the General Convention of the Evangelical Church that took place on the Lake Koronis Assembly Grounds. Pastors and delegates came from churches across the United States. I got to know the bishops of the church and youth leaders, being host state Young Peoples' Union president. Dan Ruge, president of the General YPU, and I began a friendship that continued while he was in medical school and I in seminary. In succeeding years he had a flourishing medical practice that included the President of the United States as one of his patients while my patients were those who emerged from the African jungle, yet were all equal in the eyes of God. When the assassination attempt was made on President Reagan March 30, 1981, Dan was following Reagan's limousine, nicknamed Stagecoach, in a second armored limousine, a tan Lincoln. After the shooting, Dan insisted that the President be "treated like any other patient rather than over thinking our decisions" according to a *Newsweek* article written by Dr. Joseph Giordana, head of trauma at George Washington University Medical Center. This probably saved the president's life, as a delay was prevented by a normal strip-down examination in the emergency room. Only then was the bullet wound found. Successful surgery removed the bullet lying next to the heart.

Pearl Harbor, December 7, 1941, entirely changed our lives. February 16, 1942, I registered for Selective Service. My 1-A status was later changed by the draft board at Faribault, Minnesota, when my church services were made known. They decided that chaplains were needed as a part of the service and allowed me to continue in college and then seminary training. This favored position weighed heavily on my heart as so many of my high school and college classmates were giving their last full measure of love and allegiance to our country. Long before Pastor Rick Warren wrote *The Purpose Driven Life*, we were immersed in it.

Macalester wrestling champion, Russell Sargent, on the right who went to Chile as a missionary. Macalester handball champion, me, on the left who went to Africa as a missionary.

August 2, 1942, I preached on "Be of Good Courage." August 9th was the farewell. It was difficult to say goodbye, as it is always possible you will never see certain faces again. During those two years at New Trier we had met in fellowship before God each week. We had matured in our faith – at least I felt I had. Only the future would bring a heavenly reunion.

Our family picture when I turned 21. I received a Bulova gold wristwatch promised me at that age if I did not take to smoking.

Chapter Eight

Seminary Days

It was overwhelming – awesome. More than seventy male voices were singing the "Gloria Patri"! Was I in heaven? It was the first chapel service of the new seminary year, September 9, 1942. Pastoral training was for men. They were encouraged not to marry until after graduation. There was to be no ordination of women during my three years of training. Today, seminary student bodies may be equally divided between men and women, sometimes even a majority being women.

Evangelical Theological Seminary was located in Naperville, Illinois, an hour's drive west of Chicago. Following the merger of the Evangelical United Brethren Church with the Methodist Church in 1968, ETS became a part of Garrett Theological Seminary in Evanston and was named Garrett-Evangelical Theological Seminary.

The traveling quartet from the Evangelical Theological Seminary.

I was assigned to Room 2 in Seybert Hall next to the headmaster's at the entrance. Its accessibility led to a significant social life, including fellow seminarians sneaking in to short sheet my bed. Studying was usually in the wee hours. I doubt if my room ever was locked during my three years at ETS. I never had more than a few dollars in cash (and often bereft of any), and my only other possessions were a gift Bible from my parents, used texts, a Royal portable typewriter, some well-used clothes, and a handball with accompanying gloves. Besides fellow seminarians, visitors to my room included Bishop R. H. Mueller and his brother, the Rev. H. E. Mueller, Dr. Wilbur Harr (missions professor), Dr. Paul Mayer (missionary to Japan), Dr. Frank Spong, Dr. D. C. Trapp, the Rev. Russell Praetorius, the Rev. Bill Zahl, and Dr. H. R. Heininger, president of ETS.

The three years at seminary were to be the happiest and most challenging years of my life to date. The first year class (the Juniors) represented more than a dozen states. The men were the cream of the crop. In the early fall, it was customary for the Juniors, Middlers and Seniors to have a softball tournament. With Lyndon Schendel (also from Minnesota) as my catcher, we had little trouble winning the tournament.

It was expected that the junior class would organize itself by electing officers. Dr. Heininger, president of the seminary, called me in to help with a project right when the election was going to occur. I was disappointed to have missed the important Junior meeting. After my project was completed, I joined my classmates as they were leaving. They greeted me by saying, "Where have you been, Mr. President?"

The world was at war in 1942. During my first year at seminary, I learned half of my college hockey starter teammates had already been killed. Before the war was over, there were hardly any blocks in cities without a home that had a gold star hanging in the window. The president of Evangelical Theological Seminary, Dr. Harold Heininger, expected each student to be as disciplined as our counterparts in military service. He ran a tight ship with prayers starting at 6:30 a.m. "Six o'clock in the morning, two feet on the floor!"

Finances were tight. Fortunately I was offered a job as a part-time librarian that paid 75 cents an hour. Painting with Bill Dody, a fellow seminarian, produced 65 cents an hour. Later, close friend Vernon Flynn paid me $1.25 an hour for painting with him. John Murbach cut my hair "for free."

Central Regional Planning Conference of the United Youth Movement in the U.S.

My sister, June, following her marriage to Edward Malin.

Trips into Chicago were frequent. My sister, June, worked there and always provided accommodations. That ended on December 11, 1942, when she became the bride of Edward Malin, a navy man who flew with "dirigibles" guarding the west coast of the U.S. The trips were in conjunction with committee meetings related to the Christian Youth Conference of America. My election of president of the Minnesota Interdenominational Youth Council qualified me as the representative from Minnesota to attend the Central Regional Planning Conference in 1942. There were nearly 200 delegates. A council was elected and I was chosen president. (A softball game had been played prior to the election. My fastball pitching created a stir.)

Noted speakers often spoke at the chapel services. The Rev. Karl Kuglin showed pictures of his work in Bambuka, Nigeria. Eleven years later I would be visiting him at Bambuka during our term of service in Nigeria. The same was true for Dr. Arthur Faust at a later chapel service. Speakers like Dr. Reinhold Niebuhr and Dr. D. Elton Trueblood were impressive. I included some of Dr. Trueblood's words in the preface of my 2002 book *Mine Eyes Have Seen The Glory.*

Highlights of 1943 involved being elected manager of Theologue Eating Club. Not only was food rationed, but also gasoline and shoes. My election as Inter-Seminary Representative to the seven seminaries in the Chicago area increased my trips into Chicago.

On January 1944, I spoke to the Interdenominational Foreign Missions Conference that convened in Chicago. My topic was "Practical Problems Facing Missionary Recruits." Two outstanding missionaries, Dr. Walter Judd and Dr. E. Stanley Jones, followed me. Dr. Judd was a former medical missionary to China in the 1930s during the time of the revolution. He was now a congressman from

Minnesota. The President of the United States sought his counsel during the time when there was tremendous upheaval in China. He had a staccato manner of delivery not unlike an auctioneer with piercing word phrases. Students were riveted, and certainly didn't daydream, while he spoke. His political and Christian stance did not permit any fence straddling.

Dr. E. Stanley Jones was a twentieth century theologian and Methodist Christian missionary to India and founder of the Ashram movement. He is remembered especially for his interreligious lectures to educated classes in India. His encouragement for the cause of Indian self-determination garnered friendships with Mahatma Gandhi and the Nehru family. He sought to contextualize Christianity for India through *The Christ of the Indian Road* published in 1925. The book sold over one million copies. Subsequently he published a new book annually for the next twenty years. I had heard him while attending college. I remembered seeing a tired, old, white-haired man sitting on the stage, but following his introduction and his first words into the microphone, he became animated with an angelic radiance. The student body was electrified, entranced and mesmerized in awe. He had a Christian message of world mission that was convincing. Now, years later, it was special to be able to visit with these two warm and friendly spiritual giants.

I succeeded Paul Million, past president, sitting in the row behind my right shoulder.

A great moment took place on April 28th when I was elected student body president of the Evangelical Theological Seminary. To represent such an august group of nearly 80 men deeply committed to the Lord Jesus Christ in ministry was humbling. A greater moment, however, occurred on May 23rd when my former roommate, Ervin Petznik, invited me to dinner with his wife, Beverly, and Beverly's sister, Ruth. Love at first sight is true. Ruth became the "love of my life." The entry in my journal that night was, "Ruth is grand. God willing, we are going to Africa together" – and it all came true.

An old letter Ruth had saved and was found in her things elaborates on these sentiments. It was written to my parents, dated May 28, 1944:

The Winnipeg nurse who became the love of my life.

I met Ervin Petznik's sister-in-law, Ruth Bradley. She is visiting Erv's wife, Beverly, Ruth's sister, to help a little during the time of the birth of Bev and Erv's first baby. We have been doing a lot of things together. I have met hundreds of fine girls at Lake Koronis, Lake Geneva, college, at the Christian Youth Council, at the Central Regional Planning Conference, at the Baptist Missionary Training School in Chicago, etc.

What I am getting at is that I've come to know a girl who tops all that I've ever known. What's more, she has one more year of nursing (school) before she graduates from Winnipeg General Hospital. She then intends to go to school in Chicago for some Bible study with the intent of being a missionary.

I would give anything to have you meet Ruth Bradley. Instead of taking the train to the Twin Cities I am going to take the bus with Ruth that also goes through the Twin Cities on the way back to Winnipeg. We leave Chicago Thursday afternoon and arrive about 5 a.m. in St. Paul.

I think Mother's school children and Dad's painting need a day off for once. Could you use that much gas and rubber? The four of us could have breakfast together at Mickey's.

Ruth is a very modest and sincere person. She has a spiritual quality that I never dreamed girls could have. I guess I never met the right one before. She uses a touch of rouge but no lipstick. Frankly, she looks much better than if she did. You'll have to meet her.

I'm especially anxious that you meet Ruth because for the first time in my almost 23 years, I've met one who meets all the requirements – requirements that I thought perhaps were too high.

I wouldn't expect you to make such a trip except for a very good reason. After you have met Ruth and after I have talked it over with you, I have the feeling that 'this one is going through.'

My, it's going to be hard meeting Beth this week. She is such a grand person. What I have to tell her is difficult. I haven't figured out how to be most Christian about it.
With love, Lowell

October 3, 1944, will never be forgotten. While in the lab of my premedical chemistry course, an assistant student instructor accidentally added water to a bottle that contained solid sodium that had originally been covered with kerosene. My workstation was just across the aisle – about six feet. I was deeply engrossed in my experiment. When the room became deathly silent, I looked up to find that I was the only one in the room except for several standing in the doorway about twenty feet away. I heard a hoarse warning, "Get out, it is going to explode!" As I turned away from the burning bottle, it did explode! Several of the students in the doorway received cuts from shattered glass. Apparently the explosion had arched over me and came down with debris some distance away. I was untouched and unharmed; the Lord is kind.

February 1, 1945, I was interviewed on the "Breakfast Club," a popular radio program that originated in Chicago. A week later I received a letter from Muriel Berg, my cousin, in Faribault, Minnesota, saying that she had heard the program. Several days later it was a thrill to hear the men at the Theologue Eating Club sing, to the tune of the "Doxology," a grace that I had written:

Come Holy Spirit feast with us,
Fill us with a holy trust.
Lord, bless the bread by which we live,
And bless the bread that we would give.

The next day I met with Billy Graham in Chicago. At our meeting, he requested support from the Chicago-land seminaries on behalf of Youth for Christ. Neither of us could understand why mine was the only affirmative vote for our respective seminaries to support the meetings. Days later I brought a contingent of young people from Naperville to the Youth for Christ meeting. Two of the young people made decisions for Christ.

In the closing weeks of my senior year, I had important interviews with Dr. Wilbur Harr, seminary chair of Missions, and Dr. Paul Mayer, long time missionary to Japan. On May 3, 1945, the Rev. D. C. Trapp called long distance from Minnesota informing me that I had been appointed to serve at St. Cloud and Graham churches. May 7th was graduation day from the Evangelical Theological Seminary. In the words of Jesus, we were admonished to "Go and make disciples of all nations, baptizing them in the Name of the Father and of the Son and of the Holy Spirit, and teaching them to obey everything I have commanded you. And surely I am with you always, to the very end of the age." Matthew 28:28-20

A few days later, I arrived in St. Cloud as a bona fide "preacher" without a car, with all my earthly possessions in two suitcases, and a King James Bible in my brief case.

Chapter Nine

Two Years in the Pastorate

Grace Evangelical Church in St. Cloud, Minnesota.

Ten days after graduating from Evangelical Theological Seminary on May 17, 1945, I arrived at the parsonage of Grace Evangelical Church in St. Cloud. Rosetta Bardson had cleaned it. Mother's girlhood friend, Dahly Robbins, helped me shop for furniture – a kitchen table, chairs, bed and a mattress. My money had come from a $40 loan from the Rev. D. C. Trapp. A 1937 Chevrolet was purchased from Slim Schultz for $460. Payments would come from my preacher's salary. Slim was a member of our church.

My high school buddy, Fred Kobler, had just been released from the army and came to visit me in my "new home" on Saturday, May 19th. Together we fixed up a bulletin for the Sunday service, finally getting to bed at 1:30 a.m.

It had been arranged for Mr. Will Schumann to pick me up shortly after 7:00 a.m. Sunday morning to take me to the rural Graham Evangelical Church that was yoked with Grace. He received no response to his knocking. Fred and I were dead to the world. On walking into the parsonage (people did not lock their doors in those days), he ultimately found "life" in the downstairs bedroom. He had expected to find a bachelor preacher, not two people under the covers loaned by Mrs. Robbins.

Without breakfast, we made a quick trip to Graham. We remembered the bulletins but not my sermon manuscript. My first sermon in a new charge was extemporaneous. I had gone over it so many times that I was able to preach point by point. It was a matter of surprise to some that the new preacher was preaching by only referring to an open Bible held in his hand.

Several weeks later I lost that Bible on a return trip from Graham. Within a week it was returned to me after being found on the road. It was a bit scuffed, but intact. Mother and Dad had given me this Bible during the time I had served New Trier Evangelical Church during my senior year in college.

After seeing the relatively bare parsonage, Will and Emma Schumann brought over a chair. The next day Robert Hartfield and his son, Virgil, brought over a studio couch. Folding chairs from the church next door were used for committee meetings.

On May 22nd, I received my release from the draft board. I called Ruth in Winnipeg and in the morning grabbed my birth certificate and boarded the Northern Pacific train for Canada. Ruth met me at the station. It was wonderful to be together. We had prayer and read from I John 4:1-11 which ends, "Beloved, if God so loved us, we also ought to love one another." The next day I had a chance to meet Irene, Ruth's sister, and her children Judy and Jamie, and had a nice chat with Mrs. Myrtle Bradley while Ruth was at graduation practice. Ruth and I then had a bicycle ride in Assiniboine Park. Then on May 25, 1945, Ruth graduated from nurses' training from the Winnipeg General Hospital. It was a lovely occasion and I was so delighted to meet many of Ruth's friends – Eileen McKibben, Ina Simpson, Mary Earl and Phyllis Lee. The dozen red roses I bought for Ruth was the first such purchase in my life. I was going all out, even buying "Melody of Love" sheet music for Mrs. Bradley and nuts for Ruth's sister, Irene. My journal recorded my feelings from those few days "...would so like to have Ruth as my wife."

I was back at St. Cloud the next day to prepare for Sunday services. There was a reception for the new pastor at Graham Sunday afternoon. A congregational gift of $17.50 was presented. I had been graciously "reimbursed" from my Winnipeg high spending.

The summer of 1945 was a demanding one. During the week I commuted to Chicago, as I was taking physics at North Central College in Naperville. Trains were very crowded. Often I would have to stand in the aisle the entire trip. Young men were expected to be chivalrous and give their

The rural Graham Evangelical Church.

seats to older adults and even young ladies. On almost every trip some young man would faint after standing too long without shifting his position. My preaching and making pastoral calls on weekends at St. Cloud and Graham and the intense physics course the other days was leading to a breaking point. On top of that, the atomic bomb was dropped and the August 14, 1945, V-J Day was celebrated with national rejoicing involving all the churches. I had finished physics but was totally exhausted. I slipped away from the 6:00 a.m. to midnight V-J Day activities and made a three-day trip to Winnipeg to see Ruth. Three weeks later Ruth came to St. Cloud and we were formally engaged. The world was bright and new again.

The day that Ruth returned to Winnipeg the Rev. Donald Roesti arrived for a week of evangelistic meetings at Graham. He had graduated from ETS a year ahead of me and was established in a Minnesota church. He preached powerful sermons that prompted a response – especially from young people – to commit their lives to the Lord Jesus Christ. He genuinely was pleased with the $30 stipend given him by the congregation at the end of the meetings.

A week later the Rev. John Kauffman came to conduct the evangelistic meetings at the St. Cloud church. Again there was a wonderful response to the Gospel. Both churches were experiencing a new enthusiasm in Christian living and witnessing.

In the midst of all this church activity I was taking organic chemistry at St. John's University. Father Matthew Kiess was the instructor. His arrival each day followed a routine. His cigar was removed while he intoned the "Hail Mary." The class was then addressed with regard to studies and experiments for the day. On one occasion he advised the class to consult me if they were having difficulties with the subject. Another time he warned he had replaced the laboratory's ethyl alcohol with methyl alcohol; the ethyl alcohol had been markedly disappearing beyond that was required for the assigned experiments. I learned much from Father Matthew and developed a fast friendship with him.

In mid-December, St. Cloud was host to The School of Evangelism. I shared my parsonage with important leaders in our denomination: Dr. Reuben H. Mueller (a future bishop), the Rev. D. C. Trapp, and the Rev. J. G. Heidinger. Bishop E. W. Praetorius and the Rev. Herman E. Mueller had other accommodations. At the close of the conference, I had to push Bishop Praetorius' car to get it started. What status!

Two days later, Evangeline Praetorius, the bishop's daughter, died with an undiagnosed illness, which at autopsy was found to be Guillain-Barre syndrome.

Vangie. The high school youth from Calvary Evangelical Church in St. Paul was a close-knit group. Most of them attended Central High School. Besides being together on school days, they spent many happy hours at church. Dr. F. A. Spong had a way with young people although he may have been the lowest-key pastor I ever knew. Besides regular worship and Bible studies, play productions – usually directed by Fred Kobler – were enjoyed. Bishop E. W. Praetorius and family lived two blocks from church. I spent much time with his son, Russell, who was several years older than me. He was an excellent athlete. He captained the church basketball team. We occasionally toured to places (such as Danube) to play other Evangelical Church teams. For three years he was my catcher in softball. His favorite phrase was, "Put 'er here," as he pounded his mitt. We had amazing success in spite of the fact that I was only fourteen and a half when I began playing in adult tournaments.

His sister, Evangeline, who was my age, was beautiful, athletic and artistic in nature. We spent much time together in school, in our homes, and at Lake Koronis Assembly Grounds. She went into nurses training; I to seminary. After becoming a registered nurse and serving as a public health nurse, she married a naval officer. While he was in active duty, she found it difficult to make her rounds. She spent time at her parent's home, trying to rest up. Eventually, when she could barely get up from the couch, she was hospitalized. Her progression was steadily downward.

As was the practice in the 1940s, visiting privileges were restricted. The Bishop and Mrs. Praetorius and other family members were denied visitation rights. The nurses were instructed to do their job but not engage the patient in undue conversation. One day, Evangeline was found on the floor, gasping, "I want my Mother and Dad." Still, the "no visitation" rule was enforced.

Agonizing because of this separation, Bishop Praetorius announced that he was a clergyman and was visiting a patient (who happened to be his daughter). He could not be stopped and was able to minister to Evangeline. She died shortly thereafter.

At her Christmas Eve funeral, I was one of the pallbearers. It was the saddest service I ever attended.

Three days later I was on the train to Winnipeg. At the station, I was met by Ruth. Two days later, we were married and granted a lifetime together.

Chapter Ten

Our Wedding

It was December 29, 1945, the date I had eagerly been awaiting. Friends, relatives and the congregation of Bethesda Church in Winnipeg, Manitoba, were hushed as Ruth and I stood before Pastor Thompson saying our vows and pledging our love. For the first time in my life I felt stage fright coming on. Would I be able to complete the vows? At that moment something brushed my legs. Ruth's sister, Irene, and Irene's husband, Nat, were standing up with us as members of the bridal party. Their four-year-old daughter, Judy, and two-year-old son, Jamie, were in the care of Ruth's mother in the front row. Suddenly, Jamie had broken away from grandma and began playing with a toy car. His ultimate goal was his parents, but he had to get through my legs first. The knowing smiles of the people and Pastor Thompson brought me back to reality and I truly enjoyed the rest of the ceremony.

The cutting of our wedding cake.

Following the cutting of the cake that Ruth had purchased with meager funds, we were wished well by our guests and then sped away to the Hotel Royal Alexandra in the borrowed car of my best man, Lloyd Pierce. We returned to Bethesda Church the next morning for worship services. Knowing that I was a pastor, Mr. Thompson invited me to give the pastoral prayer.

That everything went off so well was remarkable. Ruth had little help with the planning, since I was nearly 400 miles away. She was in an active nursing program at St. George's Hospital. A friend of hers had sewn the white wedding gown. The temperature was frigid – below 20 degrees. Mother and Dad endured the cold, but Mother suffered frostbite to her knees. I had no proper hat but found a distinguished Hamburg on sale the day before the wedding. It proved its worth prior to our leaving Winnipeg for St. Cloud.

Ruth had been dealing with the immigration consulate. The American consul would not approve her immigration papers. Even though I was a pastor of a church, he did not feel that I had funds sufficient to support her. With my new Hamburg hat, I confronted the consul, stating I was a church pastor with my own parsonage (and car). How could I return to my congregation without my wife? He relented, but allowed only a two-week visit to St. Cloud before having Ruth return to Winnipeg for re-evaluation. Covering letters from Minnesota church officials satisfied the examiners. Several years later, Ruth achieved American citizenship.

On Ruth's return from Winnipeg, she was looking forward to a reception from her loving husband. Instead, a heavy, cheerful, short man, Mr. Will Schumann, was the reception committee. I had been called to Graham because of the death of one of the members of my congregation.

Flanked by my parents and Ruth's mother, Myrtle Bradley, and brother-in-law, Nathaniel Blair who was also a physician specializing in ear, nose and throat.

Looking back, the wedding and the honeymoon were truly wonderful. I met and fellowshipped with Ruth's relatives and friends. Nat and Irene Blair, with their children, left Winnipeg two days after the wedding for a Saskatoon visit, leaving their bay view apartment for us. Ruth's mother seemed to have disappeared, but ultimately emerged from a friend's home. We attended New Year's Eve services at Bethesda where many meaningful testimonies were given. The next day we visited with Ina Simpson and attended a revival meeting at an evangelical church. The next night we were guests at the home of best man, Lloyd Pierce, where we played some exciting Bible games. On January 4, 1946, we boarded the Great Northern at 8:12 p.m. and arrived at St. Cloud at 8:12 a.m.

The joy and wisdom of marrying a skilled secretary was immediately realized when Ruth prepared the church bulletins. My Sunday sermon was entitled, "Following Christ in 46." At noon we were the guests of Emma and Will Schumann, an occasion we were to enjoy many times over the coming year as their "adoptive children."

On Monday, when Virgil Hartfield brought the wedding gifts to us from the station, it was like Christmas all over again. However, it brought closure to the events surrounding our wonderful and fulfilling Christian wedding. We had promised before God and the company assembled to remain true to each other for so long as each of us should live. And we did so for nearly 65 years.

Chapter Eleven

Completing Our Pastorate

Following our marriage, Ruth became a perfect preacher's wife. She attended all services, participated in the women's activities, accompanied me in pastoral calls where possible, and made the parsonage a real home that beckoned many visitors. Besides my pastoral duties, I attended pre-medical courses at St. John's University and fought with the parsonage furnace. This was to be the last time in my life that I had to carry ashes and stoke a furnace. I hated this chore, but got to be pretty good at it by late in the spring.

With our appointment to Mayer Evangelical Church, May 18, 1946, was moving day from the parsonage. There were some tears with farewells by members of the congregation. For Ruth and me it was touching to leave our first "home." Little did we know that moving would characterize our life, which included our brood of six children. My admiration for Ruth remains immeasurable. Without complaint and often with short notice, she would bundle up the family for a new move and a new experience.

Before taking on our new duties at Mayer, located about forty miles west of Minneapolis, Ruth and I had a second honeymoon at Marvin's cottages on Lake Koronis. In Ruth's words, "The cottage is cute." We fished most days in spite of the cool, damp weather until sinus trouble ended it for Ruth.

On August 15, 1946, we moved into our new apartment at 219-B 8th Avenue just five blocks from the University of Minnesota. The neighbors were kind and helpful. We traveled out to Mayer on Saturday, stayed in the parsonage overnight, preached on Sunday morning, enjoyed food and fellowship with parishioners (like Mr. and Mrs. William Hensler and Orlando and Lenora Tesch with whom we became life-long friends), and then returned to Minneapolis by late afternoon so I could prepare for a new week of university pre-medical courses. My grades were good in courses like genetics, but calculus was to be my nemesis. A mark of C+ in the spring of 1947 put me out of contention for acceptance into the medical school at Minnesota. Our world crashed. Counselors advised applying at private medical schools like Northwestern and Washington University School of Medicine in St. Louis.

The year at Mayer was truly rewarding. October 10, 1946, stands out as our first son, Tim, was born at 1:10 a.m. in Fairview Hospital. I had taken Ruth into the hospital at a late hour the night before, but the birthing process had seemed to come to a halt. Ruth insisted I go home as I would be taking medical school aptitude tests the following day. I missed the excitement at the hospital, but the results of the aptitude tests qualified me as a serious medical school applicant.

In those days, delivery patients were hospitalized for seven days. Ruth was bedridden for the first three days and was then allowed to dangle her feet over the side of the bed on the fourth. When allowed to walk on day five, she was noticeably weak. (Seven years later, while Ruth was attending the clinic at Guinter Memorial Hospital in Bambur, Nigeria, she was informed that a pregnant patient on the way to the hospital wasn't going to make it there in time. She dispatched four men with a litter. A short time later, the men, the litter, and the small baby on the litter returned – with the mother walking behind.)

My long time good friend, Fred Kobler, often visited us. On one occasion he took us out to the Radisson Hotel for a meal while being entertained by "the flaming violins." Mrs. Downy, our helpful neighbor who sometimes supplied us with delicious leftovers from the fraternity house where she cooked, cared for Tim.

Another time Fred insisted that he care for Tim while Ruth and I had an evening out. At age 93, Ruth still remembered Fred's words as he viewed his charge for the evening, "Isn't he sweet?"

We introduced Tim to the Mayer people within three weeks – to the shock of Ms. Julia Wabbe, who wondered how so young a child was transported. Again, seven years later in Nigeria, we often witnessed newborns that were strapped to their mothers' backs in the back of a lorry just several days after birth. (One difference between the U.S. and Nigeria: during the winter months, Ruth dressed Tim so well that once he developed heat rash.)

November 16, 1946, is another important date of note for it was on this day that the merger of the Evangelical Church and the United Brethren in Christ Church occurred. It proved to be very successful not only for the churches in the United States but also for the mission programs overseas.

However, November 27th was a sentimental date. During high school days, I had shoveled snow and cleaned houses, ultimately garnering twenty dollars that purchased the bicycle of my dreams with balloon tires. I had "wheels!" I still had that bicycle in good running condition twenty years later. While transporting it on the side of my car on a trip from Mayer to Nerstrand, I stopped at a gas station. The attendant admired it and made an offer of twenty dollars. I never forgave myself, for in that moment I relinquished something so dear to my heart. Perhaps I felt I was now a family man – a father – and needed to move on.

Chapter Twelve

Ready for Medical School

The winter and following spring of 1947 was a desperate time; I was finishing pre-medical courses at the University of Minnesota and pastoring at Mayer. No favorable responses had been received from the five medical schools to which I had applied.

I had not received a communication rejecting me from the medical school least known to me, the Washington University School of Medicine in St. Louis. I took courage and wrote the dean inquiring about my position. Several days later an acceptance letter was received with a request that I forward the first year's tuition of $600 if I planned to join the class of 1951. The only thing of value we possessed was our 1937 Chevrolet that bore evidence that it had rolled over in the past and for which I had paid $460. I rushed to the hardware store, bought a can of gray metallic paint, "anointed" the car, and put a "For Sale" sign on it the next morning along University Avenue. After a passing shower, it sparkled with raindrops. Within an hour, two buyers were vying for it. When asked what I wanted, without hesitation, I answered, "Six hundred dollars." The deal was closed. (The Lord knew it would work out all along.) A letter was dispatched that same day with my tuition money. I was going to medical school!

In 1996, 45 years after graduation, the Washington University School of Medicine honored me with its "Alumni Achievement Award." During the honors banquet, Ruth and I were seated next to Dr. and Mrs. William H. Danforth. He was to receive the "Distinguished Service Award." Dr. Danforth had been the chancellor of Washington University for twenty-four years and had provided exceptionally dedicated and capable service. During our conversation, I learned that while Dr. Danforth had accepted an opening at Harvard in 1947, he had also been accepted to Washington. Curious, I asked him if he could remember the date or time he had sent his letter declining the Washington acceptance. He said that it was late, just several weeks before classes were to begin, about mid-August. Apparently it was our letters that reached the dean's desk at the same time. It was a thrill beyond words to finally be able to thank the person who relinquished his acceptance that allowed me to begin medical training.

"In all things God works for the good of those who love him, who have been called according to his purpose." Romans 8:28 "...Called..."

Chapter Thirteen

Medical School

With only two weeks to make preparations to move from to St. Louis it was decided that Ruth and Tim remain in Nerstrand with my parents until I had found a place in St. Louis. I had difficulty finding a "hole in the wall' in which for us to live. Post World War II cities had little rooming space. I scanned the papers for rentals. Those available were far beyond our ability to afford.

Weeks passed and then I became caught up in a terrible scare. After the first eight weeks of anatomy, students were re-evaluated as to their suitability for a medical career. I made sure I was giving my best. However, when the test papers were returned I was not prepared for the failing grade I saw. In shock with paper in hand, I went to the office of the head of the department, Dr. Mildred Trotter. She invited me to sit down. I extended my hand with the test paper and with a voice choked with emotion said, "If this is a failure, I don't belong here." She perused it, got up, and strode into the assembly hall. She went up to the podium and announced that all of the test papers were to be passed to the center aisle where she gathered them.

That afternoon, some students were devastated when the new grades were posted while others of us were given a reprieve. An incorrect marking key had been used in the grading. I was still in medicine! Six others would not continue – some because of poor grades, but others because medicine was not turning out to be what they thought it would be. One, with whom I had become friendly, opted for a career in the FBI and became very successful.

At this time, a letter arrived from Ruth saying that she could no longer impose on Mother and Dad and was making plans to return to Winnipeg.

I literally went door to door inquiring about living quarters. One kind lady said that she had a third floor attic that was accessible by steps. There was no wallpaper on the walls. Water would be available from a washroom on the second floor and cooking would be on a hotplate. We could use it for $10 a month. This amount we could manage with the small scholarship we were receiving from First Evangelical Church in Naperville. Later, Mrs. H. S. Frank made available a few extra dollars from an agreement with the Board of Missions, but this money would need to be repaid if we did not go to the mission field.

After Ruth received my letter describing the attic, her reply letter stated, "Timmy and I are leaving for St. Louis tomorrow." The overnight trip was without incident. Tim slept the entire night in his collapsible bed-buggy. The time we spent in those humble surroundings was as enjoyable as if we were living in a mansion.

Later we found another third floor apartment only three blocks from the medical school. This time, water was available but the washroom again was on the second floor. We attended a Presbyterian church down the block. When it became known that Ruth was a skilled secretary using Greg shorthand, she was employed and given work that could be completed in our apartment. When the pastor visited us, he was shocked to see the accommodations. Within a week he presented a proposition too good to refuse. We could use an entire house, a parsonage in East St. Louis, if I would preach the Sunday sermon. With such opulence, we invited Ted and Jane Feierabend to share the upper half of it. They were in medical missionary preparation for India where Ted's parents served as evangelists their entire lifetime. Jane was a registered nurse like Ruth. The women alternated an evening shift at a nearby hospital while the men shepherded the children.

This was an ideal situation which eventually was to present a most serious problem.

The presence of an ordained pastor enlivened the church. The membership increased, the Sunday school became active, marriages and funerals needed to be conducted – all involving more and more time away from studying for medical school. I was burning the candle at both ends. Sleep was a premium. Infectious mononucleosis supervened with a ten-day hospitalization. My class was in the midst of pathology, a demanding study course, and was moving ahead. Would I be able to catch up?

The day on which I was discharged from the hospital, I remember making my way to the pathology lecture hall. I was so weak I could hardly make it. Things had literally fallen apart. Scholastically, I was in trouble to the point where I was called in by the dean who noted my standing in the class. My first year had initially found me in the middle third of my class. Why was I suddenly near the bottom?

When the dean learned of my extra-curricular activities, he was shocked. He then shared with me he was the one who had made the decision to accept me just before classes began two years earlier. He did not want to be proven wrong. Would I give up the church work and pastoral responsibilities if I were offered a Jackson-Johnson Scholarship? It was reserved for the top scholastic students with financial needs. Should he risk giving it to one in danger of flunking out? I did not disappoint him; I went from the bottom up to the top 15% in some of my later class work.

Concomitantly, Jim Vester and his wife were giving up an apartment two blocks from the medical school. Again, it was third floor but WITH ITS OWN BATH AND KITCHEN SINK! We were allowed to furnish it with surplus furniture from the parsonage. Ruth was able to convince the landlord that $15 a month was suitable. It was a delightful accommodation the last two years of medical school and was shared by Tim, as well as Mary and Beth who had joined our family in 1948 and 1950. Ruth declared these two pregnancies were the best of the six. She was cared for by an obstetrician who was tops in his field and was one of my professors. With each delivery, sedation was used and ten days were spent in the hospital. What luxury! The doctor refused to submit a charge. Barnes Hospital, host to the medical school, was also gracious.

Summers were spent in Minnesota in Mother and Dad's little guesthouse. I earned money by painting with my father. Our social life was lively with so many relatives nearby. Softball was the passion of the communities in those days, and was played at night under the lights. On June 28, 1948, Nerstrand dedicated new lights for their softball field. I pitched an extra inning game and had the thrill of hitting in the winning run. Exciting times were had pitching in two leagues – the church league and that of the surrounding towns', which included Faribault, a city of significant size. With my muscles from painting, I had no difficulty in handling prestigious teams. Four years later, after medical school graduation and during the internship at Ancker Hospital in St. Paul, the Nerstrand team wanted me to pitch in the Faribault tournament. I tried to explain that I was no longer in training. I don't know how I finally agreed to pitch against powerhouse Nutting Truck. I lasted three innings. I hung up my glove, never to use it again in an official game. Softball had always been my delight, having opened up so many avenues of opportunities. Never before had I been knocked out of the box. My softball career didn't deserve to end with a whimper.

Plans were underway to return to St. Louis by train. During the afternoon of our intended departure, a neighbor offered to sell his 1930 Model-A Ford for

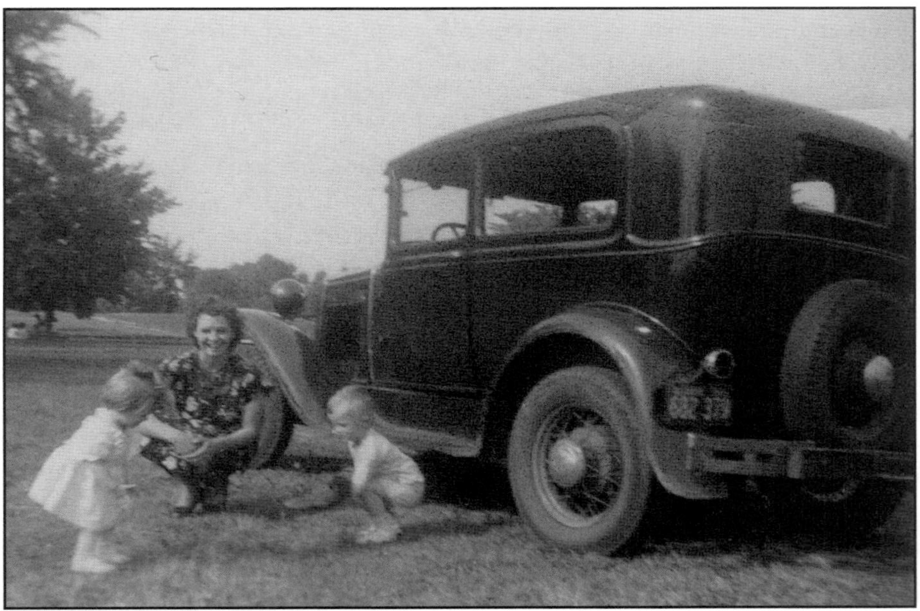

Our not-so-faithful 1930 Model-A Ford.

$275. Dad obtained insurance for it and we started out after supper. Before we had traveled 20 miles, we were pulled over by the state police. Our taillight was not working. With assurances we would have it fixed, we were allowed to go on. About the middle of Iowa I became so fatigued that I stopped for a cup of coffee. I had not had coffee in years. After a delay of time, Ruth left the family in the car and checked on me in the restaurant. She described the scene of a man hunched over, gazing into a cup of coffee as though it were poison. We safely completed the trip the next morning and continued to use the Ford during our medical school days, although something had to be fixed almost every week. When it rained and was damp, it would not start. Ruth and I pushed it to start many times. During the winter it would freeze up and not perform. My apprehension came to the fore years later in nightmares in which I would be driving in a precarious situation with the brakes not functioning. On our last trip home from St. Louis, I traded the Ford for a Nash-Lafayette that we named "Aaron," the preacher's helper. We were riding in style, my being a "Reverend" and a new "Doctor."

While the demanding "pastoral activities" of our year and a half in East St. Louis ultimately led to an imminent disaster in medical school training, many spiritual blessings were being reaped. Besides the preaching of sermons and activities with the youth as well as adults, visitations were done and decisions for Christ were made.

Chapter Fourteen

Rosalee

Home visitations were always demanding. However, hospital visits took precedent. I routinely visited the sick and the dying.

Mrs. Sweeney occasionally worshipped with our congregation, always alone. Word was that her twenty-one-year-old high strung and "wild" daughter was ill and was being cared for at the Christian Welfare Hospital where Ruth and Jane nursed. After visiting Mr. Chase, an elderly patient and former member of my congregation on his deathbed, I arrived at Rosalee's room. Mrs. Sweeney was standing in the hallway. She explained that the doctor did not want Rosalee to have visitors. However, she could not help herself and kept pacing in the hall in front of her daughter's room. She knew how ill Rosalee was. I peeked in and saw her eyes were closed. I explained to Mrs. Sweeney that the "no visitation" rule did not apply to pastors. However, Mrs. Sweeney excitedly exclaimed that no one was to disturb her daughter and asked that I not visit her.

In her role as a nurse, Ruth had access to Rosalee's medical chart that she shared with me. The diagnosis was acute leukemia. Progress notes indicated that Rosalee was beyond medical help.

During continuing visits with Mr. Chase, I would also drop in on Rosalee if Mrs. Sweeney wasn't present. I would stand by the bed and recite Scripture verses and pray briefly. Sometimes she would be conscious but not able to talk. Several days later, Rosalee rallied some and was asking the nurses for her mother and Rev. Gess. After receiving the message, I hurried to the hospital. No one was with her as the nurse ushered me into the room. I recited the 23rd Psalm, prayed, gently squeezed her hand, and left. I was apprehensive because of the strong position Mrs. Sweeney had taken about my not visiting her daughter. Several days later I returned for another visit. This time Mrs. Sweeney was quietly sitting in a chair some distance from her daughter's bed. On my entry, her eyes became wide with surprise. At that moment Rosalee spied me, raised her hand and spoke my name. Without any explanation, I moved over to the bed, read a portion of Luke 15 where the prodigal is received into the loving arms of his father, and prayed thankfully for God's willingness to forgive the past and receive the lost that they may be found. I turned to leave without engaging in discussion with Mrs. Sweeney. At the door I turned to look back at Rosalee. Her arm was raised and her hand was opened toward me. There was not to be another visit. During the night, Rosalee died. The following day Mrs. Sweeney came to the parsonage to ask if I would conduct the funeral. She said she did not have words appropriate enough to express the gratitude she felt for being able to be present during that last visit.

Following my resignation from the pastoral duties in East St. Louis on September 5, 1949, the last two years of medical training were a delight. Study time was spent meeting the requirements of the medical courses rather than preparing for sermons, church activities, baptisms, weddings, funerals and time-consuming visitations and subsequent counseling sessions. Study times were uninterrupted at the medical school's library just three and a half blocks from our "spacious" apartment. It was an uplifting feeling to be better prepared for the classes and secure a good ranking in the class rather than the lower. I had status. My relationship with the professors became open and casual. I was beginning to feel like a doctor. I successfully passed my National Board Examinations, enabling reciprocity between state medical licensing boards. Meanwhile, Ruth took her "Oath of Allegiance" to the United States of America. At the ceremony the judge picked Ruth out from the group and directed a question to "Miss Canada." He asked, "If the United States and Canada became involved in a war, where would your allegiance be?" He broke into a smile when, without hesitation, Ruth answered, "I am now an American citizen."

Even though my third year tuition increased to $700 (up from $600 the first two years), the loss of financial remuneration from the church was countered by the Jackson-Johnson Scholarship from the medical school, the missionary preparation grant from the Evangelical Board of Missions, and the annual grant from First Evangelical Church in Naperville. Each year, I would make a speaking trip to Naperville. It always was a thrill to fellowship with my former professors from the seminary and North Central College, and especially Mrs. Baumgartner with whom I struggled for two of the war years feeding budding preachers in the Theologue Eating Club. It is mind-boggling to think of the multitude of sincere Christians who helped me realize a calling to medical missions that I received as a lad of eleven years. Sacrificial gifts came from family and friends, like Harold Utzinger and Eddie Stevens, and from former parishioners at St. Cloud, Graham, and Mayer and our home church at Nerstrand.

Especially exciting during the junior and senior years at medical school was the clinical work at the hospitals. The list of "firsts" kept growing: first work ups and care of patients, first cystoscopy, first spinal tap (which prepared me for the thousands that would follow during the polio epidemic in St. Paul during internship the summer of 1951 and almost two decades in Africa), first episiotomy repair, the first eversion of an eye lid, and many other first surgical procedures. By the time of graduation on June 6, 1951, I felt I could take on the world. It had been a four-year period of stacking away knowledge of diseases and experience in handling them. A few weeks later as an intern with complete care of the patient, my tune would change. I was furtively reaching out to the residents and the visiting doctors. How could I go to Africa and be completely alone?

Several events and dates stood out during the last two years of medical school. I finally succumbed to the removal of troubling impacted wisdom teeth.

I also underwent a tonsillectomy and learned that I was especially responsive to morphine. The usual dose put me under so far that the surgeon could have done the procedure without further anesthesia. They caught me falling off the cart on the way to the operating room.

Our children – Beth, Tim and Mary – enjoying their Christmas toys in 1950. This was the first picture taken with our new $29.95 Pony Eastman Kodak camera, the biggest purchase we made during the year.

We invested $29.95 in a Pony 828 Eastman Kodak camera with which we were to capture precious moments of our family and future events. On December 4, 1950, I wrote a letter to Dr. Karefa-Smart in Sierra Leone. I do not remember the occasion or content of the letter. Seven years later I was to meet him in Freetown and realize the impact he was having on the country both medically and politically. Only irregular balloting kept him from being president of the Republic of Sierra Leone. Our friendship stemmed from the fact that in my position as Field Representative for the United Methodist Church, I sided with him against leading senior missionaries to engage more Sierra Leoneans in active leadership in the conference.

During these last two years at medical school, the development of our children was a thing of wonder. The children had many friends and shared frequent upper respiratory infections. During one episode of high fever and delirium, Mary kept singing "Away in a Manger" over and over again without waking up. The entire family had the experience of taking gentian violate because of an enterobius vermicularis invasion. Tim had an independent personally and would frequently challenge his parents. Theologically, he developed early and was praying spontaneous prayers by age three. His trustworthiness also developed early. We depended on him and his judgment even in his first school years in

Africa. Mary and Beth, who were born in St. Louis, were ladies from the very beginning. Before the age of two, Mary, too, was praying like a preacher using phrases such as, "We pray in the name of Him who taught us to pray...." She was always ahead of things – running the first day she walked and advanced in her schoolwork and accomplishments. Beth walked the day before her first birthday, so by the end of our medical school training Ruth and I were kept busy trying to keep up with children taking off in three different directions.

After taking the examinations for State Medical Boards, June 7-9, we had mixed feelings while packing "Wesley" our car for the final trip back to Minnesota, stopping on the way at the home of Pastor McIntyre in Washington, Iowa. Pastor McIntyre was pastoring there and had been the one who had made available the East St. Louis parsonage for us and the Feierabends. During the four years in St. Louis, we had grown to love the people and the place. An important part of our lives had been invested there. The thought of not seeing very dear friends again was overwhelming. It was a fact of life that we had to learn, for it was to happen again and again in the future.

Chapter Fifteen

Internship

The first house we could truly call our own.

My first choice for internship was Ancker General Hospital in St. Paul. Being highly desirable, it offered a remuneration of only $35 a month. Dr. Carl Heinmiller, in his wisdom and foresight, had arranged for us to be placed under a missionary's salary of $2,200 a year with $720 rental allowance. Never before did we have the luxury of an income of more than $10 a day!

Rentals in St. Paul were still difficult. We found a little house with a "For Sale" sign costing $5,000 on St. Clair Avenue five blocks from Ancker Hospital. Richard and Sylvia Rasmussen, members of Calvary Evangelical Church, offered to help us as struggling medical missionaries in training and provided a $5,000 interest-free loan. (A year later when we were leaving for Africa, the house was sold for $6,500.) It was wonderful to be back at Calvary where I had attended during high school and where I got started in my softball career as a very young teenager. Now, fifteen years later, the young men wanted to know if I still pitched. At a church league game during the first week back in St. Paul, I retired the first fifteen batters in a row and our team was victorious. However, the demanding internship absorbed my time day and night. With the loss of training periods, I never seriously pitched again. It had been a wonderful ride, but that thrilling sideline was over.

The sport of fishing had always given me pleasure. Between graduation from medical school and the beginning of a rotating internship, Grandma and Grandpa Gess offered to care for the kiddies while Ruth and I took off for a fishing trip.

Years earlier, Roscoe Hoiosen and I had fished a secret lake near Fergus Falls. Ruth and I headed there. We had Wesley fixed up for camping and sleeping. The fishing was great. One night it rained heavily and our car got stuck in the mud. With Ruth at the wheel, I literally lifted the car to free it. I felt something "give" in my back, which was followed by great pain that persisted the next day and made it difficult to bend over. Recurrent episodes were to happen in the following fifteen years and would keep me in bed for four or five days at a time. Finally, at the University of Minnesota, I underwent surgery. The post-op report was devastating – no improvement could be expected. I would have to stand back while Ruth handled the heavy luggage. Golfing no longer was an option. Painful episodes were to occur from time to time. An exercise program was instituted to keep me in shape that has continued to today.

After buying the house, Ruth arranged it into a lovely living place. In her enthusiasm to clean up the yard, the fire she started got out of hand thanks to a strong wind and it threatened our neighbor's house. In the melee, Ruth singed her new permanent. The prompt response of the fire department saved the day.

Being a regional hospital, Ancker had wards of patients with tuberculosis. My first clerkship was the care of thirty TB patients and their attendant needs. I came to know them well. At the time, lung lobectomies were in vogue. Post-operatively, there were critical times. In their weakened condition, some patients were not able to handle what was life saving to others. One of my patients was not recovering. Family members realized that all medical hope was being abandoned. The visiting staff member asked me to write the orders to stop medicines and supportive measures, to "pull the plug." To this day, I am surprised by my retort, "These are your orders, you write and sign them." The patient did not have a "Lazarus" experience.

In the emergency and receiving rooms, Milo Hansen, with whom I was paired in the internship, and I bravely entered the fray but only with the help of the experienced nurses. We were to be involved in the last major poliomyelitis epidemic to occur in Minnesota. Brinker machines lined the walls of the wards that would help the critically ill polio patients to breathe. It was our responsibility in the emergency rooms to make the diagnoses, which required a spinal tap. For three weeks, we went from room to room to perform this procedure. The nurses would expertly have the patient positioned and draped. We would ascertain the landmarks, insert the spinal needle, withdraw the stylet, collect the specimen, remove the needle and move on to the next patient. We became so adept at spinals that we could "feel" when the needle was in the spinal canal without even withdrawing the stylet to check for the fluid. This training was to be invaluable for Africa, as most of our anesthesia there – without an anesthesiologist in attendance – was given as local and regional blocks.

My being on duty practically night and day was a good excuse for Ruth and the children to visit her sister Irene and husband, Nat, in Vancouver. They were to be gone for three weeks. During this period there were times when I would get only three hours or so of sleep in a three day duty schedule. Besides being tired and worn out, I developed a fever and listlessness. When it became alarming, I was hospitalized. The right side of my throat and face were progressively swelling. The temperature continued to climb – 102, 103, 104 degrees with spikes even more in spite of antibiotics being administered orally, intramuscularly and intravenously. An incision to my pharynx was being considered to relieve the swelling from a "possible abscess." A fellow intern, who was doing his clerkship on pediatrics, visited me. He exclaimed, "Lowell, you've got the mumps!" All medications were discontinued, the temperature came down, and I was discharged home a week later to be with my family who had returned from Vancouver. A week later the mumps appeared on the other side, but with the easy life at home and the loving care of Ruth, a registered nurse, my recovery was uneventful – I even took the children fishing.

During my illness, I missed two weeks of the obstetrics and gynecology clerkship. I had had quite a stint in OB-GYN as a senior at City Hospital in St. Louis, and did not consider this loss of time and training important at the time. Little did I know that for the next decade this would be one of my major challenges in Africa. Besides difficult deliveries and Caesarean sections, vesico-vaginal fistulae repair presented great challenges. Prolonged deliveries and improper handling doomed young mothers to isolation with this offensive condition. Every effort was put forth to restore their social and maternal lives with corrective surgery. Even when I had finished an ophthalmology residency and was heading an eye program thirteen years after my Ancker internship, I was routinely doing emergency C-sections at Taiama, Sierra Leone.

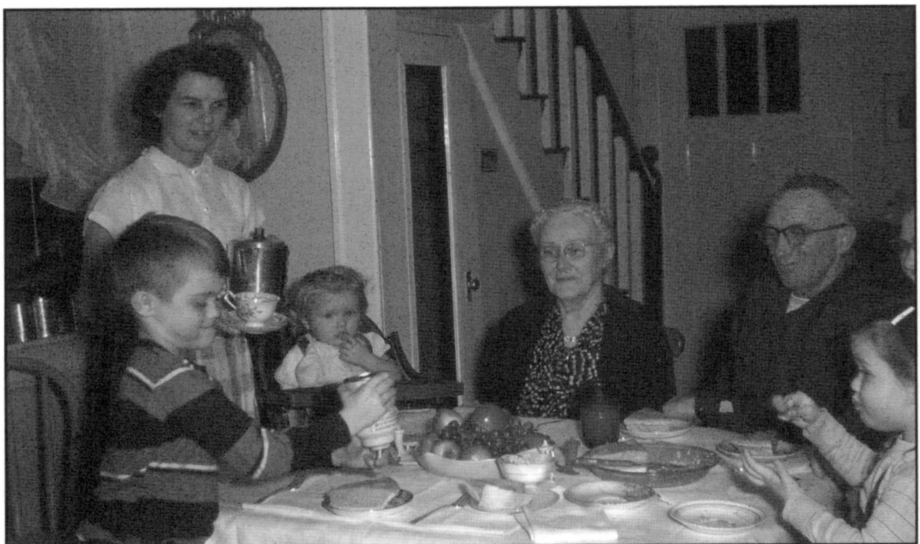

Great-Grandma Emma Wolf visits us in our new home.

Family life was the most luxurious we had known in the first six years of our married life – a whole house to ourselves. Tim started school. Mary insisted on going out with the gang on Halloween. On arriving home, she burst into tears, "I couldn't keep up. They went too far." Preparations were made for her tonsils to be removed. She took along her mask to frighten the nurses. However, she was the one to be frightened when she was being held down during ether administration. We wondered whether her trusting nature would be damaged in the future.

At the school ground, Ruth and I enjoyed the skating rink. Ruth was an expert skater, having spent much of her teen years on the Winnipeg rinks. Her younger sister, Beverly, was a speed skater who competed in places as far away as Minneapolis. I was an old Macalester College hockey player.

As the year drew to a close, we were busily engaged in "packing for Africa." Nerstrand Evangelical Church provided funds for a kerosene refrigerator. Pharmaceutical houses made available infant foods. John arrived a bit early on August 7th while we were still at Red Bird Mission helping out while Dr. and Mrs. Everett Schaeffer were on vacation, who returned the night of John's birth. During the night after attending to an emergency, I came to the Obstetrics Unit to admire our new son. He was ashen with respiratory distress. The only available suction bulb had been used earlier for a meningitis patient. I quickly performed mouth-to-mouth resuscitation, removing the obstruction. He became a pink laddie. Unnerved by this crisis, Ruth insisted that his incubator be placed at her bedside. She would not sleep while there might be some danger to her new son.

With the end of the internship and facing the real world, I was not as confident as I had been at the end of medical school. I broached the question to Dr. Heinmiller, Mission Board Executive Secretary, of taking another six months of surgical training. While that privilege was to come several years later with two years of general surgery and three years of ophthalmology, it did not fit into the schedule and needs of Nigeria at that time. We were scheduled to leave for Africa the first week in December 1952, after visiting our supporting churches in Illinois, Pennsylvania and West Virginia. It had taken 25 years of schooling to prepare us for the moment of commissioning.

Chapter Sixteen

Commissioning

A summary of my "burning bush" call to be a medical missionary.

Ruth and I were kneeling at the altar rail of Calvary Evangelical Church on November 9, 1952. On our heads were the hands of Bishop E. W. Praetorius, the Rev. Frank Spong and the Rev. Floyd Bosshardt. We were being commissioned as medical missionaries of the Evangelical United Brethren Church to Bambur, Nigeria. Calvary was part of the Evangelical Church that merged with the United Brethren in Christ Church in 1946 becoming the Evangelical United Brethren Church. The EUB Church later merged with the Methodist Church in 1968 to become the United Methodist Church.

I had graduated from the Evangelical Theological Seminary in Naperville, Illinois, in 1945. Two years were spent in the pastoral ministry in Minnesota. Following graduation in 1951 from the Washington University School of Medicine, I completed a rotating internship at the Ancker Hospital in St. Paul. Several years earlier, Ruth had obtained her registered nurse's degree from the Winnipeg General Hospital in Manitoba, Canada. We finally had come to this momentous occasion!

Ruth's Background. Ruth was born in Brookdale, Manitoba, Canada. Her banker father was posted at different locations. While in Regina, Saskatchewan, when Ruth was six years old, the bank staff lost their jobs, including her father. The family moved back to Brookdale where Ruth obtained her primary schooling. Just before she finished high school in Winnipeg, her father suffered a fatal heart attack in 1933. The insurance and savings were meager.

Ruth graduated from a business college at the age of 18 and was the main support for her mother and two younger sisters for five years at a paper products business; her secretary's salary was just $45 a month. During this time she was converted, yielding her life to the Lordship of Jesus Christ. She felt a strong call to medical missions and dreamed of becoming a nurse. Yet, financial resources were not available. She took courage and asked her boss about a raise in salary. The denial was earth shaking. In shock, she walked out the door and down the street to the principal of the business college where she had received her training. He had in his hand a letter that mentioned a position at a grain exchange. She reported the next day at a salary of $95 a month. In two years she was able to save enough to enter nurses' training.

The three years at Winnipeg General Hospital were demanding but thrilling. She became president of the Christian Nurses' Association. Time was granted to visit her sister in Naperville, Illinois, during her sister's first delivery. Her brother-in-law happened to have been my seminary roommate the year before. I was invited to their home for dinner, which had been prepared by Ruth. I was stunned by her beauty and composure – so much so, I don't even remember what I ate. (Later she informed me that it was pork chops.) Her Christian character was the one for whom I had reserved my love. Within a week, she boarded a train back to Canada, but not out of my life. Letters and visits followed.

Lowell's Background. My beginnings were at Paynesville, Minnesota. I was baptized in the Salem Evangelical Church. Along with home and school, the church was the center of my life – Sunday school, Daily Vacation Bible School, Youth Fellowship and all the social events germane to a German community surrounded by Scandinavian Lutherans to the south and German Roman Catholics to the north.

The church was our social center as well as our place of worship. Lay leader William Sack prayed for me by name. His daughter, Lily, was my early Sunday school teacher. Later, Mr. Rudolph Heitke had a major impact on my life. In spite of our squirming and rowdiness, Mr. Heitke and his prepared lessons got through to me, preparing me for my "conversion" at age of nine when, kneeling at the altar rail, I sought and received forgiveness of sins and the assurance of a new life in Christ Jesus. Two years later, again kneeling at the altar rail, I received my "call" to medical missions.

Many years later before he died, I was able to thank Mr. Heitke for his marvelous help in presenting to me the Christian message and the claims of the Lord Jesus Christ on my life. Later, kneeling at the altar at Koronis, my commitment to fulltime Christian service was sealed.

Love, Honor and Cherish. In 1945, Ruth obtained her registered nurse's degree from the Winnipeg General Hospital. On her visit to St. Cloud, Minnesota, where I was serving the Grace Evangelical Church as well as the Graham Evangelical Church, we knelt at the altar rail. Following prayers, I proposed to Ruth. She accepted my pledge of love and the engagement ring. We prayed again. The ring on her finger was fortunate as it was to ward off a previous suitor a short time later. We were married December 29, 1945. In the ensuing two years, we served churches at St. Cloud-Graham and Mayer, Minnesota, while incorporating some additional pre-medical courses.

Acceptance to the Washington School of Medicine in St. Louis, Missouri, in the summer of 1951 was the opening of the Red Sea. All other applications to medical schools had been denied. An exchange of letters with the dean just weeks before the beginning of the school year "parted the waters." The next four years were to be the most demanding of my life to date. Following the internship at Ancker General Hospital, Ruth and I again knelt at an altar rail, this time in Calvary Evangelical Church, for the commissioning service. Twenty-six days later, we were on board the *S.S. America* on our way to Africa.

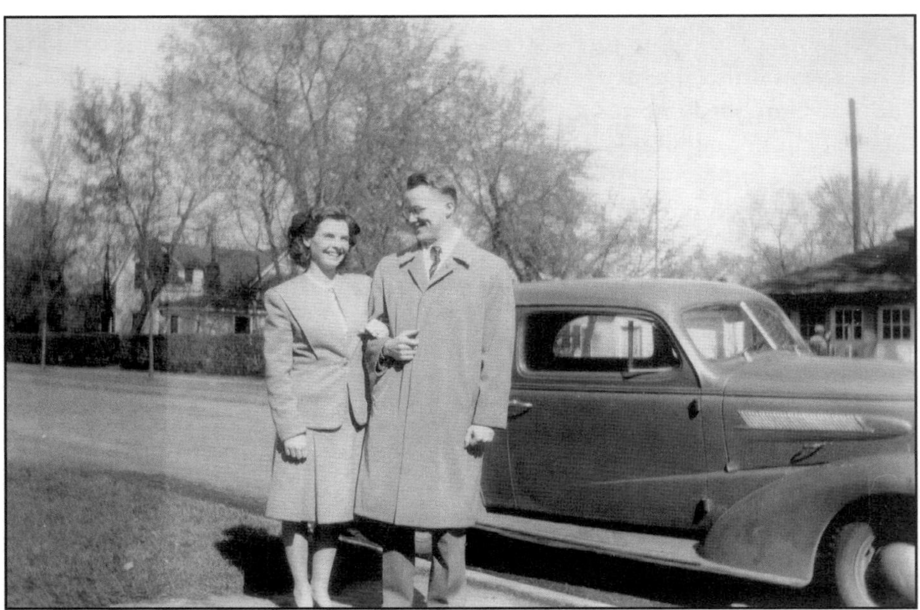

September 29, 1945, the day after our engagement.

Part II: Mission

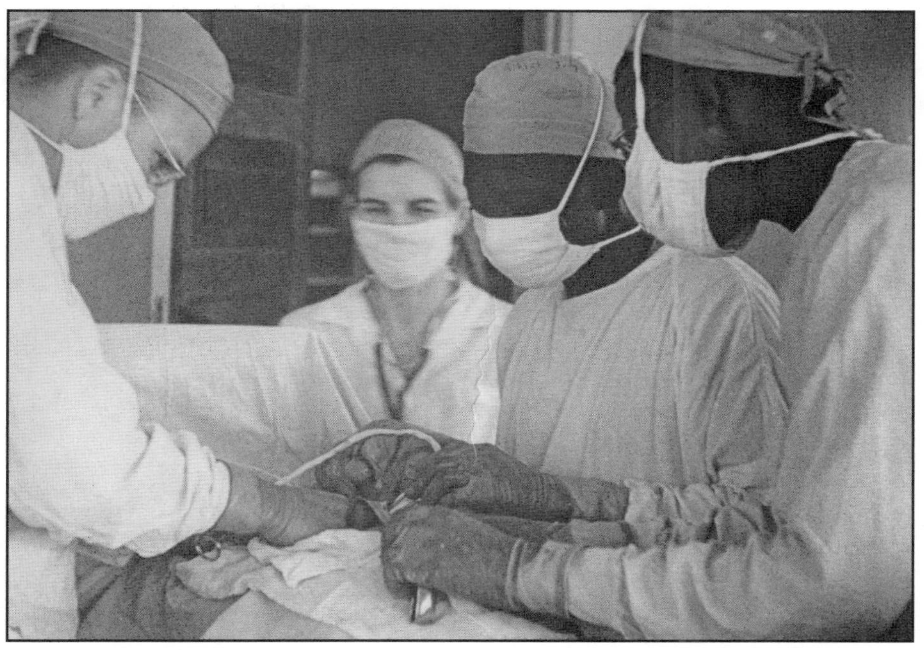

Jesus replied, "Go back and report to John what you hear and see:
The blind receive sight, the lame walk, those who have leprosy are cured,
the deaf hear…and the Good News is preached to the poor."

–Matthew 11:4-5

Chapter Seventeen

The First Surgery

Guinter Memorial Hospital, Bambur, Nigeria, Africa, 1953.

I was deep in the abdominal cavity of a young man. It was Monday, January 12, 1953. Ruth and I, along with our four children, had just arrived at Bambur, Adamowa Province, Nigeria two days earlier. The day before – Sunday – we attended church where Dr. Harold Elliot preached in Hausa, a regional dialect. (I remember other Sundays when teacher and evangelist Kura Tella held the rapt attention of the congregation.) Today was my first day at work.

Kura Tella preaching, surrounded by the Guinter Memorial Hospital staff.

The patient I was attending to had been carried by four men on a litter from an inaccessible area beyond a range of hills. At a wedding feast, an altercation had turned ugly and a spear had been thrust into his abdomen. Jean Baldwin was administering the anesthetic. Ruth was circulating. One of the hospital's five Nigerian attendants was assisting me. We had only met this morning and were not aware of each other's abilities or capabilities.

Bambur church. Mallam Tela preaching in Hausa at the Bambur church.

The small one and a half inch spear wound was enlarged to four inches to allow adequate exposure. It was evident that the bowel had been perforated. By the grace of God, the spear had impaled on the vertebral column between the vena cava and the abdominal aorta without lacerating either. I found the segment of intestine that had been lacerated and prepared to repair it. A surgical resident at Ancker Hospital where I interned, Dr. Anderson, had shown me how to do it. And yet in that moment I could not remember if it was "intima to intima or serosa to serosa." Unless done correctly, overwhelming peritonitis would prove fatal. One might have said, "Flip a coin and just do one of them. At least you have a fifty percent chance of success."

This was tragic. I was dealing with a man's life and I couldn't remember how to proceed. How could a farm boy from Minnesota be put in a situation such as this? Surely the Lord would come to his assistance.

While all of this was going through my mind, nothing was being done at the table. After about a minute, Ruth asked, "Are you alright, dear?" I responded by saying, "Let us pray. Lord bless this young man with your love and your healing. Show me how to do my part."

In that moment I clearly remembered Dr. Anderson's warning, "Be sure to carefully place the inverting serosal sutures." He didn't even mention the intima. Now six months later, it all became clear – serosa to serosa. I even remembered that in the case of intestinal laceration – with which we were dealing – his counsel was to close in a transverse diameter so as to not narrow the passage.

I was not content with a single layer closure. I fashioned a double inverting repair and then quickly ran the gut to rule out any additional lacerations. Four units of saline were used to irrigate the soiled abdominal cavity. A newly developed antibiotic, oral chloramphenicol, was given. Mildred Rebstock, a classmate of mine at North Central College, had synthesized it at Parke Davis Laboratories. Later, she was presented to President Eisenhower for her achievement. Her brother, John, a lifelong friend, had provided me with a supply of this wonder medicine just prior to our departure for Africa.

It would take some tact to explain to the patient the extensive four-inch incision when the original spear wound had only left an inch and a half opening. Furthermore, a rubber drain stuck out through the incision.

It was only after the surgery had been completed that I stopped to realize how all of this must have sounded to the nurses and staff. This was my first surgery. They had no idea if I were even a real doctor. Here I was literally coming in on a wing and a prayer. Did they, or did they not, have a doctor?

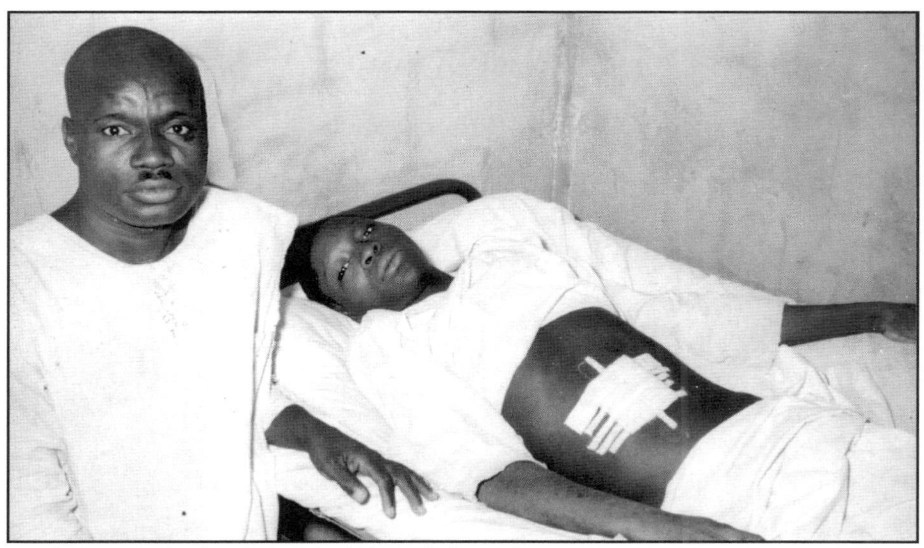

Yusufu post-op with a friend who helped him to the hospital.

In his condition, the patient – Yusufu – was willing to believe in me and to trust me. His belief and trust went beyond the care of his body. We were to realize this two years after his brush with death. An evangelist we knew learned of a Christian gathering in an inaccessible area near where Yusufu had come. Yusufu had listened to the hymns, prayers, and the testimonies of the staff during his time of recuperation. He came to trust God for his life and yielded to the Lordship of Jesus Christ. His spared life made an impact for good to his family and friends.

With the strength of his youth, Yusufu pulled through a most serious life threatening experience. I often wondered how long it would have taken for my acceptance – to staff and community – if the first patient I had touched had died.

Five decades later I still have a fond and remarkably clear memory of Yusufu and answered prayer in a time of need. My only regret is that I never had the opportunity to visit with him again as a fellow believer.

Chapter Eighteen

Love, A Beautiful Story

A young mother, who had just given birth, was brought to us. Due to a retained placenta, she was bleeding, in shock and unconscious. Her husband was one of her litter bearers. I explained to him that his wife needed to have blood or else her life would slip away. I proceeded to take a small sample of blood from each of the four men. They didn't understand why I was checking them when it was the patient who needed help. Three of them were not compatible for transfusion but one was – her husband.

We took him along with the patient to surgery. We placed him in a little room off to the side while the nurses prepared his wife for surgery. I explained to him I needed to take a little more blood. Ruth had been giving him glass after glass of orange juice and sweetened water. He didn't understand all this attention. We had him lie down and I put a needle into his vein. Underneath the bed I hid the flask that collected his blood. He looked very strong, so instead of taking just one unit of blood, I took two. We then slipped the blood into surgery and began administering it to his wife.

In the moments that followed, her life hovered between life and death. Suddenly, her pulse began to strengthen. We immediately performed the surgery she needed and her condition improved. The entire staff was elated and was beginning to rejoice when suddenly I turned and found I was looking into the face of her husband. He had tired of being in the bed in the other room and had wandered into the surgery without cap or gown to see what was going on. His gaze was transfixed on the bottle of blood. He knew it was his blood – and in Africa you don't give blood because when you "lose" blood, you die.

His face was set in a firm, hard look I had never quite seen before. I cringed because I feared what he was thinking. We had deceived him. We had taken a large amount of blood and now he saw that blood being given to his wife. No one spoke.

At that moment, his wife stirred and murmured something audible only to him and me. Unbelievable. She had spoken his name. His face melted and changed, showing genuine love and compassion for his wife.

In the days that followed, she gained strength and he walked around saying, "See my wife? She has my blood." He was proud to say that his blood was coursing through his wife's veins. The staff understood his dialect and said, "That's not unusual. You were redeemed not with corruptible things such as silver or gold, but with the precious blood of Jesus" (I Peter 1:19). This Scripture struck home and took root in his life.

During his wife's recuperation many wonderful things happened. The day she was strong enough to move, as I came to her bed she did something women never do in this part of Africa. She reached out her hand and took mine in hers and said, "Na gode Allah" ("I thank God"). Her husband, who was standing on the other side of the bed, smiled at the unusual sight of his wife reaching out to touch another man, intuitively realizing this was a laying of hands for health and healing.

"She has my blood!"

This lovely couple came to know so much of the grace of God during the time of healing that they became firm believers in the Lord Jesus Christ. They were so glad to be alive they went from bed to bed and gave all their possessions to other patients prior to leaving the hospital. Then they set off down the road, she following her husband respectfully two steps behind, each swinging their arms completely carefree.

To this very day, my eyes still swell up with tears as I see them disappearing down the road unencumbered by any possessions, simply happy to be alive. Skeptics could say that this healing wasn't special, just good nursing care and good doctors. I say, "Not so." "They shall lay hands on the sick and they shall recover." (Mark 16:18)

Chapter Nineteen

Meningitis Epidemic

During the January 1954 meningitis outbreak, the number of cases was so great that the hospital wards could not accommodate all the patients needing treatment. The magnitude of the outbreak was greater than the elders at Bambur could remember.

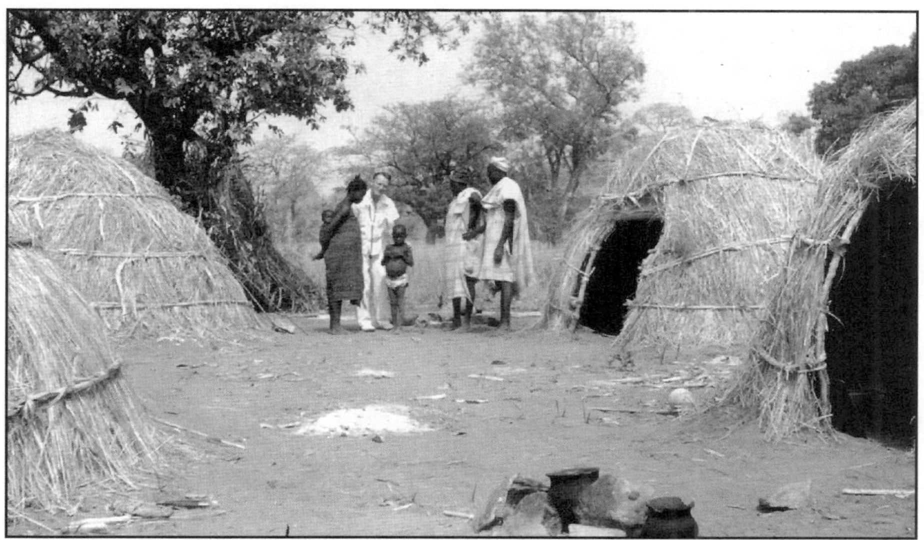

Isolation huts were built away from the hospital to keep meningitis patients from infecting others.

We kept building isolation huts a short distance from the hospital compound as everyone was afraid of becoming infected. Without treatment the mortality rate ran eighty to ninety percent. With the overwhelming numbers, we were suddenly aware of the dwindling supplies of penicillin and chloramphenical. Patients who were strong enough to take oral medications responded to triple sulpha.

The Guinter Memorial Hospital was located 300 miles from the nearest pharmacy at Jos. The roads had only recently become passable following the rainy season, which isolated the hospital from the outside world for a four to five month period. Not trusting solely in the four-wheel-drive Land Rover to get through, arrangements were also made to send runners whose one-way trip required seven to ten days over a hostile landscape.

The fateful day came when the antibiotics were exhausted. The seriously ill patients unable to swallow triple sulpha were dying.

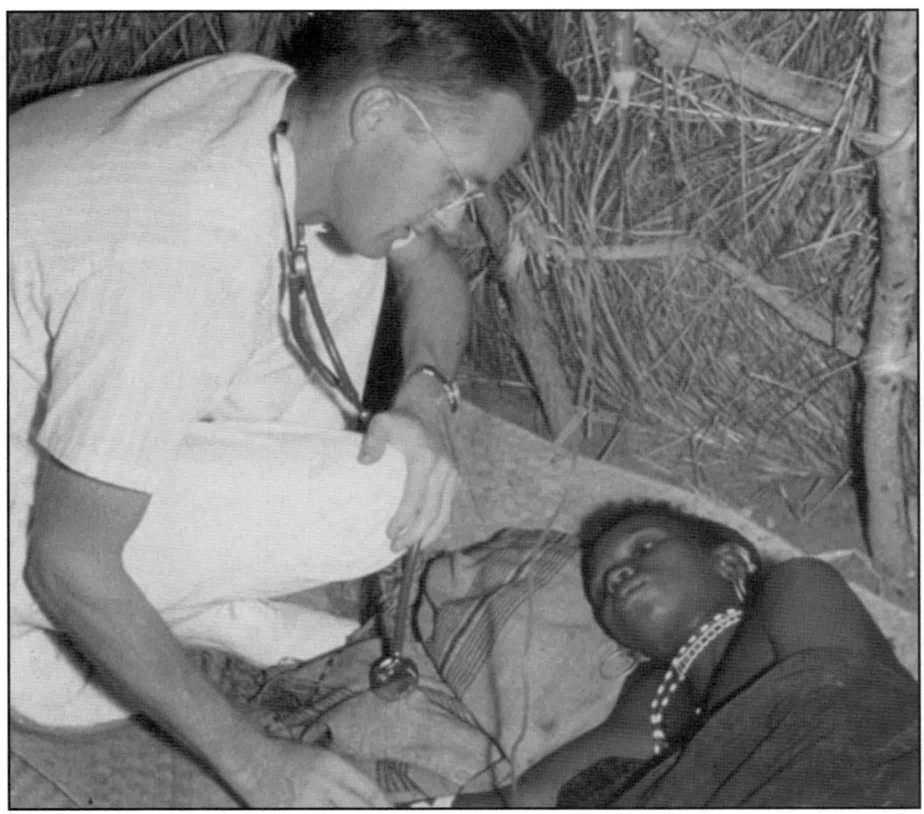

A young African mother receiving an intravenous injection in an isolation hut during the meningitis epidemic.

While kneeling in prayer over a seriously ill patient with a faint pulse, the Holy Spirit directed my thoughts: We only had one or two stomach tubes to "feed" patients the sulpha tablets, yet had dozens of patients. Using a tube was impractical and risky – especially if the tube was inserted into the lungs instead of the stomach and the patient drowned. The only plausible course was to inject the sulpha.

A mortar and pestle were sterilized and placed on a sterile towel. With cap, mask and sterile gloves on, I ground up the tablets. Saline was added for proper concentration. Then the dispensing nurses, armed with large syringes and very large needles, began the rounds of injections. We were concerned our patients might suffer from sterile abscesses because of the sulpha tablet composition, but were delighted to find that few developed. Those few who developed abscesses were considered a badge of honor – the patient was alive to have the abscesses drained! It was exciting to realize our patients' family members were not carrying away expired loved ones.

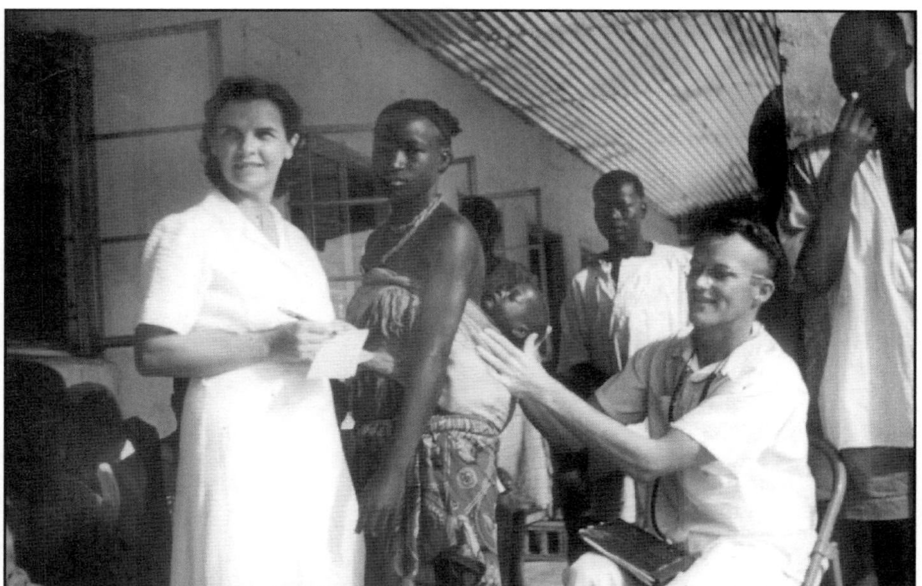

Ruth and I seeing patients on the overflow veranda.

The Land Rover did not return before the runners. A week passed before the penicillin finally arrived, and we thanked God for subsequent healing. The two runners enjoyed a notoriety of which they had never dreamed. They were the true "helping hands" in handling this epidemic. After another four or five days, as suddenly as the outbreak had begun, it vanished.

Chapter Twenty

Leprosy

A leprosy patient holding the Bible minus some of his fingers.

The man preaching at our newly established leprosy village near Bambur had difficulty keeping the pages of his Bible from turning in the wind. His fingers were missing. He was suffering from a prolonged infection of leprosy, one of the most feared diseases in the world. AIDS had not appeared on the scene. This dear man helped me check each patient to ensure they had swallowed their medicine. His form of leprosy was tuberculoid, a type with skin lesions and nerve damage with loss of sensitivity. Eventually the fingers and toes become ulcerated and could be reabsorbed by the body.

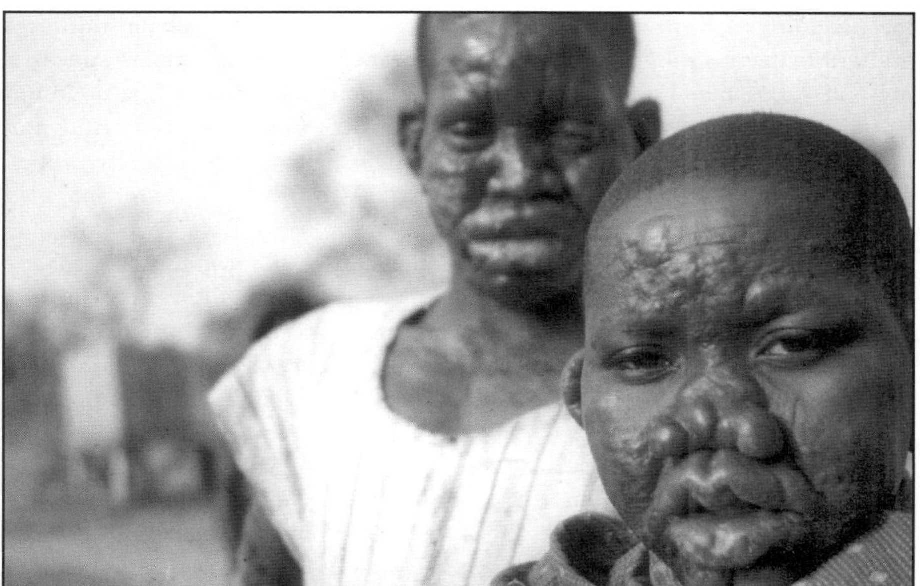

These before and after pictures of a twelve-year-old girl with lepromatous leprosy attest to an effective six-month treatment by dapsone, (diaminodiphenylsulfone, referred to as DDS). It took another year for her features to normalize.

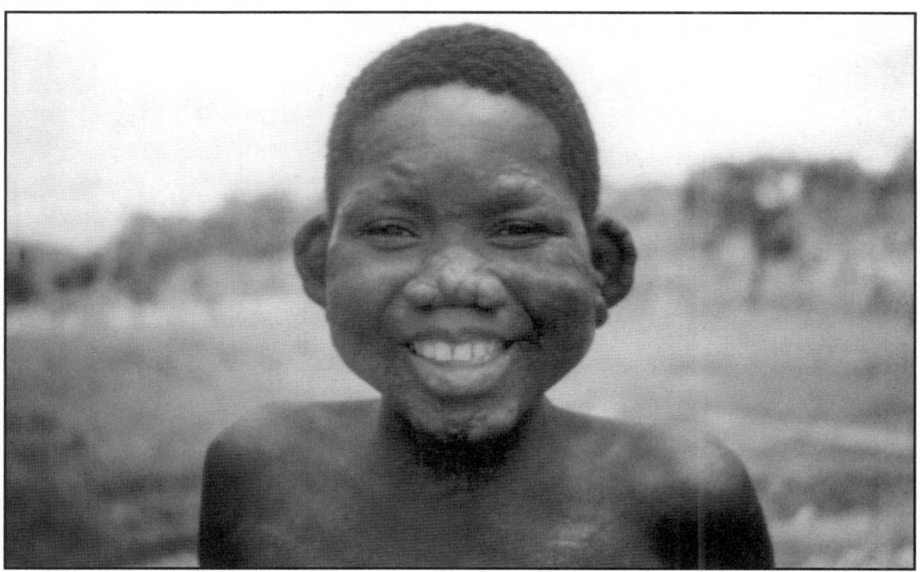

In the 1950s, leprosy medication had progressed beyond the use of chaulmoogra oil. Good results, however, were clouded by a resistance that developed when solely using dapsone.

By 1991, the World Health Organization had launched a leprosy elimination program that reduced the prevalence of leprosy to 1 in 10,000 people in ninety of the 122 countries with reported leprosy infections. They did this by instituting a multi drug therapy program consisting of dapsone, rifampin and clofazimine that prevented resistance from developing. The all too common erythema nodosum leprosum reaction was effectively treated with thalidomide, a notorious drug that in the early 1960s caused severe birth defects in many babies born of women who had taken it to alleviate morning sickness. In 1998, the FDA approved thalidomide for the treatment of erythema nodosum leprosum.

The leprosy village at Bambur no longer exists. The multi-drug therapy program cured more than eight million leprosy patients worldwide within ten years. Leprosy patients are no longer isolated as they had been going back to the time of Christ. Reconstructive surgery, pioneered by Dr. Ross, helps patients who were not treated early enough with medication that would have prevented the crippling aspect of the disease.

It is my hope and prayer that leprosy – like smallpox – will eventually be eradicated. Governments, volunteer groups and churches are engaged in a wide range of medical, surgical, educational and rehabilitation programs to provide holistic care to meet the physical, psychological and spiritual needs of leprosy sufferers and their communities. How Christ ministered to those with leprosy is the motivational force for those who care for leprosy patients today.

Chapter Twenty-One

Sharing Life's Blood

January 10, 1955, was full of surprises. The inguinal hernia repair I was performing turned out to be a "sliding" hernia with part of the urinary bladder drawn into the large herniation. An extra hour of surgical time was needed – and it was already far into the afternoon.

The long line of patients who had queued up for the day was eventually seen. One young Fulani girl was a special concern. Postpartum bleeding had left her in shock. Plasma expanders were immediately set up. She was in dire need of a blood transfusion.

Later in the afternoon, Dr. and Mrs. Ira McBride were scheduled to have physicals as the mission board required periodic health reports. At the close of the examination, Dr. McBride commented, "What I really need is a hair cut." Within moments the hospital guard was dispatched to our residence on the hill for the barbering equipment.

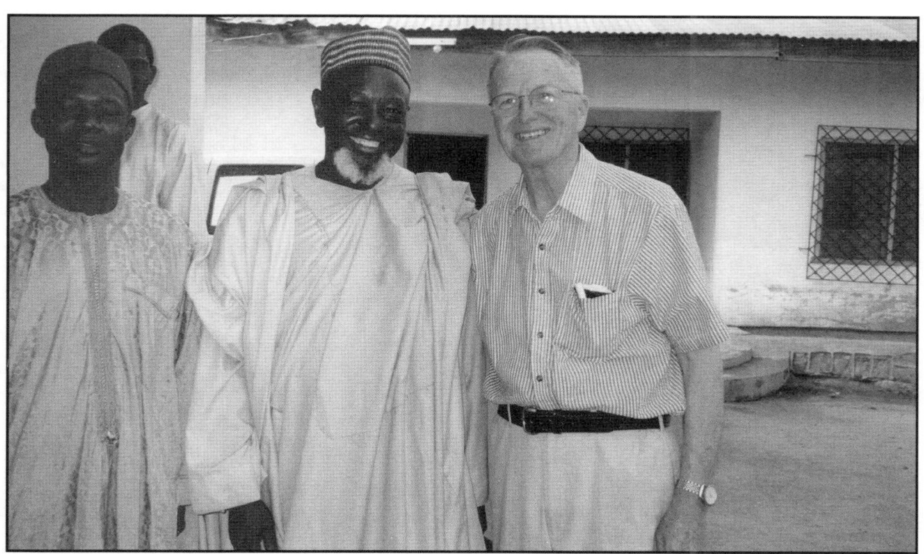

Mamman Ali Kirim, chairman of the Inter-Religious Affairs for Taraba State, Nigeria. Mamman helped us in our home during our stay in Nigeria.

While his hair was being cut, he asked about the young Fulani girl. Earlier in the day he had been hunting in the Lau swamp to secure some venison. After a successful hunt, he started home. Suddenly he came upon a small group of women and stopped to help. He learned a young mother had lost her newborn child and now was near death as a result of postpartum bleeding. He agreed to transport her to Guinter Memorial Hospital. According to Nigerian custom, men were not allowed to touch women in the delivery period, so two ladies climbed into the back of Dr. McBride's truck. Other women lifted the patient up to them. They cradled the patient for nearly ten miles over rough and bumpy roads. On arrival at the hospital, this was the patient who I immediately treated with the plasma expanders.

In my conversation with Dr. McBride, I mentioned that this Fulani girl desperately needed a blood transfusion. Relatives and friends were unwilling to donate blood. Childbirth deaths were not considered unusual.

After thoughtful consideration, Dr. McBride replied, "If my blood is compatible, I would like to finish my Samaritan act of compassion." His blood was compatible and a unit was transfused. Within an hour the patient was able to converse. The following day, she walked, though a bit unsteadily.

"For this is my blood of the new covenant, which is shed for many for the remission of sins." (Matthew 26:28 NKJ)

Chapter Twenty-Two

Nutrition and the Lau Swamp

The people in the Bambur area were meat hungry like most African tribes. Beef, pork, goat and chicken were only available on scheduled days in the local market. Many people could not afford meat. Deprived of protein, children developed kwashiorkor, a disease characterized by anemia, edema, a potbelly, depigmentation of the skin, and loss or change of hair that many times assumed a reddish hue.

This child is wearing an amulet to ward off evil spirits that could cause illnesses, a common practice throughout Africa.

Whenever we suggested an outing for the staff, the choice was always the same – "Let's go hunting." The excursion took us to the Lau swamp between Bambur and Lau where our nearest post office was located. The swamp stretched along the Benue River for 100 miles, and was approximately ten miles deep. There, kob (mariya) antelope roamed in herds. Leopards, hyenas and buffalo were present but not always seen. At any event, whenever we planned a hunt we were rarely disappointed. If by chance no large animal was captured, guinea fowl, ducks or geese could be secured.

During the dry season our four-wheel drive Land Rover could manage the swamp area. On one occasion a group of antelope was spotted. On a dare as to how close we could approach with the Land Rover, we suddenly realized that we were less than thirty yards from a magnificent buck. He refused to give way to the mechanized vehicle. He was brought down with an easy shot. We ran to the quarry. To my hunting companion I asked in Hausa, "Ina wuka?" which meant "Where is the knife?" A voice answered, "Yana nan" – "It is here." Dr. McBride, who had spoken, emerged from some tall grasses. He had been tracking and stalking this same antelope for an extended time, only to have me "drive up" and steal "his" animal at the last moment.

Gerald Faust and his father A. J. Faust bringing home three buffalo.

Sheku Bambur, my Nigerian hunting guide. Forty-seven years after our first hunt, I was able to restore his sight with a cataract operation.

The thick, tall grasses made it difficult to see which animal was being hunted. One day, Gerald Faust came upon a buffalo, which he shot three times before it finally yielded. Preparing to load it into the truck to take home for butchering, he and his father, Dr. Arthur Faust, found that they needed to load not one but three buffalo!

Protein, carbohydrate and fat were not the only dietary shortfalls for the Adamawa and Taraba people. Iodine was also not adequate, thus many had colloid goiters. Americans ingest adequate amounts of iodine through iodized table salt, but in West Africa there was no such source. Providing iodine was emphasized through the Kiwanis world outreach projects.

It is only fair to say, however, that some of the most delicious food in the entire world can be found in West Africa. Ruth and I, along with our children, loved luscious mango and guava sauces, groundnut (peanut) and palm oil stews – and above all, jollof rice, especially if prepared by Betty Carew, Teresa Renner or David Johnson's grandmother. Just thinking about it, even now, creates a strong longing.

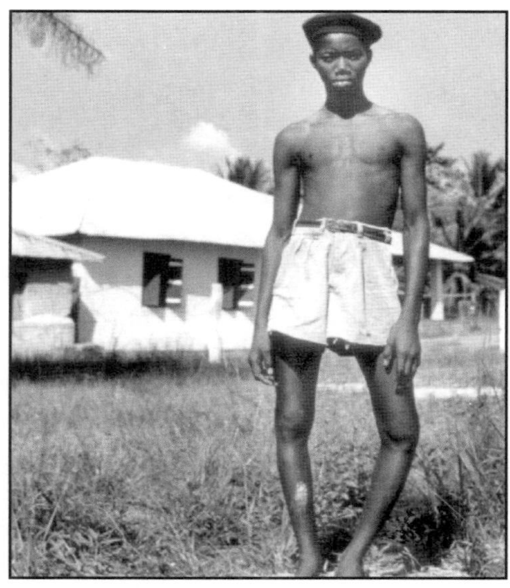

This young man had rickets – the result of a calcium deficiency. In all likelihood, his mother wasn't able to nurse him as a baby.

Ruth observing the preparation of food African style.

Chapter Twenty-Three

Malaria

It was past noon. It had been a busy five-hour morning's work in the Guinter Memorial Hospital clinic. I had a headache and was unusually thirsty and tired. In the midday heat, I could not tell if I had a fever. On my way out the door, a dispensing nurse asked me to see one more patient – a teenaged girl in a makeshift stretcher. It had taken a number of concerned family members all morning to make the trip to the hospital.

Her eyes were closed. I saw no respirations. The stethoscope indicated no heartbeat. Her forehead was still very warm. Her history of severe headache, drowsiness, confusion and delirium revealed a typical cerebral malarial infection that almost always proved fatal. I consoled the parents and expressed my disappointment in not been given the opportunity to administer treatment. Placing my hand again on her head I prayed, "The Lord bless you and keep you; the Lord make his face to shine upon you and be gracious unto you; the Lord lift up His countenance upon you and give you peace." (Numbers 6: 24-26)

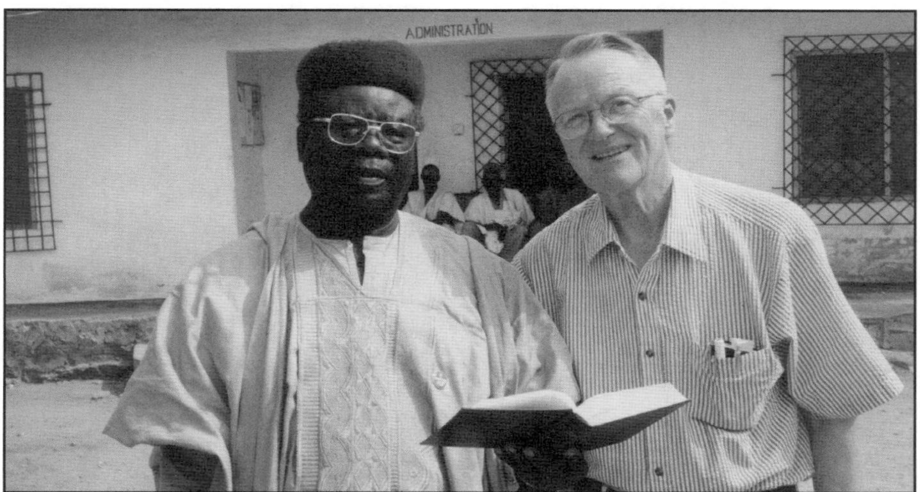

Malam Baba Jatau, present chief of Bambur, a dedicated leader who was a member of the Bambur Hospital while we served there from 1952 to 1955.

To get to work at the hospital, some days I drove the four-wheel drive Land Rover from our house on the hill down to the hospital complex below. Today, however, was not one of those days. Several times hiking up the hill to home, I paused. It seemed "I was running out of petrol."

At the dining room table that night after Ruth had served the food, all I could do was stare at it, leaving it untouched. Suddenly, I began to violently chill. Ruth helped me to the bedroom and before allowing me to lie down she brought four tablets of chloroquine and a glass of water. When I was finally stretched out on the bed, I kept asking for more blankets. Ultimately, when the blankets ran out, Ruth resorted to placing throw rugs on my shivering body.

I knew I would need another dose of medication in four to six hours. In case I began to vomit or my senses were affected, Ruth wrote down the doses of intramuscular medication that I would need to be given.

Only when the shaking chills began to subside, did I remember the teenage girl I had just attended to before leaving the hospital for lunch. She was a native Nigerian and most assuredly had experienced a gradual immunity to malarial infections. I was an expatriate, ripe for the overwhelming paroxysms that accompanied falciparum malaria. I didn't even consider the three other forms of malaria I could be suffering from. Would my fever and chills ultimately develop into cerebral malaria?

Women carried water to our home everyday.

The World Health Organization continually grapples with the problem of malaria. More than 400 million people suffer from the disease each year and at least one million die. Even though most fatalities are children, I wondered about the rest who made up the million every year who perished. I was not going to allow myself to fall asleep; I wanted to consciously deal with this crisis. However, I knew I would experience confusion and delirium, and Ruth would have to assume my treatment and care. I was still alert by the time the next two tablets of chloroquine needed to be taken. Finally I realized I needed to let Ruth and the Lord assume complete control. I dropped off to sleep.

The following day I was a bit pale – and moved a little slower – but I was back at my post.

Chapter Twenty-Four

Is Any Help Possible?

Perhaps the most deadly viper – the Echis carinatus, or saw scaled/carpet viper.

The area around Bambur had been known for many generations as one of the most dangerous places in Africa for poisonous vipers. The vipers loved to crawl onto the walking path – warmed by the sun during the day – that ran between the villages. It still retained some heat in the evening. While serving at Guinter Memorial Hospital, we were aware of two pastors who were bitten by vipers while on the way to their churches. Tragically, both pastors died following their bites.

We had brought snake anti-venom with us. We felt that with this in our treatment bag we would be able to help people who were bitten by poisonous snakes. And yet each time we were presented with a snakebite victim, the patient died in spite of all the care we gave. In addition to anti-venom, we also used some new treatments – such as wrapping the extremity in ice in order to slow the absorption of the poison. We were able to do this at the hospital compound because there were a number of missionaries who lived on this compound who had kerosene refrigerators that made ice cubes.

One evening around 8:00 p.m., a ten-year-old girl was brought to the hospital after being bitten by a snake. She had already begun to hemorrhage from her gums and later on she profusely threw up blood. We treated her with all our known armamentarium, but within eighteen hours she was dead.

It was obvious we were dealing with a problem that was unaffected by our anti-venom serum. Not only was the venom of this snake hematoxic, causing bleeding, it was neurotoxic as well and caused paralysis.

Soon after, a sixteen-year-old young man who had been brushing the school compound that afternoon was brought in with a snake bite. He was a recent convert to Christianity and had been warned by his Muslim family for making a commitment to Christ. They felt calamity would befall him.

Within a very short time of his bite, he was brought to the hospital. His friends were wild-eyed with terror. We had 100 percent failure with other patients. In addition to the overwhelming neuro-shock they had experienced, blood loss was also a key factor leading to their deaths. Patients lost blood even at the sites where the anti-venom and antibiotics were injected. We could not let this boy die. We asked for blood donors and ten students volunteered, three being compatible. As he was receiving the third transfusion the following day, he slipped away.

The Christian community was devastated. We prayed for spiritual guidance and read Mark 16:18 (Good News Bible) where Jesus says that one of the signs of those who believe will be that they "one can take up the serpent and not be harmed." It was apparent what we were doing was not adequate.

After researching what type of snake we were dealing with, we discovered it was a saw-scaled viper. We could not find any anti-venom for this type of snake. The Echis carinatus was of the family viperidea, found in deserts and other arid regions from northern Africa to Ceylon. While probably the most venomous of vipers with an often-fatal bite, it rarely exceeded more than 60 cm (two feet) in length. We were able to find no anti-venom that was specific for this type of snake. We would have to make our own.

Chapter Twenty-Five

Handling Vipers

Following some Spirit-filled prayer meetings, it was finally decided we would pursue the production of Echis snake anti-venom. During this time it was not unusual to hear the expression, "Oh, help, Lord."

Dr. Dean Olewiler and I met a caravan while visiting the ECWA Eye Hospital in Kano.

Dr. Dean Olewiler and I visited paramount and district chiefs in the area. We expressed to them our desire to help save the lives of those bitten by poisonous snakes. They were quite willing to help and all we asked of them is that if anyone saw or was aware of one of these snakes, please have someone tell us immediately so we could come and capture it.

We placed these snakes in secure pens and fed them mice from time to time. It was our intention to "milk" their venom and then send it off to have anti-venom produced. Dr. Dean Olewiler and myself shared the milking chores.

When milking a snake, normally I would pick it up with a stick that had a looped cord at the end. After securing the snake in this cord, I would grasp its head behind the jaws and bring it to the rim of a small vial. Instinctively, the snake would open its mouth as the vial touched it and squirt out venom through a pair of fangs. On one occasion, I was preparing to milk a snake when it suddenly turned its head and sank its fangs into the stick by the looped cord. The fangs stuck in the stick. I put the snake back in the pen and assumed that now without its fangs, it would not be able to capture the mice we fed it.

Milking venom for the production of an anti-venom.

The next week I included this snake with the others that were being milked. It performed normally. We learned later it had five extra pairs of fangs on the roof of its mouth so that if a pair was damaged during a bite, another pair would move down into its place. For many years afterwards, I had occasional nightmares in which a snake was wriggling within my grasp and a lethal bite was imminent.

After harvesting a number of snake venom ejections, we learned that only South Africa had the facilities for anti-venom production. South Africa was isolated from other African countries because of apartheid. The venom therefore had to be carried to New York by missionaries and then sent to South Africa from the United States. The anti-venom was returned to us reversing this process.

Soon after the return of the anti-venom, an Echis viper bit the son of Mai Doki our cook. He was the first life to be spared with the use of this anti-venom. There was great praise in the church and in the community.

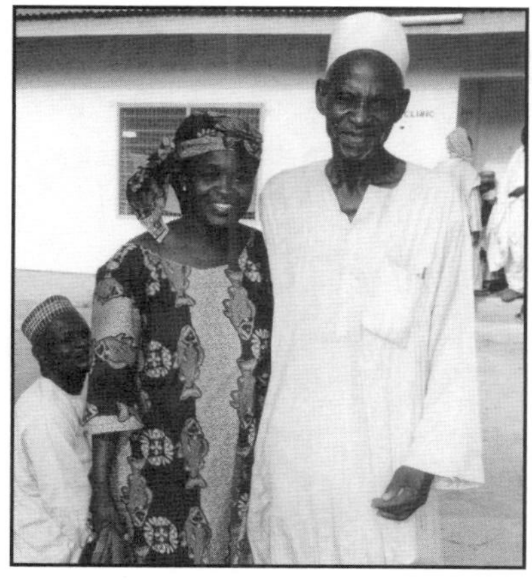

Mai Doki, our gifted cook at Bambur.

During the time we were milking vipers – but prior to receiving the anti-venom – a dramatic incident happened. While cutting grass, the hospital yardman was bitten on the back of his hand. I was at lunch. A hospital messenger breathlessly appeared at the door of our house. In the excitement, his Hausa, the native dialect, was too rapid and complex for me to understand. Our seven-year-old son, Tim, standing at my side, tugged at my leg and said that I was to hurry to the hospital as a snake had bitten our yardman.

I had just finished a surgical procedure at the hospital and everyone had rushed away for the lunch break. The instruments, no longer sterile, were all laid out as they had been left. Following a quick local injection of anesthetic, the tissues on the back of his hand were removed, leaving only the tendons. We were later able to graft his hand and rejoice in a functional hand as well as the first successful treatment of an Echis bite without anti-venom!

As parents of small children, we wondered if ever a day might come when a finger or some other part of the body might have to be sacrificed to preserve life. Thankfully, all six of our children survived their time in Africa with all body parts intact.

Chapter Twenty-Six

Venomous Snakes Fifty-Five Years Later

Since the time when all these dramatic experiences happened fifty-five years ago, much has been learned about snakes and how to handle their bites. Snake venoms can be categorized as neurotoxins, hemotoxins and cytotoxins. The bite of an Echis snake is one of the most deadly. We were well aware of the affects of these bites in the 1950s, but now they are classified. There were marked cardiac and vascular changes, to be sure. It is now known that they also caused problems with coagulation and changes in vascular resistance, which caused massive bleeding into injection sites. We were aware – as is now pointed out – that bleeding occurred from the orifices of the body, from the gums, from the stomach, in the lungs, peritoneum, kidneys and the heart. Cadaver studies carried out in succeeding years substantiate what we unhappily experienced more than five decades ago. Neurologically, the patient's nervous system essentially collapsed; they could not control their muscles and their minds became confused. Thankfully, they may not have been conscious and aware of their peril in the latter stages prior to death.

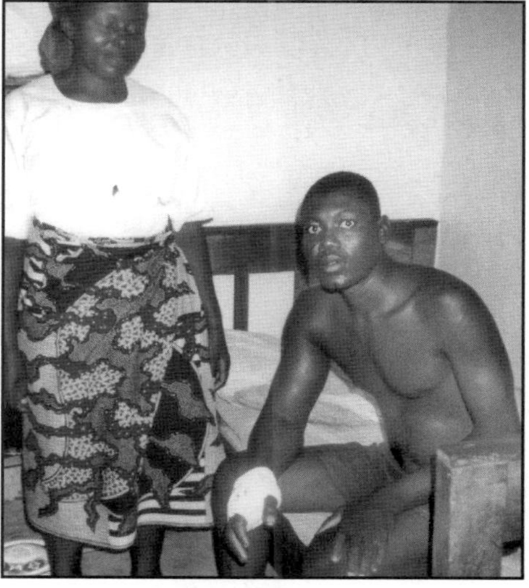

This is a young man who had been bitten by an Echis viper in 1999. He was at the hospital in the United Methodist Mission Outreach at Zing. His right arm is swollen and has tissue breakdown. The wonderful thing, however, is that he is alert and alive. He was one of the fortunate people living when Echis anti-venom is available. We continue to thank God for the help of all involved in producing this life saving anti-venom and for those who are ministering in these outreaches.

Dealing with cobras was somewhat different. Cobras had fixed fangs. In order to successfully inject their venom, they deliver multiple bites. They are also accurate up to ten feet in spitting in their quarry's eyes.

Miss Vivian Olson was much closer to a snake in the middle of one night. She awakened to the sensation of movement in her bed. To clear her senses, she got up and took a shower. Finally, fully awake, she returned to her bed and gingerly lifted one corner of the sheet. Her breath left her when she saw part of the black body of a cobra. She screamed for the night watchman who came running with a long stick and dispatched the four and a half foot spitting cobra that never was given the chance to spit.

Miss Olson's experience of the feel of the snake is an electrifying one – especially when one does not have control of the situation. I had been laid up for more than two weeks with type A viral hepatitis. I had already gone through lack of appetite, malaise, nausea and vomiting. The fever was supposed to end when dark urine and jaundice appeared and should have felt better despite my yellow eyes and skin. However, this was not the case. An abnormally high temperature developed and both Ruth and I feared I'd experience delirium. When Ruth heard my call from the bedroom to bring a shovel, she assumed that I was "out of my head." Dutifully, however, she came running with the shovel in hand.

She found me standing in the bed, wild-eyed, pointing to a green four-foot snake slithering out the doorway. With the help of the visiting mission superintendent, Rev. Clyde Galow, the snake was never allowed to rejoin his family.

In a half sleep, I had suddenly become aware of something moving over my feet. On opening my eyes, I saw the snake was in the process of going from point A to point B. He never made it because every muscle in my body contracted at the same moment. The snake was sent flying into the air and I called for the shovel.

Ruth and I were concerned about the persistence and progression of my fever. Our medical backgrounds made us aware that a favorable prognosis or outcome could not always be guaranteed since Hepatitis A had a mortality rate of ten to fifteen percent. It was a sobering thought as to which persons make up those figures.

Thankfully, however, following the snake incident I began my recovery under the care of Dr. Sama Banya, who in later years was to politically guide the destiny of Sierra Leone. Eventually I was able to return to work – and its privilege had never been sweeter.

While all these incidents have a happy ending, such was not the experience of our family's favorite black cat that courageously tried to stand up to a cobra. The cobra spit into the eyes of Blackie and she became wild with pain, literally clawing at her eyes. It was apparent that the cat would be blind, and so in the tradition of the rider who places a gun to the head of his horse with a broken leg, we mercifully sacrificed our cat.

Chapter Twenty-Seven

Beyond the Help of Human Hands

While serving at the Guinter Memorial Hospital, our fifth child was born – a bonny boy! Apparently there was some contamination along the way at the time of his birth and he developed an infection. He was treated with massive antibiotics, but the infection was so serious that ultimately he began to convulse. When a patient convulses with fever, it usually means the body is being overwhelmed.

Paul was convulsing. In spite of treatment, he continued to have repeated episodes of convulsion the entire day. The spasms even continued throughout the night and into the following day. Dr. Dean Olewiler and the attending nurses were wonderful in their care. Everything possible was done. However, there was a general consensus that our little boy was beyond the help of human hands. We continued to give antibiotic injections as well as medications to control convulsions during that second day. Repeatedly, in our minds, we knew "there are some things that we have to accept, sometimes diseases get beyond human control, and we have to accept them as the permissive will of God." We realized that medicine was not always the answer. We continued to pray for Paul's renewal.

As the second evening approached, we were beginning to accept the inevitable. We had helplessly seen so many patients die from meningitis whose situations were also beyond the reaches of medical help. A question troubled us: Had Paul's general infections invaded his central nervous system? I had to know. This meant doing a spinal tap on this very small infant, our son. Would Ruth agree? I feared that she would draw back and clutch the baby more closely. However, with a look of trust and possibly resignation she positioned him on the dining room table and the procedure was done without difficulty. My heart sank. There was no spinal fluid.

During the polio epidemic in 1952 at Ancker General Hospital in St. Paul, as an intern I was required to perform spinal taps by the dozens day and night. I could tell without the shadow of a doubt when the needle entered the spinal canal. At that moment in faraway Nigeria dealing with my own son, I knew that the needle was in the proper place and there was no spinal fluid. That was the moment of greatest anguish. He really had gone beyond the point of return. We had to let go. We had to let God, in His sovereignty, to be in control. Ruth gathered Paul in her arms and we huddled together on the front room couch.

After a period of prolonged silence, Ruth spoke, "We haven't even baptized him." I went to the kitchen and got a cup of water. We opened the Bible to Matthew 19:14, where Jesus says: "Suffer the little children to come unto me, forbid them not, for of such is the kingdom of heaven." We baptized him with the name of Paul. Ruth prayed, I prayed. Emotionally exhausted, we continued to sit on the sofa. We truly felt the presence of the Holy Spirit and were relieved that we had finally come to the place where we were willing to let go of our son that he might return to God, our Creator.

About a half hour later Ruth said, "Lowell, he's not convulsing. Oh...he's gone." Instinctively, I took out my stethoscope and placed it over his heart. It was beating normally and strongly. His breathing was regular. And then that wonderful moment – he moved his arms and shortly began to nurse.

The recovery was rapid.

It was now close to midnight. The other children were in bed. After Paul finished nursing, we too went to bed. We took Paul with us and put him between us. One of us tried to sleep while the other one watched. We were not going to let anything happen now!

Our healthy baby boy, Paul, approximately six months after the peril that almost took his life.

In the years that followed, Paul developed into a beautiful boy. He was a joy to his parents. He knew the Lord as his Savior. Although we wondered about the sequellae from such a serious illness, it was exciting to see him develop and become strong. On the football field he starred as an all-state tailback for a championship football team. He was committed in his loyalty to the Lord Jesus Christ. He was willing to get on the loud speakers and address his fellow high school students about upcoming prayer meetings and Bible studies. Being a big jock, the students listened to him. He went on to college and played championship soccer. At Fuller Theological Seminary, he completed a Masters degree and is now a family and marriage counselor.

The Lord had much in store for him following that midnight baptism.

Paul (second from left), who was thought to be beyond the help of human hands, with his brothers. Left to right: Timothy, Andrew and John.

Chapter Twenty-Eight

Nigeria, Land of Our Calling

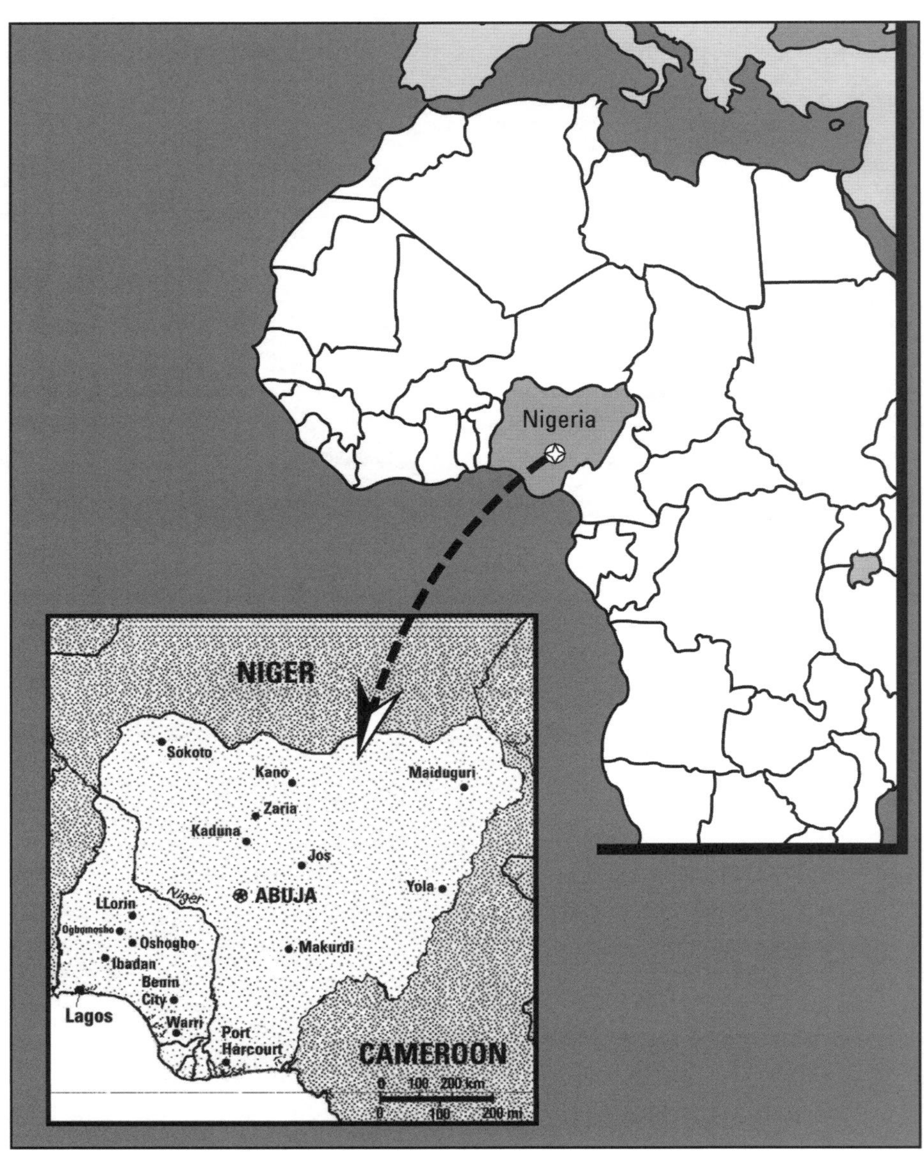

In 1952 when we set foot in Nigeria, West Africa, it was already the most populous country on the African continent numbering about 80 million people. In 2011, it was estimated to be 140 million. In geographic size it measures slightly more than twice the size of California (which has somewhat over 32 million people). Lagos, the capitol in those days, was a teeming metropolis with steamy heat.

We were dead tired after the trying events of the day. We had arrived without a visa. British authorities took it as an affront that we would continue our journey from the U.S. and then from the UK without official documentation in our passports. Up until the last moment before boarding the *S.S. America* liner in New York, we had been scurrying around for word about our visa. We were all ticketed, and it was decided to get on board for our trip to England. Surely the visa to Nigeria would catch up with us there.

During the five-day layover in London, I kept contacting the mission board in New York while visiting the American and Nigerian embassies in London to see if the visa papers had been sent to them. When no word arrived, we needed to make a desperate decision. Elder Dempster's steamship, *Accra*, was departing from Liverpool the next day. Our freight had been put on board automatically from our first ship of passage. It would be detrimental to not accompany our baggage and remain in London for an extended time until another ship left for Nigeria.

We decided to present our tickets and our passports at the boarding gates. A missionary doctor and nurse with four small children must have distracted the officials, and we were politely ushered on board and given our staterooms.

It was quite another story at the other end. The British officials called me into the captain's office and explained that allowing us to disembark the ship would be a breech of policy and law. How could we have been so presumptuous? In hopes of righting the situation, I explained the intense activity we had during the trip. My statement that we felt called by God to minister in Nigeria caused an extended silence. Apparently the official did not feel that he could subvert the will of God and finally relented. We were the last to leave the ship.

It was New Year's Eve. We were happy to arrive at the comfortable missionary guesthouse in Lagos. Thankfully the children were able to drop off to sleep. Such was not the case for Ruth and me as the seemingly greatest of all New Year's celebrations was taking place just outside our window. We ushered in the early hours of 1953 very much awake.

The next stage of our journey was by train. It took two days to reach Jos, which is on a plateau rising to more than 4,000 feet above sea level. Understandably, the engine of the train required much more time on its ascent than it did on its return trip to Lagos.

After having left Lagos, we passed through jungle foliage with myriads of birds and animal life. The savanna territory gave us an extended view of the countryside with the many villages and their grass roofed huts.

Our home at Bambur.

Jos was delightfully cool. The missionaries at the Sudan United Mission guesthouse assumed complete care of our family. The children were bathed and fed early in the evening. After 8:00 p.m. the adults sat down to English cuisine, which occasionally included brussel sprouts. The matron insisted that we be as independent as possible. Instructions were given as to how we were to communicate with the in-house Nigerian employees. "Kawo mani ruwan sha" meant "Please bring some drinking water." "Kawo mani ruwan wanke" indicated that we needed water for washing.

The view from our Bambur home.

The final segment of the trip to the Guinter Memorial Hospital was a long, dusty, and hot day's journey. Leaving the elevated plateau and returning to the savanna countryside brought stifling heat. Shenge Pass had to be maneuvered just outside of Pero. Riverbeds needed to be crossed. Those which still had not dried up necessitated negotiating a four-wheel drive vehicle through water that occasionally came up as high as the headlights.

We received a genuine Christian welcome when we finally drew up to what was to be our home on a hilltop overlooking the hospital complex for the next three years. Those years were to be some of the most delightful yet dangerous times of our lives. It should be said, however, that occupying the house was delayed nearly four weeks while Dr. Harold Elliot and his family packed for their return to the United States. We were made comfortable in the new maternity ward of the hospital.

After three weeks of traveling the high seas and crossing jungles, savanna and plateau lands, we were finally "home." As was our practice throughout our life with the many homes we occupied, we gathered as a family and thanked God for his presence and preservation "this far" and for the assurance of "future care."

Background of Guinter Hospital. The Rev. C. W. Guinter arrived in Nigeria in 1906. He served under the Sudan United Mission, which had been formed two years earlier. In 1909 after a furlough, he returned to Wukari with his new bride, the first white woman to see that part of Nigeria. Many times during her first weeks at the compound, the matting on the fence was deftly parted to permit curious dark eyes to peep at the new arrival.

The Women's Missionary Society of the Evangelical Church assumed the support of the Guinters and his station in 1918. By the time of the merger in 1922 of the two Evangelical churches, Dr. Paul H. Eller reported in the "History of Evangelical Missions," the W.M.S. had in hand $12,744.06 for the founding of an African mission. The Rev. and Mrs. I. E. McBride offered to accompany Guinter back to Africa if they received an appointment by the Board of Missions. The church officially declared its support of the Wurkum District as their denominational mission field, and later granted additional appointments to the Rev. and Mrs. J. J. Armold and the Rev. and Mrs. V. E. Walter.

Missionaries, with their understanding of "cleanliness is next to godliness," were in a position to minister to those with debilitating ulcers as well as problems created by contaminated water and food. They were unable to deal with serious diseases, either among the Nigerians or among their own number in spite of the fact that in 1937 the British government had made it mandatory that all missionaries have six months of instruction in tropical diseases. The evangelistic staff did as much medical work as they were capable of doing while continuing to make urgent requests for the appointment of a doctor. Death stalked the mission as Ruth Lowell McBride was taken on October 10, 1933, and Elizabeth Conboy

McBride on March 25, 1941. Dr. McBride narrowly escaped death himself while experiencing "black water fever."

In my teens, I remember Bishop E. W. Praetorius at Koronis Assembly announce on a number of occasions the need for a doctor for Wurkumland, Nigeria. I felt he was speaking directly to me, but I resolved to answer the call to Christian ministry – and not as a doctor in some far off deep jungle in Africa. Ultimately a doctor was found in the person of Dr. Harold Elliott. Instead of a mud-walled dispensary, a concrete block hospital with wards was built in 1950 to 1952 under the supervision of Mr. Chester Reinhardt and Mr. Woodrow Macke. It was dedicated as the Guinter Memorial Hospital. A succession of doctors followed: Dean Olewiler, Lowell Gess and David Hilton to name a few.

Guinter Memorial Hospital dedication.

The nursing staff included Swiss deaconess Emmy Tschannen and Americans Crystal Springborn, Jean Baldwin (wife of Eugene "Hank" Baldwin), Florence Walter and Ruth Witmer who eventually married and settled with her husband in Switzerland. Couples serving as evangelists included: Dr. and Mrs. Arthur Faust, Rev. Karl and Tekla Kuglin, Rev. Armin "Tex" and Margaret Hoesch, Rev. Walter and Ruth Erbele, and Rev. Martin and Ruth Stettler.

In the training of future missionaries and doctors, the present United Methodist church now numbers about six times as many as those noted by Dr. Dean Gilliland during his 1999 trip back to Nigeria from his professorship at Fuller Theological Seminary. Government-appointed Nigerian doctors now administer Guinter Memorial Hospital. The Banyam Bible School library is a wonder to behold.

Expatriate nursing staff at Guinter Memorial Hospital in Bambur, Nigeria.

Chapter Twenty-Nine

1957

Following two years of residency in general surgery at the Akron General Hospital in Akron, Ohio, we were ready with our seventeen barrels and six crates to return to Sierra Leone. On the drive from Akron to Boston, we bought cowboy hats for the children. On the way to the Boston airport a traffic officer stopped us for speeding. Our driver was the Rev. Richard Kunz who showed great composure in dealing with the officer. When the officer expressed surprise at seeing in the car an enormous amount of luggage and five children wearing cowboy hats, he inquired after us. Learning we were medical missionaries on our way to West Africa, he was quiet for a few moments and then, shifting his hat, dismissed us without writing a ticket.

Once on the plane, we began to relax until we realized we weren't taking off. After an interminable ten minutes, the pilot announced we were ready for takeoff. He explained that the delay was necessary to burn off fuel as we were overloaded. The psychology of that report had a devastating impact on the passengers. We were starting out over thousands of miles of ocean and he was burning up the plane's fuel before we even got off the ground. Thankfully we landed safely at Santa Maria in the Azores on the long leg of our flight.

Transferring planes in Dakar, Senegal, on our way to Sierra Leone.

A cablegram from Dr. Carl Heinmiller on December 5th had decided our future. We were to go directly to Rotifunk without any delay for language study. However, I did attend a leprosy conference directed by the famous Dr. Robert Cochran at Ganta Hospital in Liberia from December 7-19. Dr. Cochran had also been the director of the workshop that I had attended three years earlier in Kano, Nigeria.

Returning to Freetown and my family, I spent December 21st at the quay trying to locate our luggage that had been shipped as ocean freight prior to our departure on the plane. While watching the steamship *Accra* being loaded for travel to England, I noticed one of our steamer trunks going up on the hoisted platform. It contained all the clothes for our family. I frantically waved my arms, trying to gain someone's attention and finally was permitted to go on board where arrangements were made for the off-loading of this important trunk.

On December the 30th we arrived at Rotifunk. This was to be our home for the next three years.

Our home in Rotifunk.

Chapter Thirty

Deliveries and Three Hours of Artificial Respiration

Caesarean sections are sometimes referred to as "Caesars." It was obvious that the young mother with a cephalo-pelvic disproportion I was examining would not be able to deliver her baby normally. Several times in her presence, the term "Caesar" was mentioned. The fact that thousands of mothers die each year in childbirth was common knowledge in Sierra Leone, so when she was told she would need an operation, she readily agreed.

The next day the mother was up and even smiling. While cradling the newborn in her arms, Ruth asked the mother what name she was giving to her son. She replied, "Julius Caesar."

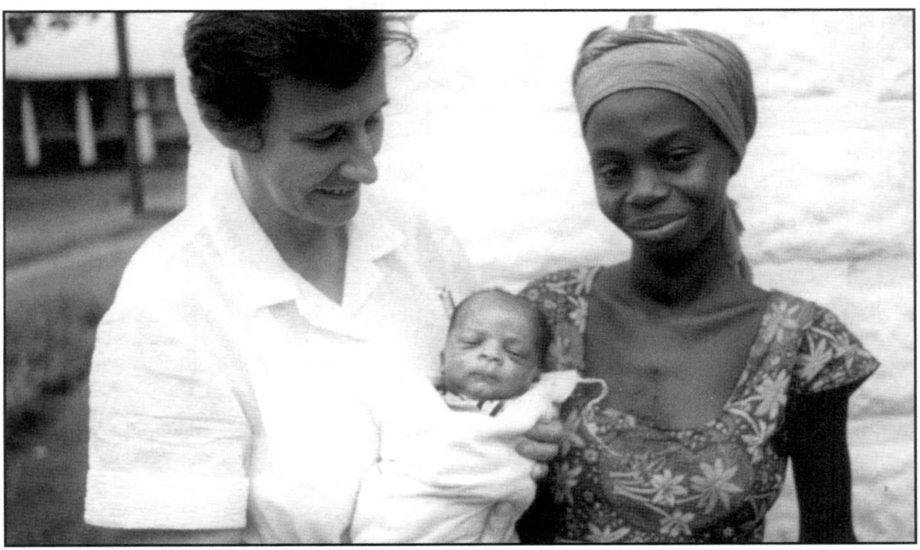

Midwife nurse, Betty Beveridge, holding "Julius Caesar."

One day, a breathless runner informed Ruth that an expectant mother was on the way to the hospital. He declared she was not going to make it in time, so Ruth dispatched four men with a litter. They returned shortly with the little newborn lying on the stretcher, the mother walking behind.

The maternity staff at the Rotifunk Hospital, under the direction of nurse-midwife Betty Beveridge, was solicitous and considerate of the doctors who occasionally were asked to participate in difficult deliveries. Often the doctor would be called from his sleep only at the last moment when everything was ready. One night, half asleep, I staggered over to the hospital and was presented with a patient who had been brought in a lorry from Taiama more than fifty miles away. Dr. George Harris, who had stopped at Taiama on his way to Bo, had advised transferring the patient to Rotifunk for a possible Caesarean section.

The head of the baby was in the birth canal. I reached for a forceps that was on the surgical tray. Turning back to the patient, I discovered that the baby's head had disappeared. Instinctively, I grabbed the scalpel and made an abdominal incision. Up popped the baby free in the abdominal cavity. Two large clamps were placed on each side of the uterus to stop the mother's profuse bleeding. The umbilical cord was clamped and the baby handed to Miss Beveridge.

The uterus was shredded beyond repair, and since the mother already had five children, a hysterectomy was performed after Dr. Mabel Silver had been summoned to administer a general anesthetic.

The next day when the mother was asked about the original incision that rescued her baby, she replied, "I thought it was another labor pain."

Three Hours of Artificial Respiration. Sometime after midnight a patient was brought to the Rotifunk Hospital in severe pain. A hernia, which had been troubling him for several years, had suddenly protruded dangerously and he could not reduce it. If it swelled any more, it could become strangulated, and if not attended to could lead to death. He was aware of this and was wild-eyed with pain and panic. Non-surgical reduction was no longer possible, so we began to prepare for surgical intervention.

I was always most comfortable when Ruth administered the anesthetic. As husband and wife, our communication was good but now at 2:00 a.m. in the morning, she needed to stay at home with our children. Another nurse was called to give non-inflammable chloroform, since the procedure would have to be done with lanterns because the hospital generator had been torn down for repairs. The substitute nurse thought I was teasing when I asked her to count out loud the number of drops being placed on the mask. She had never used chloroform before and simply poured it on as though she were using ether. In several minutes, the patient was "out." More than that, he had stopped breathing. With such profound relaxation, the hernia was reduced by manipulation after all – yet we had to "breathe" for him using the EMO anesthetic machine. Three hours later as the sun was coming up, he opened his eyes and spoke to us. Sometime later, his hernia was definitively repaired.

Few patients have ever had a continuous prayer being said over them for three hours. His awakening was like the stone being rolled away from the empty tomb.

Chapter Thirty-One

From Death to Life

Looking down the line of patients, I noticed the limp body of a small girl who was tied to her mother's back. It was apparent that the child was not in a normal sleep. Suddenly, I became aware of a foul, putrid odor.

The mother loosened the ties around the unconscious child, laid her on the tying-cloth and lifted a makeshift bandage from the left leg. From the knee down her leg was shredded, rotting flesh.

A pre-operative picture of the little unconscious girl with the rotting lower leg.

Usually patients are taken from the hospital when we confide to their relatives there is nothing more we can do. In this case, the mother was bringing the child to the hospital after everyone knew that the leg was beyond repair and that she was only moments from death.

Ordinarily, I would have said a quiet prayer over the patient and then moved on. However, the mother knelt in front of me and pled in Temne, a tribal dialect. A nurse interpreted that she wanted me to use the "knife" – meaning to do surgery. To this very day, I do not understand my reaction that moment. Apparently, the thought flashed through my mind that "where there is life there is hope." Although the little girl was not conscious, she was breathing and her heart was beating. Swiftly, the nurses bathed her and positioned her on the operating table. We made sure she was still alive before applying antiseptic and prepared the decaying lower leg for amputation since its toxicity was poisoning her entire system.

We had taken the precaution of starting IV fluids in the event that they might be necessary. Lidocaine was used to infiltrate the area, but she didn't move or react to the injection. Massive antibiotics were given. The amputation was done in less than ten minutes.

The IV fluids helped her regain consciousness a short time later. We were able to feed her a healthy diet, so within a week this sweet and winsome little darling had recovered. A prosthesis for the left leg was later successfully adapted. Glory to God!

The little girl who moved from death to life.

Chapter Thirty-Two

Crocodile

Occasionally our family would picnic on weekends. The children loved to jump into the Land Rover and drive to the swamp along the Benue River. Wildlife was almost always seen. On one occasion, we went all the way to the Benue and arranged for a cruise in a large dugout canoe. We intended to see the wildlife along the banks, which would include large birds and animals that had come down to drink. Above all else, we anticipated seeing crocodiles sunning themselves on sand bars.

During the course of the trip, the children were not very comfortable and there was some complaining. By the time a creature was seen and the children pointed in the right direction, it had disappeared. The sun was high and it was very hot.

Crocodile.

On the return to the beach, the children begged to have a little time to splash in the water. None of the children ever gave a thought to the fact that the waters might be dangerous and it wasn't until possibly twenty five or thirty years later that our oldest daughter, Mary, learned that during this outing her father had sat nervously on the bank with a loaded high-powered rifle at the ready with the safety off. Perhaps if I had known at that time how silently crocodiles could approach the shore and spring out for their prey, I would have been less willing to allow the children to have their swim in the Benue River.

Chapter Thirty-Three

First Eye Surgery

The first eye surgery was done in 1958 at the Hatfield-Archer Hospital in Sierra Leone. I had been sent to the Rotifunk Hospital to assist in the general surgical program. Dr. Mabel Silver had labored at that hospital for more than twenty years. Her medical success made Rotifunk famous and one of the four premiere hospitals in Sierra Leone. Dr. Silver, however, declined to do surgery.

I was posted at the Rotifunk Hospital to work with Dr. Silver. The program soon became so busy that Dr. George Harris was also brought in to help. While still performing surgeries, Dr. Harris' presence allowed me to visit churches and help with their programs as the board of mission's field representative. Dr. Harris and I did the full compliment of surgery, but herniorrhaphies and C-sections demanded most of our time. Dr. Harold Adolph in *Today's Christian Doctor* noted that in Africa only one in twenty women needing a C-section receive the operation. Only 15 percent of hernia patients get the operation they need even if their hernia is strangulated.

During one surgery session, we were honored by the visit of Dr. John Karefa-Smart. A decade earlier he had been the surgeon doing the procedures in the very room in which we were working. He had been appointed to the Rotifunk Hospital in the early days when Dr. Silver was directing the medical program. Several decades later, Dr. Karefa-Smart again visited the Kissy UMC Eye Hospital in Freetown. He was in political leadership in Sierra Leone for many years and went home to be with his Savior in 2010.

Dr. John Karefa-Smart.

It was troubling to see so many patients come to the hospital who were blind and no treatment was available to help them. I mentioned this to an ophthalmologist friend of mine in Akron, Ohio. To my delight, some months later I received a set of eye instruments and a cataract surgery "how to" book. I devoured the book and practiced mock cataract surgeries with the surgical assistants. I reasoned that my knowledge of general surgery might help me attempt the demanding ophthalmological procedure and give blind patients a chance to see.

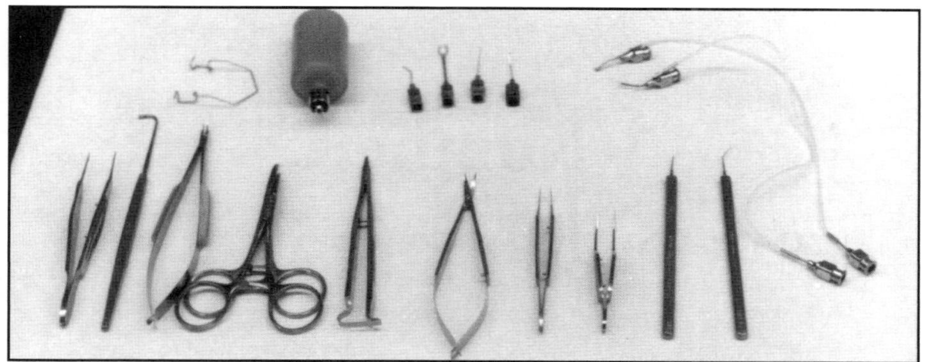

Eye surgical instruments.

The day came when arrangements were made for the first eye operation. Three totally blind people were selected. It was hoped that possibly one out of the three might obtain some vision. I asked Dr. Mabel Silver if she would participate – especially in providing a covering of prayer. She prayed in Temne. The patients followed her prayers with arms extended, hands open as was their custom.

It was at this point I nearly panicked. How could I have come to such a place as this – a farm boy from Paynesville, Minnesota, whose main activity had been cultivating corn with a team of horses that needed special expletives to make them go? The only time I had cut into an eye before was in the cadaver room as a freshman medical student. In a few moments, I was to cut open a living eye. It would bleed. The opaque lens would have to be removed if the patient were to see.

With the support of Dr. Silver's prayer, I set about doing the task at hand. It was I, then, who prayed, "Lord, help me do this effectually with precision that there may be the blessing, not only of physical sight, but also of spiritual insight into your love as revealed in Jesus Christ."

In a wonderful way, the Lord blessed and healed the patients. All three were thrilled with new sight. They wanted to dance. The success of these opened the floodgates for other blind patients in Sierra Leone. As word spread, the blind were brought to us from every corner of the country.

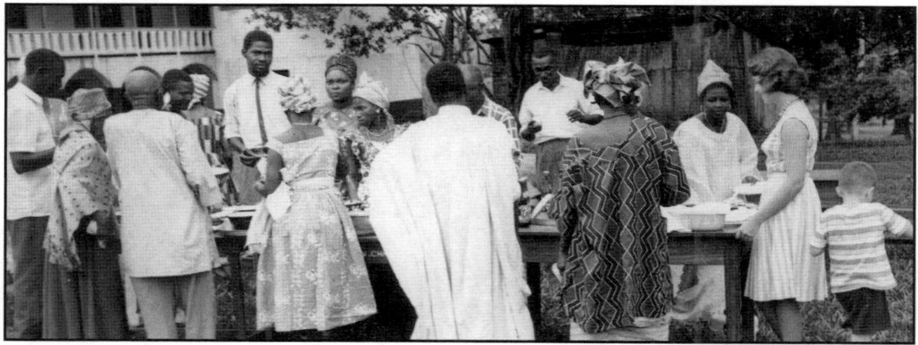

Ruth providing a buffet luncheon at Rotifunk where food found its way to plates and handbags.

Chapter Thirty-Four

Kombe: From Begging to Praising

"What do you want me to do for you?" Jesus asked Bartemaeus. The blind man said, "Rabbi, I want to see." "Go," said Jesus, "your faith has healed you." Immediately he received his sight and followed Jesus. (Mark 10:51-52 NIV)

Kombe was a totally blind pagan who daily begged for alms at the gate of the Taiama United Methodist Church in Sierra Leone. Compassionate Christians raised money for his trip to the Rotifunk Hospital for remedial surgery.

Following the usual pre-operative prayer and while waiting for the local anesthetic to take effect, I visited with Kombe, as he spoke English well. I said, "Kombe, we are happy that you are here at the hospital, that you are submitting to surgery in order that the Lord may give you new sight. Remember, we also prayed that you might accept the Lord Jesus Christ in your heart. Renewed sight will pass away again someday, but to those who give their lives to Christ, to those who know Him, they see forever." It was at this point I asked if he had the choice,

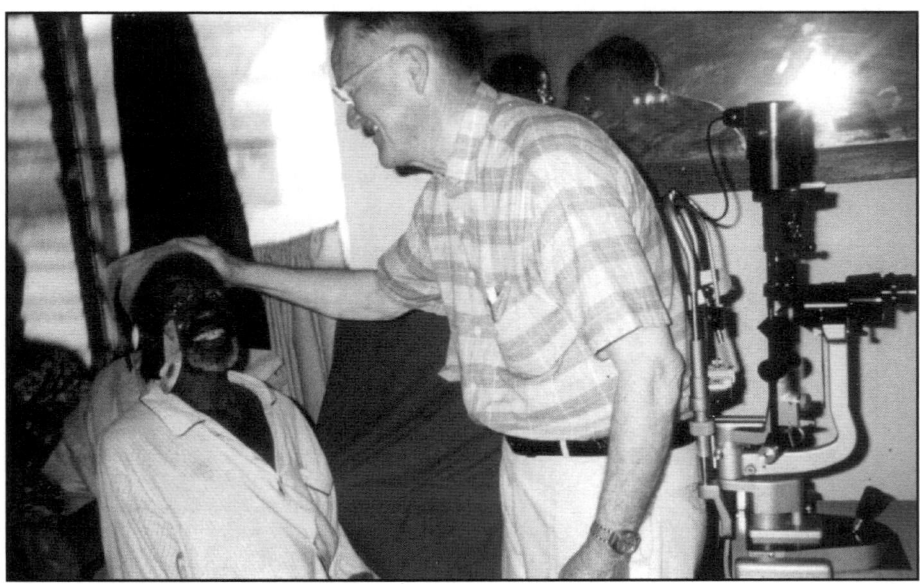

Kombe after his successful eye surgery.

would he rather be a new person in Christ for eternity or have new vision for the rest of his physical life? After a slight hesitation he replied, "I would rather be a new person in Christ!" There were some smiles behind the surgical masks. No one really believed him. He was just saying the respectful thing, as he knew he was being ministered to in a Christian hospital. Then after another short pause he quietly added, "I want to see again, too."

Our prayers for him were answered. Following a successful surgery, he prepared to return to Taiama. He could see and was now independent. He joyfully left the hospital, without being led, walking out of our lives and our thoughts.

A year later I was a guest preacher at the Taiama United Methodist Church, referred to as "The Cathedral in the Bush." It was a vibrant church pastored by the Rev. B. A. Carew. People from prayer groups in the surrounding villages would attend the Sunday services. At the close of the service, communion was served. Pastor Carew announced that those who had committed their lives to Jesus Christ – those whose love and loyalty were to the Lord – were invited to come and kneel for Holy Communion. Several hundred baptized members out of the thousand-member congregation responded. At the last table, as I was passing the bread, I noticed a man who was healthy, well-dressed and wearing thick glasses.

Thick "cataract-type glasses" were unusual for someone in this far off place. Returning with the cup, he took it, raised his face and smiled. My heart leapt within me. I was looking into the face of Kombe. He really meant what he said when he desired to become a "new creation in Christ."

Once he was a beggar. His clothes now indicated he was gainfully employed. Once he knew constant hunger. No longer thin, it was obvious he could buy adequate food. Once he was a lonely man. Now he was experiencing the fellowship of the Christian Church. Once he was without faith or hope. Now, by his kneeling at the communion rail, he was laying hold of the Lordship of Jesus Christ and the promise of eternal life.

"If any man is in Christ, he is a new creation; old things are passed away; behold, all things are become new." II Corinthians 5:17

Loving God,
We thank you for the joy of sight.
Thank you for the revelation of new insight into your love as revealed in Jesus Christ.

Chapter Thirty-Five

Train Wreck

It was Christmas Eve 1959. I was repairing a rocking chair. Ruth was singing "Love Lifted Me" as she cradled our three-month-old son Andrew. Our home on the Rotifunk Hospital compound overlooked the Sierra Leone railroad tracks to the southwest. The express from Bo to Freetown was due any time.

Suddenly we heard it – the train's whistle and screeching brakes as the engine pulled into the station several hundred yards to the south. Within moments, a train employee ran up the incline to our home. At our gate, he frantically called for the doctor. I grabbed my doctor's bag and went down to meet him. His report was brief. Eight miles back on a curve, five cars had left the track and rolled over. Only the engine and coal car remained on the tracks. These had been dispatched to Rotifunk where they knew there was a hospital and surgical staff.

I was bundled into the engine cab along with Tim, our twelve-year old son, and we took off for the site of the accident. During the trip the story began to unfold. The crew and passengers were all eager to get to Freetown on this special afternoon of the year and the train was going faster than usual. The speed of the train was too great to negotiate one of the curves. Tragedy struck.

Train wreck.

A train terminal at Bauya was seven or eight miles to the east of the wreck. The terminal there had dispatched an engine with some empty passenger cars.

There was such an entanglement of cars at the site of the wreck that the train could not continue on to Freetown. It could only go back to Moyamba, a district headquarters, where there was a government hospital.

On dropping down from the cab, I was hardly prepared for the scene – bodies were lying in the ditch, some pinned under the overturned passenger cars. Blood was splattered everywhere. The moaning of the injured drowned out the crying and shrieking of relatives and friends. Thirteen already were dead.

Realizing the urgency of the situation, I gave my supplies and bandages to others and hurriedly did a triage – going from body to body to determine if care could be given. The wounded were put on the Bauya train for transport to Moyamba Government Hospital and I rode along with them. I spent the rest of Christmas Eve until 1:00 a.m. Christmas morning doing emergency surgery.

Ultimately the situation came under control so I could leave the doctor and staff at Moyamba to care for the remaining injured. A four-wheel drive Land Rover had been dispatched from Rotifunk to take me back home. The driver was Ruth, accompanied by our children and Metra Heisler, a nurse from Rotifunk.

Arriving at Rotifunk in the wee hours of the morning, dead tired, I was informed that there was an injured child lying in her mother's arms at the door of our Rotifunk Hospital. Approaching the mother and three-year old daughter, I couldn't believe my eyes. I had seen this child at the wreck. When we had moved this unconscious child to examine her, her head had flopped onto her back. Her neck had been cut from side to side, completely severing the muscles that held her head forward and erect. I had spent no time on this hopeless case and had moved on to the next patient.

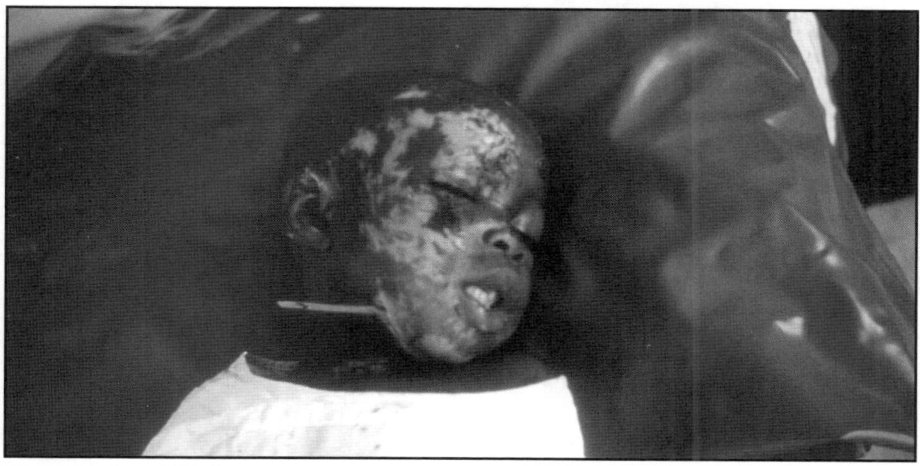

The unconscious child after surgery.

The mother had stuffed leaves and grass into the gaping wound in an attempt to control the bleeding. She then carried the child eight miles down the track to Rotifunk where I met them nearly eight hours later. The child was still unconscious but alive!

We immediately took her to surgery where we found her major arterial vessels still intact. Only the venous vessels had been severed along with the sternocleidomastoid muscles. A surgical repair was quickly done during which a depressed skull fracture was discovered. No anesthesia had been used since the patient was unconscious. Towel hooks grasped the depressed fracture, relieving the pressure on the brain. At the completion of surgery, multiple drains were left sticking out from her head and neck because of the gross contamination. Supportive care was instituted and we all dropped into our beds.

In the morning the child, Marie Jones, was still alive. She received excellent care through the night, as the nurses hovered over her hour by hour. That afternoon a nurse came running to report that Marie was responding and crying for her mother.

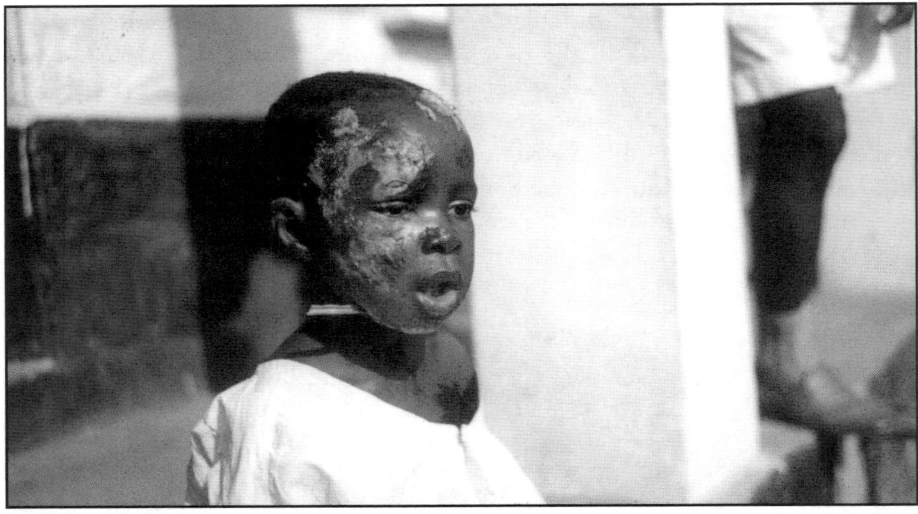

Marie Jones awake – and walking about – the next day.

In the days that followed, Marie became a pet of the nurses. Frequently they would tie her to their backs in typical African style. Ultimately the day came when Marie left the hospital. The mother asserted that she had been thoroughly spoiled by all the attentive care of the staff but there was such joy as they left – this time Marie tied to her mother's back. The Lord is kind. This little flower was allowed to bloom.

Seven years were to come and go when one day at Taiama where we were then conducting an eye program, a mother and her daughter came to the door. They were all smiles – as though we were supposed to know them. Both were beautiful. Suddenly I noticed some slightly perceptible scars on the neck of the daughter running all the way across. And there it was, the scar on her right forehead where the depressed skull fracture had been elevated. She had not only developed normally, but was also a bright student in one of our Christian schools.

We were never to see her again, but there was a deep feeling in my heart that confirmed the call to enter a medical missionary career so many years before on the shores of Lake Koronis.

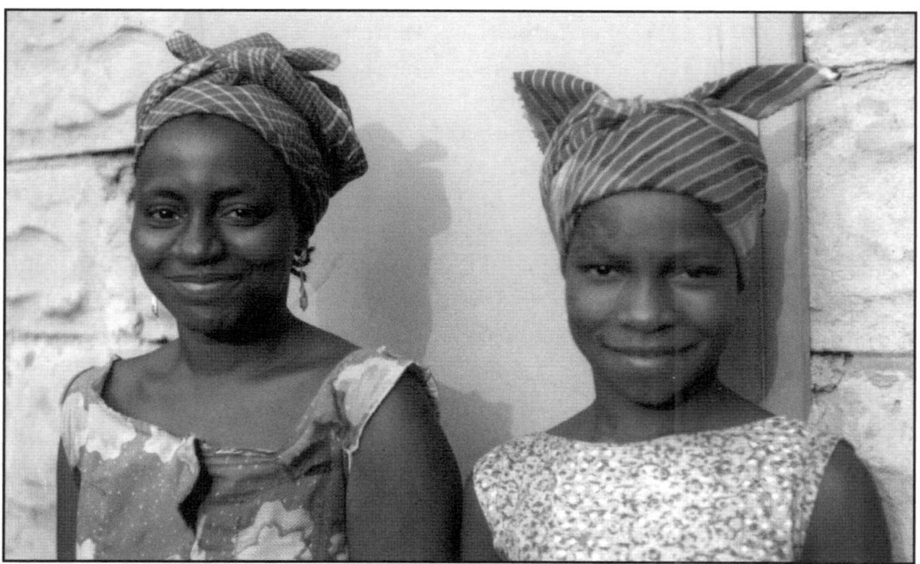

Marie Jones with her mother seven years later.

Chapter Thirty-Six

Konoland

In the final months of our three-year term at Rotifunk, significant treks were taken to Konoland. Sanford Price made annual trips to help with the buildings and maintenance of property at Rotifunk and Jaiama. We had seen him during a trip to Kurabunla in April. We had chatted about an advertisement in *Time* magazine touting Rolex watches that had accompanied mountain climbing teams. A Rolex watch would accompany me one day on a mountain climb.

We set out for Kurabonla April 20, 1960, after having had a Rupp Memorial School committee meeting chaired by Gareth Wiederkehr. The road proved difficult. David Kindy, Don Theuer, David Johnson (our surgical assistant from Rotifunk) and I were in one vehicle. David Rupp's vehicle carried the others. Due to serious road conditions, we had to walk the final three miles into the village; carriers managed our medicines, supplies and climbing gear.

Medical and surgical patients were waiting for us. On the first day we did three cataract extractions. The second day included more eye surgery but also femoral and inguinal herniorrhaphies. The early morning eye surgery on April 23rd was canceled because the patient had a violent cough and we were afraid it might cause complications.

Our surgical "safari" at the base of Mount Bintumani.

Leaving David Johnson to care for the post-ops, six of us set out for Sukurela at the base of the mountain. We had great camaraderie, good meals cooked over an open fire, and bathed in open streams. As was our practice, times of Bible study and worship were held each day during which the villagers were invited to participate. My assignment was to conduct a Bible study of II Timothy.

Up at 5:15 a.m. on April 25, we had devotions and a final packing session. Six official porters, one for each climber, accompanied us to the base camp at 4,900 feet where our camp was erected. On the way, Gene Ponchot missed capturing a bush goat that would have provided meat for the entire party of twelve that night. With the denial of that feast, our spirits sank. However, just before dark while it was still raining, one of the porters spotted a huge black boar that at first I thought was a buffalo. I was the only one who was still shouldering a rifle. Two porters dashed off with me downwind of the meandering animal. We had delicious pork that night. The excitement of the hunt was overshadowed by the discomfort of being wet and cold throughout the night.

Having had success hunting the previous day, I stayed in camp to fix it up, fill water bottles with a hand filter and better secure the tents for a drier night. During the day, Dave Rupp captured two red pigs.

Mount Bintumani, the highest peak in West Africa.

The next morning we enjoyed pork steaks and liver for breakfast. All six of us (Russ Birdsell, Don Theuer, Gene Ponchot, Dave Rupp, Ken Rupp and myself) made the final climb to the 6,390-foot summit. We tarried to have pork sandwiches along with tea and then enjoyed a Bible study on top of the world in

Sierra Leone. The view was breathtaking. We planted a British flag, since Britain still claimed Sierra Leone as a colony in 1960, independence coming the following year in 1961. I placed a slip of paper in a sealed bottle with our names and the inscription of II Corinthians 4:5: "For we preach not ourselves, but Christ Jesus the Lord; and ourselves your servants for Jesus' sake." After returning to base camp, Dave Rupp went out alone on a hunt to "sneak up on a buffalo." He did, was successful, and beef was added to our menu.

Coming down to Sukurela the next day, we were caught in a raging tropical storm. For more than an hour I huddled beneath a banana plant. We hardly considered the pouring rains as we had come upon fresh elephant spore. Baboons were barking on each side of us. Perhaps the baboons could smell the heavy loads of pork and beef the porters were carrying. Meat was shared with the chiefs and their people in the area. The people were especially attentive to the witnessing service prior to the distribution of the hunting catch.

Then it was off to Kurabonla, which we reached by noon. We were hardly prepared for the excitement that was taking place at our eye camp. David Johnson had been dressing the surgical patients. Eye patients who had been blind now could see. We were grateful to have had a part in the Lord's healing.

On our return trip we stopped at Kamron and were graciously received by Jake and Ruth Schierling who encouraged us to tarry and get cleaned up at their facilities. The night was spent at the Monko Resthouse where we concluded out study of II Timothy.

The following morning we finally arrived back in Kabala. It was a joy to see our children, Tim, Mary and Beth. Another student, Ron Baker, heard us relate the interesting stories of the eye surgery and the mountain climb. More than forty years later when speaking to some pre-medical students at Huntington College, he related the incident of how these blind patients near the Loma Mountains were able to SEE AGAIN because of a missionary's trek to that far-off place. Hearing our stories of how we were able to bless the blind with sight prompted him to consider medicine. He served as a medical missionary in Sierra Leone for many years.

We had another school board meeting and then Gene Ponchot, David Johnson and I set out. We stopped at Magburaka where Wilbur Warner and his wife invited us to share their supper. David and I continued on to Rotifunk where by God's grace we arrived by 10:00 p.m. Within ten hours I was back in the Rotifunk surgical theatre.

The final medical trek of 1960 to Kono began June 10th. At 3:00 p.m. after having completed a total hysterectomy at Rotifunk, a stop was made at Taiama where eight sputums had been prepared for examination by Lois Olsen. Five of the eight were positive for tuberculosis. Along with onchocerciasis and the many tropical diseases, tuberculosis was one of the most dreaded diseases in Sierra Leone. AIDS was not on the scene at that time.

Going on to Bo and Manjama, equipment was delivered to Les and Winnie Bradford. A warm welcome greeted us and we enjoyed a delicious meal with the Ben Clossans. The following day breakfast was with Clyde and Gladys Galow and then we headed our Land Rover toward Jaiama where we found Tonda Thomas, daughter of Delores and Jack, covered with a measles rash. Measles requires appropriate care or vision and life-threatening complications could arise.

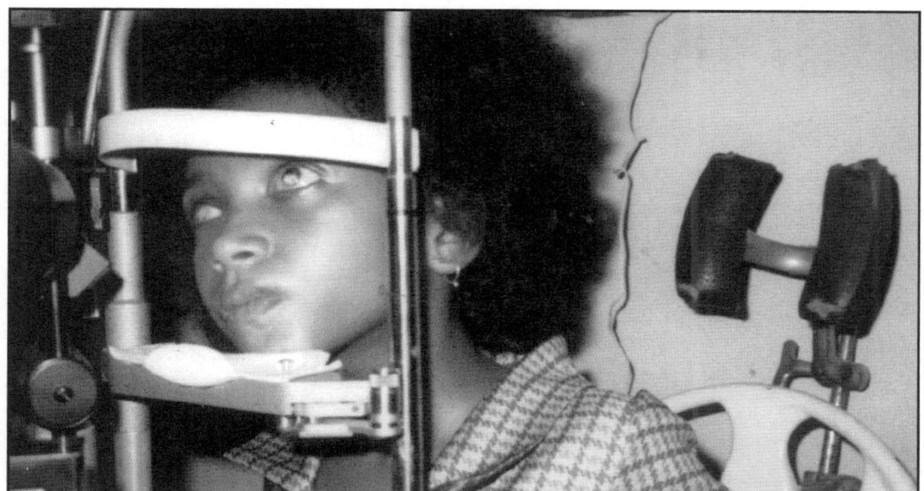

Measles complications.

On beginning the surgical program arranged by nurse Betty Esau at Jaiama, we were met by such procedures as supracervical hysterectomies, cataract extractions, herniorrhaphies and vesico-vaginal fistulae repairs. On the way to lunch after doing a thyroidectomy, I mentioned to Ruth that some day I might have to face the complication of "nicking" the recurrent laryngeal nerve. The next day I was devastated. The thyroidectomy patient could not talk! After two agonizing days of self-recrimination, on the third day I was greeted by the patient whose voice had returned. Edema had temporarily blocked nerve transmission. Along with the patient, I was alive again in this dangerous world.

These types of operations were repeated the following days. The number of surgeries was astounding. On June 16th one of our patients nearly went into a potentially fatal asthmatic crisis. Our urgent prayers and available ephedrine and aminophylline thankfully saved the patient. We were humbled when our patient, Paramount Chief Moriya from Kangama said, "Thank you for saving my life." The reply that came forth from my lips was, "I wish you the blessing of the Lord Jesus Christ." Nothing more was said.

Later in the day Paramount Chief Dudo Bona took Joseph Solo Cole, the surgical assistant, and me to see a diamond mine. I could not help but share with him Jesus' story of the "Pearl of Great Price" – possessing the Lord Jesus Christ as personal Savior.

Chapter Thirty-Seven

An Eye Doctor to Taiama

The day came when the executive secretary of the board of missions, Dr. Carl Heinmiller, visited the Rotifunk Hospital. Noticing the many blind people sitting around, he inquired as to what was being done for them. It was explained that they were waiting for their surgery as time allowed between the regular general surgical cases. He declared that something had to be done about this situation. He would secure an ophthalmologist and send such a specialist to meet this tremendous need.

Months passed – nearly a year – and no ophthalmologist was found. He then asked if I would be interested in training as an ophthalmologist to help all these people. Ruth and I made this a matter of prayer, realizing that it would mean going back to school again for another three year period. However, the need was real so we made preparations for a residency in ophthalmology.

Ophthalmology residency openings were almost non-existent at this time. Some doctors had waited for one, two or more years to get into an eye residency. Wanting to be near my parents in Minnesota, I sent my application to the University of Minnesota eye program. Dr. John E. Harris was sympathetic after hearing my story of the need in Sierra Leone and made available a place for me in the program. Later on, I learned Washington University School of Medicine also had accepted me in their eye program, but our plans had already been made to go to Minnesota.

Following the residency in eye training, we were posted back to the Hatfield-Archer Rotifunk Hospital in Sierra Leone. After about six months, the Sierra Leone conference decided to transfer the eye work to Taiama, centrally located in the country. It was on the highway with Freetown 118 miles to the west, Bo sixty miles to the east and a railway station eight miles to the south. We were to learn that Taiama was a stopping off place for travelers between eastern centers such as Bo, Kennema and Freetown on the coast.

Since Ruth was an R.N., the medical board reassigned Miss Metra Heisler to another needy area as was done so many times in her life, but always with her understanding and cooperation. Ruth was to care for the general medical problems; I was to do the eye care and Ruth's referrals, especially cardiac patients.

The move to Taiama in February of 1965 meant starting all over again with the eye program. The $20,000 that had been raised for the new eye facility originally planned to be at Rotifunk had been used for upgrading the general surgery program. A contingency fund of $1,700 was all that remained. By counting blocks, sand, cement and metal sheeting for the roof, an optical building was put up at Taiama with that amount in less than a year.

During the building, spare rooms at the end of the clinic were set up for examining and refracting lanes. An area was partitioned off in the maternity ward for an eye theatre. A well was dug. A carport was set up. The cisterns were repaired. An old generator that had been on its last legs for several years was repaired. One electric line was strung to the clinic and one to the residence, which could only be used when the clinic was not using power. The three buildings were connected by covered walkways to protect the staff and patients from the heavy rains. Don Appleman, Les Bradford, Les Shirley and other missionaries installed electrical wiring, tiled floors and contributed to the major repairs of the clinic and missionary residence.

The program rolled along; the number of operations – general as well as ophthamological – increased daily. Obstructed and incarcerated herniae could not be turned away. Ma Abby Johnson and Yebu Smart with their busy maternity program presented patients in need of emergency C-sections.

The Taiama staff.

There were many other emergencies. On New Year's Day 1965, a hysterectomy needed to be done. We had no IV stand. A nurse held up the bottle until the carpenter could put together an appropriate stand.

Joe Solo Cole, Alfred Bangura, Willie Williams and Joseph Sowa handled the flow of eye patients. Mr. Stewart visited us frequently from Njala University and serviced the optical equipment. We began edging lenses and producing finished glasses.

The Taiama eye clinic building on the left was built by local labor for $1,700. The eye program was vibrant.

Slit lamp examinations revealed live swimming microfilariae of onchocerciasis in every other patient. Many patients were already at the end stages of their disease with irrevocable blindness. We began the dangerous treatment of onchocerciasis with banocide and antrypol. Severe skin reactions occurred.

It was Ruth's challenge to monitor the oral steroids patients needed for protection. Alfred Bangura became expert at intravenous injections. The wonderful discovery of mectizan (ivermectin) by Merck, Sharp and Dohme was still not available for the more than twenty million people infected with onchocerciasis, also known as river blindness.

It was a busy program that worked hand in hand with Pastor B. A. Carew and his church across the street known as "The Cathedral in the Bush." Things were coming together and were under control.

We were privileged by the occasional visit of Sister Hillary, director of the Catholic Hospital at Serabu. It was wonderful to talk "shop" with one of the best surgeons in Africa. Her wit and charm made her visits a high point for our children.

Sister Hillary.

Most of our family was together during the summer of 1965 as we had the pleasure of Tim and Mary's visit during a break from their studies at Westmar College in LeMars, Iowa. Tim observed some eye surgeries and scrubbed in on a herniorophy emergency for a non-reducible incarcerated bowel. Beth was at the Hillcrest School in Jos, Nigeria, as a junior. John, Paul and Andrew were with us during their vacation from the Rupp Memorial School in Kabala, Sierra Leone.

Then IT happened!

Chapter Thirty-Eight

Hepatitis

Diary Entries 1965

August 20. Paul came down with hepatitis. We promptly injected Tim, Mary, John and Andrew with gamma globulin.

August 21. It was too late for John. The following day he developed clinical signs and symptoms of hepatitis. Then I noticed a chill. Was it malaria? Bile in the urine proved that I, too, had hepatitis. Obviously we had been exposed to contaminated food.

August 23. Dr. Sama Banya, physician at Njala University, came to attend us. Thirty-five years later in 2000, he continued to attend to the entire country of Sierra Leone in his position as foreign affairs minister.

August 26. Tim and Mary left Taiama to fly back to the U.S. I was unable to leave my bed to see them off. For the next eight days I was too ill to even make entries in my journal. On September 4th, news came of Dr. Albert Schweitzer's death that intensified the depths of my despair. I was getting weaker and more icteric (yellow) by the day. I could not eat.

September 5. Pastor and Mrs. Carew visited. Their prayers were a great blessing. Later in the day Eustace Renner and his wife Zainabu dropped in on their way through Taiama. He too prayed, actually kneeling by the bedside. His uplifting prayer was truly appreciated. Except for these prayers, I was at the lowest of my life, wondering if there would ever be a change for the better. I was weak and had liver pain, diarrhea and frightening episodes of 103 to 104 degree fevers. This was not typical of the disease. I began to wonder who constituted the five

Dr. Sama Banya, my physician during my hepatitis illness.

percent who did not recover from hepatitis. I decided to take chloramphenicol, the same medication that helped our first surgical case in Nigeria thirteen years earlier. It is especially effective against typhoid-type diarrheas. Within two days I began to improve in spite of being very icteric.

September 6. Andrew mentioned that he didn't feel well, but he and Ruth set off for the school at Kabala with Mr. James Simpson, his children and the Spencer's children.

September 7. Andrew and Ruth came back the next day. He was experiencing abdominal pain and his urine was dark. How many more would be affected? Banya dropped in. (Andrew recovered two weeks later.)

September 8. Ate lunch! Urine less dark.

September 9. Allis Ribblett and Clyde Galow here for lunch. It was at this time that the dramatic incident occurred of a snake crawling up onto my bed and over my feet. Fred and Margaret Gaston brought medicines from Freetown as well as a lawnmower for our large Taiama compound.

September 10. Les Bradford and Les Shirley dismantled the electric generator to take it to Freetown for rewiring.

September 11. Was out of bed today! Jack and Delores Thomas stopped by for a visit.

September 12. Dr. Sylvester Pratt and his nurse stopped in and stayed for supper.

September 13. Les and Grace Shirley, Les Bradford and Clyde Galow dropped in for a visit to encourage me in my recuperation.

September 15. Am now walking, but weak. Dr. Shadeke dropped in and prayed with me.

September 16. Took the top off the mower to show Ali how to engage the starter gear. Dr. Banya arrived while I was doing this. He laid down the law: "No activity or work for another two weeks."

September 17. Dean and Ramona Spencer, Howard and Mary Mueller dropped in to visit. Mary needed her glasses fixed.

September 19. Virginia Pickarts and Vivian Olson arrived at 4:30 p.m. The Spencers and the Muellers stopped in on their way back to Freetown.

September 20. Les Bradford picked up Andrew to take him to school at Kabala.

September 21. Jim and Cleo Simpson with their children, Carol and Tim, here for lunch.

September 22. Four mothers delivered from 7:45 a.m. until 11:00 a.m. Abby Johnson, Yebu Smart and Gladys are all very busy. Dr. Sylvester Pratt re-checked on me as he journeyed to Freetown. Les Bradford brought the rewound generator and electrical supplies.

September 24. Dressed in street clothes for the first time in three and a half weeks.

September 25. Kurt and Hilda Hein here working on the optical machine.

September 26. Clyde Galow preached at "The Cathedral in the Bush" church across the street. His wife Gladys and their son Robbie came along. Robbie accidentally spilled kerosene on our cat, which paralyzed it for a short while.

September 29. Clyde Galow, along with Methodists Don and Viola Redman, stayed for supper. The union of the EUB and the Methodist church would take place three years later.

September 30. Jim Beck from the Peace Corps welded our clothesline poles. Vivian Olson arrived 9:00 p.m.

October 1. Left for Freetown.

October 2. Slept most of the day at Hamilton Beach.

October 4. Returned to Taiama. A new mother had just died with a retained placenta. The nurses were in tears.

October 6. Aggressively began antibiotic treatment for seriously ill Everett Carew, son of Pastor and Betty Carew. A spinal tap revealed cells that were indicative of an infection.

October 7. Did a Swan Scleral imbrication, burying a rod of synthetic material on Mr. Wright's superior temporal tear and temporal separation.

October 8. Treated Fred Gaston's chronic ear infection plus rales in his left chest. After the eye cases, I did a right indirect inguinal herniorrhaphy on a patient who was having difficulty reducing his hernia.

October 10. Fred much improved. He and Margaret stayed for supper. I slept most of the day following the church services.

October 13. Dr. Willie Fitzjohn, Dr. S. M. Renner and Mr. Max Bailor visited. A little later, dear Mr. Kundaba from Mano dropped in. I thoroughly enjoyed these visits without feeling tired. I must be well. Thank God. Finally Ruth will receive some needed help with the busy Taiama clinic.

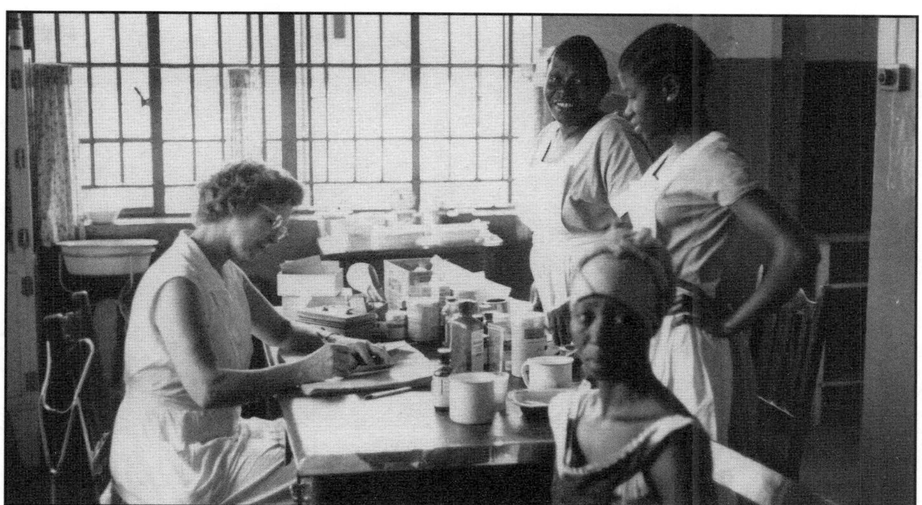

Ruth attending the clinic at Taiama.

Chapter Thirty-Nine

Burn Care

During our time at the Taiama Eye Clinic, Ruth conducted a general clinic. On one occasion she was presented with an overwhelming burn challenge, involving weeks of intensive personal care. The story in her words:

"The clinic was closed for the day when I was called to admit a severely burned woman. Her right arm and neck were covered with agonizing burnt flesh. She became our special concern for many weeks. Lowell had recently read that a new treatment for severe burns was being investigated using compresses soaked in a diluted solution of silver nitrate.

"We patiently compressed the patient with this solution day after day. Then came the period of delicate skin grafting, taking pinch grafts from the patient's waist for her arm and neck. I can still hear her pleading, 'Mawo, mawo,' which means 'Wait, wait,' when we changed the moist dressings. Amazingly the skin grafts took, and she was finally discharged from the hospital.

"With the help of Betty Carew translating into Mende, we were able to share our reason for being in Taiama and the message we brought of God's Son and His love for all.

"She came from a distant village and we didn't think we would ever see her again. She did return later wearing a new dress and presenting us with a tray of beautiful rice she had grown. She wanted to say, 'thank you!' What joy!"

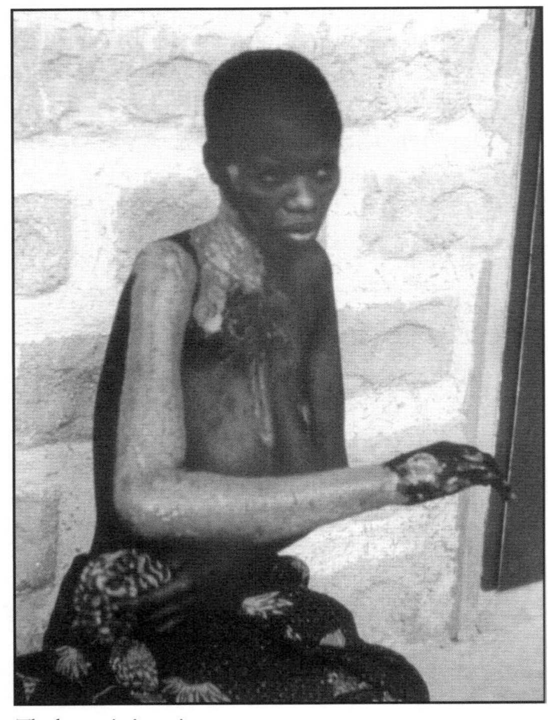

The burn victim prior to treatment.

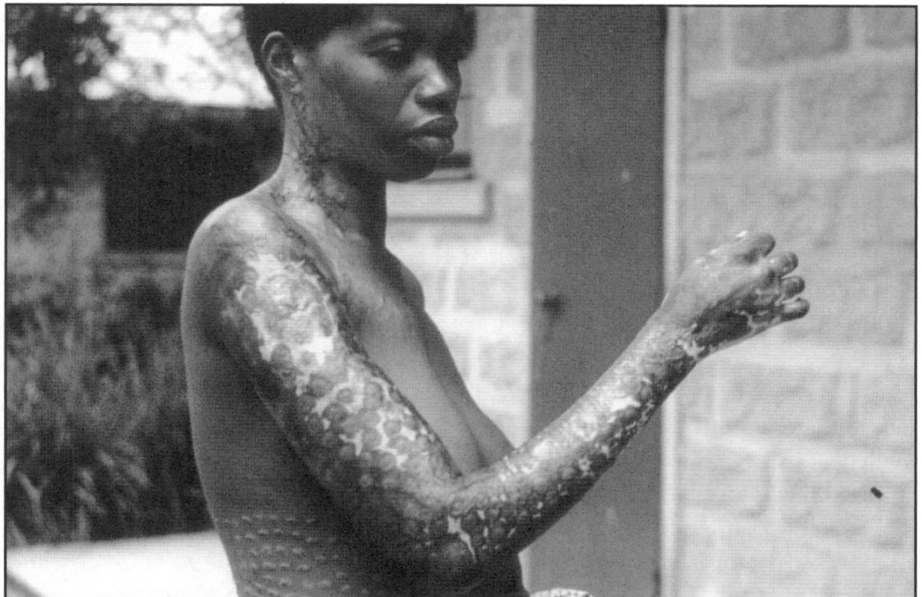

After pinch grafts.

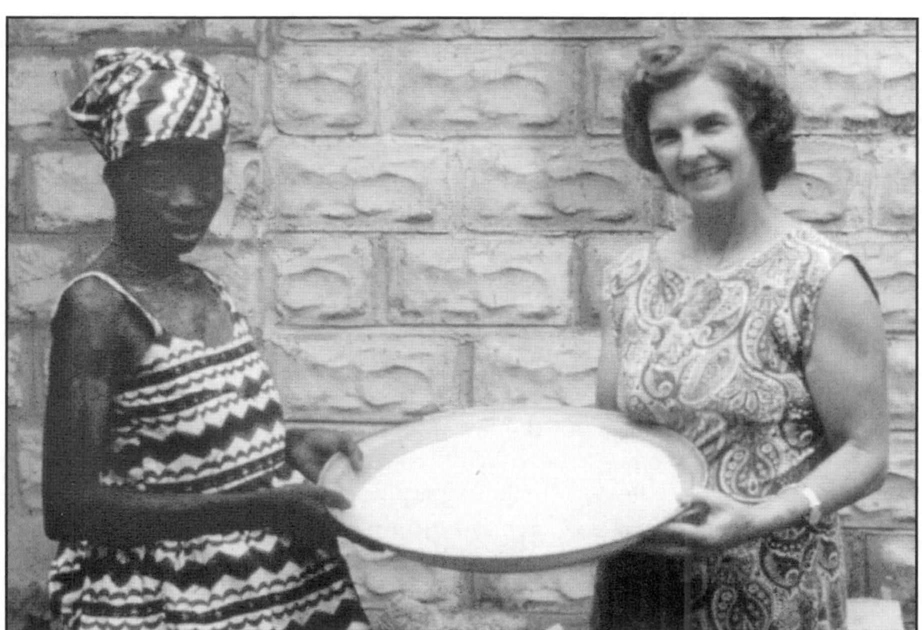

Marvelous healing after burn care.

Chapter Forty

Fish Bone Surgery

He was only twelve years old, but like a man Simeon Thomas stood tight lipped between his father and his uncle. Occasionally an uncontrollable cough erupted, eliciting a grimace caused by the pain. The father explained that while eating fish, he began to gag. In spite of vomiting, "it" remained "stuck."

I became especially concerned when I learned that two days had passed before they had come for help. The fact that they had come to an eye hospital at Taiama did not deter them. My worry was that the bone could have already eroded into the mediastinum. A dear friend, the wife of a trial lawyer, almost died from an infection after an esophagoscope had perforated her esophagus during a routine examination.

Surgical companies and their representatives had always been generous in sharing instruments no longer on the cutting edge but still of good quality and use. I had been given several esophagoscopes and bronchoscopes with claw forceps twenty inches long. Perhaps I should have given them to other hospitals, but here they were at an eye hospital. I loved good instruments – the very feel of them gave me a measure of delight. I had used instruments of this kind in my surgical residency. In the back of my mind I thought I might need them someday.

The boy was lying on the operating table. We had invited his father and his uncle to come along into the surgical suite. They were standing on one side of the table, Ruth on the other. As was our custom, we prayed before proceeding. Simeon grasped Ruth's extended hand. "Dear Lord, you made the lame to walk, the deaf to hear, the blind to see. Bless and heal Simeon. In Jesus' name, amen."

Simeon showed no signs of fear. We had learned years before patients can go into shock from overwhelming pain while still remaining stolid and uncomplaining. He opened his mouth for topical anesthesia and cooperated perfectly in positioning the esophagoscope. He did not squirm or fight while the tube was being inched along down into the esophagus.

Suddenly, it appeared – an unbelievably large and jagged fish bone half way down the esophagus. I slipped the long grasping forceps down the tube. It was apparent that the bone was too large to be drawn into the instrument. Trying to control my emotions and with as low and steady a voice as possible, I instructed Simeon not to move. I extended the forceps beyond the end of the tube and grasped the bone. Slowly the forceps and esophagoscope were withdrawn as one. Had the boy jerked or moved, the forceps would have slipped off. In spite of all the pain he did not even move so much as a finger.

Within several seconds we were able to show Simeon the "big fish" he had caught.

Chapter Forty-One

Operation at Saiama

Our trek to Saiama where the children had never seen a white person.

I had never been this far away from the hospital at Rotifunk, in fact it was nearly the border of the Republic of Guinea. Evangelistic missionaries, Jim and Nancy McQuiston, who were familar with that far off corner of Sierra Leone, had made arrangements for a trek. Ruth and I had previously done volunteer surgery at Kayima. But even this was not as far out and as far away as Saiama. In order to get to Saiama, we had to ford rivers with water nearly up to our chins. Also we had to climb a very long mountain of pure rock before ultimately getting to the area. Once we entered the village, our arrival was announced by children screaming and running off into the bush. Apparently white people had not been seen in this remote area before.

The village elders received us and helped us set up camp. By that afternoon some patients were seen and preparations made for surgery the following day. There were people in need of surgery, but for the first day there was only one who was presented to us. In order to allay fears, all of our preparations were done outside – even scrubbing our hands – prior to surgery. Careful attention was spent on providing a sterile field for the operation, which was done successfully. The following day when the bandages were removed, the patient was able to see for the first time in years.

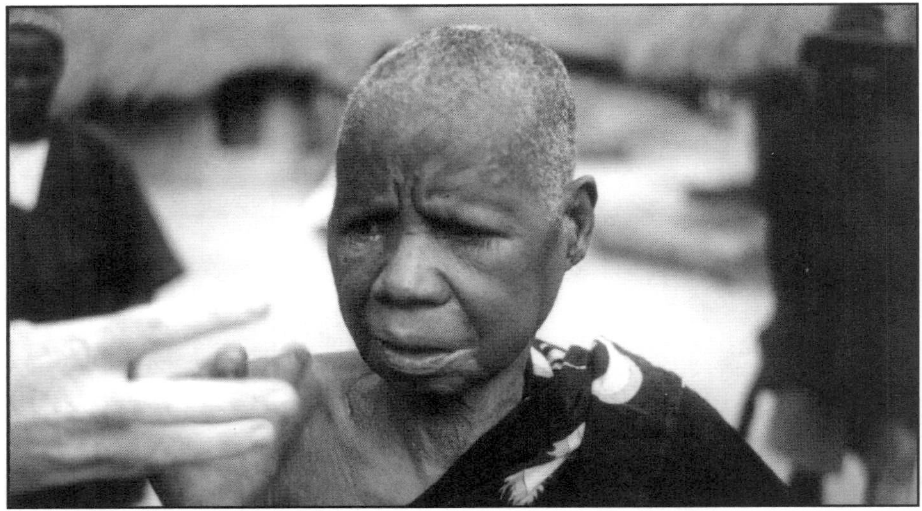

The "sacrificed" lady seeing for the first time in years.

Later we were to learn that this old lady had been "sacrificed" by the village elders to honor "the white visitors." They felt that little damage could be done by offering an old lady who was entirely dependent, needing food to be brought to her and led wherever she went. With the newfound sight, the patient was able to be independent and even productive. The realization of this finally took hold in the community and we were welcomed by the presentation of other patients who needed surgery to see again.

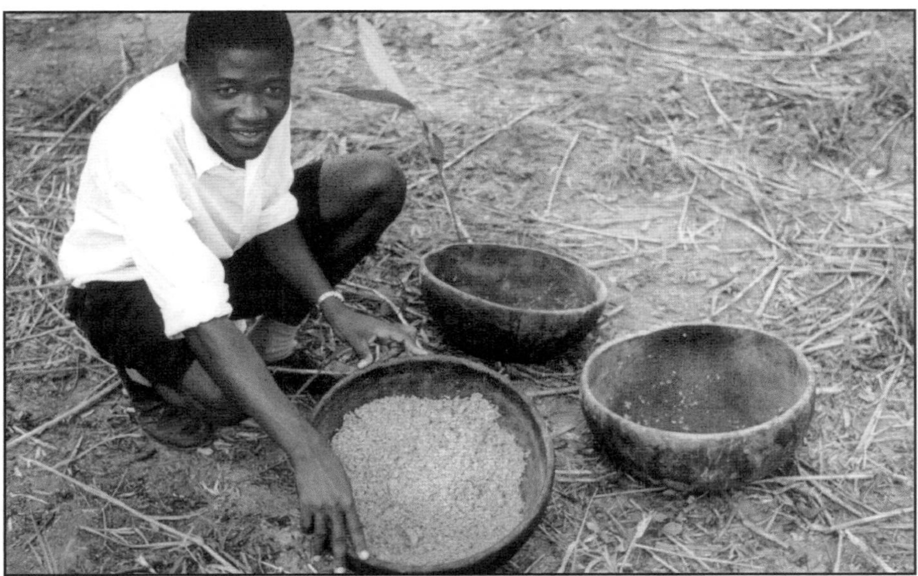

Rice being sacrificed.

It was a time of rejoicing for the people, and we took this opportunity to share how the knowledge of Jesus Christ as Savior brings joy into the lives of people. Respectfully they listened to our testimonies. Our far-out visit proved to be as great a blessing to us as to the people to whom we ministered. Our only disappointment was that of witnessing a spirit-worship ceremony during which calabashes of rice were thrown into the bush to appease the spirits while hungry children stood by.

Chapter Forty-Two

The Bridge Over the River Tai

This tranquil scene depicts a baptismal service where I assisted 119 people with their immersion into their newfound faith in Jesus Christ as their Lord and Savior.

As an ordained pastor as well as a medical doctor, I was able to assist in the baptism of many, including those in the Tai River. The bridge's right pillar is grounded on a large and immovable rock. On this rock in 1898 Pastor and Mrs. McGrew were beheaded during the Hut Tax War, a general uprising of the people against the British colonialists who levied the hut tax to institute a source of revenue for political, social, medical and educational development. Many African civil servants who were a part of the British rule lost their lives. All white people, including missionaries, were in great danger. It was to this rock that the Rev. and Mrs. McGrew were taken and killed. At the Hatfield-Archer Mission Hospital at Rotifunk sixty miles away, an even larger tragedy was taking place. Dr. Hatfield, Dr. Archer, nurse Ella Schenck and evangelists Rev. and Mrs. Cain all were killed.

There is a saying – and not without truth – that the church of Jesus Christ is built on the blood of the martyrs, as it was hardly a year before new and dedicated missionaries came to take up the work. Strong churches evolved where they had been destroyed. The church at Taiama, "The Cathedral in the Bush," was to be one of the largest churches in Sierra Leone.

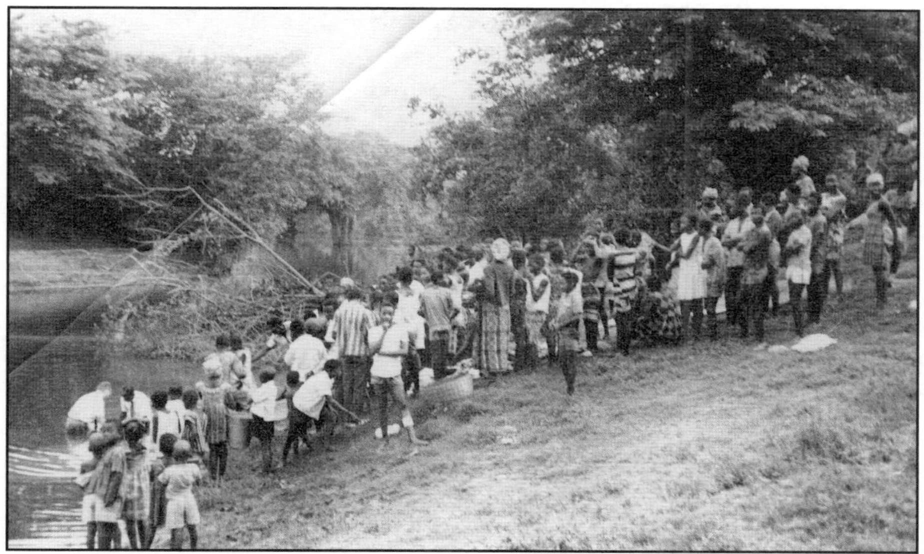

The Taiama UMC congregation participating in a baptismal service.

Chapter Forty-Three

Theologically Proper

During our five-year leave of absence from 1967 to 1972, there was the merger of the Evangelical United Brethren and the Methodist churches. When Ruth and I indicated we were ready to return to the mission field, we found that a reassessment and a re-evaluation was required. Our early service was with the Evangelical church and subsequently with the Evangelical United Brethren church.

Examination involved medical internists and even a psychiatrist. Returning missionaries were also brought before a panel of jurisdictional church representatives which included youth delegates.

One college student from Hamline University probed deeply into our spiritual motivation for medical missionary service. The scene was turning into a courtroom drama. Ultimately, I paused and I asked her what United Methodist church she attended. Her reply had the effect of a lead balloon, which ended the interview. She said, "I am not a United Methodist. I am a Christian Scientist."

We were on our way back to Bo in Sierra Leone.

Chapter Forty-Four

Methanol Poisoning

During our time of service at the Bo Eye Clinic in Sierra Leone we had the occasion to successfully treat an expatriate of Russian descent who, at a later date, presented us with a gift of appreciation. On opening it, we found a large bottle of vodka. We didn't know quite what to do with it so we put it on a shelf in a storeroom. When sometime later someone saw it and commented on its presence, we decided that perhaps there was no real use for it. We "liberated it" by pouring it out.

It could not have been more than three or four months later that a nineteen-year-old student arrived at the clinic led by several of his friends. He was nearly blind. We tried to get a history but were not successful in determining the cause of the blindness. Examination showed a rather sluggish pupil reaction and funduscopic examination showed some hyperemia of the disc. At this point we asked if by any chance he had ingested some sort of poison. Ultimately, we learned he and several of his buddies had surreptitiously taken a bottle of methyl alcohol from the laboratory of his secondary school and had imbibed. More than two hours had passed. We knew there were real problems ahead for him without aggressive treatment. Visual impairment, fortunately, could prove to be his salvation.

We immediately dispatched a runner to the downtown of Bo to try to find rum, vodka or something of at least fifty percent alcohol content. While unorthodox, this was the best course of treatment. Methyl alcohol, when broken down, forms formic acid and formaldehyde that produces an acidosis, which causes gastroenteritis, pulmonary edema and retinal damage. However, if a patient with methyl alcohol poisoning is given a large amount of ethyl alcohol, the ethyl radical replaces the formaldehyde radical and prevents the poisoning effect of the methanol. This was the first time in my life I encouraged someone to have a "second glass." In fact, we encouraged him to take an adequate amount but not enough to make him dangerously drunk.

We were successful in getting an adequate level of alcohol in his system. We also treated the patient's acidosis with sodium bicarbonate. I am happy to report that within a four-week period the patient came to the clinic without being led and eventually was able to read again in spite of the fact that he had initially lost his central vision. After this experience, we would have second thoughts about "liberating" vodka the next time it was given to us in appreciation for services rendered.

Chapter Forty-Five

River Blindness

Six men, blind from onchocerciasis (river blindness), being led by a small boy.

One of the saddest scenes I ever witnessed in Sierra Leone was that of six men, ages twenty-five to forty-five, being led by a small boy. All were irrevocably blind. This was happening in a country where in our early days of medical missionary service the medical community declared river blindness did not exist in Sierra Leone. And yet, these blind men were representative of the twenty-five to thirty million people in the world afflicted with onchocerciasis, commonly referred to as river blindness.

The culprit that causes river blindness is a microfilarial worm that is transmitted to humans through the bite of a small black fly that breeds in fast moving streams where people bathe and launder their clothes. The adult worms can attain a length of six inches and reproduce millions of microfilaria for up to fifteen years. These microfilaria burrow under the skin, causing intense itching to the point of making a patient suicidal. If they invade the eye, an inflammation develops that in fifty percent of cases results in secondary glaucoma and if left untreated destroys the eye.

These six men had received no treatment. My heart went out to them, for they were at a stage at which I could be of no further help. It was too late for the harsh and dangerous treatment with diethylcarbamazine and suramin, the commonly used medications in the 1970s. The World Health Organization (WHO) was trying to help countries in Africa eradicate the black fly by spreading insecticides over the streams with low flying airplanes. Surely there should be some way that this tragic blindness could be prevented. It became a matter of serious prayer.

It was at Bo that we began to focus on eliminating secondary glaucoma. Pioneer work by Dr. Cairns in England produced a new procedure called trabeculectomy that incorporated the formation of a protective scleral flap. However, we had a success rate of only about thirty percent. The plight of the remaining seventy percent was a matter of intense prayer. Was there some way to prevent so many from becoming blind? Consulting surgical textbooks, an old method of creating a drainage path using iris tissue piqued my interest. Instead of smoothing the iris tissue out flat and having the scleral edges closed over it, the thought came to me to allow the tongue of iris tissue to curl up on itself with the pigment layer lining the formed tunnel. Theoretically it should stay open, as the iris pigment was known to not stick together or grow (heal) to itself.

New surgical patients granted me permission to use this untried procedure. It soon became apparent that onchocerciasis patients we were treating for secondary glaucomas had a success rate of more than eighty percent!

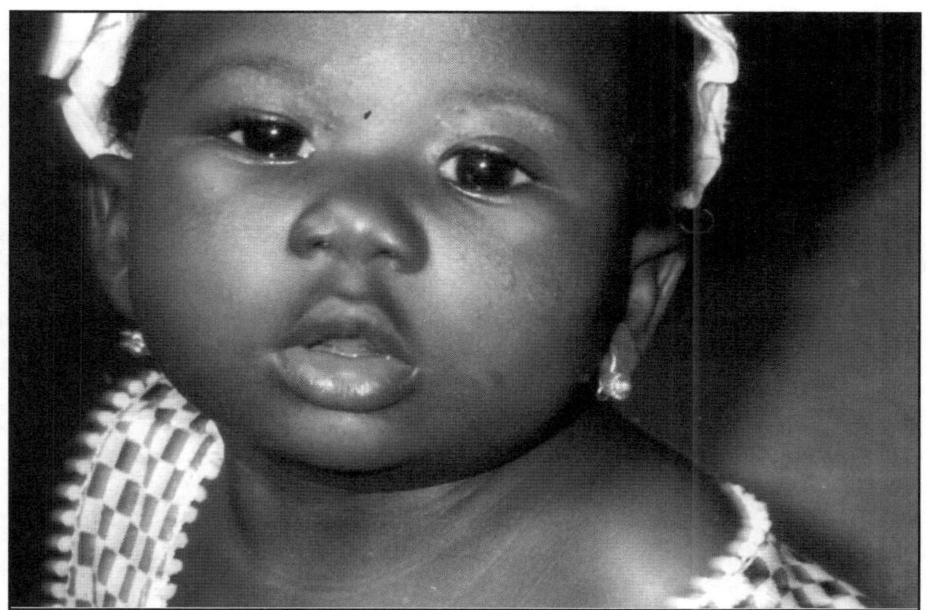

Congenital glaucoma unrelated to river blindness causes the eyes to enlarge, a condition that requires surgery to correct.

Subsequent series were done at Lunsar Baptist Eye Hospital by Dr. Eleanor Koeth and Dr. Ingrid Graelle. I did a study of fifty Caucasian patients. Success rates were in the high eighty to low ninety percent even without additional glaucoma medication. A subsequent series by Dr. Robert Barbe did not show a statistical difference in this new approach, but Dr. Norval Christi, doing a series of 5,000 surgeries in Pakistan, felt it was beneficial.

The real breakthrough came when Merck, Sharp and Dohme developed ivermectin (mectizan), which reduces the microfilaria more slowly and limits systemic and ocular reactions. Treatment needed only to be repeated at six to twelve month intervals.

Those who developed this drug at Merck – that saved the sight of millions of people around the world – must have been elated. The financial rewards would also be tremendous. Yet, the patients who needed ivermectin were poor and indigent. There was no way they could pay for the medicine. In a truly ennobling decision, Merck offered ivermectin free of charge to the World Health Organization (WHO) if they would manage its distribution.

At one point in Sierra Leone, slit lamp examinations revealed microfilaria – looking like wiggling silver threads – swimming around in the anterior chamber of patients' eyes. About half of all the patients examined would have these little worms. A decade later, I could go an entire day without seeing the microfilaria. Nodulectomies (removing small worm masses that grew under the skin) also helped reduce their production.

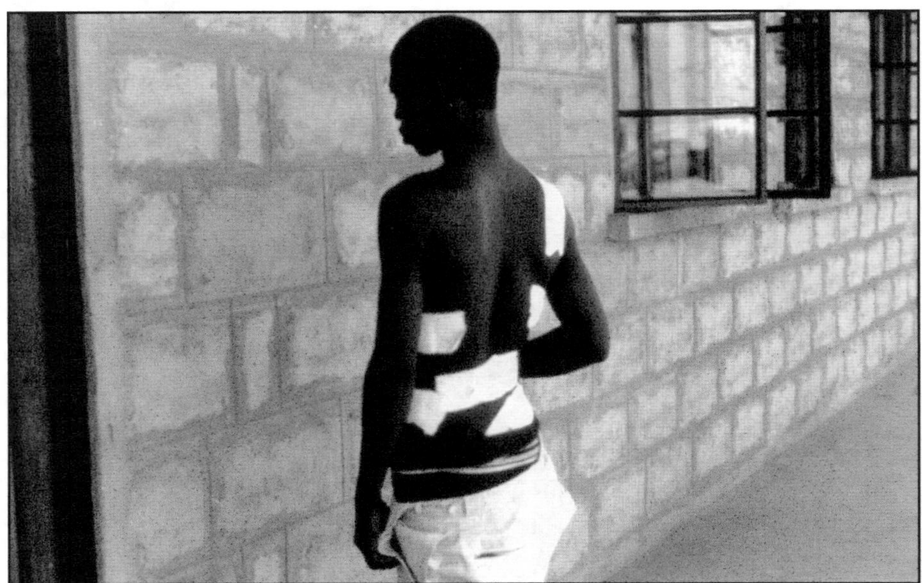

Noduclectomies for onchocerciasis.

After the development of ivermectin, it was a joy to assure patients with river blindness that they weren't going to be blind from the disease. I often thought of the decision Merck made to make the medication available to the world without reaping great financial gain. Their helping hand exemplifies the wealth of goodwill that still can be found in the world today.

Chapter Forty-Six

"When Hope is an Eye Clinic in Bo"

by Esther Groves

The middle-aged African woman lies face up on the surgical table as missionary ophthalmologist Lowell Gess observes, "If no one intervened, this patient would go completely blind with glaucoma. What we will do is make a hole in her eye to serve as a sort of overflow. If we were just starting work here in Bo, we would not do this operation because it may or may not be successful. One cannot have reverses in the beginning or people will say the place is not worthy. Now they trust us and we can do it."

A young African assistant, Andrew Josiah, swings the surgical tray into position above the patient. The masking cloth is fitted over her face with only her eye showing through the oval hole in the center. The lower edge of the cloth is attached to the tray so that she can breathe easily. There is no oxygen.

Seated behind the patient's head Dr. Gess separates her eyelids with a lid speculum as assistant John Morlai, fly-swatter in hand, scans the room for any insect that may have accompanied patients into the clinic.

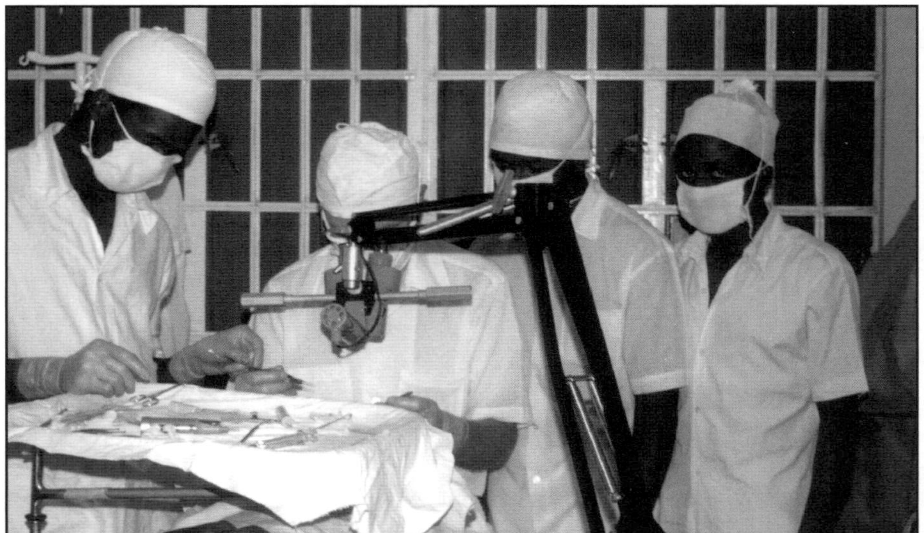

Surgery setup at Bo.

Gess now incises the cornea at the top and with forceps removes a speck of iris. It leaves a hole that can be seen as a tiny dark spot. As he sews up the incision saline is inserted, creating a balloon that rests on the pupil, a sign of watertight closure.

"For the rest of her life we will want to see that bug (the tiny dark spot). It's her lifeline to sight. Let's see how she does with this before we do anything to the other eye." As it turns out, the operation is successful.

This is what the Bo Eye Clinic means to West Africans – the difference between blindness and sight. Only a year ago many blind persons sat in darkness listening to a world of sounds. Some were babies and children with congenital cataracts, some were adults with worms in their eyes. They were led here and there by relatives, they went to native doctors, they experimented with native medicines, sometimes with dire results. A few lived in pain.

Then in September of 1972, Sierra Leonians began to hear that a puumoi (Western) doctor had come to Bo. They began to show up at the clinic before it was officially open, so United Methodist missionaries Lowell Gess and his wife Ruth, a nurse, paused in their preparations to treat them. Soon the first white eye patches were seen in bush villages.

The Gesses took on five Christian high school graduates to train as assistants. When the clinic opened on October 20, this training continued in and around eye examinations, treatments and surgery; gradually skills were sharpened and the work gained momentum. News spread that the blind could see and before long patients filled the clinic and overflowed onto the front veranda.

A day at the clinic begins between 7:30 and 7:45 a.m. as the assistants (there are now six) come to work. Patients are already entering the T-shaped one-story concrete building and taking places in the front room that serves as waiting room, office and optical shop.

At the rear door a white Land Rover Cruiser pulls up with the Gesses and Justin and Marge Sleight. Dr. Sleight is an ophthalmologist with a private practice in Lansing, Michigan, here for one year of voluntary medical service at his own expense. Marge Sleight helps with secretarial routines. Both couples live in the same duplex and arrive every morning in time for 7:45 a.m. devotions with staff and patients.

Almost before the last note of the closing hymn has died away, the staff is in action. Francis Boyo makes out number slips for patients, John Morlai asks a youngster, "Are you a patient?" and Ernest Kroma checks the vision of a young woman in traditional handkerchief, tie-dyed top and wrapped skirt. Other patients watch so that they will know what to do in turn.

The two doctors and the other assistants, Andrew Josiah, Joseph Mosima and John Fornah go to the five-bed ward to look at post-surgery patients and change dressings. The ward is the right wing of the four-room T, the surgery room the left wing. In the center is the room with examining and refraction lanes. Limited space has been used well; refraction lanes normally twenty feet have been halved to ten feet with mirrors and reverse-letter eye charts.

Now seated by his slit lamp, Gess examines quickly and carefully but shows friendly interest in the person before him ("And how is so-and-so?"). Constantly busy, neither doctor seems hurried, and the patients respond with trust. Gess is looking at a thirty-four year old man totally blind in one eye and almost blind in the other. "Pressure out of control here – iris plastered against the lens – bleeding in anterior chamber." Perhaps with an operation the man will be able to see well enough that he won't have to be led around.

By this time, the doctors and their wives are the only light-colored faces in a sea of brown. Sleight looks at the growing crowd and observes dispassionately, "It's going to be a wild day." Four persons are visiting relatives in the ward, which holds male patients one week, female patients the next.

Dr. Sleight is examining a little girl, Fatmata Gbondo. "This began as a measles complication," he says. Measles complications are not unusual in Africa; children frequently die of measles here. "Most places would have thought this eye completely lost. She was given antibiotics to protect the inside of the eye and medicines for the outside, and the eye was patched to give it support. The eye broke out but the perforation is healing. Yesterday when she was tested she had 20/50 vision. That eye will be saved."

Justin and Marge Sleight, Ruth and Esther Groves.

"An unusual case," Gess comments as he looks at a small boy. (Sleight points out later that most cases here are unusual compared to the States. People with cataracts are in their 40's and 50's compared to 60's and 70's in the States, and the cataracts are more advanced.) "The cornea is deteriorating and losing its thickness. At this rate the eye will open, the inner contents extrude and the iris will plug the hole." Gess sketches the little boy's condition on the patient card as Joseph Mosima tells the mother, "Only for the left eye, four times a day." The eye drops cost four leones; Gess decides the patient can be charged two leones and shows the mother how to apply the drops.

In the background the air conditioner hums quietly under a steady rhythm of low-pitched voices – doctors talking, assistants translating, patients answering. Occasionally Marge Sleight comes to ask about a patient card or invoice, or Ruth Gess would come in to consult about a letter or telephone call. Ruth shuttles between rooms like a weaver drawing many strands together, catching loose ends and working them into place. Between them the women make possible a steady flow of patients and free the doctors of nearly all business and housekeeping chores.

In the surgery room, assistants Andrew Josiah and John Fornah prepare to operate on a white-haired woman with nodules on her hip. Such nodules contain worms that cause onchocerciasis ("river blindness," so called because the fly and worm breeding cycle occurs partly in fast moving water). The progeny of the worms migrate under the skin to the eyes, so nodulectomies are routinely performed even though they are not eye operations. Andrew and John have been trained to handle them except for nodules on the chest wall or in a critical area of nerves.

Andrew makes two light cuts over the nodules. As John pulls back the edges of the incision with speculae, he snips around the increasingly visible nodule and brings the whitish lump into the open. A few more snips and it comes free. The young surgeon probes the incision, locates two smaller nodules and removes them, sews up the incision and moves on to another lump, repeating the entire process. A large nodule the size of a plum is removed, then a smaller one. Soon the two young men help the old lady sit up and she walks out by herself as Andrew removes his cap, mask and gown. Not bad for a high school graduate!

Ruth Gess is treating a man who has what looks like goose bumps on his chest. A patient with onchocerciasis needs hetrazen and eventually antrypol injections to kill the worms under the skin. The body reacts to the presence of dead worms with fever and other symptoms – the patient becomes ill. Then Ruth performs a delicate balancing act, giving the patient just enough steroids to provide relief until his body adjusts so that higher dosages of medicine can be given.

By this time the waiting and examining rooms are more crowded than ever. Marge Sleight is busy with invoices for glasses that have just arrived from London. Charges need to be refigured in leones and people notified by mail, phone or through friends that their glasses have arrived. Gess explains to a young man that his new glasses are mostly a gift from the clinic. What he does not say is that the balance must be made up by gifts. ("I like to think the Lord provides.")

Mohammed Tholley, a twenty-one-year-old from a village ninety-six miles away, sits down by Sleight's slit lamp. He has had pain in his eyes for nine years, has permanently lost the sight in one eye and has a cataract in the other. He can barely distinguish light from darkness. Sleight will operate on him this afternoon but the chance of sight is remote; even though the cataract is successfully removed, the retina may be found to be damaged. But Mohammed is still a young man and he has begged to take the chance.

The doctors discuss his case and operation. "We will lift the iris off the lens before we penetrate the lens," Justin Sleight decides. Lowell Gess says to Joseph, "I wonder if Andrew knows that it's an aspiration first?" and Joseph goes off to tell Andrew, who is assembling packs to be sterilized for each operation.

Gess looks at Kalu Tullah, an older man led in by a relative. "Ruth, this will be the second patient for this afternoon's surgery." He does not – cannot – promise Kalu Tullah sight, only "We will try." Sleight is examining seven-year-old Posch Komara from Freetown, 167 miles away. Both of her eyes are completely involved with congenital cataracts. She is told to come back at 1:30. If the first two operations go well they will operate on her, too.

The two doctors look at a middle-aged Lebanese who had sought medical help in Lebanon to no avail. They detect lid-lag, a retraction of the upper lid that is a sign of a thyroid condition. "It takes an opthalmologist to detect this!" says Lowell with a twinkle. "We know what's wrong with you but we don't treat this here. You need to go to the hospital." Ruth takes notes for a letter to be sent with the man and goes off to type.

Now a dark trembling old lady is lowered into the chair by Sleight's slit lamp. "I think maybe she can see a little bit today," Justin says, holding a glass lens in front of her eye. She does see, and laughs a little, then relaxes as the doctor gently swabs her eye and administers drops. Justin and Joseph apply the new dressing like one man with four hands, so smoothly does the gauze, shield and adhesive go into place.

A tiny bald-headed boy is led in wearing a makeshift pair of glasses so large for him that the handles curve around his ears and back past his cheeks. Joseph brings the new little pair of glasses and tries them on him; the child's mother smiles to see her son's improved appearance. A minor adjustment is made and the docile little fellow tries them on again, fingering the tortoise shell frames and looking about through the thick lenses.

Assistant Ernest Kroma has become proficient in grinding prescription lenses by hand. A semi-automatic machine now does the work but Ernest's skills are still needed. On occasion the clinic has even provided a pair of prescription glasses in the chosen frames an hour after the examination!

By 1:30 p.m. Mohammed Tholley is on the operating table, taking his long chance, covered to the chest with a white sheet. He hears a prayer in his own tongue, Temne. Dr. Sleight is seated behind Mohammed's head and Andrew is ready as scrub nurse.

The cornea is slit deftly and the eye flooded with saline. Justin reaches under the cornea to the cloudy mass in the center. Andrew, steady as a rock, holds the pediatric scalp vein needle in place in the eye with one hand while reaching with his other hand for the next instrument needed. The milky mass in the center of the eye is grasped and moved; it fluctuates with the injection of more saline but the nucleus is stubborn and will not come out. Gess, entering in cap and mask, agrees with Sleight that a larger incision is needed.

Andrew is sponging the eye with a homemade swab – a cotton-wrapped toothpick. ("We roll our own," says Gess, "It's cheaper and the others aren't always available.") Sleight laces the cornea further back, reaches in, seizes the pale mass and begins to move it out. Another instrument. Then the cloudy mass yields and it is drawn out, and the stitching up begins.

The patient's eye with the lids drawn back seems as large as the eye of an immobile giant staring upward. Fingers move in and out of the bright pool of light, weaving the fine strong filament like a spider magician, and the incision is closed. Next comes the dressing and shield. Assistants help Mohammed Tholley sit up and he puts on his sandals and walks between them to the ward. The operating area is cleaned up and the next patient prepared.

Now it is Gess's turn. He addresses Kalu Tullah as "Pa," the term of respect for older men. "Pa, we are going to give you a small shot." He injects the local anesthetic and John Fornah prays in Temne. Quick, sure cuts bring the cornea away from the eye. Gess threads loops with a curved short needle and Andrew snips the ends. Then a slender white cylinder of frozen carbon dioxide is touched to the lens, which freezes to it. Out comes the oval lens intact. A saline bubble falls into place above the pupil as the incision is closed. "In the States they use freon," says Gess, "but in Europe they use carbon dioxide because it is cheaper and so do we. We do have freon on hand, and if we had to do this on two patients in a row, we'd use freon for the second."

Bo Eye Clinic staff, 1973.

Other assistants, finished with duties in the outer rooms, don caps and masks to watch the third operation. They are keenly interested in their work, even borrowing books to study eye pathology in the evenings. Their interest and high morale is due partly to the Gess' thorough training, partly to the Christian ideal of service-with-love that the missionaries personify and teach. Together they can provide translation in nine languages, an indispensable service.

Andrew carries in Posch Komara and lays her gently on the table. Her black crinkly hair is braided neatly in cornrows; gold-color earrings pierce her ears. She lies quietly under the sheet, eyes closed, a lovely little girl.

"Tell her she will feel only some pricks but nothing else," Lowell says to John Fornah. "The main thing is to get her to accept the injection." But at the first injection Posch cries, "Mammy! Mammy!" and begins to turn her head before the needle is withdrawn. They talk soothingly to her, Justin and John hold her, and when the rest of the injections are given she whimpers only a bit. John takes her hand and prays.

Gess inserts the pediatric scalp vein needle, Andrew holds it in place, and Sleight controls the saline flow. (With a child you float out the cataract.) Like the two before, this will not be an easy operation.

Gess says, "I'm going to make just one little opening here, (to Sleight) that chamber is beautiful, you're doing a perfect job – I can't get it off all the way, I'm going to stop." Then everything comes loose and Lowell hands up the tube with the cloudy nucleus at the end of it, suctioned out. He is looping stitches into place when Ruth appears at the doorway and asks, "Was she good?"

"Yes, she's nearly asleep – Doctor Sleight's sleeping potion!" Lowell says as an afterthought, "I saw on the box that it cost 20 leones."

"It's worth every penny of it," Justin replies. Posch, though conscious throughout, has not moved once during the operation thanks to the special anesthetic from the U.S. She cannot afford it but perhaps some gift will cover the expense.

By this time the room is very hot and everyone is sweating. Ruth and Justin discuss the possibility of an exhaust fan in the surgery room that would draw in cooled air from the centrally located air conditioner in the examining room. But that would take money, and medicine and glasses come first.

John carries Posch to her bed on the ward. It isn't women's week but the arrangement will work with little Posch. One of the assistants is on duty with patients all night, tending to their needs and dozing in between.

After the operations Mr. Bangura, who has a hole in his head, shows up for his daily check and change of dressing. For years he went from hospital to hospital with an infected draining right sinus that cost him his right eye. Gess saved the other eye by making a hole in his forehead that brings drainage outside. Today as usual the sinus is irrigated with hydrogen peroxide and freshly dressed, and Mr. Bangura goes off in comfort with his young, attentive wives, each one, however, already a grandmother.

A young girl comes in for a check, wearing a false eye that is absolutely undetectable. Justin Sleight had fashioned a prosthesis to fit, an eyepiece resembling a specially built up contact lens which fits over the useless eye and turns with it.

At last the day is at an end. Four weeks later Mohammed Tholley's long chance has paid off. He can actually see somewhat. His eye is being kept quiet with steroid medications. Kalu Tullah had not received much hope from the doctors beforehand because of the pathology in his eye. His eye is slowly – very slowly – clearing. Little Posch is coming along well and will have her second operation in a little while. It had not been an easy afternoon, but Lowell Gess and Justin Sleight and their supporting staff can feel happy about the day. Perhaps – one can always hope – other ophthalmologists like Justin Sleight will volunteer anywhere from six months to a few years to help keep the clinic running. Because for Mohammed, Kalu, Posch and many, many others, hope is an eye clinic in Bo.

Chapter Forty-Seven

Bo: 1972 to 1975

On September 1, 1972, we docked at Freetown, Sierra Leone. Happy to be back in the land of his birth, our youngest son Andrew kissed the ground. Days later he became a teenager. Within a few more days he was attending the Rupp Memorial School in Kabala, a six-hour journey away.

Our eye program was to operate in Mende country. Bo was the second largest city in Sierra Leone. Our mission compound bordered the main road leading in and out of Bo. A small headquarters building was altered and adapted to house the Bo Eye Clinic of the United Methodist Church. The optical equipment that had been used at Taiama and stored at Rotifunk was brought up to Bo. John Morlai helped Ruth and me clean and restore items that had been tucked away in boxes that mice, cockroaches and lizards had felt comfortable. Even while the clinic was being set up, we could not refuse eye treatment to many disparate eye conditions.

Officially, the Bo Eye Clinic was ceremonially opened November 1, 1972. The first patient, Pastor J. B. Vandy Rogers of the large Centenary United Methodist Church, was discovered to have glaucoma. Medicine and surgery protected his vision for the following twenty-eight years. Air service within the country of Sierra Leone allowed patients from Freetown and elsewhere to speedily get to the Bo Eye Clinic. One of our favorite patients whom we met at the airport from time to time was Mrs. S. M. Renner. She, too, needed management for her glaucoma.

The Bo UMC Eye Clinic.

Ultimately, the Bo Eye Clinic became well established. Early on, the number of patients we saw each day rarely exceeded fifty, but as the numbers increased we not only saw patients each day but also had a daily surgical schedule. Little did we dream that as many as 166 patients would eventually be seen and treated on a single day. Everyone pulled together to meet the challenge. The African staff worked long but effective hours.

We looked forward to a new and full year at the Bo Eye Clinic but we did not anticipate how eventful and sometimes dangerous it could be.

1973. In February 1973, the United Methodist Church, Sierra Leone Conference, consecrated the Rev. B. A. Carew as its first bishop. Bishop Maynard Sparks, from the General Board of Global Ministries participated, along with Dr. S. M. Renner, Dr. J. K. Fergusson and other council members. The new Bishop Carew had a history of an unusually successful pastoral ministry. As bishop, his wise guidance was to lead the United Methodist Church in Sierra Leone to new achievements.

Before they were captured, members of a Black September gang terrorized the Bo area. Twice the United Methodist Church compound in Bo was invaded. Our two watchmen were usually asleep whenever we checked on them. The people in our area took matters into their own hands and captured one thief whom Gil Olson, a missionary evangelist living on the same compound, delivered to the police. Sadly, another thief was the object of the people's fury and was beaten so badly he subsequently died.

As a delegation, the missionaries went to the police to inquire about protection for the Bo Eye Clinic and the Bo Bible Training Institute, as one of our members was severely harmed during one of the break-ins. Several days later, I was summoned while examining an eye patient and was presented to the Sierra Leone chief of police and the director of the CID (Criminal Investigation Department) from Freetown. They sat down and visited about the trauma suffered by our missionaries and gave assurances they would do all in their power to prevent further happenings. Within several weeks, we learned that the loot had been found and the gang apprehended and sentenced.

We were to see a number of Moorens ulcers in the years to come. The first one had a deadly impact on the staff and me. Chali Bangali was a youth of eighteen. He was popular at school and a good student. He was brought to the eye clinic by a member of our staff and was assured that his painful eye could be helped. One look with the slit lamp confirmed a diagnosis of Moorens ulcer. This was also the first viewing of a Moorens ulcer for visiting opthalmologist, Dr. David Stayer. The marginal ulcer had already excavated tissue at the limbus a quarter way around the cornea. It did not respond to antibiotics, corticosteroids or surgical excision. Relentlessly, it completed its circle and destroyed the eye. Our only constructive service was fitting him with a prosthesis that looked and fitted very much like a normal eye. Sue Robinson, area representative from the General Board of Global

Ministries, had just two weeks earlier brought a set of appropriate sizes and colors.

In July 1973 we had the pleasure of entertaining Ray and Arlene Harrison and their children; Daniel, their eldest, was born at the Taiama Eye Clinic. Gareth and Treva Wiederkehr, with their sons Wayne and Wes, also dropped in. We were shocked and saddened later to hear that Wayne had been bitten by a squirrel while attending school in Kabala and was overwhelmed with toxicity before help arrived. Few tragedies can be as great as to have a small son die in his father's arms while on the way to the hospital.

While at Bo, we had the help of longtime dedicated missionary, Dr. Jenny Gibson, who would come over and give general anesthesia for our pediatric patients from time to time. However, a number of weeks later I finally figured out how to anesthetize children using ketamine.

Trips to Freetown were made frequently, as the 118 miles were paved. On one occasion I was called upon to give a paper to the Sierra Leone Medical and Dental Society on the topic of onchocerciasis. Sometime later, doctors in Freetown were made "believers" that onchocerciasis did exist in Sierra Leone.

1974. Early in 1974, I attended an eye workshop in Liberia while Justin Sleight minded the store at the Bo Eye Clinic. Our sons, John and Paul, assisted our clinical staff with some of the school surveys conducted at Jaiama (1,300 students) and Yengema (1,200 students). It was discovered that a number of students were in dire need of glasses. Other eye ailments were also uncovered that we could treat at the Bo Eye Clinic.

Our four sons sang at Leader Memorial Church in Bo. Ruth and I especially enjoyed hearing them sing "My New Life I Give to Thee."

While there was much gaiety during the visit of our four sons (who arrived just before Christmas for a month's vacation), they were productive as well. Utilizing the optical equipment, both John and Paul examined patients and fabricated glasses. Without television to occupy their time, it was rewarding to know that besides family devotions and prayers, John read C. S. Lewis's *The Great Debate* and Paul read William Barclay's *Ethics in a Permissive Society.* On their return flight to the U.S., John and Paul stopped off at Francis Schaefer's L' Abri community for a short visit. This entire three-month visit was underwritten by the General Board of Global Ministries to help keep families together. It was a great blessing.

The eye program had developed to such an extent that even with Justin's help, we were being unduly pressed to accommodate the large number of patients who needed glasses, medical treatment and surgery. We were doing many retinal reattachments while caring for a host of trauma patients.

Alfred Bangura, who had received optometric training in Houston, Texas – along with the support of Dr. and Mrs. David Stayer – played a significant role in the examination of patients. It was a great disappointment that he was unable to obtain his official degree in optometry. However, the Sierra Leone army was happy to have his commissioned eye service. With the developing civil war and the continued encroachment of the rebels, Alfred was pressed into combat leadership. Tragically, he was killed in this bitter civil war.

Another stark tragedy happened to Dr. Yilla, our friend and fellow physician in Bo who was referred to a London hospital for neurosurgery for a slipped disk. During the operative procedure, the surgeons were concerned about some "white thread-like structures." The anesthesiologist reminded them that Dr. Yilla was from Sierra Leone, suggesting a Guinea worm infestation. A biopsy was taken. Analysis revealed aberrant spinal nerves. Dr. Yilla never walked again.

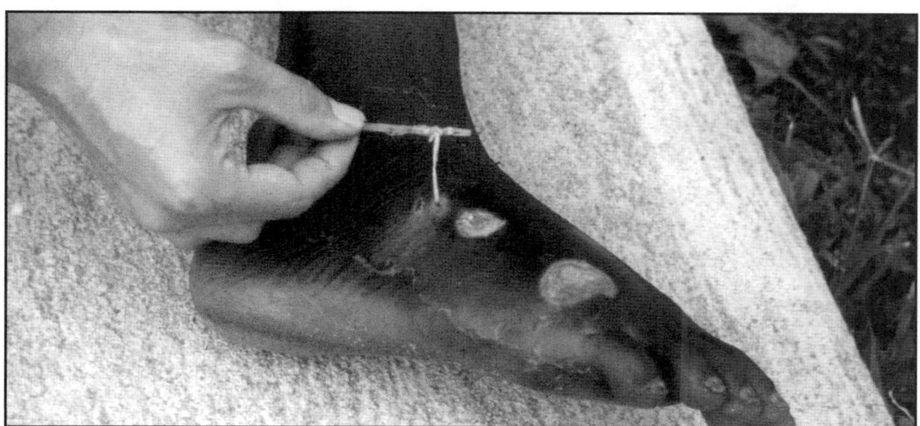

Guinea worm disease.

1975. The years of service at the Bo Eye Clinic went by very rapidly with such an intensive schedule. We never anticipated that our patient load would exceed fifty or sixty a day, but often it was more than 160 during the latter half of the tour.

Surgeries were done four or five times a day. During January and February our son Tim lent a hand. He helped with every aspect of the program and on January 27, 1975, recorded his first complete cataract extraction. By the end of February, he was doing four or more cataract procedures each day as well as an occasional glaucoma operation (trabeculectomy).

The spiritual tone of the community of missionaries was a special blessing at Bo. Prayer meetings were life directing. While Chalky and Elaine Cox, Phillip Dean, Jenny Gibson, Richard and Carol Jackson and David Griffith represented Protestant, Catholic and other independent denominations, during prayer times all hands were raised in praise and supplication to God. It was a foregone conclusion that the baptism of the Holy Spirit could and would happen.

Preparation for our departure from the Bo Eye Clinic was an involved process. Paul, who had not as yet started his work at Fuller Theological Seminary, flew out to help with the packing. Most of the instruments and technology were our own. We donated some to the Lunsar Baptist Eye Clinic where the Sierra Leone Baptist Church was beginning an eye clinic. Our trained staff was transferred as a body to this new work at Lunsar.

When packing was completed, nineteen barrels and four crates were ready for shipment. While some crates contained slit lamps and other optical equipment, one crate held the dismantled parts of a Honda trail mini-bike from which Andrew could not part.

Paul's help was invaluable. I was going day and night trying to minister to all the people who needed help before the Bo Eye Clinic closed. The ongoing Christian fellowship and prayers kept us healthy and sane.

The Bo Eye Clinic years were to contain some of the deepest spiritual experiences of our lives.

Flowers for Ruth after losing thirty pounds following her third pregnancy. (Pg. 282)

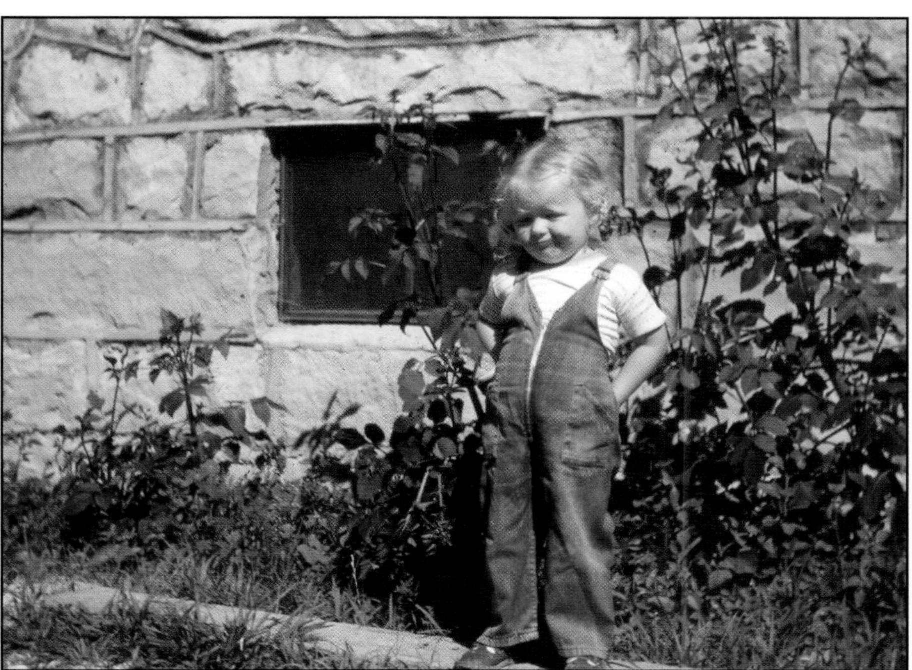

Beth (under two years of age) discovered applying lipstick was not as easy as it looked. (Pg. 317)

Several months before our first trip to Africa and just before John was born, the family went fishing on Lake Koronis. Our two-year-old, Beth, caught the most fish as we secretly kept putting the same little fish on her line. (Pg. 65)

Yusufu, my first surgical patient in Africa, post-op. (Pg. 73)

The children's pet monkey at Bambur, Nigeria. (Pg. 103)

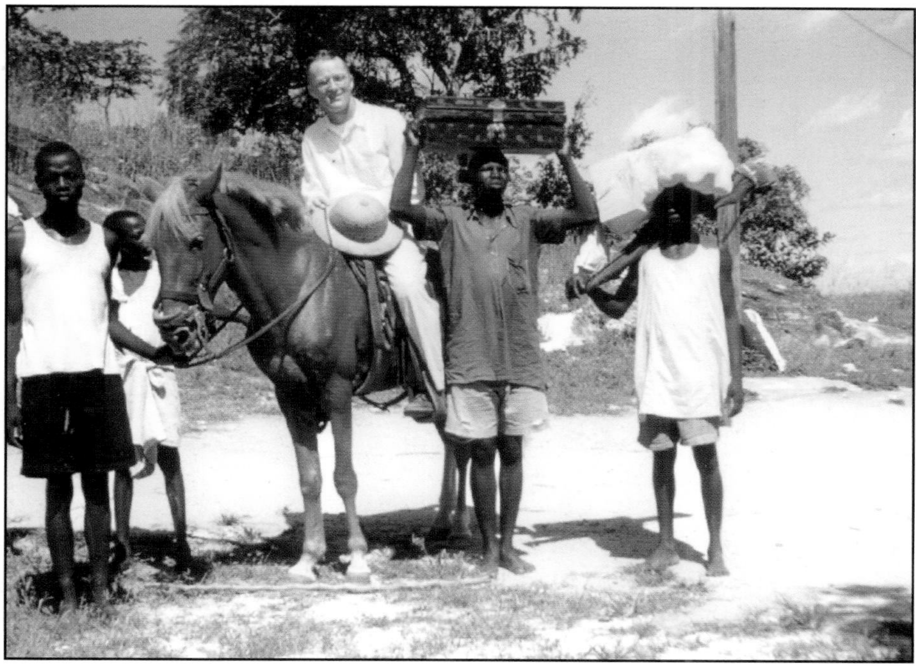

When roads washed out, clinic visits to Pero required a horse rather than a Land Rover during our first year as medical missionaries. (Pg. 103)

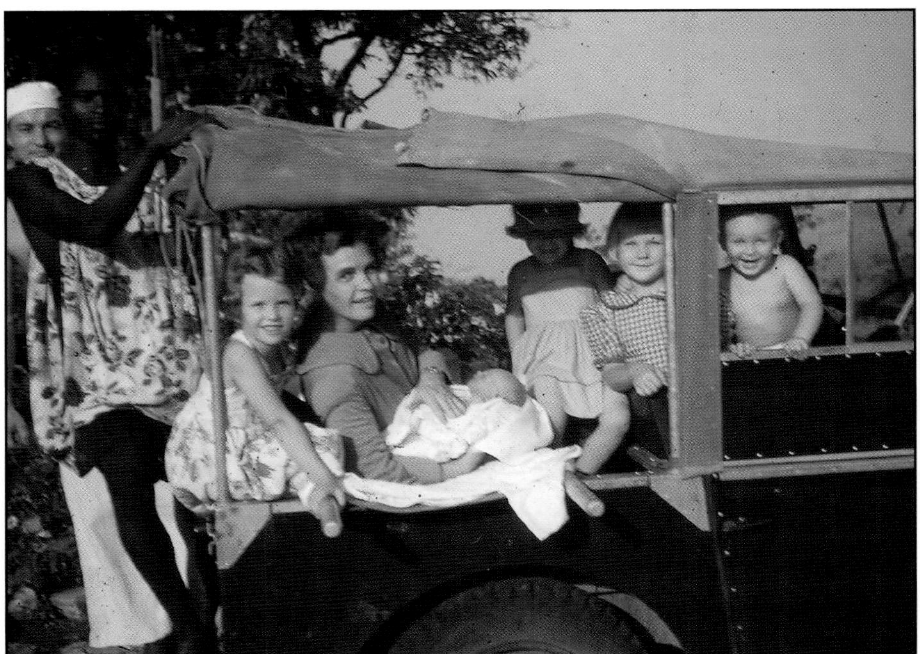

Ruth was brought home from the hospital an hour after the delivery of Paul. She had a cheering section of the other children as well as Dr. Olewiler and the chief nurse, Bila, who rode on the back of the Land Rover. (Pg. 97)

Our son, Paul, second from left, who was thought to be beyond the help of human hands; other sons left to right–Timothy, Andrew, John. (Pg. 99)

The family in the Land Rover that had faulty brakes. (Pg. 283)

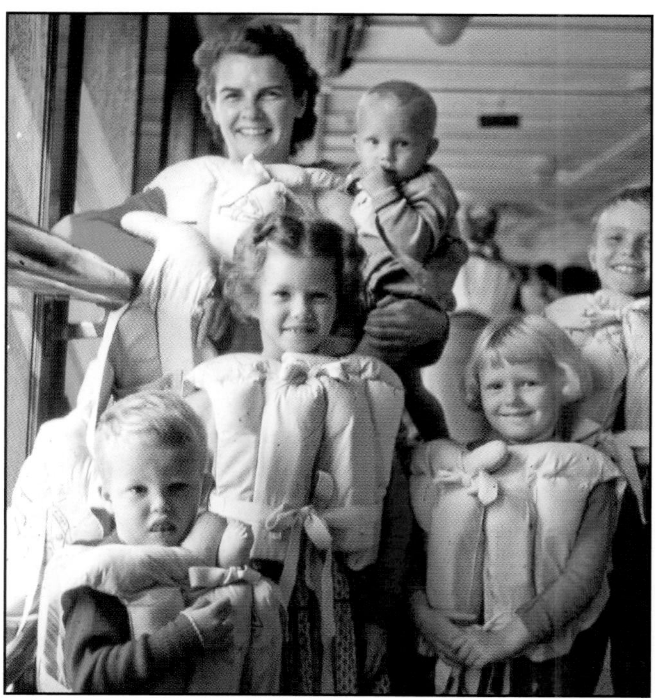

Boat drill on the *HMS Accra* returning from our first tour in Nigeria. (Pg. 283)

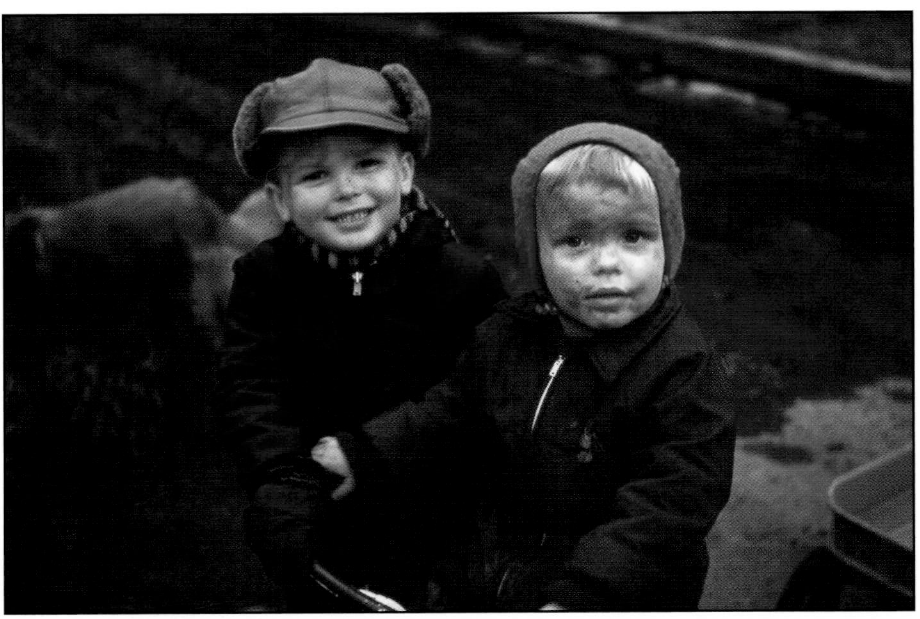

As an extrovert, Paul (right) was at the center of most activities, willing to take on any challenger. (Pg. 115)

John, Paul and their favorite playmate at Rotifunk, Jacob. Paul apparently was too much in a hurry to get his shoes on properly (they are reversed). (Pg. 323)

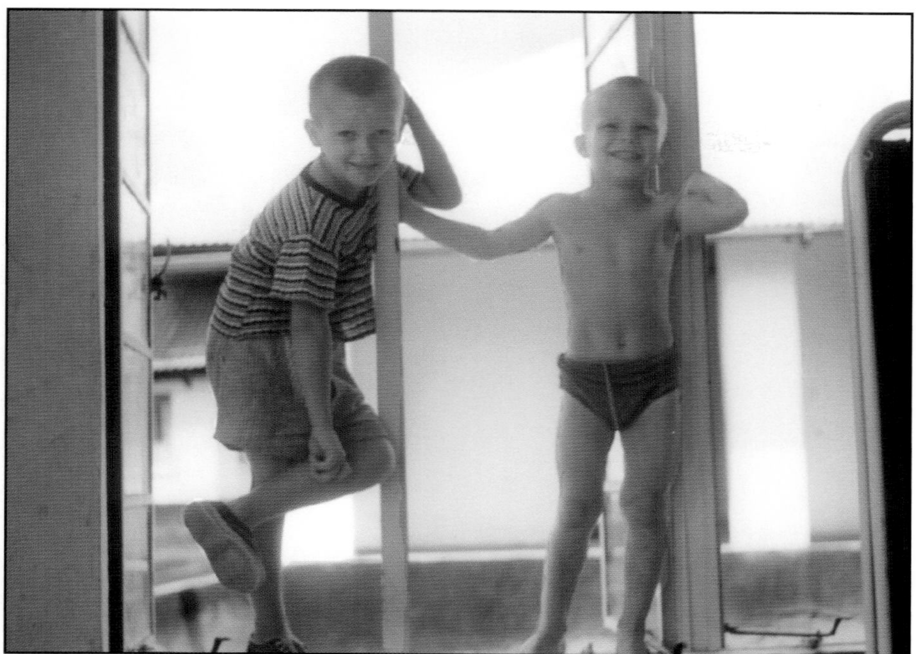

John and Paul in the surgery window waiting for their mother to finish administering anesthesia. (Pg. 115)

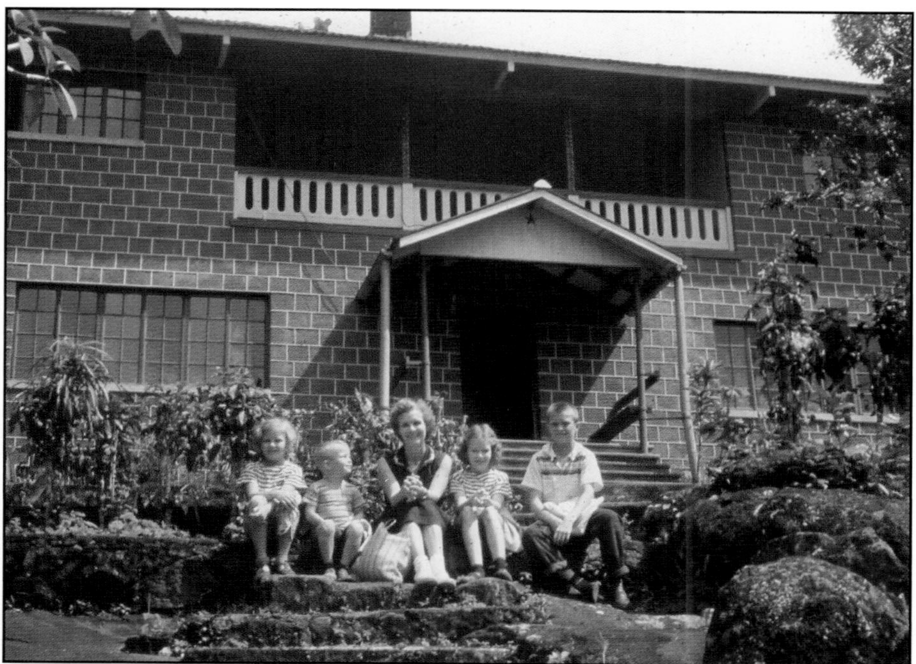

UMC Rest House for missionaries located at the highest elevation of Mount Leicester until the Sierra Leone Radio-TV station was built at the very top. (Pg. 162)

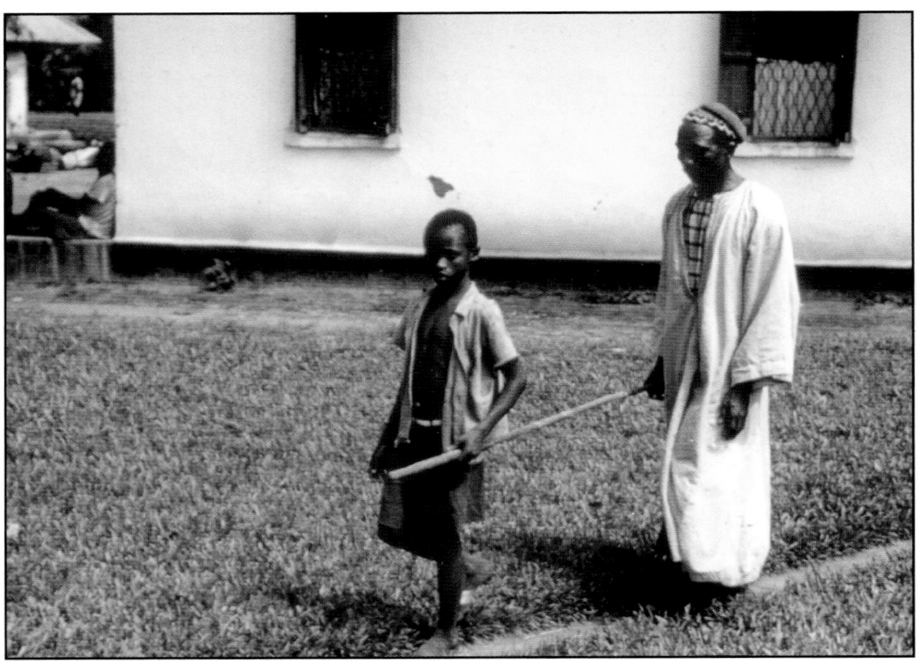

Blind Kombe being led to the hospital by a small boy. (Pg. 116)

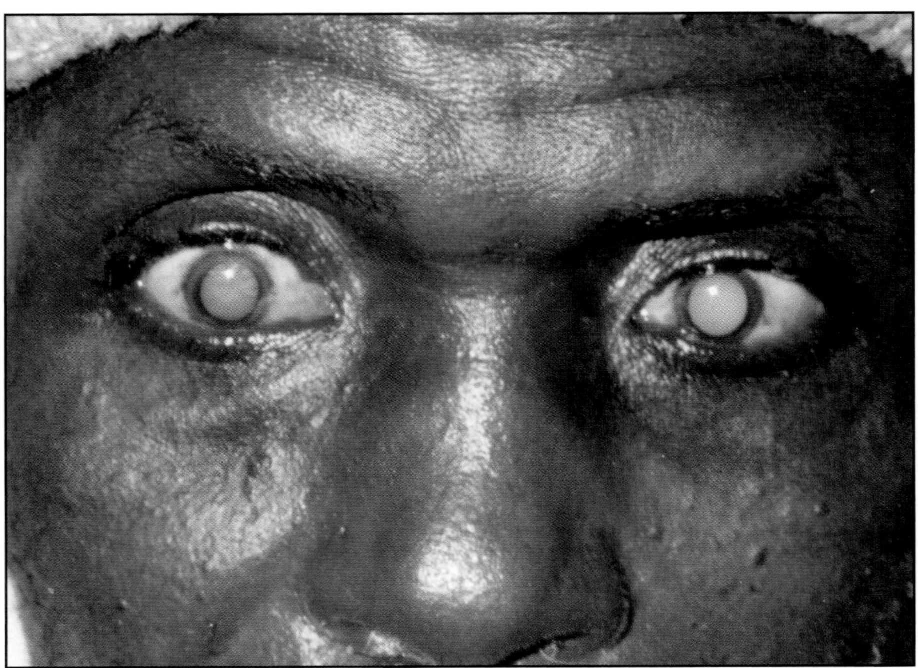

Bilateral blindness from mature cataracts is common (picture taken at Rotifunk.) (Pg. 116)

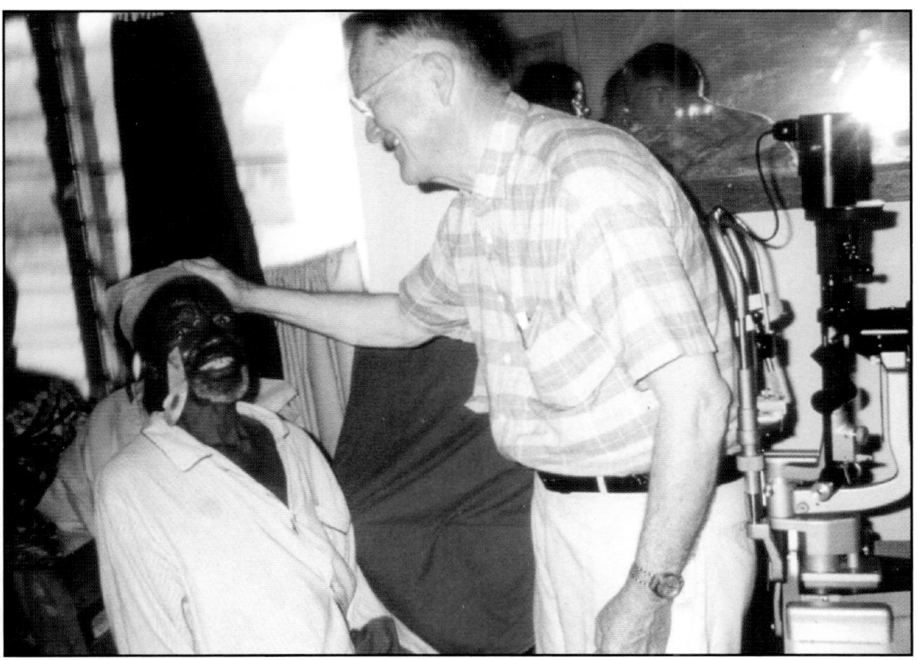

Kombe rejoicing with vision on the day following surgery. (Pg. 116)

Kombe, no longer blind after his operation, walks without being led. (Pg. 117)

Ruth being escorted to the hospital by Dr. George Harris for Andrew's delivery. (Pg. 327)

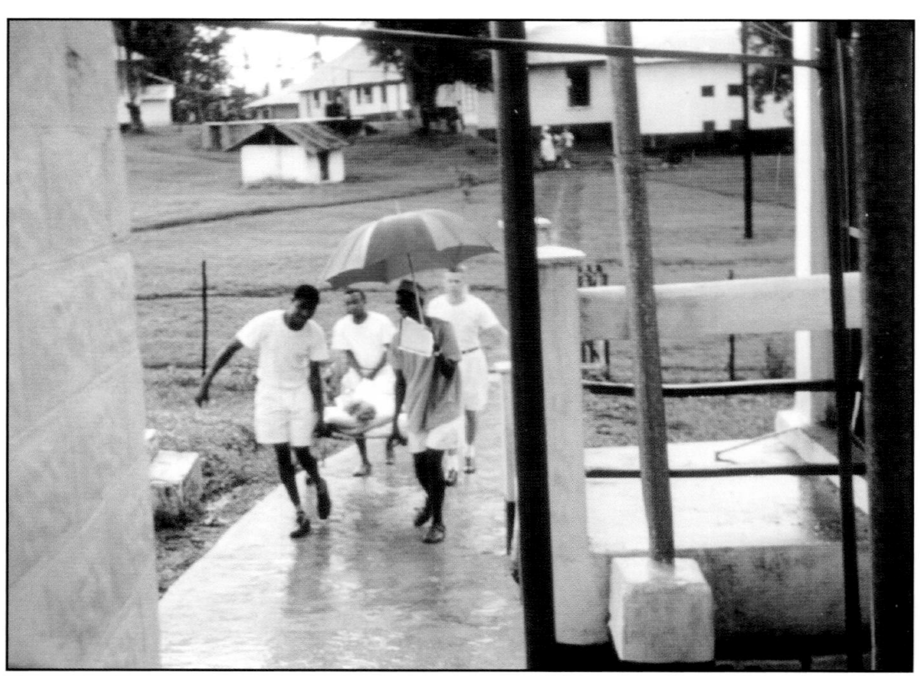

Ruth being carried home after Andrew's delivery. (Pg. 327)

Andrew carried on back of nurse Tatar Bagrav. (Pg. 327)

Ruth being thanked with a gift of flowers by a leprosy patient; Ruth had shared food and clothes with several leprosy patients. (Pg. 359)

Ruth's Sunday school class at Rotifunk. (Pg. 289)

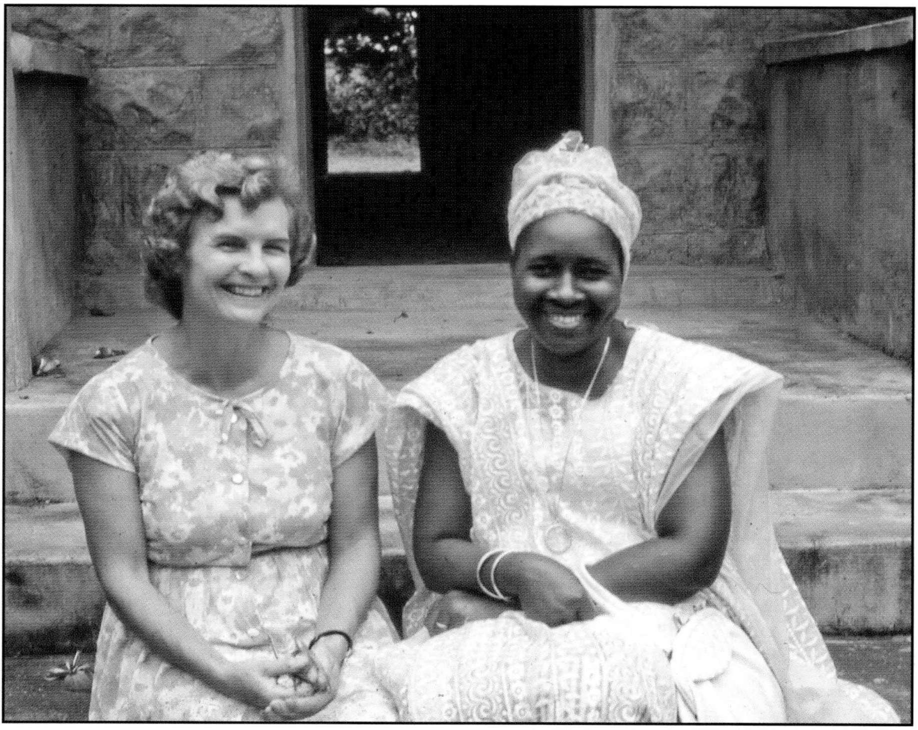

Ruth with long time friend Betty Carew, wife of Bishop B. A. Carew, the first African United Methodist bishop in Sierra Leone. (Pg. 87)

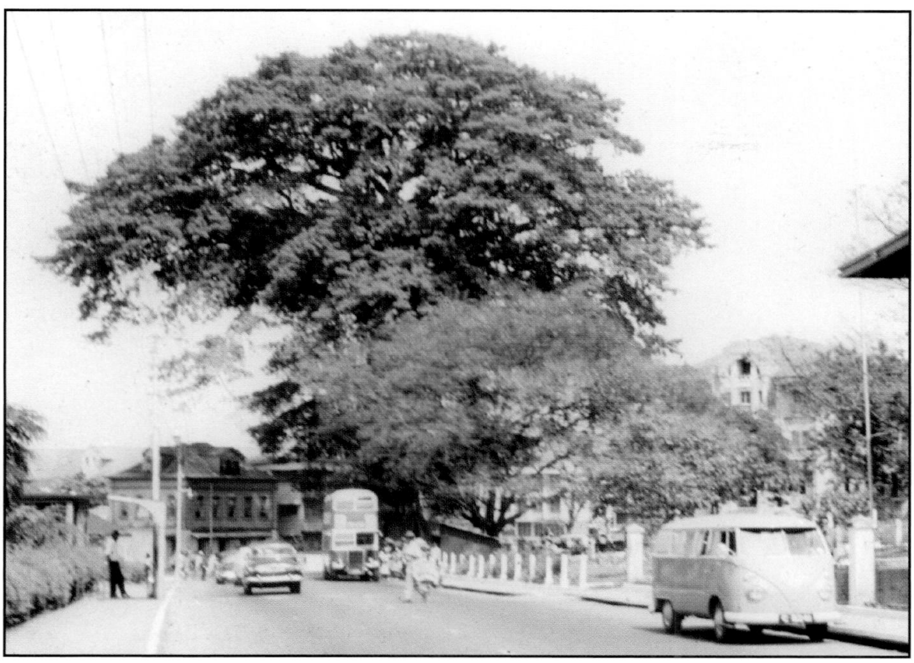

Under this cottonwood tree in Freetown slaves were sold – many of whom were sent to America.

Surgical trek in 1960 to Jaiama, more than 250 miles from Rotifunk. Betty Esau Wight is the nurse on the far left. (Pg. 122)

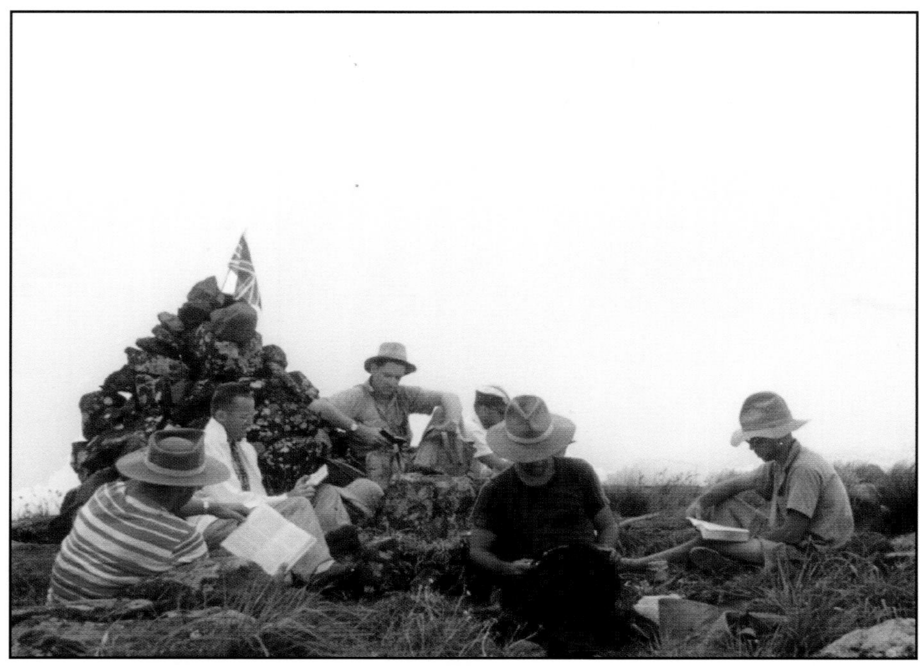

Our Bible study on top of Mount Bintumani. My lifelong habit of not wearing headgear led to skin cancers in later years. (Pg. 123)

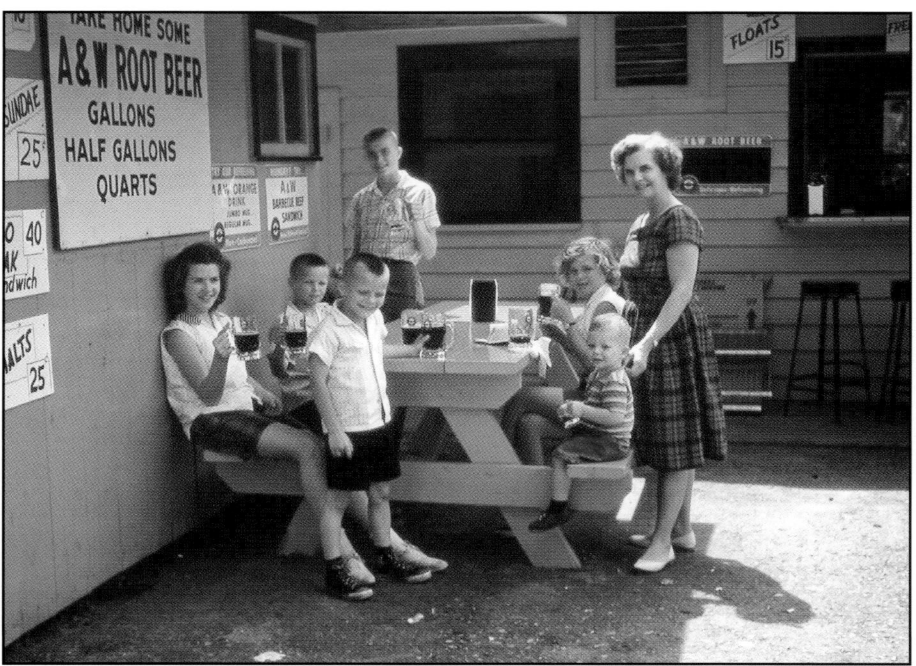

Ruth and the six children drinking A&W root beer. (Pg. 283)

A rare event when the children got me into the water. Demonstrating a backstroke almost did me in. (Pg. 342)

Baptism of 119 new Christians in River Tai. In the background is the bridge with its right pillar resting on the stone on which Rev. and Mrs. McGrew were martyred in 1898. (Pg. 138)

The results of river blindness (onchocerciasis) – six men aged twenty-five to forty who were irrevocably blind. (Pg. 142)

The five original Kissy volunteers: Roger Reiners, builder; Arvid Liebe, pharmacist; Loren Ebsen, builder; James Mundwiler, mortician; Floyd Bohn, accountant. (Pg. 164)

The staff at Kissy UMC Eye Hospital. (Pg. 169)

Gate to the Kissy UMC Eye Hospital. (Pg. 166)

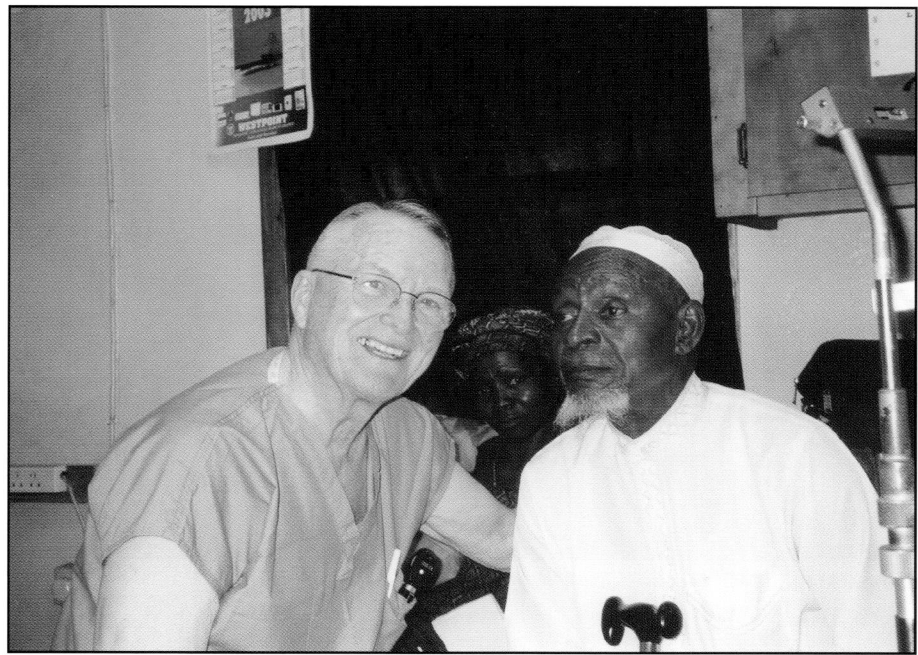

This gentleman was one of the first eye surgery patients I had at Kissy. On this visit thirty years after the surgery he could read the paper without glasses. (Pg. 166)

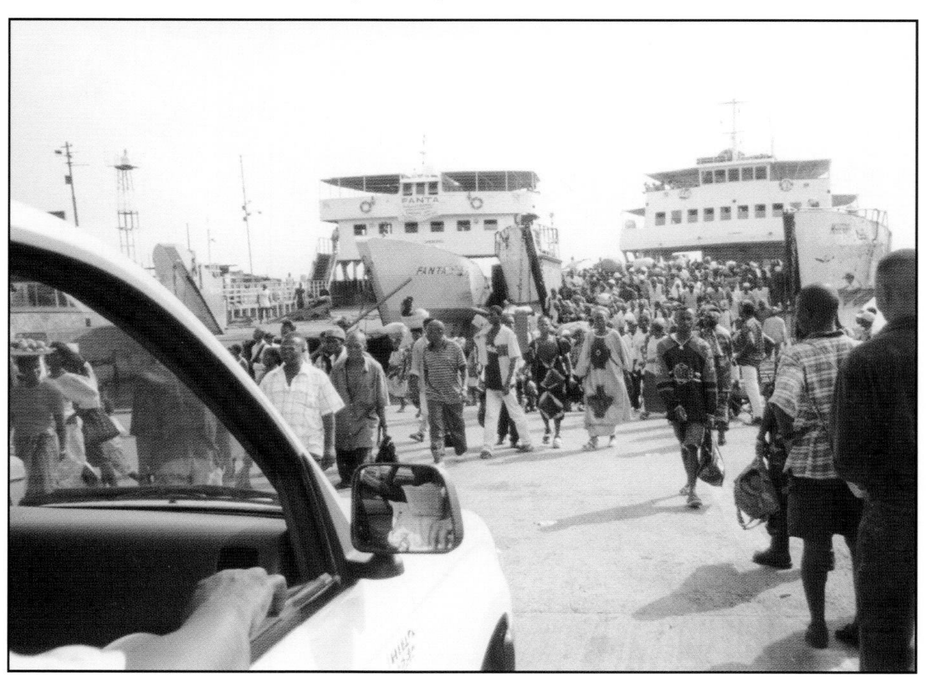

Ferryboats connect Freetown with the Lungi Airport across the bay. (Pg. 213)

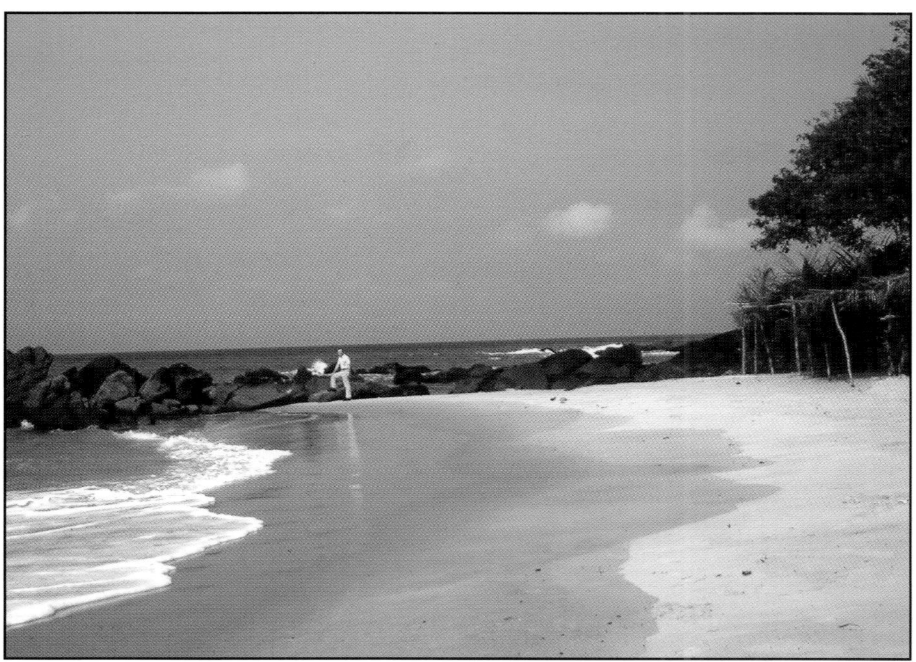

At the end of our missionary career when the family was no longer with me, I made a sentimental trip to Hamilton Beach in Sierra Leone, which holds so many precious memories for our family. (Pg. 316)

Dr. C. William Simcoe (center), a famous intraocular lens surgeon, pioneered many instruments and lenses; his wife is on his right. Dear friend, Dr. Walter Paschall, is on the far left while his wife, Jan, is second from right. (Pg. 370)

Visiting with Dr. S. N. Fyodorov (in white), internationally known ophthalmologist, while attending the International Eye Foundation meeting in Cairo, Egypt, in 1984. (Pg. 370)

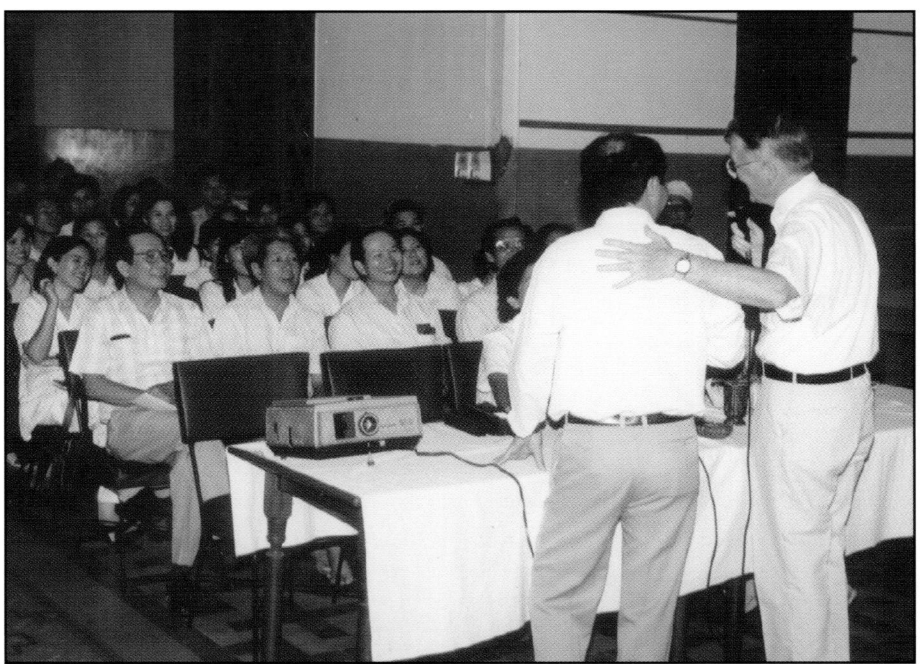

In Ho Chi Minh City, Vietnam, I shared ophthalmological intraocular lens expertise with more than thirty eye surgeons who then placed more than 25,000 lenses in patients during the next two years. (Pg. 242)

Tim's family. Front row (from left): Elly, Debby with daughter Sophie, Sarah with son Landon, Becky with sons Miles and Mason. Back row (from left): Brett, Eric, Tim, Joanne and Matt. (Pg. 312)

Mary with husband Steve, daughter Jennifer, and son Christopher with wife Gabby. (Pg. 315)

Beth's family. Back row: Christy, Beth, Bob, Becky. Front row: John Robert, David and Becky's husband, Jesse. (Pg. 319)

John's family, from left: Peter, Britta Lisa, daughter-in-law Rena, Adam, Ruth and John. (Pg. 322)

Paul's family, from left: Jason, Joshua, Aaron, Arlet and Paul. (Pg. 325)

Andrew, his wife Carrie, and daughters Anna (left) and Aimee. (Pg. 329)

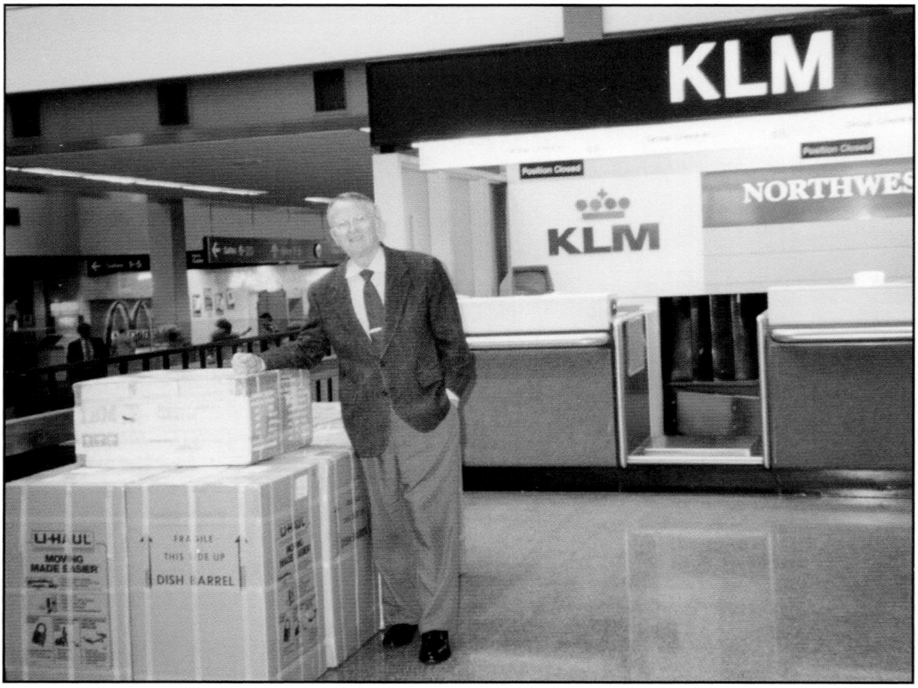

With 182 ocean crossings, KLM often allowed free freight for our medicines and supplies. (Pg. 175)

The Milbank, South Dakota, support group. (Pg. 170)

Mr. Ibrahim Conteh, Ruth's favorite student, now Kissy's eye hospital administrator.

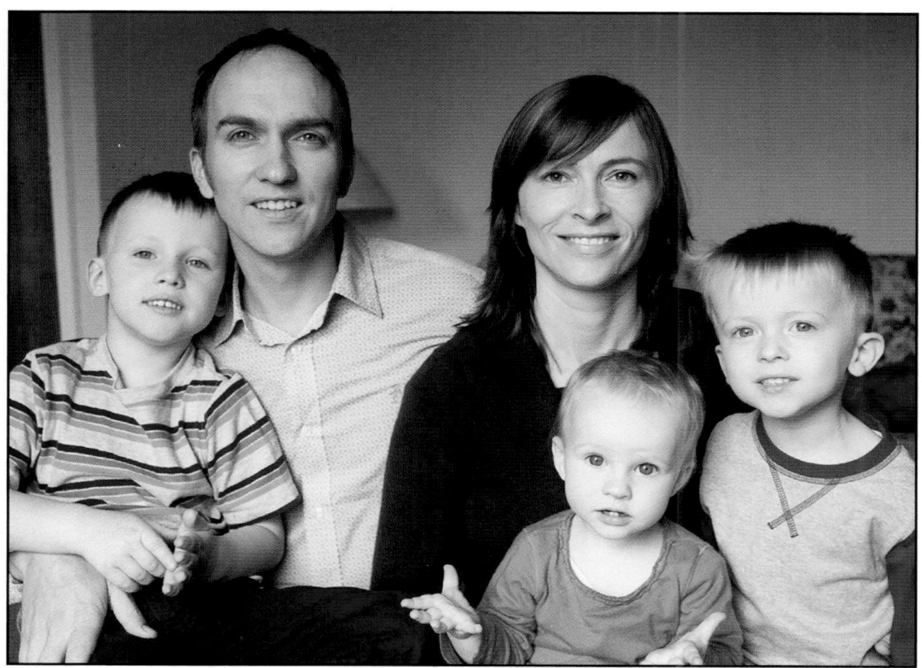

Dr. Buchan and wife, Anne, with Calum, Zoe and Josiah. (Pg. 224)

Guide, Lee Olmschenk, holding a forty-inch muskie I landed. Subsequently I landed a forty-seven inch ("four foot") monster weighing thirty pounds. I released each of them to go back to their families. A replica of the latter one hangs on the cabin wall at Lake Miltona. (Pg. 260)

Tim has the luxury of having on his staff his wife, Joanne to his left; daughter Debby on his right who is an ophthalmologist; daughter Becky who is a registered nurse on the far left; daughter Sarah, next to Joanne on the far right; and Debby's husband, Eric, far left second row, who is assuming an administrative role previously held by Joanne. (Pg. 311)

Bishop John Yambasu, Sierra Leone's current dedicated and respected United Methodist spiritual leader, and me.

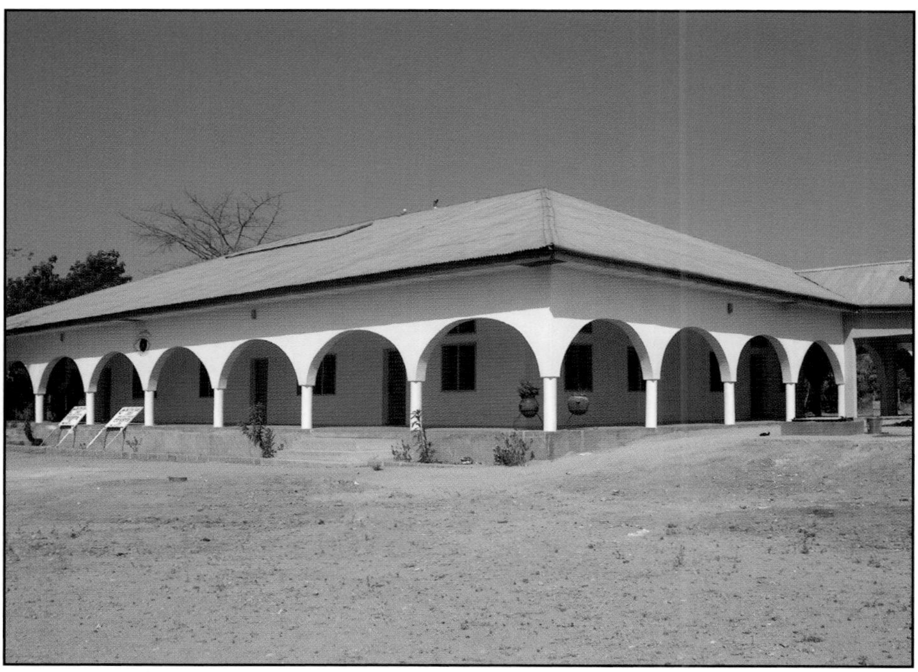

The new Zing Eye Centre to which Reuben Schneider of Paynesville, Minnesota, gave a grant of $100,000. (Pg. 253)

My last volunteer trip to Zing before Dr. Mefor and Dr. Avar brought the new Zing Eye Centre to great heights. (Pg. 256)

Precious children and grandchildren. (Pg. 364)

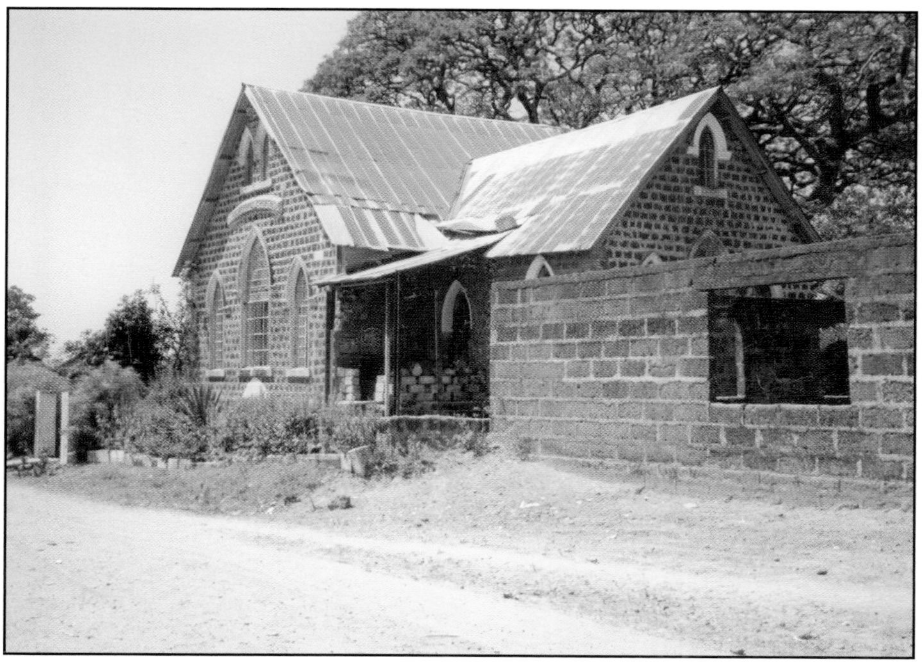

The Martyrs United Methodist Church in Rotifunk damaged in the recent rebel war. (Pg. 186)

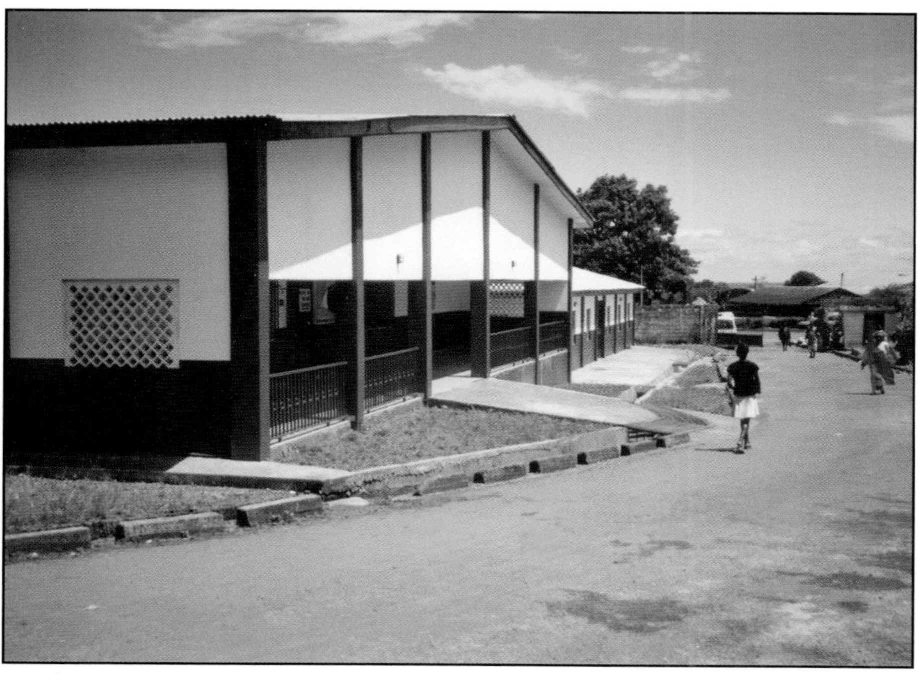

The expanded Kissy clinic and hostel built by Christian Blind Mission. (Pg. 231)

Dr. Isaac Sesay, who received his degree in November 2011. His prayers are directed toward doing eye surgery at Kissy in the future.

When Ruth and I visited Beth and Bob in Alaska, this silver salmon became friendly. (Pg. 318)

When Ruth and I visited in Canada, this twenty-five pound northern hit my 67-cent lure.

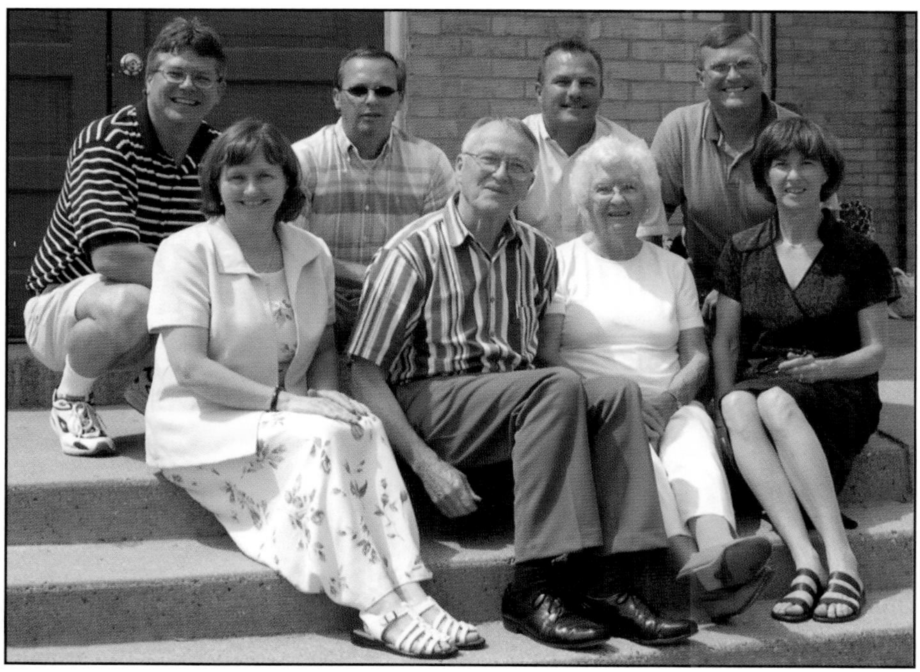

At a family gathering at Salem Church several years ago. (Pg. 261)

One of us is having a 90th birthday. (Pg. 259)

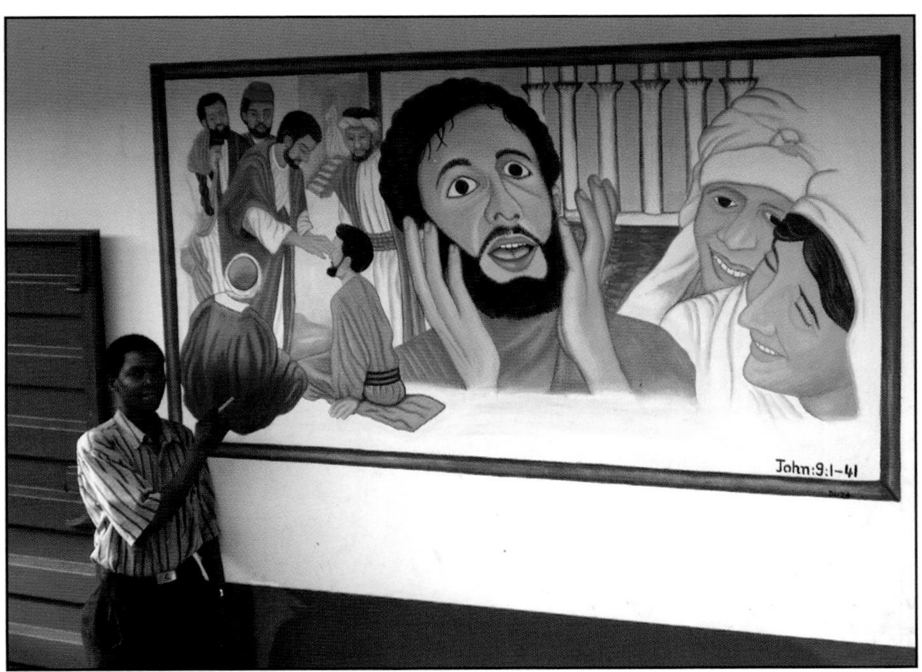

This painting on the surgical wall at Kissy is of the blind man's reaction to being healed by Jesus as in Matthew 20:34 and John 9. The artist is standing next to the painting. (Pg. 370)

Chapter Forty-Eight

Ruth's Trips to the U.S.

It had been two years since Ruth had seen "her girls" with their babies. A windfall estate gift enabled Ruth to make a special trip back to the U.S. During the visit, she consulted a physician by phone about a recurring pain in her back. She was reassured and returned to Bo in Sierra Leone.

The two men to Ruth's left – Peter Conteh and Ishmael Jobbie – were wonderful friends and expeditors at Lungi Airport.

Within six weeks, she became violently ill with gall bladder symptoms. The General Board of Global Ministries promptly authorized passage for her, as well as for me, to Frankfurt, Germany. The cost of the tickets was comparable to the cost of going all the way to the United States, so we stayed on the plane with the help of pethadine injections to handle the pain. We arrived unannounced at John F. Kennedy International Airport. Bob and Connie Dietrick, UMC missionaries who served at the Kissy UMC Urban Centre, were waiting for the arrival of Rob's brother from South America and happened to see us disembark. We were unable to contact the GBGM office because of it was a holiday. The Dietricks took us to their home and then transported us to the Newark airport where we took a direct flight to Rochester, Minnesota and the Mayo Clinic. Surgery was promptly done and within two weeks Ruth and I were back at our posts in Bo.

Chapter Forty-Nine

Family Volunteers

While still in medical training, our son Tim visited us at the Bo Eye Clinic. He flung himself into the program. Following his marriage to Joanne Anderson, the two of them served for six weeks doing volunteer eye surgery at the Lunsar Baptist Eye Hospital.

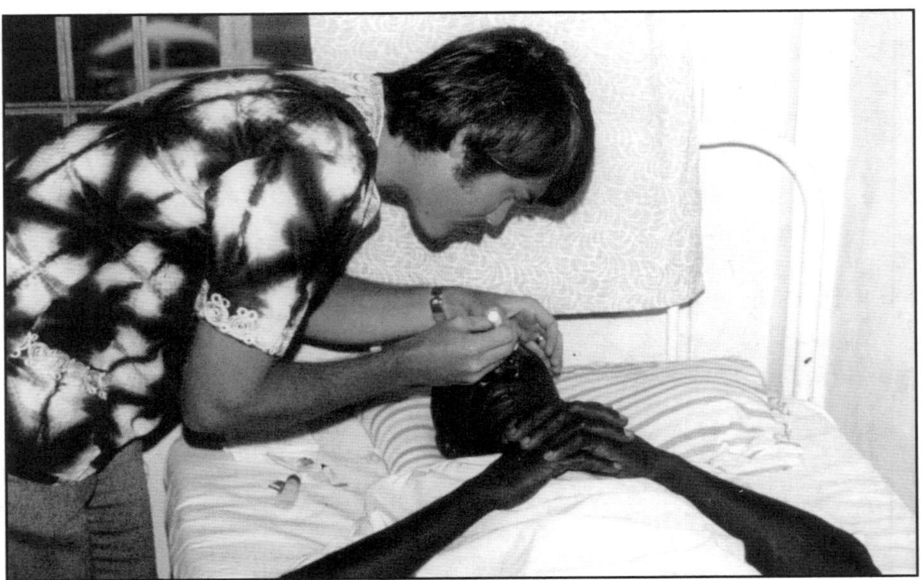

Tim preparing a patient for surgery.

In the 1970s, it was the policy of the General Board of Global Ministries to underwrite field visits for family members whose parents were under appointment. Ruth and I had been at the Bo Eye Clinic for more than a year and a half when we were delighted to have our four sons visit at Christmas. It created quite a stir when these four young men appeared with long hair and beards. Ruth and I had determined not to blink an eye at their appearance. We were just happy that they chose to visit their parents.

Since John and Paul had spent a large portion of their lives in a mission situation, it was easy for them to go hunting or help in the eye clinic. Both became expert at fabricating glasses – edging lenses to size and then fitting them into appropriate plastic frames. Simple refractions were done for patients who had good distant vision and only needed presbyopic corrections for reading.

One morning while John was hunting, Paul came to the clinic early and examined a patient. He measured him for glasses, did the edging, placed the lenses in a plastic frame and sent him off completely happy in less than ninety minutes. The examination included a glaucoma tonometer check by brother, Tim, and a funduscopic exam by me. Significant is the fact that Paul returned to graduate study at Fuller Theological Seminary and became a family counselor. The absent John pursued an optometric career, refracting patients and fitting glasses as his life's work.

Twice in later years Andrew accompanied us during our visits to Sierra Leone. It was a joy for him to visit the country where he was born. He was able to renew boyhood friendships at Rotifunk, Taiama, Bo and Freetown. Andrew participated in staff and patient devotions at the Lunsar Baptist Eye Hospital and Kissy UMC Eye Hospital. Especially helpful was the expert video filming Andrew did of the eye hospital patients, facilities, program and staff. Donors are encouraged when they visually witness the lively and extensive program in Africa.

Chapter Fifty

Overlooking Freetown

Overlooking Freetown.

I have overlooked the city of Freetown many times from varying heights, but there was one experience that I have not – and perhaps will not ever – forget.

It was 1976 and I was on my way to perform eye surgery upcountry at the Lunsar Baptist Eye Hospital. The road I traveled on wound around Mount Leicester. At the highest point, more than a thousand feet above Freetown, I stopped at the side of the road where it met the mountain. On the other side there was a perilous drop. At this elevation, thick enveloping clouds often made it impossible to view the surrounding country.

On this day it was clear. As I moved to the open side of the road, I could see the bustling city lying at my feet with traffic resembling the movement of little ants. During the dry season, the backdrop was brown but when the rains came, it was green everywhere.

After viewing the breathtaking scene for a period, I was suddenly struck with the realization that there were a million people at my feet. Along with the more than ten million people of West Africa, they needed modern eye care. In that moment I felt a Christian compassion that prompted a resolve to continue a yearly volunteer eye ministry to Sierra Leone for as long as the Lord would lend me breath. "To this very day (thirty-five years later) I have been helped by God, and so I stand here giving my witness to all..." (Acts 26:22, Good News Bible).

With the completion of our three-year tour of service at the Bo Eye Clinic in 1975, we retired as medical missionaries. We established a practice in Alexandria, Minnesota, but could not forget the continuing need for eye surgery in the country of Sierra Leone. With the understanding of the Douglas County Hospital and the community in general, Ruth and I continued to return to Sierra Leone for approximately three months each year – January, February and March. Local patients were willing to wait for their eye surgery until our return to Alexandria.

During the initial returns to Freetown we had a temporary facility set up at the Kissy Urban Centre. The term "Kissy" represents an area of eastern Freetown predominantly settled in early years by members of the Kissy tribe from upcountry. Between visits, we would store slit lamps, operating microscopes and refractive equipment. The Annual Conference of the United Methodist Church in Sierra Leone ultimately felt that a more permanent facility should be built, encouraged Mr. Henry R. N. Jusu, UMC Sierra Leone Conference treasurer, and Ms. Anna Morford, a representative from the conference office of the General Board of Global Ministries. Mr. Jusu hired an architect and plans were drawn up for an eye hospital. The building was to be fifty feet wide by eighty feet long, which would accommodate all that was needed for a comprehensive eye program. A second floor above the surgical wing was to be built as an apartment for visiting ophthalmologists. Over the years, forty ophthalmologists have spent from one to three or more months doing volunteer eye surgery at the Kissy UMC Eye Hospital.

Kissy UMC Eye Hospital.

The money to underwrite building the hospital was to come from the General Board of Global Ministries. However, the $70,000 allocated was not adequate for the entire building. To supplement the amount, women from the Missionary Society of the Alexandria United Methodist Church mailed appeal letters to more than 10,000 ophthalmologists in the United States. The letter challenged eye doctors to help build the Kissy UMC Eye Hospital in Freetown. It was suggested that the revenue from a single intraocular lens implantation procedure be donated for this hospital. Surprisingly – and wonderfully – a number of doctors responded and the hospital was completed.

The five original volunteers from Central UM Church, Milbank, S. Dakota: Arvid Liebe, pharmacist; James Mundwiler, mortician; Loren Ebsen, contractor; Floyd Bohn, accountant; Roger Reiners, contractor.

It is a thrilling story as to how the hospital was built. The Reverend Walter Erdman, a pastor in Milbank, South Dakota, had invited me to speak to his church about medical missions. After the presentation, he mentioned that he had some men in his congregation who were enthused about missions and might be challenged by a project such as building a hospital in West Africa. In less than four months, five volunteers from his congregation were on their way with the supplies and equipment needed for the hospital. Interestingly, there were only two contractors among the five, Loren Ebsen and Roger Reiners. The other three gentlemen were Floyd Bohn, an accountant, Arvid Liebe, a pharmacist, and Jim Mundwiler, a mortician. Others also came repeatedly to help with the construction and repair of the eye hospital such as John and Frances Rebstock. Not only have these helpers and volunteers actually laid block upon block, down through the years they have continued to pray for the work and to contribute financially to the ongoing program. Many people, including individual doctors, churches and interested people have shared in the ongoing expenses of the Kissy eye program. It continues today as the premiere eye care center in that part of West Africa. We thank God for the concern and compassion of so many people for the eye needs of people in Sub-Saharan Africa.

Chapter Fifty-One

History of the Kissy UMC Eye Hospital

During 1976 to 1982 when Ruth and I made our annual three-month pilgrimages to Sierra Leone, there were many open avenues of service. We provided medical services in Rotifunk, Taiama, and Bo, but the principal opportunity was at the Lunsar Baptist Eye Hospital. The surgeon, Dr. Eleanor Koeth, was well trained in ophthalmology and was quick to develop surgical skills for cataract and glaucoma procedures. Some years later, Dr. Koeth, Dr. Ingrid Graelle and I published an article titled "Trabeculectomy with Iridencleisis," *British Journal of Ophthalmology*, Volume 69, No. 12, (December 1985), pp. 881-885.

The gate to the Kissy UMC Eye Hospital. Will it always be available for those in need?

The Lunsar administrator, Sister Ursula Schwemmer, made Ruth and me welcome during our visits. She would bless us by sharing precious choice foods sent in gift boxes from family and friends in Germany. She was a master builder of staff houses and hospital wards. Building suppliers were invariably prompted to give her unusual discounts. Sister Margaret Breitling, a co-worker, was one of the best surgical assistants with whom I ever had the privilege to work.

Dr. Herb Friesen, accomplished and dedicated eye surgeon to Pakistan and Afghanistan, and his wife Ruth spent time at Lunsar further developing the surgical program prior to the arrival of Dr. Jan Stilma, surgeon extraordinaire. Dr. Stilma did extensive research in glaucoma and onchocerciasis (river blindness). Dr. Robert Barbe, Dr. William McElroy, Dr. Richard Wilson and Dr. Ralph Buhrman made significant contributions, especially in educating optical assistants, which Dr. Barbe initiated and oversaw for a number of years. It was a privilege to work with these outstanding skilled and Christian motivated medical missionaries.

When Lunsar was showing progress in developing their program, I spent more time in Freetown. Some surgery was done at the Connaught Government Hospital where Dr. E. B. Ceesay and Dr. Dennis Williams conducted the program, but more and more work was being carried on at the Kissy Urban Centre. We examined pastors and laypersons at King Memorial United Methodist Church during the annual conferences. Glasses were provided. Eventually, we were given accommodations at the main building of the Kissy Urban Centre, which included a patient waiting room, a surgical prep room, and a small six by ten foot room for the surgery. An air conditioner was supported in a small window, which made the close quarters livable.

Dr. James Foulkes and his wife, Martha, of Kasempe, Zambia, visited us for a period. He took extensive notes and participated in some of the procedures. On his return to Zambia, he developed an eye clinic and became proficient in cataract extraction with intraocular lens implantation. In recent years, besides doing volunteer general surgery in the Sudan, he has given instruction and oversight for eye procedures in Zambia.

The response to the medical and surgical care of eye patients at Kissy was overwhelming. By 1981, it was obvious to the leadership of the United Methodist Church Conference that an eye program was greatly needed for Sierra Leone based in Freetown. It was at this time that Mr. Jusu engaged Ms. Muhleman, a qualified architect, to draw up architectural plans. Three lovely mango trees were sacrificed for the hospital plot. The foundations were begun January 15, 1982, and the walls began to go up. Later in the year, the five volunteers from Milbank arrived. Before they returned to South Dakota, a roof was in place.

Some nine months later, others joined the original five volunteers. The hospital rooms and the apartment above surgery were outfitted. Patients were seen and surgery begun.

Chapter Fifty-Two

Triumphs and Tragedies: 1984 and 1985

The Kissy UMC Eye Hospital was dedicated February 18, 1984. Bishop Thomas S. Bangura officiated, assisted by Bishop Arthur F. Kulah from Liberia with future Bishop Felton E. May in attendance. The President of Sierra Leone, Siaka Stevens, cut the ribbon. The scripture noted at the entrance was taken from II Corinthians 4:5, "For we preach not ourselves but Christ Jesus the Lord, and ourselves your servants for Jesus' sake." (KJV) This verse was etched in the framework.

President Siaka Stevens cutting the ribbon at the Kissy UMC Eye Hospital dedication, February 18, 1984. Left-to-right: Bishop Arthur Kulah, Vice President Kamara Taylor, President Siaka Stevens, Bishop Thomas S. Bangura, Dr. Frank B. Davies.

The selection of a staff was of primary importance. Deference was made to Mrs. Gess for this responsibility, as she had overseen the business management of the clinics down through the years. She chose Leticia Williams as administrator. John Fornah and Ernest Kroma, who worked with us at the Bo Eye Clinic, were drafted from the Lunsar Baptist Eye Hospital. Mr. Fornah headed up the surgical department and Mr. Kroma the refraction. With the growth of the hospital, twenty-three people eventually joined the staff.

When the rebels threatened to overrun Freetown in 1997, Mrs. Williams and two of her daughters escaped to live with her relatives in Gambia. The assistant administrator, Hannah Koroma, and her three daughters were caught in the onslaught. One of her daughters was kidnapped. It was to be nearly a year before her whereabouts were known and arrangements made for her release.

With the dedication, the eye program expanded. The early surgical emphasis was continued and enhanced by surgical volunteer specialists coming for one to three months at a time. The first surgeon in 1984 was Dr. Russell Boehlke accompanied by his wife, Donna. Seven times over the next sixteen-year period they came with valuable medicines and supplies to do surgery and clinical work.

Kissy UMC Eye Hospital staff.

The second volunteer was Dr. Hal Bryan and his wife, Greta. At customs, the listings of the items they brought totaled over $80,000. They returned in 1985 and again in 1992.

Other 1984 volunteer eye surgeons were: Dr. John S. Dunn, Dr. Winston T. Cope, Dr. Ricky Russell and Dr. Frank J. Cerny who, besides doing eye surgery, played the organ for services at the Brown Memorial United Methodist Church located on the same compound as the eye hospital.

The handling of this complicated program was well managed by Mrs. Leticia Williams. Her previous training in the UK, where she assisted in eye surgery, was extremely helpful. She possessed administrative skills that brought leadership to a disparate band of newly hired staff.

The Sierra Leone Conference of the United Methodist Church took an active role in guiding the new eye program. Dr. F. B. Davies, pastor and general practitioner, gave leadership as chairman of the Conference Medical Board. It was at this time that he and his family suffered the tragedy of having their son killed in an automobile accident.

There were other disappointments in the early part of 1984. On January 5, 1984, Mr. Ernest Kroma, one of our staff members, was given the responsibility of protecting eye equipment that had been placed on the veranda that had not yet been moved into the main building. A pellet from his warning shot, aimed above the intruders' heads, struck one of the would-be thief's in the left eye and removal was required. Subsequently, the patient was fitted with a prosthesis, which appeared normal but disappointingly provided no vision. The CID incarcerated Mr. Kroma for nearly a week's time. When released, he gave his testimony at the Brown Memorial United Methodist Church in which he told of sharing Christian songs and witnessing during his time of imprisonment.

In January and February 1984, the Milbank volunteers completed cabinets in the hospital as well as in the living quarters above the surgery. They completed a highly efficient kitchen, living room, two bedrooms and two baths in the apartment that housed volunteers. The team consisted of Roger Reiners, Bernice Ankeny, Rev. John and Fran Rebstock, and Rev. Ralph Dunn. Other volunteers from Tennessee came to serve in the dentistry program.

During the latter part of February, I needed to make a trip to Cairo, Egypt, where I presented a paper on trabeculectomy with iridencleisis. During my absence, Ruth awoke one morning to see that our Toyota Corona station wagon was resting on stones minus all four wheels, the battery and its tools. The philosophy of some in West Africa is that if property is not appropriately guarded it is fair game for the community to appropriate.

This attitude was underscored one night when Ruth and I were awakened by the sound of scratching on the screen in the living room. Getting out of bed and investigating, I saw a hand reach in through the cut screen and grasp the radio that had been resting on the desk close to the window. With a forceful vocal rebuke from me, the hand released the radio and the body plummeted to the earth and sped off in the darkness.

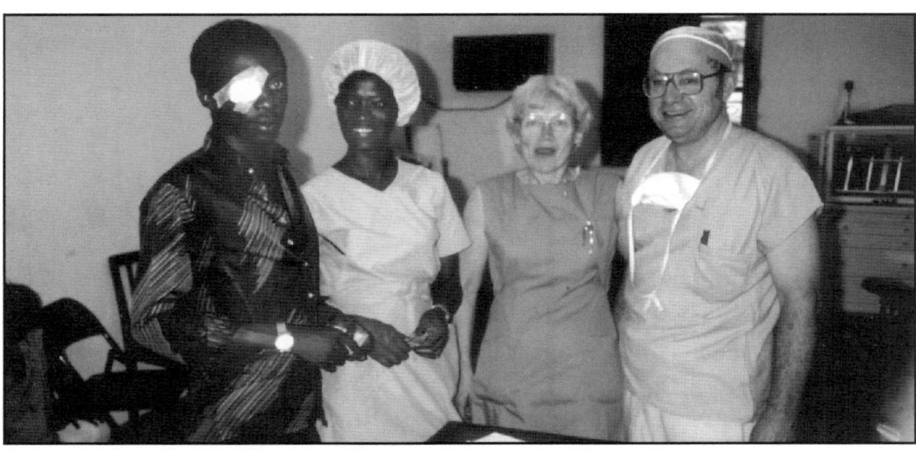

Dr. and Mrs. Russell Boehlke with Lettie Williams and patient.

1985. Early in the year, the mission was privileged to have a visit by Mr. Spurgeon Dunnam who was the reporter/editor of the *United Methodist Reporter.* His visit to the Kissy UMC Eye Hospital took place at a time when Dr. Knute Guldjord was present. Dr. Guldjord's practice was in Bremerton, Washington. He had arranged to spend a month away from his private practice in the United States to join in the work at Kissy. He dealt one by one with a long line of patients with eye problems and enjoyed the fellowship with them at the time that Mr. Dunnam interviewed him.

Dr. Guldjord was not at Kissy as a part of any structured mission. He had met me at a medical convention and agreed to come as a volunteer. He spoke appreciatively of the clinic's equipment and facilities. He said that he was happy to be a part of ministering to the needs of people in West Africa when they had so few opportunities for treatment. When he was asked why he responded to the invitation to come to Kissy, he said, "We all like to feel we are doing something worthwhile in life and doing God's will. I feel a very deep relationship to God as I use my talents here among these people."

Dr. Ingrid Graelle, Ruth Gess, R.N., and Dr. Eleanor Koeth.

It was a privilege to welcome Dr. Ingrid Graelle, an ophthalmologist living at Jui, while her husband taught at the Bible and Theological College. She did not have a background in intraocular lens implantation, but during her visits to the Kissy UMC Eye Hospital she readily took up this new modality and became an expert in doing this procedure. On one visit, she became aware of the subdued tone of the hospital where on the previous day an unusual tragedy had occurred. Mrs. Fattu Jalloh, while having a cataract extraction, went into an asthmatic crisis and experienced respiratory failure. In spite of successful intubation and medical treatment, Mrs. Jalloh could not be revived. She was to be the only eye fatality of many thousands of patients in West Africa.

During the second week of February 1985, one of our most significant Africa trips was taken to visit Rev. D. H. Caulker in Konoland. During this 200-mile trip, we stopped along the way at the Lunsar Baptist Eye Hospital where we visited Sister Ursula Schwemmer and Dr. Jan Stilma. They told of the tragic death of Mr. Joseph Ngeba, one of their most promising nurses in training. He had been struck and killed by lightning as he crossed the road in front of Lunsar Hospital to buy bread. Joseph was especially adept at English, due in part to being a close friend of our sons John and Paul when we served at Bo.

Our visit with Rev. D. H. Caulker was one of the most inspirational Ruth and I had ever experienced. In his 113th year, his love for the Lord's work was undimmed.

Our return to the Kissy UMC Eye Hospital on February 14, 1985, was especially meaningful. On this trip to Sierra Leone I received a lovely valentine from Ruth. I received this same valentine while in Africa for the next twelve years.

Chapter Fifty-Three

The Eye Program in Full Swing

Nineteen eighty-six was a banner year. More volunteer ophthalmologists participated in the Kissy UMC Eye Hospital program than ever before. Early in the year, Dr. Albert H. Bryan, better known as Hal, returned with his wife Greta, and performed as many as fifteen to twenty intraocular surgeries a day. He was followed by Dr. Robert Searle, Dr. Jack A. Aaron, Dr. Hillmer A. Fonken, Dr. Norman F. Woodlief and the return of Dr. and Mrs. Russell R. Boehlke. Dr. Richard A. Yook brought his entire family with him. This struck a responsive note with the Kissy staff. Their visits were always anticipated. Ms. Vivian Olson volunteered seven months at the hospital doing clerical work and balancing the books. She had been an appointed missionary for more than thirty years and was well known for her Christian compassion. Many people came to the hospital with the intent to see "Miss Olson."

The year was one of political stability but inflation was beginning. Ultimately, the devaluation of the leone was to assume such a proportion that a large amount of currency needed to be carried in a handbag to pay for purchased items. With this handling of large quantities of leone notes, a practice developed where waiters and clerks would announce that the payment, after being counted by the cashier, was short – never was it reported to be in excess. To deal with this, customers made it a practice to have a second person count the money before giving it to the waiter or cashier. If the amount was stated to be "short," the reply was simply, "Oshe" (sorry) and the customer would take his leave.

It was an important time at the Kissy UMC Eye Hospital when the Zeiss OMPI-6S microscope arrived. It had all the recent improvements in optics as well as zoom features, x-y movement and foot panel controls. This instrument, along with the Yag Laser, five Haag Streit slit lamps, a DBR 310 Ascan, and B & L phoropter, impressed visiting volunteer eye surgeons. It was a pleasure to be able to use excellent instruments in this faraway place in West Africa.

Ruth and I were informed early in the year of a serious automobile accident involving several United Methodist missionaries. One of the passengers, Miss Metra Heisler, was brought some thirty miles to Freetown for care. Ruth and I were made aware of her presence at the Nethland Hospital by Rev. Joseph Humper and Rev. David Caulker. Immediately, we visited her and found that she had been hospitalized for nearly a day and a half and had yet to see a physician.

She had a serious leg injury and she complained of chest pain. We prevailed on the administration of the hospital to allow us to care for Miss Heisler at our Kissy UMC Eye Hospital. We stopped on the way out of the hospital for X-rays of her chest, which were read as normal. In bed, she needed to be propped up in order to breathe. It was obvious her rib cage was compromised in spite of the negative X-rays. On her return to the U.S., she was diagnosed with a hemothorax and five fractured ribs. We thank God she was stable until definitive treatment was made available.

Shaking hands with President Dr. J. S. Momoh.

On January 30, 1986, Ruth and I had the pleasure of being presented to his Excellency Dr. J. S. Momoh, president of Sierra Leone. The purpose of the occasion was to recognize the volunteers who came to Sierra Leone. When asked to respond, I reminisced about shaking hands with the past president Siaka Stevens in 1956. It had been thirty years since that handshake and I asked that a new handshake be done with the hope and prayer that President Momoh would have strong and sturdy shoulders to assume the mantle of leadership for Sierra Leone.

Following this service, we were invited along with Rev. Susan Messenger and Rev. Franklin Messenger to have dinner with Rev. Crispin Renner and his wife Theresa, an excellent cook. Over the years, they repeatedly invited us to their home to share a meal, as well as brought food to us while we worked at the Kissy UMC Eye Hospital. The Christian fellowship with this family was one of the high points of our repeated visits to Sierra Leone.

At the beginning of our return trip to Kissy UMC Eye Hospital the second week of December 1986, we needed to transfer planes at Chicago's O'Hare airport.

We were informed by a KLM official that they would not be able to take along all of the seventeen boxes of eye medicines we were carrying as excess baggage. Previously, KLM had been helpful and supportive in graciously accepting our many boxes that weighed up to seventy pounds each. We at once realized that if the boxes did not accompany us to Amsterdam and then on to Freetown, we would not have the use of the medicines and supplies during the early weeks of our visit. We explained this to the KLM officials, but they insisted the cargo was more than KLM could manage.

Dejected, we returned to our seats, trying to understand their decision. Suddenly it came to me – Christmas was only a week away. There just might be some confusion with cargo because of extra Christmas baggage. Innocently, I went up to the baggage department and asked for the person in charge. I explained to him again the great need we had for the medicine contained in our baggage, that it must accompany us in order for us to give sight-saving operations in West Africa. And then out of the blue I said, "If, by any chance, this eye medicine is being bumped because of the need to carry holiday spirits on the plane, it would not be a very good story for the press." Letting it go at that, I returned to my seat.

It was hardly ten minutes before a new high-ranking KLM official came to visit Ruth and me. He explained that KLM was making arrangements to take our excess baggage with us in order that we might continue our work. We had a very pleasant flight and a most rewarding time of surgery in Africa over the holiday season.

We enjoy our many trips with KLM Airlines.

Chapter Fifty-Four

1987 to 1988

Shortly after arriving at the Kissy UMC Eye Hospital for our time of service in 1987, a newborn was brought to us whose upper eyelids had become everted during birth. There was great swelling, not only of the eyelids but surrounding tissue as well. The situation was frightening to the mother and local attendants. Witchcraft was believed to be involved. A sympathetic neighbor not related to the family had brought the infant to us. In this case, surgery was needed to restore the lids to a normal position, unlike a similar case we had witnessed in Abak, Nigeria, where the head nurse was able to remedy the problem without anesthesia.

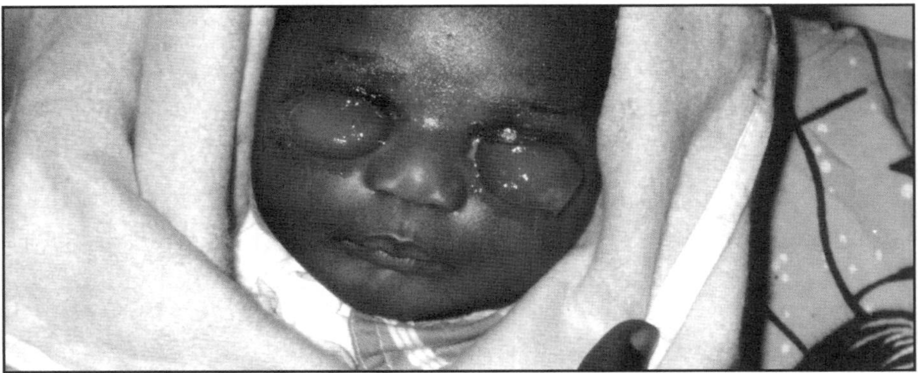

Newborn with everted eyelids.

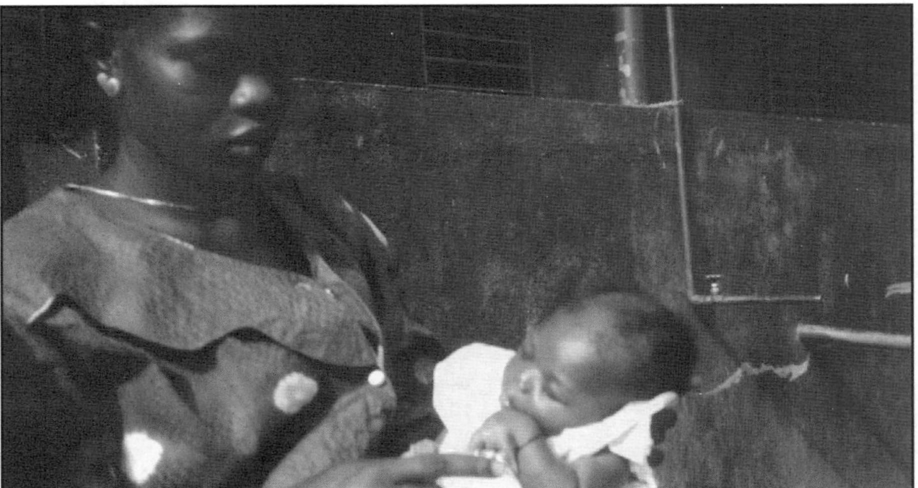

Eyelids restored to a normal position.

The time of service in 1987 was not without excitement. During one night I was awakened by a strange noise below our bedroom. I knew that trustworthy and honest Bossie Kamara was on guard duty and dismissed the thought of following up. The next morning we learned thieves had made their way through a window and actually lifted out our Honda generator. It was inconceivable that a machine of such size and weight could be handled so deftly.

1988. As we were about to make tentative arrangements for our annual trip to the Kissy UMC Eye Hospital, I visited my ninety-two-year-old father in the Faribault Rest Home. Since he was not doing well, I mentioned Ruth and I would skip our visit to Africa this year. He nearly bolted out of bed, declaring, "I'll not be responsible for blind people in Africa not receiving their surgery. I insist that you go."

We made our trip to Africa, but our premonition proved correct. With my sister June at his bedside, he slipped away February 13, 1988. The news of his passing came to us by cable several days later, written by our son, Tim. It read, "Grandpa went to be with Grandma February 13 at 12:10 p.m." The severe frost that winter in Minnesota delayed his burial for a number of weeks. By then, we had returned and were able to participate in the committal service at historic Salem Evangelical Church four miles north of Paynesville. Mother's death had preceded his by five years.

As a staff, we had an immense thrill when a Fulani couple presented themselves to the hospital. Both the man and woman were tall and regal with striking good looks. I can say that perhaps there was never a more beautiful African woman who had visited the hospital. She was totally blind and had been so for fifteen years.

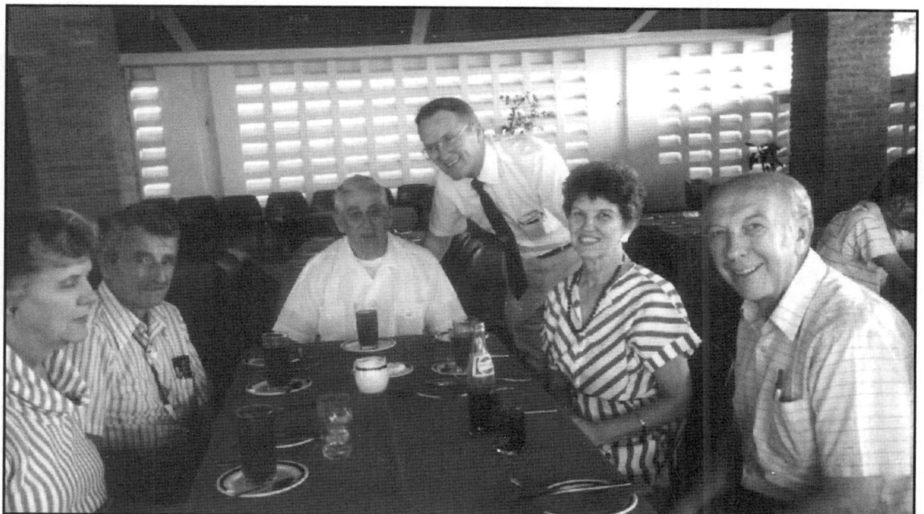

Wonderful volunteers. From left to right: Enid and Loman Young (artist), Everett (Pete) Shearer (well digger), Joyce and Richard Reeves (volunteers to Sierra Leone and African University, Zimbabwe).

Following her cataract operation and intraocular lens implantation the following day, she took her first steps without being directed. Her husband was perhaps even more thrilled. He had been lovingly solicitous all those years and now she was able to resume her responsible place in their home.

We shall always remember Ayub Fawaz, a Lebanese merchant in Freetown, who developed cataracts subsequent to his diabetic condition. He realized the risks involved in surgery but did exceedingly well, developing better than 20/20 vision in each eye following surgery. In his enthusiasm, he was our greatest supporter in bringing patients to the hospital. On one occasion he brought Major Momoh, brother to President Joseph Momoh, and along with them the First Vice President, A. K. Kamara and his wife.

It was during 1988 that Paul Tarawally and I had the thrill of setting up the new OPMI-6S operating microscope with the x-y and zoom functions controlled by foot panel. We also set up a brand new 900 series Haag Streit slit lamp.

Mrs. Gess usually hired the hospital staff. A very bright and promising young man applied for work in the surgery department. Mrs. Gess was not happy about taking him on. We could not understand her position, as he was the one person who was needed in the expanding surgical program. Within a week, IV administration sets as well as IV solutions began to disappear, not dreaming that this capable new employee would be the cause. Ultimately, it was discovered that many items were being "liberated" by this gentleman, the discovery made by another member of our staff. We sadly let this promising young man go, but learned later he had turned completely around and was gainfully employed.

In 1988, Dr. Randolph Nugent of the General Board of Global Ministries of the United Methodist Church honored us with a visit, which occurred during the Sierra Leone Annual Conference. At the eye hospital, we had him start the new generator that had been installed the previous day. Whenever I turned on the generator, thoughts often went back to Dr. Nugent's visit to the Kissy UMC Eye Hospital.

Over the years, the General Board of Global Ministries has been most supportive of the eye outreach. They have underwritten Dr. Ainar Fergusson as a PIM (Person In Mission). Also, they made available the Advance Special, a fund to which individuals and churches can give toward the eye program. This fund has enabled the purchasing of medicine, equipment and supplies.

Our flight in 1988 to Sierra Leone involved excess baggage of nineteen seventy-pound boxes. Northwest and KLM Airlines were especially helpful in making possible the transportation of the many needed items for the hospital, discounting the cost of more than half of them. The Kissy UMC Eye Hospital has been the recipient of tremendous good will over the years.

A few weeks after the end of 1988, Don and Lilburne Theuer arrived (February 23, 1989), to spend several months upgrading the hospital's accounts and general program. While in Sierra Leone, Don was asked to do an extensive evaluation on the Rotifunk Hospital related to future growth and development. Their past appointments as mission accountant and mission host and hostess enabled them to understand the West African way of doing things, which enhanced the effectiveness of their work.

Chapter Fifty-Five

A Unique Situation

The Kissy UMC Eye Hospital under the administration of Mrs. Lettie Williams didn't have a regular ophthalmologist in residency. Mrs. Gess and I would return each year for January, February and part of March. The remaining months would find other volunteer eye surgeons coming to address the eye needs of Sierra Leone and neighboring countries.

It has always amazed me that an excellent and high quality eye program could be carried on by volunteers coming and going. Over the years, sub-specialists have done retinal work, strabismus care, and corneal transplantation in addition to the usual cataract extractions and intraocular lens implantations. Every effort was made to ensure the capabilities of visiting eye doctors. Usually checks would be made with other doctors about their expertise.

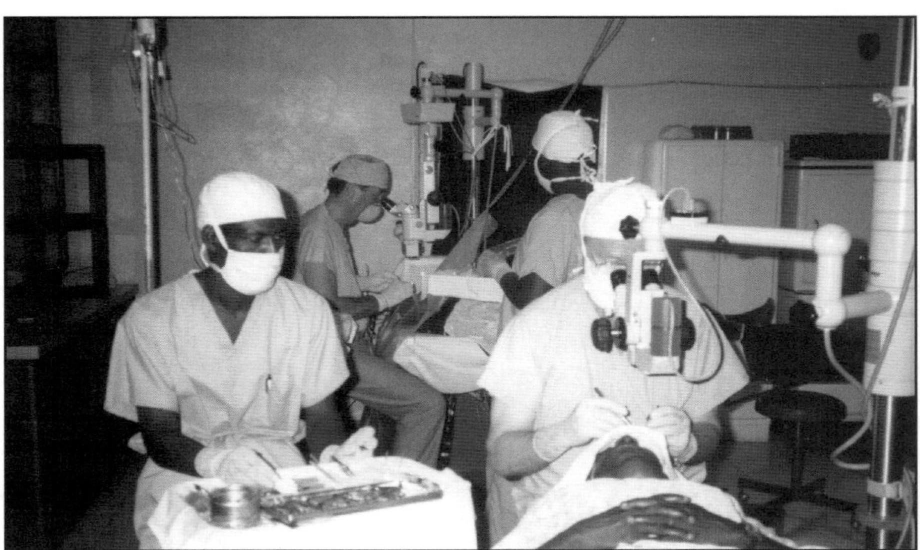

Volunteer eye surgeon Dr. Charles Carter (in the background) using the Zeiss OPMI-6S.

One time I received a sobering call from a Florida ophthalmologist who learned that an acquaintance was scheduled to do eye surgery at Kissy. He told me that the doctor in question had had no training in intraocular lens implantation. To my dismay I learned that the doctor had already set out for Freetown. Emails and faxes were not available in those days. The hospital had no telephone for trans-Atlantic calls. There was no way to warn the staff.

I learned later that the surgical assistants at Kissy UMC Eye Hospital realized immediately the doctor had not been trained in intraocular surgical procedures. They intercepted the scheduled patients and the following day removed the operating microscope, table, and other equipment and began painting the ceiling and walls of the surgical theatre! During the remaining time, the doctor did an excellent job evaluating patients for eye diseases.

Chapter Fifty-Six

Trouble on the Horizon

Our first trip to Kissy UMC Eye Hospital in 1991 began on New Year's Day. On landing in Freetown, we were met by Rev. Angie Myles and Larry and Marge Chambers. The Chambers were spending a year at Rotifunk restoring the hospital.

We flung ourselves into the work at Kissy and oriented Dr. Kai Lewis, an eye doctor who trained and practiced in Liberia, to the program's nuances. Liberia was going through the throes of a civil war. Dr. Lewis and his family escaped to Freetown. The Sierra Leone Conference of the United Methodist Church and the General Board of Global Ministries of the United Methodist Church in New York had sought his services for the Kissy UMC Eye Hospital. However, in a short time he made plans to leave for the United States to further his training in preventive eye care.

Volunteer and appointed United Methodist missionaries in 1991. In 2001, there were only four missionaries in Sierra Leone.

During January 1991, the Gulf War erupted. During this time, Dr. and Mrs. Ainar Fergusson were in Freetown on leave from their work at Abha Hospital in Saudi Arabia. They chose not to return to Saudi Arabia because of the conflict and cultural differences. Knowing of the Kissy UMC Eye Hospital in Freetown, Dr. Fergusson's interest and commitment led him to the hospital first as an observer, then as a helper and finally as the staff doctor who was to continue his work there for at least another decade.

During the Gulf War, we were careful not to share political views as some of our Muslim patients heartily supported Saddam Hussein. On one occasion, we were invited to a meal with a Muslim family just prior to the active three-day hostilities. With the defeat of the Iraqi aggressors, mention of Hussein's role was never again broached.

The Rev. Bodo Schwab, predecessor to Dr. Thomas Kemper, general secretary of the German Mission Board, visited Sierra Leone and gave encouragement. The German United Methodist Church invested heavily in personnel and finances in the Jaiama Nimi Koro Medical Clinic. Miss Brunhilde Goebel and Miss Renata Horn did extensive tours of service. The last German-supported nurse was Ms. Fritzie Carlson, whose life was miraculously spared time and again during the rebel incursion. She lived through terrible times only to die in childbirth several years later in her own homeland.

Besides being involved in the training of two eye doctors during the year, I also had the privilege of tutoring Madianna Myles, daughter of Joe and Angie Myles. Madianna was preparing for acceptance into a registered nursing degree training program. In spite of the war and the political collapse of the country, she eventually attained her degree, following in her mother's footsteps.

Our second trip to Sierra Leone began on April 23rd. Excess baggage cost more than a thousand dollars (which on a previous trip had reached $1,700). Shortly after our arrival, we were invited to the investiture at the statehouse to receive the "Office of the Civil Division of the Order of the Rokel" in recognition of service in Sierra Leone over the past thirty-eight years. The Rev. David and Mammi Caulker along with Mrs. Regina Bangura represented the United Methodist Church at this occasion. In anticipation of this august meeting, Ruth had bought a white hat, something which she hadn't done for several decades.

Three days later, we made the promised trip to Rotifunk to see the repairs that Larry and Marge Chambers had accomplished at the Hatfield-Archer Hospital where we had served from 1957-1960. It gave us immense pride to see the hospital restored again. Little did we realize what was happening at Kissy while away those two days.

Plans had been made to stay overnight in Rotifunk with the Chambers', which allowed us time to visit Rev. W. B. Clay and walk through his plantation of fruit trees. This plantation was two and a half miles from Rotifunk, but he made this trip by foot each day. We also had a chance to visit with Laura Kandeh, daughter of Rev. and Mrs. C. V. Rettew, prominent early Christian leaders in Sierra Leone. We were surprised also to be able to see Bossie Koroma with whom we had worked more than thirty years before.

The following morning on our way back to Freetown, we stopped at Taiama to treat the eye patients who had gathered for our announced visit. We also had the opportunity to see friends that we had known during our 1964-1967 time of service.

On arriving home at Kissy we were met by somber faced Lettie Williams, Angie Myles and David Caulker. During the night, thieves had broken into the hospital through the window of our bedroom which providentially we were not occupying because of our trip to Rotifunk. They carried off the medicines and supplies we had just bought. They also took the refrigerator, TV, VCR, radio, typewriter, tools – and Ruth's new white hat.

Ruth's white hat.

Losing those items was not the serious part of the incident. Volunteer ophthalmologist Dr. John Barker and his daughter Susan were terrorized in their upstairs apartment. The thieves threatened to break down the door, but Dr. Barker placated them by passing all the money that he had through a hole in the barred window screen. He threatened them by saying that he would call the police. They laughed and taunted him saying "we are the police!"

After hurriedly taking their loot, gunfire broke out. The hospital guards had been tied. One guard was able to free himself from the wire bands and eventually made his way to the police station. The police investigation turned up one of the thieves who had been shot dead. He still was cradling the radio I had purchased just days before at Schipohl Airport in Amsterdam. The police identified the corpse as a repeat offender who only recently had been released from prison. I was never able to reclaim my radio, as the police "needed it for evidence."

We rejoiced with returning surgeons Dr. Charles Carter, Dr. Michael Cunningham and Dr. Michael Gottner. New was Dr. Richard A. Bowers with his wife Miriam Rader, who extended their stay to several months. They loved the patients and staff at Kissy and the patients and staff loved them in return. Like Dr. Charles Carter, they have continued to be supportive of the program over the years.

Besides Dr. John S. Barker, the other new volunteer, Dr. Jerry D. Harrel, was a retired Air Force ophthalmologist who served more than a decade at the Lighthouse for Christ in Mombassa, Kenya. In subsequent years, he frequently referred to the meaningful prayers offered preoperatively for the patients at Kissy, often by John Fornah.

Nineteen ninety-one was the year that storm clouds appeared on the horizon. Foday Sankoh, the rebel leader, adopted the tactics of Liberia's president, Charles Taylor, in Liberia's civil war. Initially, he kept to the jungles near the Liberian border, but by the end of the year he threatened the democratically elected government headed by President Joseph Momoh. This was the beginning of one of the harshest, most brutal and cruel civil wars the world has ever seen.

Chapter Fifty-Seven

Coup

In April 1992, I was in Sierra Leone alone. Ruth and I had been there earlier in January, February and the first part of March. Now on April 18th, I was delivering some additional medicines and supplies. I immediately became immersed in the busy surgical practice. Dr. Richard Lockwood and his family were still at the Kissy UMC Eye Hospital. At that time, we were training Dr. Ainor Fergusson in some of the procedures. On the 29th, a Wednesday, we were in the midst of surgery when suddenly there was a loud blast as though a bomb had exploded. It turned out to be an anti-aircraft gun that had been fired along the main highway entering Freetown just a half block away. This was the beginning of a coup that toppled President Joseph Momoh's regime. There was much confusion. Dr. Lockwood and most of the staff left immediately.

The shift in power from President Momoh to junior officers was the result of an unhappy situation where the soldiers felt they were not being treated well at the front lines of the civil war. They revolted and took over the leadership of the country. President Momoh escaped to Guinea.

The following day, anarchy reigned. Roaming bands looted houses and businesses. There was a great amount of destruction and burning. The large Datsun dealership just a block away from the hospital was ransacked and all the cars were taken. The building itself was severely damaged. The Honda dealership

Destruction from the coup.

five blocks away experienced the same fate. The looters destroyed equipment and appliances, such as stoves and refrigerators. The supplies of rice from a storage dock two blocks away were all taken. No one was safe.

At the door of the hospital a former patient, whose corneal transplant Dr. Donald Doughman had done the year before, met me. He had been trying to protect his home when looters burst through the door and manhandled him, damaging his operated eye beyond repair. It was necessary to eviscerate the eye.

In spite of the mayhem, we decided to keep the doors of the hospital open rather than have them broken down. We were aware that on all four sides of the hospital, houses and garages were being broken into and vehicles taken. By keeping the doors of the hospital open, we were able to care for patients who presented themselves with gunshot and grenade injuries. One man had a live grenade go off in his hand. The hand was severely damaged and his whole body was bloody. Somehow the shrapnel missed vital organs and he did not bleed to death. One of his eyes was completely shredded and was removed; the other eye was less damaged and was salvaged. In the days and weeks to come, we were happy that he not only lived but also was able to see and move about independently.

Thoroughly exhausted, I finally left surgery and climbed the stairs to our apartment. On looking out the window, I realized there was not a single light to be seen in the entire city of Freetown with a population of one million. I quickly turned off the solar light, not wanting to be a target for a flying missile.

For four days and nights we continued the policy of not locking the hospital doors. Everyone cowered in their homes. While I slept in my bed, it would have been wiser to have been under the bed because of the flying bullets. The former President, Siaka Stevens, literally sought refuge under his bed during a period of unrest. It was wise not to turn on any lights and give occasion for someone to shoot through the window. The nights were long. I remembered Psalm 91:5-11: "Thou shalt not be afraid for the terror by night; nor for the arrow (bullets) that flieth by day; for he shall give his angels charge over thee, to keep thee...." I took comfort in Isaiah 26:3: "Thou shalt keep him in perfect peace whose mind is stayed on Thee." In spite of being alone, I truly tried to keep a positive attitude. Nights don't last forever, as "weeping may endure for a night, but joy cometh in the morning." (Psalm 30:5)

Food was a problem. I only had two boxes of corn flakes and some powdered milk and the occasional orange or banana slipped through the window. No one was on the streets, as there was a strict curfew. Somehow a messenger got through to me with a note instructing me to report to the U.S. embassy downtown. This was almost impossible to do because of roadblocks, but I dutifully got into my car and went from roadblock to roadblock. Because my skin was white, apparently they didn't feel I was a threat and allowed me to pass through the barricades. When I got to the embassy, it was completely boarded up. No one was around. I saw one man standing near the corner. I asked him, "Is there anyone here at the

U.S. embassy?" He whispered, "Oh yes, there are marines inside, but they are not showing themselves." I asked him, "Is it possible to report, as I was asked to come down?" He apparently was out there officially and said, "No, there is no way in which they will open the doors."

I returned to the Kissy UMC Eye Hospital. The next time I ventured out I had the good sense to take along with me my passport as well as a few personal items. I went to the Bintumani Hotel, which was deserted. I retreated to Wilberforce to see if Ted and Rosemary Townsend were there. Happily, I met a number of missionaries who, when they saw me, said, "Where have you been?" They had been trying for several days to find me to tell me that we were all being evacuated in the morning. I stayed that night at the Townsend residence and left my vehicle in the garage we had built several years before. When I got to the Mammy Yoko Hotel, I met several hundred people, mostly expatriates. At least a hundred missionaries were being evacuated. During the time of signing up to be evacuated, I felt that since I was able to freely go through roadblocks, I should stay and complete my work. There were a number of post-op patients who needed care over the next few days. At the last moment, I took my name off the list and prepared to stay.

It was Sunday and I returned with my 1987 Honda Civic to the King Memorial United Methodist Church. A policeman had asked to ride along. With him by my side, barricades presented no problem. An enthusiastic worship service was in progress. My appearance caused some surprise because it had been assumed that all the white people in Sierra Leone had been evacuated. I later learned that the evacuation had been to warships as well as to the airport from which people were flown to the neighboring city of Conakry in Guinea.

After a week, things began to stabilize. The patients were doing well; I prepared to go on to Ghana for a planned visit with Dr. Herb and Ruth Billman at their eye clinic in Cape Coast. When I got to the airport to take the Ghana flight I was told, "Oh we're very sorry but the Ghana flight flew over Freetown. They didn't want to risk landing." That meant I was isolated.

I saw on the runway a small plane with turning propellers. I asked where that plane was going. They informed me that it was leaving for Monrovia, Liberia. I frantically asked, "Is there any room on it?" The only man present took my small bag and went out with me. I was able to get the last seat on the plane, which was located next to the pilot. With that, the plane took off for Liberia. I transferred and eventually got to Accra, Ghana, where Dr. and Mrs. Billman met me. I stayed with them for six days, and then had the wonderful experience of returning to Alexandria. Finally, I was home with my loved ones. On getting into bed that night, I was relieved to not hear shellfire around me.

Chapter Fifty-Eight

1993 to 1996

With the relative political stability in Sierra Leone in 1993, the hospital truly had a banner year. A concerted effort was made to address the many corneal conditions that affected West African people. Dr. Donald Doughman of the Department of Ophthalmology of the University of Minnesota brought more than a dozen cultured corneas for transplantation. His expert anterior segment surgery gave the hospital added status.

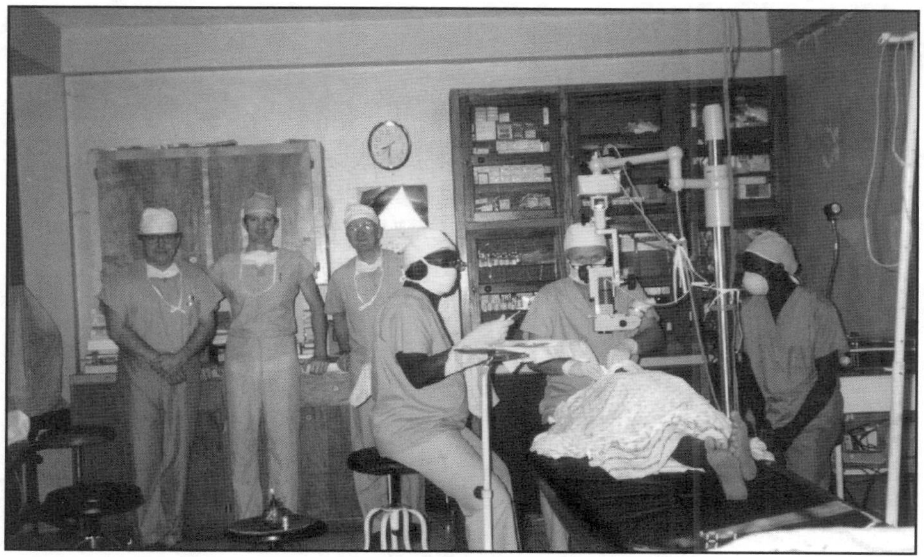

Dr. Donald Doughman, corneal specialist; Dr. Richard Lockwood; Dr. William McElroy (at the microscope.)

One day during his visit, we had four ophthalmologists doing surgery at three operating microscopes. Dr. Bill McElroy came to join Dr. Rich Lockwood and myself. It was great fun to have outstanding help in a faraway place on the earth. An international flavor was added to this assembly of volunteers when Dr. Anne-Liese Lauffemburger from Switzerland arrived.

On Ruth's and my 1993 trip to Sierra Leone, we were met at the airport by Dr. Richard Lockwood. He informed us that the mercy ship, *Anastasia*, was docked at the Freetown quay. I was privileged to board the ship and visit with Drs. Bob Dyer and Bert Souryal. In the past we had fellowshipped with them at Christian Ophthalmology Society meetings along with other outstanding ophthalmologists such as J. Lawton Smith, Mike Siatkowski, Brad Ferris and Arthur Pellicaine.

The *Anastasia* docked at Freetown. Volunteer ophthalmologist, Dr. Bert Souryal, is standing to my left.

On January 10th, I fulfilled my promise to Pastor Coker of Bombara Town United Methodist Church. I had agreed during our 1992 September-October tour to preach at his church. It was fortunate I had two months to prepare for my topic, "I Will Build My Church" as I was surprised to see Bishop and Mrs. J. C. Humper in the congregation. Ordinarily, he preached and I was in the congregation.

A high point of the year was the visit of our son Andrew in September born exactly thirty years earlier in Rotifunk. The low point came on a return trip from Zimbabwe where we had been working in Karanda with Dr. Daniel Stephens. Our booking home took us by way of Johannesburg, South Africa; Sydney, Australia; the Fiji Islands; the Hawaiian Islands, and then Los Angeles. It was on the last leg of this trip from the Hawaiian Islands to Los Angeles that Ruth became seriously ill with a developing stroke. It was later diagnosed as a blockage of the left posterior cerebral artery that resulted in loss of vision to the right eye and an inability to name persons or places. Thankfully recovery was rapid, allowing Ruth to return to Africa within a year's time. The Lord is kind.

1994. Still recovering from her stroke, Ruth was unable to accompany me on January 1, 1994. Instead, our grandson Christopher Boehlke, a junior at Macalester College majoring in philosophy, used Ruth's ticket. Chris is the son of our daughter Mary, a practicing clinical psychologist, and her husband, Steve, a corporate management consultant. Chris' exposure to medicine and mission outreach was a turning point in his life. The purpose of his going to Africa with me was originally to provide a strong back in helping to transport eight boxes of

Grandson Christopher Boehlke with Pastor W. B. Clay at Rotifunk.

medicines and supplies, each weighing up to seventy pounds. He was an old pro at carrying eye instruments; at the age of thirteen he carried a heavy portable YAG laser for several blocks to the servicing shop.

Once at the Kissy UMC Eye Hospital, Chris participated in the flow and care of eye patients. His outgoing personality enabled him to become an integral part of the staff. Not at all squeamish, he observed cataract surgery and IOL implantation through the operating microscope's second scope. We did some community-based eye care trekking that took us to places where his mother had lived as a girl – Rotifunk, Taiama and Bo. It was at Bo that we met with Dr. Dennis Williams and observed the remarkable program and facility of Sight Savers (the Royal Commonwealth Society for the Blind). The visit at Rotifunk found us treating more than fifty patients. It was a pleasure to work in the restored hospital, thanks to a year of volunteer service from Larry and Marge Chambers. It was also thrilling to be with Tator Carew, Julia Caulker, Marian Caulker and Nancy Judy with whom we had worked in years past. Eventually, I was privileged to help restore Nancy Judy's eyesight with IOL implantation in both of her eyes.

Chris and I could not visit the Kabala Rupp Memorial School, as the distance was great and there was the problem of political instability and the activity of the Revolutionary United Front (RUF). Chris was an innovative chef and was hard to beat at Shanghai, a game popular with missionaries. Our common interest in philosophy, in which we both hold majors, brought up topics and personalities such as Socrates, Plato, Aristotle and especially Augustine and Kierkegaard. He saw patients at the Kissy UMC Eye Hospital were not only receiving physical sight, but also spiritual insight of lasting worth.

In medical school, Chris ranked high and became chief resident in his eye residency program. Following a corneal fellowship, he went into practice. He still has an interest in volunteering his services in Africa as an accomplished surgeon. Two other of our grandchildren are also ophthalmologists. Dr. Debby Gess Ristvedt, who assisted her father, Tim, on a trip to Kissy in 2003, is now practicing with him in the Alexandria Eye Clinic. Dr. Adam Gess, John's son, is within months of beginning a corneal fellowship following his three years of eye residency.

Especially touching during our 1994 trip was the concern our Sierra Leone friends had over Ruth's health. One of the most meaningful prayers I have ever heard and experienced was that of Angie Myles' for Ruth's healing. There were also the wonderful prayers of Bishop Humper and David Caulker for the Rev. Ken Green, hospitalized in Connaught Hospital. He was hanging onto life by a single thread of faith, beyond further help from the doctors. In God's time, he was to return to the pulpit as one of the most effective preachers in Sierra Leone.

We helped a fellow colleague, Dr. Moses Mahoi, with whom I had worked at Rotifunk Hospital during our 1957-1960 tour. He needed cataract surgery. His entire career had been spent in general practice in Sierra Leone. Most of the doctors had fled the country, yet he continued to spend his days helping those in need in the Lumley area of Freetown. Some people traversed the entire distance of the city for his care.

He was crippled with arthritis. He used an assistant to record his findings and directed treatment after someone else placed his stethoscope on the patient's chest. Mentally, he was sharp. His spirit was at peace with the assurance of forgiveness for what he referred to as his faults and hurts to others during his life. I last visited with him in October 1998. Several months later, while his country continued to be torn apart in the vicious civil war, he was laid to rest.

Lee Weaver operating a well digging machine brought out by Pete Shearer.

The Kissy UMC Eye Hospital had been dedicated in February 1984. Ten years later, forty volunteer ophthalmologists had shared their time, tithe and talents with the people of West Africa. Of the nearly 10,000 surgeries performed, eighty-five percent were cataract extractions with intraocular lens implantations and ten percent were glaucoma operations.

It is a thrilling experience to have 100-150 patients present each day when the staff leads a service of hymns, scripture, prayer and testimony. I am sure that the angels are impressed by the staff's choruses which many of the patients know and in which they are quick to join in. Often quoted is Luke 7:4: "Unto many who were blind Jesus gave sight." We are happy when people like Yateh Glulah, who had his sight restored a year ago subsequently accepted Jesus Christ as Lord and Savior. Ruth and I counted it a privilege to minister in a program of healing in which people received sight both physically and spiritually.

1995. By mid-March 1995, I was the only American missionary left in Sierra Leone. Being conspicuous by my white skin, help was given me at every turn. I have never had such royal treatment. Baggage, immigration and security checks were expedited in an unbelievable way.

Sierra Leone was in the greatest crisis in its history. This once beautiful and cultural jewel of West Africa was in the throes of an internal war. The rebels, known as the Revolutionary United Front under Foday Sankoh, were taking over rural Sierra Leone step-by-step as Charles Taylor did in Liberia five years earlier. They moved from place to place at will, killed village leaders and then burned their homes. By intimidation, they forced children and teenagers to join their ranks who then were caught up in the ritual of killing and destroying. They kept themselves supplied through looting.

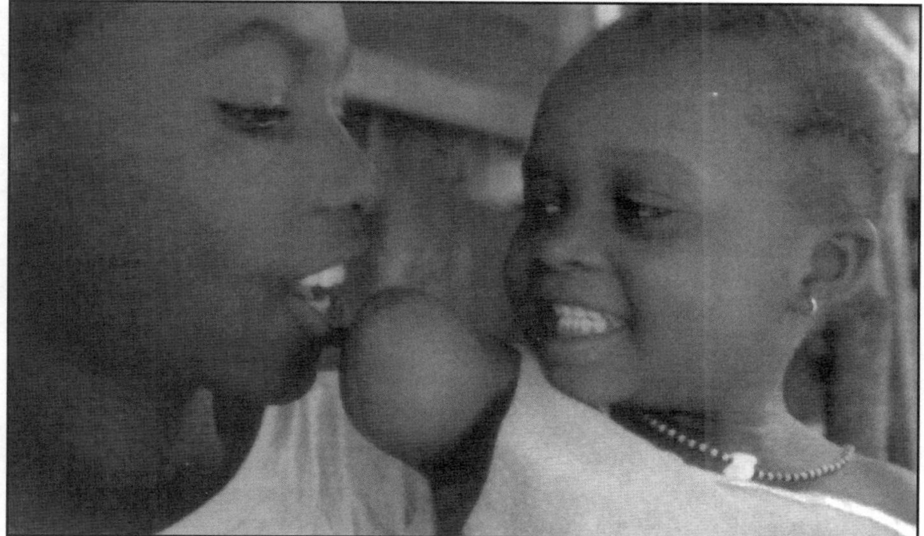

The rebels amputated limbs as a terror tactic, irrespective of age.

It was never known if their AK-47s were real and functional. In the attack on Bo it was learned that most of the arms were imitation – with only ten of the more than fifty attackers actually having real armament.

It was inconceivable that the insurgent rebel forces used such brutal tactics on the young and old to subjugate the populace. Amputating limbs and other disfigurements became a ritual – yet, pictures of a child with a stump for his arm and a little girl with an eye destroyed by a machete seemed unreal. Children, God's gifts, are to be loved and protected.

In the wake of what happened to thousands of maimed people, how was it possible to live with the perpetrators of such evil acts? Was forgiveness possible – was it necessary? Could a truth and reconciliation commission actually become a reality? (The commission did become a reality and completed its work. In fact years later former soldiers and those who were maimed were able to come together without threat of retribution.)

Jesus' parable of the Good Samaritan speaks to this problem. In spite of the wounded and dying man being his enemy, the Samaritan's compassion saved the man's life. The prodigal's father was able to forgive his wayward son, even though the brother could not. The Christian cannot risk chronic hostility and unforgiveness without being destroyed. Stress of this nature is destructive to the spiritual life as well as to the cardiovascular system. Forgiveness means accepting what has happened and deciding not to seek or take revenge. "...If anyone is in Christ, there is a new creation: everything old has passed away, everything has become new." (II Corinthians 5:17)

The day before I flew out of Sierra Leone, the rebels attacked Moyamba, killing and burning everyone and everything in sight. Paramount Chief Madam Gulama's compound of houses was entirely destroyed. I had examined her eyes just forty-eight hours prior to this catastrophe.

Most leaders crowded into Freetown. All hospitals and health centers upcountry were closed. The UMC Clinic at Jaiama was especially hit hard; all its equipment and a large supply of medicines was looted by the rebels. The Kissy UMC Eye Hospital was in operation in Freetown, along with the Connaught hospital and several small private ones. It was providential that the Board of Global Ministries had placed Dr. Ainor Fergusson, a Sierra Leonean eye doctor, under salary as a Person In Mission. He had developed into a competent eye surgeon and was now the only hope for surgical eye care in that part of West Africa. In March 1995, while the civil war was raging in Sierra Leone, Dr. Fergusson was doing four to six cataract extractions with IOL implantation each day. More than one hundred patients were daily cared for at the hospital.

The day before leaving, I also ministered to a pastor who narrowly escaped death and who had family and church members killed or maimed at the hands of the rebels. He had lost all of his possessions, even his glasses. The villages of his parish had been looted and burned. He was sober when I saw him, and not the usual ebullient, outgoing, cheerful person we had known before. It may take generations to erase the havoc the war created in Sierra Leone.

Amidst this tense situation, the church stood firm in the faith that God in his love would prevail. While some maintained that "hell isn't bad enough" for the rebels who killed and maimed innocent men, women and children, most were willing to put their Christian convictions on the line and "pray for them that persecute you" (Matthew 5:44). What stability that remained in this devastated country was due to the faith of Christians that God's righteous people would prevail, and that peace would follow tragedy.

The Islamic community in Sierra Leone is largely Sunni and doesn't practice radical fundamentalism. Regardless of our own religious persuasion, Ruth and I sought to obey the Lord to love and serve whomsoever was in need of healing and restoration of sight – both physically and spiritually. We were happy to be a part of the medical outreach of the United Methodist Church and its emphasis on agriculture, education and evangelism. The Church is feeding the hungry, giving water to the thirsty, taking in the stranger (refugees), clothing the naked, and visiting the sick and imprisoned, especially those imprisoned in the chains of superstition and sin.

At such a precarious time in Sierra Leone's history, some may have questioned my trip to the Kissy UMC Eye Hospital. It definitely was questioned by the U.S. State Department. Once they learned of my presence in Sierra Leone, I was required to register with the embassy even though I was scheduled on a return flight to the U.S. several days later.

My trip had a practical side to it. I delivered seven seventy-pound boxes of medicines and supplies. Other shipments had been held up. Saving the eyesight of patients – especially children – was of utmost importance. Secondly, it was important for me to mentor Dr. Fergusson, who was still new to the field of intraocular lens implantation. And thirdly, my being there when other expatriates had been evacuated was of great encouragement to the staff. As native Sierra Leoneans, they had been caught in this tense situation. They had nowhere else to go. My willingness to spend some time with the staff meant a great deal. I will never forget the firmness of their faith and the depth of their Christian convictions. It was I who was inspired by them.

1996. Our return trip to Sierra Leone in January 1996 was not without incident. A delay of two and a half hours in Minneapolis while a cabin door was being repaired caused us to miss our KLM connecting flight – Amsterdam to Freetown – by ten minutes. As a consequence of those few minutes, we had to spend five full days in Amsterdam waiting for the next flight. Mrs. Kootje Stilma, wife of Dr. Jan Stilma, took us in hand and made our stay pleasant. Her husband, Dr. Jan, was on a six-month sabbatical teaching in Harare, Zimbabwe.

At KLM's expense, we were billeted at the Victoria Hotel. We attended an English service in a nearby Catholic church, had tours of Amsterdam, followed the Desert Storm war on television, and witnessed diamond cuttings. We wondered whether or not the diamonds were from Sierra Leone. The world learned later how important a role diamonds played in the Sierra Leonean civil war. Rebel forces purchased arms and ammunition with diamonds. By 2000, a ban was placed on Sierra Leone diamonds except for those legally processed through government agencies.

By February 1st, we arrived in Freetown. Miss Ingrid Holmgren and Mr. Joe Skasko were busily engaged in helping orphans and other abandoned children. We learned of the present political and economic situation from Dr. June Holst Ronness, a general practitioner and former mayor of Freetown. Her husband, Rolf, a dentist, was the ambassador to Sierra Leone from Norway.

At Kissy UMC Eye Hospital, we were faced with an emergency – no water due to poor water pressure. To meet our water needs, eye surgery patients were required to have relatives bring three buckets of water as part of their pre-op regime. To correct the issue, adequate water pressure was only assured if we tapped into the pipeline leading to a nearby brewery. Pastor Alfred Karimu of Brown Memorial United Methodist Church judiciously and delicately dealt with the personnel involved in the hookup. Our conscience was guilt-free for siphoning off a portion of the brewery's water, as our supply ran through a meter that allowed us to pay Gumma Valley Authority for the water used.

Kissy UMC Eye Hospital moved right along with the expanding technology. Lawyer Bob Swenson and his wife Bea had donated an excellent IBM-compatible computer. Cassandra Fergusson, wife of Dr. Ainor Fergusson, was a computer expert who taught computer courses. She set up the computer in the hospital and in a short time Mohamed Rogers and Elsie Fornah were successfully using it. Unfortunately, during the rebel intrusion into Freetown, it was destroyed. The happy ending to this story is that the Swensons donated a replacement that is being used today.

Sister Kalon, a prominent nurse in the UMC program, had previously been in charge of the clinic in Taiama before being driven out by the rebels. Now she was at the Kissy Health and Maternity Centre. Decreasing vision made her work difficult. A cataract extraction with intraocular lens implantation returned her to 20/20 vision. She decided to postpone her other blurred eye for a later date, at which time during the procedure a sterilizing mishap occurred. For a time it was feared she might lose sight in her second eye, but mercifully her good health and the power of prayer led to useful 20/30 vision.

As we prepared to fly home from the Lungi International Airport on February 23, 1996, we witnessed the ballot boxes arrive that were to be used in the upcoming democratic election. We wondered whether or not such an event could take place during all the political instability. Pressure had been brought

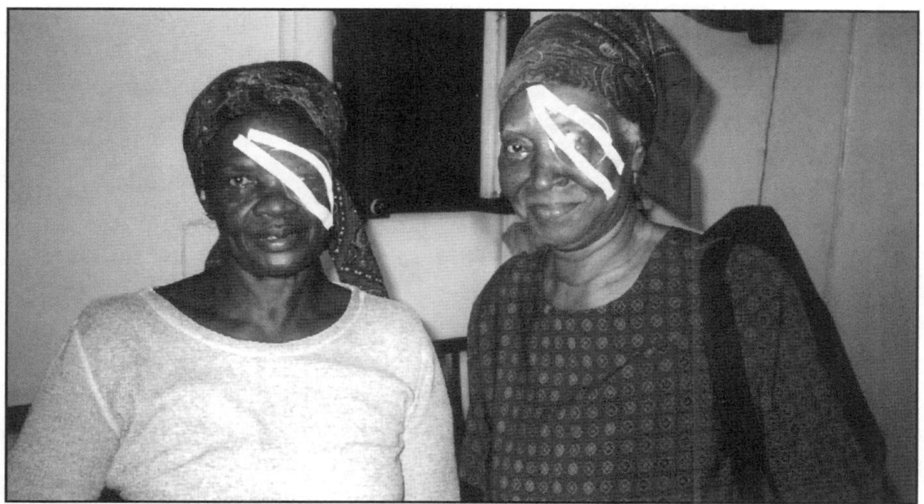

Sister Kalon, stalwart United Methodist nurse, on the left.

by civilian groups to establish a duly elected leadership rather than a military-led government. The brave and determined women of Freetown achieved what the male dominated parliament could not. They repeatedly marched through the streets in great crowds. It was obvious they would not be placated. Elections were scheduled.

The election was close between Alhaji Ahmad Tejan Kabbah and Dr. John Karefa-Smart, who had served at the Rotifunk Hatfield-Archer Hospital years earlier. Dr. Smart had been prominent in political affairs down through the years. Tejan Kabbah, however, had a long term of service at the United Nations representing Sierra Leone, and prevailed in the election. President Kabbah had a stormy career. Within several months of his election, he was forced to flee to Guinea for his life.

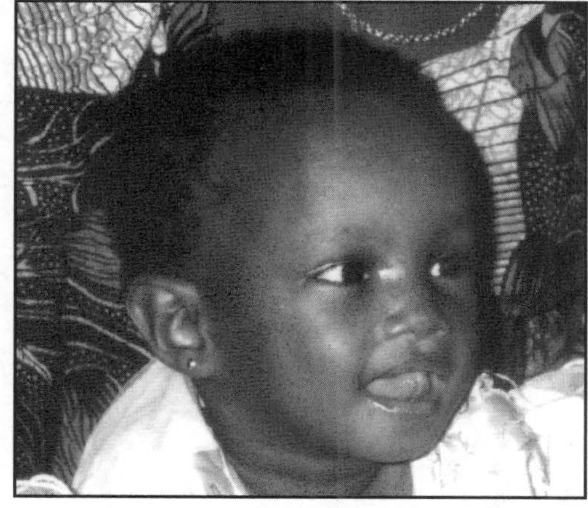

A happy child after congenital cataract extraction.

The visit in the fall of 1996 proved again how close to death some patients came. At the end of a congenital cataract procedure on a two-year-old child, he aspirated. Thankfully, the procedure had been completed and the eye securely closed with nylon sutures. This enabled us to lift him up by his feet, slap him on the back, and use an aspirator to remove the occluding mucous. He promptly cried like a newborn and in our relief and joy we cried along. I missed Ruth who usually monitored these delicate anesthetics on infants and children. During this visit, she had remained at home.

A number of pediatric patients required surgery for congenital cataracts and glaucoma. Kwitkow's direct, external goniotomy was used on two patients whose corneas were too opaque for standard goniotomies.

There were scenes of joy for patients, relatives, and eye staff when patients who had been blind were able "to see." Especially moving was twenty-nine year-old Safia whose Christian faith was willing to accept blindness but prayed for a miracle. She brought an audiocassette she wanted played in the surgical theater during her operation. She and her church had recorded the hymn, "There is Power in the Blood." The eye that was to be operated on could only see light – a complicated cataract obscured other forms of sight. Following the cataract extraction, she could see the movement of people for a period of time but eventually the world closed in on her again. Her unshakable faith did not waiver, for she had true insight into God's love.

Another patient was a blind beggar who sat daily begging in front of the mosque. Soon he begged us for help. We told him we would gladly help him and requested that he bring a friend to accompany him during his postoperative care. We understood that he had no money but believed a Christian would provide the money to help him, a Muslim.

The day after surgery, he came into the hospital and triumphantly said, "IT ME – I SEE!"

We were able to share with him that the eye hospital was here because many Christians felt "sorry heart" for him and his blindness and wanted him not only to have new vision but also the knowledge of God's Son who loved him and died for him.

The blind beggar, Ruth's special patient.

Chapter Fifty-Nine

The End of a Surgical Career?

I was on my third cataract extraction with intraocular lens implantation when it happened. I could not release the mosquito forceps holding the superior rectus suture. First assistant John Fornah came to my rescue.

I had recently been experiencing pain in my right hand – especially the right thumb. While putting up the Christmas tree, I had over-exerted tightening the base. I thought the discomfort would go away in a few days.

It had now been six weeks and the pain was still there along with weakness. The delicate maneuvering of eye instruments was not a problem. I only needed help for heavier instruments during the three-week period of surgery.

I was aware that on occasion the distal phalanx of my right thumb would "snap" when moving it up or down. During the night following my last scheduled surgery, I was awakened out of a deep sleep by a sharp pain in my right thumb. The distal phalanx had snapped down and would not go back. It took considerable force to return it to its normal position.

The terror that night was not about pain. It was the thought that perhaps I would not be able to wield instruments in the future. Agonizingly I prayed, "Lord, is it over? Will I be able to help the blind in the future?"

I did not want another episode of "locking" of this trigger finger. The thumb was splinted as we packed to return home as well as on the trip itself. In Alexandria, Dr. David Larson graciously had me come in immediately for an examination. The next day I was in surgery.

Healing was complete. Today I cannot imagine I ever had a serious brush with being incapacitated for doing eye surgery. To use one's hands for health and healing in the name of Jesus continued to be a great joy.

Just hours before leaving, I had the opportunity to visit with Pastor Matthew E. L. Philie. Our friendship extended back for more than thirty years. I respected him as a preacher who was always concerned about the spiritual and physical welfare of his congregation and family. He was a master tracker and hunter, which impressed me. Whenever possible, we would team up to hunt.

The most dramatic incident we had together was going after a buffalo. We were aware that these wily and dangerous animals sometimes would circle around and come up behind their tracker and spring a fatal surprise.

In thick bush, the buffalo we were tracking sped off away from Pastor Philie. He got off a shot from his shotgun. He always prepared the ammunition he used, ensuring extra powder and a single slug. It was apparent that he had hit his mark, as a trail of blood was evident on tall grass and bushes.

At this point, the other members of the party decided to call off the hunt. They knew the danger of trying to follow a wounded buffalo. Just months before, one of their friends had been mauled by a buffalo and had thankfully lived to tell the story.

Since I had the high-powered rifle, it was my role to proceed first. I sensed the danger of having a wounded animal in front and another loaded gun behind. We came to the small draw of a dry stream and followed the trail across it. Once on the other side, we realized the trail turned around and went right back at an angle. With my hair standing on end, I wheeled around and there it was – the buffalo in a crouched position! Reflexively, I fired. The animal shook with the impact of the missile but did not change his position. Pastor Philie's first shot had caused the buffalo to bleed to death while in an upright and crouched position.

The "dangerous" buffalo.

Suddenly, everyone in the area was willing to help. Pastor Philie's congregation had a great church supper, the community rejoiced and the staff at the eye hospital enjoyed steaks.

Now, in the midst of the Sierra Leone civil war, I was prompted to do away with my shotgun. I wanted to give no appearance of being armed. I had already "loaned out" my powerful 300 H & H Magnum rifle.

Would Pastor Philie allow himself to possess a firearm in these tense days? When offered the gun, he was overwhelmed with emotion. His handling of the pump action shotgun was like a tender caress. He had always made do with a single shot firearm. He walked away in a daze with the gun under his arm. A few minutes later he returned, and with composure expressed thanks for being given the type of gun he had hoped for during most of his hunting career.

We were living in perilous times, witnessing perhaps the lowest point in the history of Sierra Leone. On May 25, 1997, a second coup led by AFRC Chairman Major Johnny Paul Koroma replaced the democratically elected government headed by President Alhaji Ahmad Tejan Kabbah. Instead of hiding upcountry, RUF rebel soldiers were brought into Freetown to join the junta, which was universally condemned by the UN Security Council, ECOWAS (the sixteen-nation Economic Community of West African States), the European Union and the UK Commonwealth. Under the primary leadership of ECOMOG, sanctions were enforced with embargoes on arms and oil. Food supplies dwindled and became expensive, as did fuel. The country's infrastructure crumbled. Hundreds of thousands fled the country. Law and order broke down. People lived with apprehension and fear.

Hooligans had their own way robbing, looting, raping and dispossessing people of their homes by simply moving in and forcing the owners to leave. At Rotifunk, three hundred homes were burned to the ground. We learned of ghastly tales of barbarism where beheading often climaxed rituals of torture. All this was happening in Sierra Leone, the pearl of West Africa, to which other countries in the past sent their gifted young people to study at Fourah Bay University – the Athens of West Africa.

In the midst of this chaos, the staff of the Kissy UMC Eye Hospital continued to minister to patients. It was not unusual for them to have twenty to thirty relatives who were refugees living in their homes. It was difficult to provide food for such numbers. Dr. Ainor Fergusson and I often did more than ten surgeries a day during the brief time of our visit. Most of the surgeries were cataract extractions with intraocular lens implantation, but we made a special effort to surgically help glaucoma patients. These patients needed surgical intervention, as glaucoma medications were often not available, their cost was prohibitive and patient compliance was poor. Twenty trabeculectomies were done with the hope that vision would be preserved. A fourteen-year-old boy underwent successful strabismus surgery. His straightened eyes gave him a new confidence and composure.

Chapter Sixty

1998 to 2001

An unplanned trip June 24, 1998, was made to the Kissy UMC Eye Hospital. A container arranged by Mr. Pete Shearer had docked one week earlier with a cargo of rice and other food products and clothes. It also carried medicines and supplies for the eye hospital.

Dr. Ainor Fergusson already had arrived in Freetown to begin eye surgeries on a backload of more than a hundred patients. These were only the tip of the iceberg. Along with Mr. Samuel Coker, whom we had taught suturing and basic cataract techniques a year and a half earlier, surgery was restarted. Together we did 207 intraocular lens implantations in a four-week period. I had planned not to have any surgeries the day before I left but relented and actually did five more.

It was wonderful to set foot on Sierra Leonean soil where Andrew, our youngest, had been born. The welcome was overwhelming. No missionary had been seen for more than a year. During that year, the Kissy staff and the people of Sierra Leone had lived and died through some of the worst brutalities in the history of West Africa.

When the junta (the AFRC-Armed Forces Revolutionary Council) took control May 25, 1997, they freed all criminals and political prisoners and invited the rebels (RUF-Revolutionary United Front) to join them in a new administration, supplementing the democratically elected President Alhaji Ahmad Tejan Kabbah. The anarchy spilled over into 1998. Augustine Macauley, our previous optician, recounted being stopped by an eleven-year-old with an AK-47 demanding sweets. An altercation between several people was taking place a few feet away. The boy moved over and executed one of them.

People were afraid to appear on the streets during the day and spent sleepless nights awaiting the invasion of their homes. A ploy the soldiers often used was to come to a home and offer protection if the people would care for them – which they did. When the soldiers were ready to move on, certain people were ordered to pick up slips of paper with instructions written on them. They read: "cut off right hand," "cut off left arm," "kill this one," "let this one go," "cut off right ear," "put out left eye."

There are 2,000 amputees in Sierra Leone. It was estimated that only twenty to twenty-five percent of those who suffered atrocities sought help before they died of complications. The UN established a sixty-bed hospital in Freetown for amputees. The U.S. donated millions toward primary care and future prosthetic fittings.

Burned out church.

Upon arrival, I was greatly surprised to see as many buildings standing as there were. However, along Kissy Road there were many houses and businesses with only naked, burnt out walls. Kissy UMC Eye Hospital had been in the direct path of the ECOMOG and AFRC/RUF confrontation. Miraculously, the hospital had not sustained a direct hit. The roof had to be replaced because of damage from shell fragments, but the Zeiss operating microscopes, four of the six Haag Streit slit lamps, the keratometer and the A-scan were left intact. Lunsar Baptist Eye Hospital was not so fortunate. Buildings were burned to the ground, and eye equipment (including a Zeiss OPMI-1) was willfully damaged, rendering them inoperable.

Staff members sent me individual reports, which I still have. Some were able to flee to remote places upcountry while others went to Conakry, Guinea Bissau and Gambia. Those who remained in Kissy went three to four days without food. While this was debilitating, their greatest fear was being summarily and randomly executed.

Rev. David Caulker was a pillar of strength during these terrible days and months before the February 1998 liberation of Freetown by ECOMOG forces. Although he preached the truth in love, he was not arrested or thrown into jail with the thousands of others who refused to support the junta in their reign of terror. He stated it was difficult to preach compassion for the captured junta and the rebels who brought death and destruction. He asked me to preach on July 5, 1998. I shall never forget facing a congregation of about 1,000 worshipers who filled King Memorial UM Church to the rafters. I was led to preach on Luke 10:33, where Jesus tells of the Good Samaritan who showed compassion and offered help to his enemy. As followers of Christ, He might expect us to do the same.

Pastor David Caulker.

When we arrived at the airport in October 1998, it was eerily subdued. Peter Conteh, a security officer and friend of long standing, did not have his usual smiling face. Forty-eight hours earlier, twenty-four officers and men of the former junta ruling party were executed, including Peter's brother and a cousin. Also condemned to death were fourteen civilians who had abetted the junta.

After being checked three times under military scrutiny, I was able to join Paul Tarawally for the trip to Kissy UMC Eye Hospital. The staff had made elaborate plans to have the hospital in tiptop shape with supplies ready for the start of surgery at 7:00 a.m. the next morning. Along with Dr. Ainor Fergusson, the resident ophthalmologist, we usually did nine to ten procedures each day – most often cataract extractions with intraocular lens implantations. Since the visit was to last less than two weeks, surgeries were also done on Saturday.

Besides surgery, many repairs were needed for the hospital. A repaired operating room table was installed and a Zeiss OPMI-6 operating microscope was delivered by Operation Classroom. This third operating microscope allowed Dr. Fergusson and me to each have our own microscope while Mr. John Fornah used a third for lid procedures, pterygia and enucleations. Mr. Mohamed Rogers and Mrs. Isatu Sesay, surgical assistants in training, helped the ophthalmologists. Later in the day a new computer was set up, and unlike previous instances, no parts were missing!

After checking the eight post-ops from 7:30 to 9:00 Sunday morning, I was on my way to the Brown Memorial United Methodist Church. I had not stepped off the veranda before a patient met me who was suffering from a right eye rock injury. Applanation revealed an intraocular pressure of 64 mm Hg. Not being a total hyphema, timoptic and diamox medicines were administered to see if the pressure could be lessened without surgery. The day before, I was to have attended a 3:00 p.m. meeting with the UMC Conference treasurer, but again on the way out of the hospital, a five-year-old child with a stick injury to the right eye met me. Under ketamine and local anesthesia, it was discovered that the right globe had been ruptured and the eye eviscerated by the trauma. John Fornah did the enucleation and completed the lid repair. We still made it to the meeting. The Conference treasurer, however, had forgotten about it, so the hurried trip was used instead to purchase some supplies for the hospital.

Forty-two surgeries were done before the return trip to Lungi Airport. The ferry had broken down, so the trip was made in a hovercraft. It rained in sheets and the wind whipped up the waves, but wonderfully the seagoing craft skimmed over the ocean with hardly a shake.

1999. The civil war in Sierra Leone had been going on for more than six years. Internet news reported a peace initiative between President Kabbah and the rebel leader Foday Sankoh during their meeting in Togo.

The eye ministry at Kissy had been active in spite of the war. In 1997, Dr. Ainor Fergusson was targeted for imprisonment or execution by the revolutionary junta. He escaped with only the clothes on his back to Conakry, Guinea. Christian Blind Mission (CBM) transferred him and his family to Bissau in Guinea Bissau. In June 1998, CBM provided him with a plane ticket so he could perform eye surgeries at Kissy, as ECOMOG forces had stabilized Freetown. While in Freetown, Guinea Bissau had a coup. His family was rescued by the UN and brought back to Freetown. I worked with Dr. Fergusson in October and November of 1998. We did 122 surgeries in less than a three-week period.

On January 6, 1999, the rebels stormed into Freetown. Dr. Fergusson and the other twenty members of the Kissy staff were holed up in their homes for two weeks before ECOMOG forces drove the rebels out of Freetown.

Sierra Leone boys at play.

Unlike the "soldier boys," the thirteen-year-old boys who played at Kissy UMC Eye Hospital were exuberant and playful, splashed about in the water from the overflowing hospital tank. The thirteen-year-old soldier boy who sat in front of me was a sullen youngster I fitted with an ocular prosthesis. A rocket-propelled grenade had malfunctioned in the launcher, so he was fortunate to have survived and only lost one eye. We were happy to say to him, "We can help you." After the fitting procedure, he was placed before a mirror. All agreed he looked handsome. Yet he stood there quiet with no smiles. The next moments were sobering to all of us. We saw tears coursing down his cheeks. I turned to John Fornah, who had helped with the selection of the prosthesis, and asked him what had caused this supposedly hardened soldier to cry. John explained – "He thought he would see with it."

Soldier boys.

It is a dreadful, appalling story. Children who fought in the Sierra Leone civil war – aged ten, eleven and twelve years – were kidnapped. At first they were used as carriers and performed other menial tasks. Eventually, under great intimidation, they were taught how to handle and operate weapons. To prove their manhood, they were forced to take lives, sometimes even of family members. Failure to comply meant their own deaths. Boy soldiers were easy to feed and clothe. With an innocent bravado, they made up the advancing line that was exposed to enemy fire. Under the influence of drugs, they recklessly plunged themselves into the battle, seemingly unaware of the dangers. Graduation came when they carried out grisly amputations of limbs and other parts of men, women and children. Even infants were not immune from this barbarism.

Child soldiers were denied the normal schooling afforded to others in their age group. Their only families were other child soldiers and commandants. However, after carrying out terrorist acts, they were no longer welcomed back in their own families or villages. They are a lost generation devoid of education, social and ethical graces. What was true in Sierra Leone in 2000 was also true in the Congo, Angola, and other places in Africa, Asia, Latin America and Europe.

It was eerie to drive along the main streets of Freetown. Thousands of homes, businesses, and public buildings had been burned. I saw the charred remains of churches – Anglican, Baptist, and non-denominational. King Memorial UMC was torched but failed to burn. The reason for the church burnings was that "the enemy" – defenseless women and children – were taking refuge in them. Amputations were a part of the invasion, again including women and children.

With the signing of the peace accord July 7, 1999, people faced soldiers who killed and maimed their families and friends. How far could peace, forgiveness and reconciliation go? Especially difficult was the child soldiers' plight. Often they had fought with no particular allegiance – some on one side and then on the other.

It was exciting to arrive at the Kissy UMC Eye Hospital and see it standing yet again. The rocket propelled grenade destruction to the doors, windows and roof was glossed over with makeshift repairs. The staff was there with a warm Christian welcome. Their faces did not betray the fear, anguish and deprivation they had experienced day and night for several months. None of the enrolled staff had been killed. Several had their homes burned. All of them lost most, if not all, their personal possessions. They had gone for extended periods without food while they were in hiding. And yet here they were, greeting me with phrases such as "Kabo, how da bodi!" "We tank God." (We welcome you! Are you well? We are thankful to God.)

It was hard for them to understand I was only there for one night before going on to Ghana where I did thirty-five sight-restoring surgeries at the Cape Coast and Sunyani eye clinics of the Christian Eye Ministry. In a series of meetings with the Kissy general staff, Rev. David Caulker, Rev. Angie Myles (Medical Program Coordinator), Lettie Williams (the administrator) and Dr. Ainor Fergusson (the resident ophthalmologist), important issues were decided.

All this was done with a sense of urgency, as everyone had to be off the streets by the 9:00 p.m. curfew. I was then left with Mohamed Rogers to survey the damage; he stayed all night as a sentinel.

After everyone except Mohamed had slipped away, the tour of the facilities began. Manhandled, the $17,000 Nikon Automatic Refractor no longer gave accurate digital readings. Lens sets had been scattered and broken. Some were

Our apartment before the looting.

missing. The trial frames were all gone except one. Trial frames were later seen being worn on the streets of Freetown. The spectacle loops of my Keeler indirect microscope had been torn away leaving only cords and the transformer. All the ophthalmoscopes were gone. Lenses, frames and equipment in the store and optical room had been emptied from their drawers and strewn about with some breakage. Only one operational fan of five was left. The drug room had been cleared of valuable medicines, supplies and financial receipts. The surgical theater was in complete disarray. The staff went to great efforts to restore the surgical supplies to their proper places, including the intraocular lenses. Parts of the video equipment were missing, as was the video camera that attached to the Zeiss operating microscopes. Headlamps were destroyed, but the three operating microscopes were operational. The $39,000 YAG laser had maliciously been destroyed. None of the vandals had known how to open the sterilizer that contained two complete sets of eye instruments valued at more than $5,000.

The final survey was done in the upstairs apartment. Looted were optical and surgical equipment, mattresses, sheets, towels, kitchen articles, maintenance supplies, tools, sofa cushions, etc., etc. Dexamethasone, gentamycin and viscoelastics stored in one of the rooms was scattered about or taken thoughtlessly away; they were of little use to people unqualified in their medical usage.

Until 3:00 a.m., I sifted through the debris to salvage usable optical parts. The bed, prepared with a secured net, felt so good. Lettie had been able to find a mattress. I don't know who contributed the sheets and pillow.

Up at 5:30 a.m., I found the washrooms to be in good shape. The hot shower could not be used, as electricity flashed as it was turned on. The staff all agreed that the most important item not destroyed was our 30 KVA generator, in spite of the fact that the three vehicles had been taken and all other equipment looted.

Our apartment, over the surgical wing, after the looting.

The staff had astutely pieced together equipment. The medical and surgical program would resume in full force with the arrival of the boxes of medicines and supplies.

In 1999, I was honored to be able to participate in the Partnership Consultation (U.S., Germany and other countries in Europe) of the Sierra Leone Annual Conference of the United Methodist Church in the wake of the July 7, 1999, Lome Peace Accord. The brutal, vicious and barbaric civil war had destroyed many properties and infrastructures, and brought various ministries of the church in Sierra Leone to a standstill. Both general and committee meetings planned for rehabilitation, reconstruction, resettlement and relief programs and projects of the Conference.

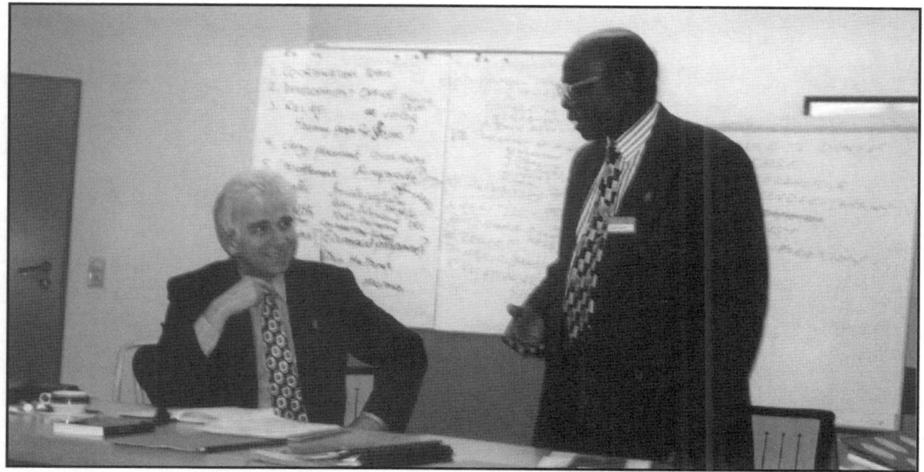

Bishop Walter Klaiber and Bishop Joseph Humper of Sierra Leone.

Chaired by Bishop Walter Klaiber, the consultation was conceived by the Rev. Joseph and Carolyn Wagner of Operation Classroom and Dr. Thomas Kemper of the Evangelical Methodist Church World Mission. It received the broad report of Bishop J. C. Humper of war damages and the need for $9,000,000 to establish or rebuild churches, chapels, parsonages, schools, health centres, conference buildings, trauma and HIV/Aids counseling centres, women's training centres, the Bo Bible Training Institute, camp and retreat centres, and other ministries. Prominent leaders were in attendance from Europe. Dr. Zebediah Marewangepo, Dr. Paul Dirdak of UMCOR, and Ms. Maxine West of the Women's Division represented the General Board of Global Ministries of the United Methodist Church.

Involved in medical missions for more than five decades, I have a deep love for Sierra Leone. While serving as the General Board of Global Ministries' field representative, I had the opportunity of crossing the country from Freetown to Bunumbu and Koidu and then down from Kabala to Shenge, visiting the churches and schools of the United Methodist Church which shaped the lives of people such as Sir Milton Margai and others. Albert Academy at Harford, and the other 212 primary schools and sixteen secondary schools, mean much to the development of Sierra Leone. I can still remember the Christian witness of our school at Kayima where for the first time I heard students heartily sing the song, "They crucified my Savior, and laid Him in the tomb," and then rang out with the chorus, "He rose, He rose, He rose from the dead, and the Lord shall bear my Spirit home."

2000. With the intensity of the savage civil war in Sierra Leone, visitation to the Kissy United Methodist Church Eye Hospital is not always possible. A window of opportunity, however, was presented during February and March of 2000, when more than 13,500 peacekeepers were deployed from Nigeria, India, Ghana, Kenya and Guinea.

School being conducted under a tree.

Mrs. Gess and I arrived at the Lungi International Airport in Freetown along with our four large boxes of medicines and supplies. We were given a VIP reception in an air-conditioned room. Attendants took our passports, tickets, and vaccination records and completed our clearance. Every effort had been made to make Lungi International Airport as up-to-date as possible.

During travel to Africa, I provided my own mosquito net – this time in Lagos, Nigeria.

While waiting to take possession of our luggage, pandemonium suddenly broke out. A baggage handler's hand had become enmeshed in the gears of the conveyor, and he was being drawn into the mechanism. Before the machine could be stopped, his hand and lower arm were shredded. Uniformed workers hurriedly carried him outside for transportation to the nearby government branch hospital.

Ishmael Jobbie, our airport friend of more than twenty years, arranged for our $40 helicopter tickets to Mammy Yoko heliport where we were met by Paul Tarawally. He drove a brand-new four-wheel drive Toyota Hilux, a gift to Kissy UMC Eye Hospital outreach from Christian Blind Mission. The two hospital vehicles and our Honda Civic had been burned and destroyed in the wake of the January 6, 1999, rebel invasion of Freetown.

On arrival at the Kissy UMC Eye Hospital, we were relieved to see it relatively intact. Doors and windows had been repaired and the roof was in the process of being replaced a second time. Rocket-propelled grenades had again created the damage.

Our living quarters above the surgery had also been ransacked and looted, but Lettie Williams, the hospital administrator, had again supplied it with kitchen utensils, beds with mosquito netting and even curtains on the windows. A delicious meal of jollof rice was waiting for us to enjoy. We were home again. We collapsed into the beds for a good night's sleep.

The next day (Monday), Ruth managed to get the gas-stove working and water flowing in the filters. I went down to the clinic and arranged the slit-lamps for the imminent invasion of up to 150 patients. Very soon, the waiting room and the verandas were filled – some of the patients were totally blind. Dr. Ainor Fergusson and I prepared to perform up to ten surgeries a day with the help of four surgical assistants. The entire staff numbered twenty-three, which included the trained ophthalmic assistants as well as three watchmen.

During our two-week visit, forty-eight operations were done, most of them cataract extractions with intraocular lens implantation. My last surgery was a difficult "complicated" cataract. The patient's other eye was not amenable to surgery. We were overjoyed the next day when the bandage was removed, his face lit up with true surprise and joy. He could see – and see well. We watched him leave the hospital and step out in front of the family member who had been accustomed to leading him for years. We had counseled the patient that we could not predict the success of the operation. All thanks were given to God.

It was a wonderful experience for Ruth and me to be with our hospital staff for two weeks. In spite of all the fears and dangers, they had remained at their posts, ensuring the only continued eye care in the entire country.

We also had the opportunity to see our friends of many, many years. During the last week, the Sierra Leone Annual Conference of the United Methodist Church met at the Brown Memorial United Methodist Church adjacent to the eye hospital. We were showered with African food and words of appreciation for bringing sight and healing to the blind and providing needed eyeglasses for pastors, many of whom had lost all of their possessions in the recent war.

Dr. Craig Cameron, orthopedist, flanked by his pastor and an assistant.

Our flight home from the Lungi International Airport involved a helicopter ride across the bay from Mammy Yoko Hotel where our driver, Mr. Paul Tarawally, introduced us to an elderly woman with a left arm amputation and a young man with both arms missing due to rebel attacks. Also present was Mr. Mark Kindy with whom some of our children had attended the Rupp Memorial School in Kabala. He had been working with volunteer members of the project Limbs of

Hope established by World Hope International. We had the opportunity to visit with Dr. Craig Cameron, an orthopedist, whose account of his visit is reported in Focus on the Family *Physician*, March/April, 2001. During his participation with the team, 147 patients were fitted with prosthetic limbs. After learning how to use the prostheses, the victims of this horrible abuse were able to put on and take off their own limb, wash, dress and feed themselves, light a lantern with a match, prepare food, carry a bucket of water, and shovel and hoe in a garden. The newfound independence and productivity gave them hope for a better tomorrow.

2001. The Ghana Airways plane set down at Lungi International Airport on Sunday evening February 18, 2001, after several hours of delay. On board the plane we sat next to Mr. Kamara who was returning from New York where the Rotary Club had arranged for prosthetic fittings for his double amputation. He remained a proud man unwilling to let his disability destroy his life. This is true also for the more than 2,000 amputees who survived. At minimum, that same number died following forced grisly and vicious amputations often performed by child soldiers not strong enough to do a clean machete or ax stroke. Only worse were the victims whose eyes were intentionally blinded.

The ferry from Lungi to the government wharf was in service, which allowed us to cross the bay by water instead of helicopter. The apartment over the surgical wing at the Kissy UMC Eye Hospital had been cleaned and made comfortable for our late arrival. The security of a mosquito net over our bed was comforting.

On Monday morning it was a glad reunion with our staff of committed Christians still at their posts after having their lives threatened and their property and personal possessions destroyed. Mrs. Lettie Williams had administratively held things together. Dr. Ainor Fergusson each week had performed twenty or more cataract extractions with intraocular lens implantation. They welcomed our

The white, sandy beaches of Sierra Leone.

four seventy-pound boxes of medicines and supplies. Mrs. Hannah Koroma, our assistant administrator, underwent cataract extraction during our stay. With her absence in the clinic, Ruth filled in for her in handling the flow of patients.

Together Dr. Fergusson and I performed seventy-one eye operations – sixty of them cataract extractions with IOLs and eleven trabeculectomies for out-of-control glaucoma. Some eyes had such unusual conditions we could only provide partial improvement. One volunteer eye surgeon who performed surgeries for a month several years ago stated that he never did a really "normal" cataract extraction the entire time he was at Kissy.

The need for eye care is great. Kissy UMC Eye Hospital is the hope for millions of people in West Africa. In spite of the continuing standoff between the democratically elected government of President Alhaji Ahmad Tejan Kabbah and the RUF (Revolutionary United Front) people tried to live normal lives under the heavy protection of more than 10,000 UNAMSIL soldiers. There were indications that the RUF was weary of the continuing conflict that had spread from Sierra Leone to neighboring Guinea. As many as 135,000 refugees from Sierra Leone and Liberia were thought to have been caught up in the "parrot-beak" area between the warring factions and were without food or medicine for as long as three or four months, but later dispersed into the bush and jungle areas as the refugee camps emptied. A UN representative called the state of affairs in this area "the greatest humanitarian crisis in the world today." We continue to pray for peace in our beloved Sierra Leone.

Our return flight to Accra, Ghana, from Freetown was not delayed but rather cancelled. Two extra days were involved with working our way home back to Alexandria, Minnesota. Home was never more sweet. Ruth and I felt privileged to have been able to minister to a destitute people and country during very difficult days in Sierra Leone.

Our home in Alexandria, Minnesota.

In October 2001, it had been six months since our last visit to Kissy. Freetown, at that time, had the largest concentration of United Nation troops in the world. Refugees flooded the streets and brought traffic to a near standstill for periods of every day. The short distance from downtown to Kissy UMC Eye Hospital normally required 10 to 15 minutes; with various impasses, it often took two to three hours.

Our Hilux four-wheel drive vehicle donated by Christian Blind Misssion to assist in mobile eye clinics throughout Sierra Leone threaded through the mass of humanity crowding the streets. Thankfully, no pedestrians were injured during our passage. We were happy to arrive at Kissy UMC Eye Hospital after our trip from Alexandria via Amsterdam and Accra, Ghana. Members of the staff were there to greet us and help us with our luggage, which included 350 pounds of medicines and supplies. Alcon Laboratories and S.E.E. International had generously supplied us for our three-week stay of volunteer eye surgery, which included 106 eye operations. Eighty-five percent were cataract extractions with intraocular lens implantations with the remainder consisting of trabeculectomies and procedures for pterygia and lid alterations.

During the following days of a busy clinic and surgical schedule, we continued to be amazed by the upbeat attitude of the staff. They considered their work as God's calling. They took turns reading scripture, praying, witnessing and hymn directing once the hundred or more patients were registered for the day. Their deep Christian commitment was a challenge to Ruth and me. Without exception, they returned to their posts at times of great danger. None were killed, but some lost all of their personal possessions. Three had their homes burned during the rebel intrusion into Freetown.

Being able to help blind patients is a soul inspiring experience. Many were bilaterally blind, making them dependent on others to lead them. Their joy at being independent and productive is vicariously experienced by the surgeons and staff. Dr. Ainor Furgusson, a native Sierra Leonean, not only performed eye surgery four days a week at Kissy but occasionally flew to Guinea Bissau to help in the CBM sponsored program there.

While I was thrilled to be a part of renewed sight for these blind patients, it was a special event to do a second intraocular lens implantation on Mr. Josef Caulker, a radiant Christian, who on March 4, 1984, received a personally designed Alpha Omega intraocular lens. Seventeen years later, he saw "perfectly" with that left eye but wanted to have the blind right eye restored as well. His hopes and prayers were realized.

Isata Kamara had been blind for several years. Because of the nature of her condition, she required an anterior chamber intraocular lens. Thinking she might not have much vision, we did the other cataract extraction five days later – again requiring an anterior lens. A few days before returning home from our visit to Kissy, Isata walked through the door, followed by her daughter who was carrying a baby on her back. Previously, the daughter had led the mother. The daughter explained that before coming to the clinic, she found her mother in the market having a wonderful time. Along with the many smiles, there were a few tears of joy.

Samuel Kamara, a soccer standout, realized that something was wrong with his sight. The eye examination revealed he could only perceive movement in his left eye. Vision in the right was drastically constricted. Since eye medications are not always available in West Africa, he chose to undergo a trabeculaectomy on his better eye. Postoperatively his anterior chamber was dangerously shallow. Mr. Conteh, who originally diagnosed the glaucoma, prayed for Samuel. Two days later, the chamber returned to a normal depth and pressure. Malcolm Albert broke out with his beautiful baritone voice singing "The Doxology." A half dozen others joined in, including the patient.

I cannot help but strongly encourage ophthalmologists and other doctors to share their time and skills as volunteers to a needy world. The impending visit of ophthalmologist Dr. Cathy Schanzer that December was highly anticipated along with the visits of Dr. Samuel Pieh and other members of the Mid-South Africa Link team who included Taiama in their volunteer work schedule. Other organizations around the world are still at work to bring to fruition Alan Harkey's vision of sight for the world by 2020. A doctor is never the same again after participating in the service of love.

While going from Jericho to Jerusalem, two blind men pleaded with Jesus to help them regain their sight. In compassion He restored them. The wonderful ending to this incident was that after their healing, "they followed Jesus." There are patients who were treated at the Kissy UMC Eye Hospital who received not only physical sight, but spiritual insight into the love of God as revealed in Jesus Christ.

Part III: A World to Serve

For God so loved the world that he gave his one and only Son,
that whoever believes in him shall not perish but have eternal life.

– John 3:16

Chapter Sixty-One

Penniless at Forty-Six

Our children? They never knew.

They realized that other children often had nicer clothes, more toys and extra spending money, but as adults they are adamant that they have no terrifying memories of our being poor (cashed strapped). Ruth and I always dwelt on how rich we were spiritually – and the mission-provided housing and travel funds allowed us to live far better financially than the people among whom we served.

However, stretching a rubber band just goes so far.

Ruth had once supported her mother and two sisters on $45 a month as a secretary for five years. In 1967, she was managing a family of six children who needed food, clothes, school supplies, swimming lessons, etc. The children and I have no memories of going to bed hungry at night. I hope that was true also for Ruth.

Tim and Mary had secured some scholarship assistance to attend Westmar College. Beth was to begin college training. Our missionary salary support ranged from $2,800 in 1952 to $8,000 in 1967. The rubber band was breaking. We were annually granted a leave of absence. An ophthalmologist's salary for five years at the Quain and Ramstad Clinic in Bismarck, North Dakota, stabilized our finances and met our needs.

Our home in Bismarck, North Dakota.

The interlude at Bismarck was a definitive time. We had the pleasure of building our first dream home. The eye practice with Quain and Ramstad Clinic was busy and rewarding. Cryotherapy, the use of freezing carbon dioxide, came into its own for cataract removal and retinal therapy.

Corneal grafting became possible, as American patients accepted tissue from a deceased person, which was not the case in Africa. The first procedure I performed was done on a patient who followed me from the Veterans Hospital in Minneapolis. The donor, sadly, was a high school senior who when playing basketball had jumped for the ball and then collapsed on the floor. His parents were anxious to donate his corneas so a living person might benefit from his short life.

I also took some time away from the clinic to complete the examinations that qualified me to become a Diplomat of the American Board of Ophthalmology.

Ruth was in demand as a missionary speaker in North Dakota as well as neighboring states. She had the pleasure of organizing Bible study groups. She was able to participate in the lives of our six children since no patients waited for her services, as was her role in the clinics in Africa.

During our time in Bismarck, Tim began medical school. Mary and Steve Boehlke were married as well as Beth and Bob Hopkins. John and Paul attended Seattle Pacific University; they had enjoyed soccer as children in Africa and played the game well in the U.S. Andrew developed a love for hockey.

I finally agreed to surgical intervention for my back problems. The day after surgery the head neurosurgeon at the University of Minnesota gave me the sad news that no improvement could be expected. The fact that I could still walk was comforting, as a colleague in Sierra Leone had his back surgery done in London and was never able to walk again.

In 1972, we could no longer resist the leading of the Holy Spirit to return to Africa. We had been reminded by our African friends how great the need was for a trained eye surgeon. We sold our house, paid off the mortgage and set sail for Africa.

When we returned to Sierra Leone (from 1972 to 1975), we established an eye program in Bo. It was one of the most thrilling times of our missionary career. Bo is the second largest city in Sierra Leone, and at that time had air service so patients as far away as Freetown (about 110 miles) flew in for eye care and surgery. (The distance was nearly double by road and often more difficult in the rainy season.) We enjoyed the support of other missionaries stationed in Bo. We had the luxury of Dr. Justin and Marge Sleight volunteering their services for an entire year. Our children were in post-graduate training or college. Our youngest, Andrew, was in high school at Hillcrest, Jos, Nigeria. But… Ultimately, our finances gave out. At age fifty-five, I had to face reality – we were broke again.

It was not easy to resign as missionaries – it was our life's calling. We found a hospital in Alexandria, Minnesota, the Douglas Country Hospital (one of the

100 best hospitals in the United States) that had been unsuccessful in recruiting an ophthalmologist. On assessing the situation, other candidates did not believe this small rural community could support a specialist. One remarked: "I would also have to take in washing." To further encourage our coming to Alexandria, the hospital was willing to allow Ruth and me to return to Africa three months each year to carry on volunteer missionary services. They even provided space in the hospital for our practice.

The secretary of the hospital's administrator scheduled eye appointments during the summer of 1975 while I completed deputation work for the General Board of Global Ministries. We had a filled schedule from day one of general and surgical patients. While we ministered in Sierra Leone during January, February, and March, cataract patients went to warmer climes as "snow birds." When they and we returned in April, about two months of scheduled surgeries were met. Their willingness to wait for our return was due in great part to having intraocular lenses inserted after cataract extraction. Mayo and the University of Minnesota still did not accept this practice in those early years. For a time, Alexandria was the place to have immediate sight following eye surgery.

The three months spent each year in Sierra Leone prompted a great response. Eye care was done at the Government Connaught Hospital in Lunsar and at the Urban Centre in Freetown. The Sierra Leone Annual Conference suggested an expanded program. They arranged for architectural planning for a facility at the

Volunteer builders of the Kissy UMC Eye Hospital.

Mango Brown mission compound at Kissy. The GBGM approved $75,000 for the Kissy UMC Eye Hospital. Money from interested people and churches – including ophthalmologists in the U.S. – provided the additional funding. Forty board certified ophthalmologists volunteered their services between one to three months for more than a decade following the dedication of the Kissy UMC Eye Hospital in January 1984.

Our practice in Alexandria met our financial needs. We felt we were still "missionaries" for the subsequent thirty-five years.

Kissy UMC Eye Hospital under construction.

Chapter Sixty-Two

Official Missionary Retirement

In the early summer of 1975 we completed three years of missionary service at Bo and officially resigned from being commissioned missionaries of the United Methodist Church. Our staff was transferred to Lunsar where the Baptist church was beginning an eye care clinic. The building in which we had conducted our work in Bo was returned to the Sierra Leone Annual Conference. The equipment – including the operating microscope, Haag Streit slit lamp, sterilizer, and instruments – was stored at the urban center for use during the months of January, February and March in the succeeding years.

Beginning in January of 1977, Ruth and I returned each year to perform eye surgery at various places in Freetown, including the Urban Center in Lunsar, Kissy Maternity Hospital and even King Memorial United Methodist Church. In 1982, construction on the Kissy UMC Eye Hospital began; it was dedicated in January 1984. Christian Blind Mission assisted us in our program by appointing Dr. Richard Lockwood in 1992 to serve as a fulltime ophthalmologist. Dr. Nick Cook followed him in 1993. During their tours of service, Dr. Ainor Fergusson, a Sierra Leonean with eye training, became a permanent member of the staff. The ten-year civil war stopped the visits of the volunteer eye surgeons, but Ruth and I continued to help Dr. Fergusson, who eventually had to flee for his life.

Dr. Ainor and Mrs. (Cassandra) Fergusson faithfully served at Kissy UMC Eye Hospital for fifteen years.

During the civil war in Sierra Leone, the hospital was heavily damaged. Rocket propelled grenades were used to access the building through doors and windows. Instead of having the doors blown apart, I left them open and bravely attempted to minister to those who were wounded. While I was there, each group gave ground so that one time we cared for the rebels, another time for government forces.

I remember one patient who was brought in with his face and body in shreds. A grenade had exploded in his hand, which he had held near his upper body. Some of his fingers had been blown off and one eye was destroyed. The other eye was cut, but since he was alive, we took him into surgery to try to save some of his sight. We noticed his face, neck and chest had many wounds, but miraculously no vital organ had been penetrated. The patient lived and was blessed with sight in his remaining eye.

It was a thing of wonder that the opposing sides did not attempt to loot or destroy the hospital. Gunfire damage amounted to $120,000. The Minnesota UMC Annual Conference covered this $120,000 and the hospital was restored. (Bishop John Hopkins had challenged the eight hundred Conference members by giving each of them five dollars and then asked what they could do to earn more. The next year $120,000 was returned, the exact amount needed to restore the hospital.)

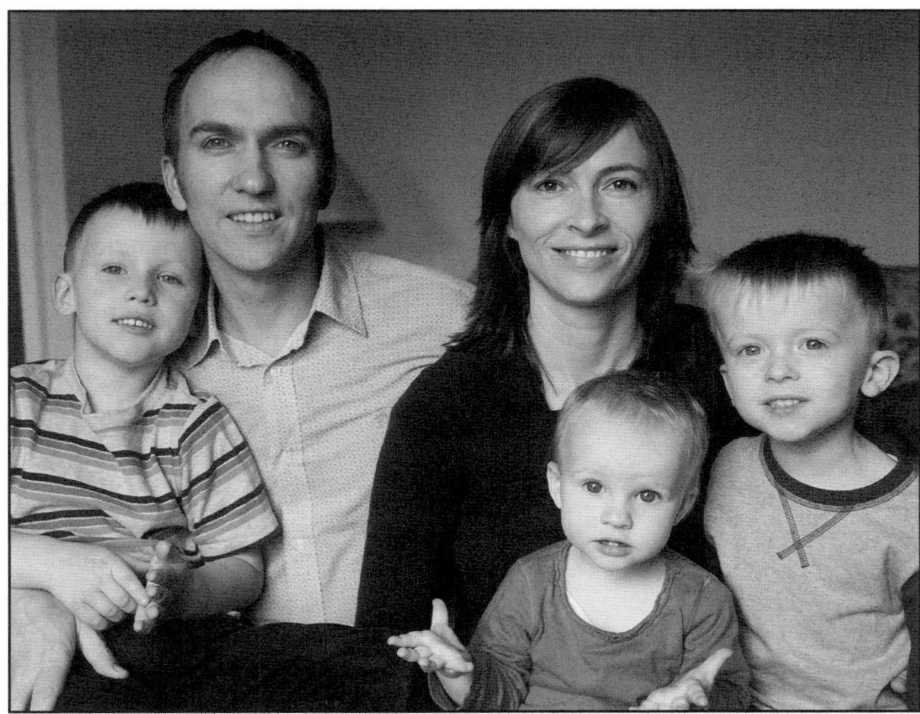

Dr. John Buchan, his wife Anne, and children Calum, Zoe and Josiah, will be at Kissy until 2013.

The hospital program was restarted, but did not resume its position of excellence as had been known prior to the war. Dr. Fergusson died from a fatal heart attack in 2007. Volunteer ophthalmologists were no longer willing to come to Sierra Leone because of reports of atrocities. Only Dr. Kiru, an outstanding eye surgeon from Canada, came to help with his wife, as well as Dr. Bill Wilson, who had formally worked at Lunsar, and Dr. Giselle Baghy of Hungary, an outstanding ophthalmologist who had served with Dr. Kiru at Kano, Nigeria.

Through the intervention of Dr. Allen Foster, president of Christian Blind Mission, Dr. John Buchan signed up for a four-year term of service beginning in mid 2009. The hospital is now making huge strides in meeting the eye needs of Sierra Leone.

Chapter Sixty-Three

Home in Minnesota

In 1975 when we arrived home in Minnesota, the Vietnam War had just ended. We had made tentative arrangements to have an office in Bloomington, Minnesota. When I saw it was next door to Dr. David Chizek, a very busy and popular ophthalmologist, I was not prepared to compete with someone of his stature. We needed to look elsewhere for a location. (Dr. Chizek later became a generous benefactor of our mission work, donating an operating microscope, phaco machines, medicines and supplies.)

Ruth and I visited possible places in Minnesota to open our practice, starting with Faribault, which was near Nerstrand where my parents lived. However, an ophthalmologist from a nearby city covered the Faribault area. Looking at Northfield, we learned that they had just signed up with an ophthalmologist a month earlier. The situation in Apple Valley was not acceptable. Accompanied by son, Paul, a trip was made to the northern part of Minnesota, including Crookston, Grand Forks, Moorhead, Detroit Lakes and Alexandria.

While walking through Douglas County Hospital in Alexandria, we were met in the hallway by the administrator, Bill Flaig. We learned they hadn't been successful finding an ophthalmologist. When they knew that we were available, they made every concession possible. They arranged to have the administrator's secretary take appointments during the summer while I was completing deputation for the UMC. They provided office space by using part of the obstetrics section. By the time I finished my summer deputation for the General Board of Global Ministries, we had a full schedule of patients for examinations as well as surgeries.

Eventually, our office moved to larger quarters in the basement of the hospital next door to the Orthopedic Department. At that time our son Tim, who began his ophthalmology practice in 1978, joined us. A year later, I purchased and remodeled a house next to the hospital, which made an excellent clinic. Tim built a new facility next to us and covered for Ruth and me during the many periods that followed when we returned each year to Sierra Leone.

Alexandria. On arriving in Alexandria we needed to purchase a home but found that our assets amounted to only $1,700. I spent $1,500 of that to secure certification so we could implant intraocular lenses. That meant that our remaining assets were $200. We consulted the president of the Savings & Loan regarding a mortgage loan. Unfortunately, we had no money for a down payment. When the president knew of our situation, he did something he had never done before. He authorized a mortgage for us without a down payment. Apparently because we were returning missionaries and I had good potential earning power as an ophthalmologist, he took a risk. We did not disappoint him. Within a year, we made arrangements to purchase another house across the street from our clinic at 111 15th Avenue East.

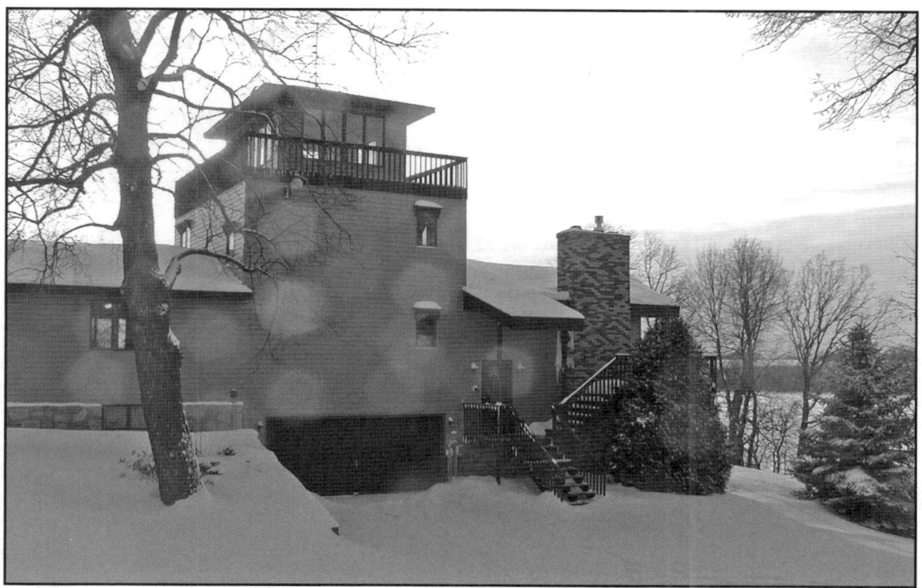

Our home on Lake Burgen, Alexandria.

Eight years later in 1983, Ruth realized her dream home that we built on the east shore of Lake Burgen. We had purchased this lot from our son, John, who was building his own home on the lot next door. The building of this new house knew many strange inconsistencies. We had neglected to get a permit to build the house. Somehow, the builder had not thought about it either. And when the house was up, it was found to be too high according to code, as it was in the general area of the Alexandria Airport. Fortunately, the lot next door was available for sale and the inspectors helped us by suggesting that we move some ground from the next-door lot to build up a higher point alongside our house so the house would be "shorter" and satisfy the code. Also, it enabled us to build another garage in the future so that there was a happy ending to a very confusing story.

The fifteen years of active practice were a joy. The practice prospered and the Eye Research and Development we conducted was exciting – there was success with new models of intraocular lenses. We received 100% accreditation from the oversight committee.

On one occasion, the chairman of the surgical committee of Douglas County Hospital came upon an article in medical economics telling of an elderly surgeon who wouldn't stop doing surgery even though he no longer was effective and had to be bailed out by younger surgeons on occasion. Investigation of the ages of the surgeons at Douglas County Hospital revealed that I would be seventy years old my next birthday. A committee was formed to meet to deal with age qualifications.

I could not envision myself appearing before a committee of my peers who would decide whether or not I was capable of doing eye surgery when these were the years of incredible development of intraocular lenses and the expertise of how they were used – all of which I was pioneering. Talking it over with Ruth, we decided that as of midnight December 31, 1989, I would resign from the Douglas County Hospital. Within two weeks, Ruth and I were back in Africa enjoying complete freedom as volunteers.

We began to receive invitations from other countries, a total of fourteen, which included Sierra Leone, Uganda, Nigeria, Kenya, Zambia, Zimbabwe, Malawi, Mozambique, Haiti, Honduras, Bolivia, Vietnam, China and Mongolia. What these countries wanted was an ophthalmologist to teach them how to implant intraocular lenses following the extraction of cataracts. What followed was one of the most enjoyable periods of my life, marred only by Ruth' stroke in 1993 while returning from a volunteer trip to Africa.

The fifteen years of active ophthalmological practice in Alexandria and the succeeding years of volunteer surgery were an absolute delight. We enjoyed every aspect of the practice as well as the community of Alexandria.

Chapter Sixty-Four

Intraocular Lenses

We had been under appointment to the General Board of Global Ministries from 1952 to 1975. I was fifty-five years of age. We had no financial assets. Three of our six children were in graduate school. An annual missionary's salary of less than $10,000 was inadequate to meet our needs. It was necessary to establish a private ophthalmological practice. The opportunity was found in Alexandria.

Starting a new practice, I was concerned patients might be skeptical of the skills of an aging missionary and feel, perhaps, I was not adequate for modern medicine after having been in deepest Africa for more than twenty years.

I needed to prove I was a bona fide eye surgeon. That opportunity came on my 1976 return visit to Africa with a layover in London. I had developed a friendship with Mr. Peter Choyce of England over the years. During my layover, he invited me into his home. In surgery with him, I had hands-on experience as he deftly placed anterior chamber intraocular lenses after extracting intracapsular cataracts. He was exceptionally skilled at it, as he had developed a procedure over time that was safe and effective. He had chronicled the do's and don'ts of this new modality as he had assisted Mr. Harold Ridley as a resident during the first history-making intraocular lens implantation in England in 1949.

Mr. Ridley had noted that PMM (polymethlmethacrylate), a plastic, was an inert material. Fragments of this plastic from exploding canopies struck by anti-aircraft fire had been observed in the eyes of flight navigators of the Royal Air Force. The canopies had been fashioned with PMM. Consequently, he asked Raynor, an optical house, to fashion some artificial lenses of various strengths and began inserting them into patients' eyes following cataract extraction. The era of intraocular lens implantation had begun with vigor.

Mr. Choyce gave me fifteen intraocular lenses that I took back to Alexandria. To qualify to perform intraocular lens implantation, I attended workshops both in California and in Florida. I hung up the framed certificates and on February 16, 1977, I did my first Choyce anterior chamber intraocular lens implantation.

The drama surrounding this occasion was almost as stressful as my 1952 first general surgery in Nigeria and my 1958 first eye surgery at Rotifunk. Mrs. Annie Halvorson wanted to have vision restored in her right eye. She had been legally blind for several years. Her blurred left eye prevented her from reading road signs. We mentioned to her the availability of a lens that could be put inside her eye following removal of her cataract. The advantage was that it would still allow her to use her better left eye along with the operated eye. The standard operative technique required a thick lens in her glasses, which did not allow for a balanced use of vision between the operated and unoperated eye. She would have to use only her right eye to avoid double vision.

The advantage of the IOL appealed to Mrs. Halvorson, and she elected to go with it even though I explained I had never done it before. She asked, "Do you think it will work?" I answered, "Yes."

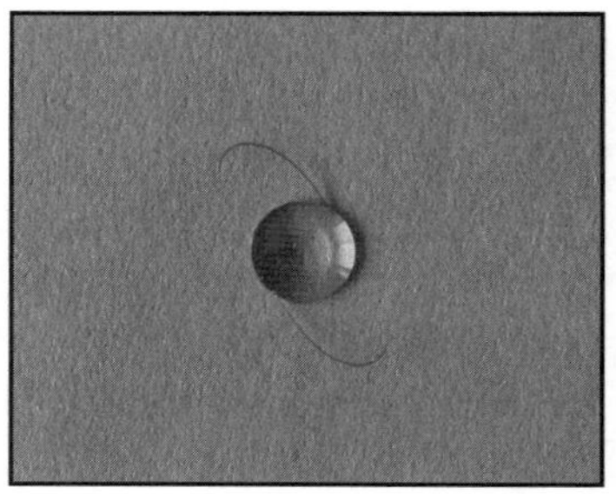

The most common type of intraocular lens in the years when they became acceptable.

An Alpha-Omega intraocular lens.

Mrs. Halvorson was the first of more than 17,000 IOL patients I was able to help. The outcome of her surgery? A delighted patient, a delighted surgeon!

Patient satisfaction spread like wildfire. Through word of mouth, prospective patients learned from former patients where intraocular lens implantation was available. Patients came from Minneapolis and St. Paul as well as some from states surrounding Minnesota. The intraocular lens age had definitely begun.

I was not the only ophthalmologist befriended by Mr. Peter Choyce. Dr. Thomas Ellingson visited Mr. Choyce at "South End on the Sea"; through his subsequent busy and successful practice, the opthalmological world was alerted about UGH (uveitis glaucoma hemorrhage) syndrome. Dr. Richard Horns also visited Mr. Choyce. Dr. Malcolm McCannel utilized implants other than Choyce's Mark VIII and contributed the famous "McCannel suture" for IOL stability.

During a relatively short period of time, Tim and I successfully placed more than 150 anterior chamber lenses in patients in Alexandria. While a significant number of early lenses needed to be removed by other surgeons, we were spared that complication.

In those early days, there was significant resistance and disapproval of the use of IOLs in the medical community. Doctors who used them were referred to as "dangerous buccaneers." Since we were hidden away in the "boondocks," it was almost a year before the University of Minnesota's Department of Ophthalmology learned that IOLs were being implanted at the Gess Eye Clinic in Alexandria. In 1978, Dr. Richard Lindstrom, chief eye resident at the university's eye department, invited me to describe my experiences with the first 150 lens implantations. It was a humbling experience to address my peers who had been immersed in the best eye care for more than twenty years while I was off in Africa – and then to be the one to describe the newest procedure available.

The pre-eminence of the anterior chamber IOL was not to last indefinitely, even though ophthalmologists appreciated them since they were able to continue with their intracapsular extraction technique.

Led by Mr. John Pearce of Bromegrove, Warwickshire, England, ophthalmologists began to see the value of extracapsular cataract extraction, first performed by Mr. Harold Ridley in 1949. Dr. James Gills and Dr. Robert Welch were sensitive to this new emphasis and conducted training periods for the removal of lens and cortical material. I was fortunate to be one of their early pupils and later have one-on-one training with Mr. John Pearce himself. Mr. Pearce graciously invited me to stay in his home and to participate in his surgery. He described the benefits of having the IOL placed in the posterior chamber rather than the anterior chamber. He emphasized that this was what nature intended. What he was actually saying was that the lens should be placed where God had originally placed the natural lens of the eye.

My first posterior lens implantation was on December 4, 1979. From that moment on, I chose to place the IOL in the posterior chamber following an extracapsular cataract extraction. In subsequent years, I was invited to a number of countries to teach and demonstrate this technique.

It was inevitable that this procedure was eventually performed in Sierra Leone. Previously, patients had been fitted with +10 heavy aphakic glasses. In time they were lost, broken or stolen. Placing a refractive lens inside the eye provided excellent vision without glasses. Acceptance in Africa of this new method was again slow in coming. Within seven years Christian Blind Mission, a funding partner of the Kissy UMC Eye Hospital, realized its merits and offered financial help in providing intraocular lenses, viscoelastic and instrumentation for inserting intraocular lenses in more than 100 countries where they supported eye centers.

In a telephone conversation I had with Dr. Jerry Herrell on November 10, 2010, we re-visited the early days of our participation with Christian Blind Mission. Dr. Joe Taylor, who guided the eye care of Christian Blind Mission, had taken a firm stance against the placement of IOLs. Christian Blind Mission's medical consultant, Dr. Allen Foster (now president of Christian Blind Mission), an ophthalmologist who had served in Tanzania, however, had been interested in the results of our IOL patients in Freetown. Unlike Dr. Taylor, he offered reserved encouragement. Dr. Taylor continued to do eye surgery and on one occasion when he did a volunteer surgical outreach in Nigeria at Bambur and Zing, he came across some of my IOL patients. He wrote me a letter asking if I could overlook his early objection to the use of IOLs at Kissy in Freetown. Few other letters have ever brought tears to my eyes.

Dr. Allen Foster

Chapter Sixty-Five

Patent

With the experience gained by my association with Mr. Peter Choyce for anterior chamber lenses and Mr. John Pearce for posterior chamber lenses, I was in a unique position that interested optical companies in the United States. Precision Cosmet of Minneapolis was pioneering a good portion of intraocular lens research within their sophisticated facilities. They worked with Dr. Jerald Tennant, whose angled modification of Mr. Choyce's Mark VIII anterior chamber lens, alleviated pupilary block syndrome that plagued early designs. Precision Cosmet specialists, Mr. Noel Bissonette and Mr. Charles Gay, were knowledgeable about design, testing and manufacturing.

Of the five models I drew up for fabrication, three were used in a series of patients – two were anterior chamber lenses while the third, called the Alpha Omega lens, could be used either as an anterior or posterior chamber lens. The use of these lenses was closely controlled by strict guidelines and local hospital surgical committee surveillance. Members of the committee included medical and surgical doctors, as well as a hospital administrator, a lawyer and a clergyman from the community. Successful results continued, making the committee no longer necessary. My son, Tim, a phacoemulsification specialist also doing surgery at the Douglas County Hospital, was extremely successful with this procedure, producing consistently higher results with a greater numbers of cases. He was to remain the only "phaco" surgeon in North Central and Western Minnesota for nearly a decade.

With the success of the new IOL designs, I was encouraged to pursue a patent. A lawyer was engaged. As with many legal affairs, the process was slow. Ultimately, the drawings and descriptions were sent in late spring 1983 to another lawyer in Washington, D.C. who specialized in patents. The letter lanquished on his desk throughout the summer while he was on vacation.

Meanwhile, outstanding ophthalmologist Dr. Charles Kelman and his "bank" of lawyers presented a similar design in mid-summer. It was actively processed.

When my application was received at the patent office, a letter was written informing me that my patent application infringed on the recently accepted Kelman lens. It is of great satisfaction to note that Dr. Kelman's lens has true character and is being used on occasion to this very day.

Another model of mine was accepted – No. 4,409,690 on October 18, 1983, signed by Mr. M. C. Henry. It never was developed beyond the original series of patients in which it was successfully used, as Precision Cosmet was taken over by

IOLab and only a handful of the many models produced by Precision Cosmet were continued.

Nevertheless, I am a patent holder. It is unlikely that this achievement has ever impressed anyone. Only my loyal wife and the cleaning lady have ever viewed the license certificate hanging in my office.

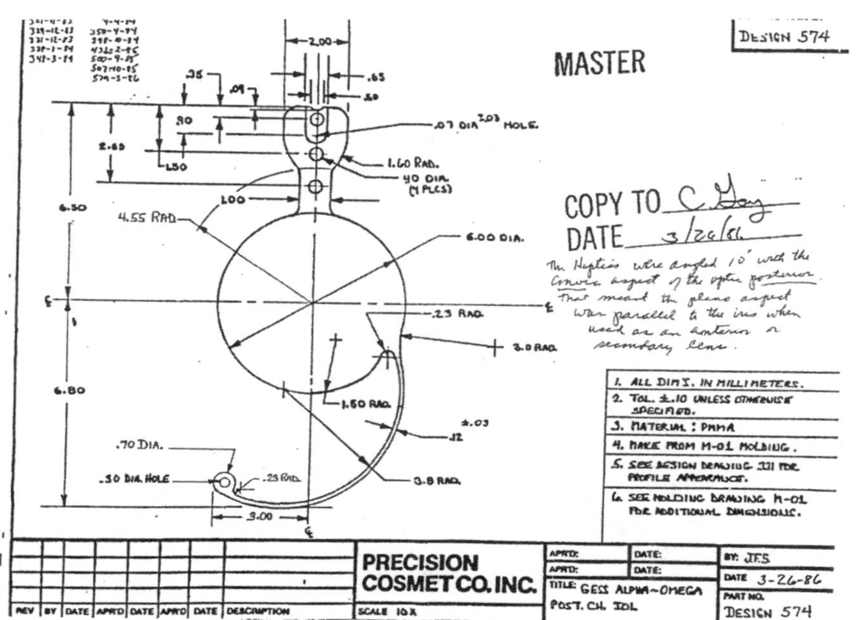

[1] **The Alpha-Omega IOL.** The haptics are angled 10 degrees with the convex aspect of the optic posteriorly when used as a posterior chamber lens. When used as an anterior chamber IOL or as a secondary lens, it is flipped over with the plano surface of the optic parallel with the iris (the convex portion then being anterior). Scleral fixation is secured by utilizing a small hole recessed in the solid haptic. The end of a 10-0 prolene suture is threaded through the hole. The heat of a cautery causes the end of the suture to shrivel up into a smooth, round ball which cannot be pulled back through the hole. The needle on the other end of the suture is passed through the ciliary body (several red cells on one occasion in 303 cases), and buried in the sclera under a flap or by passing the suture horizontally half the thickness of the sclera and then bringing cautery to the suture's end forming a smooth, round ball which prevents it from being pulled back into the eye. The ALPHA-OMEGA lens was used successfully both anteriorly and posteriorly. The series which used 10-0 prolene fixation for posterior IOLs also was without complications when placement was in the capsular bag.

Chapter Sixty-Six

Following God's Path

It was the fall of 1989. On my next birthday I would be in my seventieth year. A prominent doctor on the surgical committee at Douglas County Hospital happened upon an article in Medical Economics describing a difficult situation in which an elderly surgeon, past his prime, needed to be rescued from poor decisions and performances. He refused to give up his practice or his hospital privileges.

It seemed wise to review the ages of staff doctors at the Douglas County Hospital and have a special meeting to prevent such a tragic situation developing in Alexandria.

Ruth and I were stunned. Was the Lord telling us something? Should we shift our practice to Sierra Leone where there was no completely trained ophthalmologist? Along with primary surgery we could also teach and upgrade other doctors in the underserved world.

The next day we drafted a letter of resignation and made preparations to close our practice as of midnight December 31, 1989. We made a presentation of more than 25,000 charts to our sons, Timothy, an ophthalmologist, and John, an optometrist.

Following our resignation from the Douglas County Hospital surgical staff, Ruth and I needed to appraise the challenges for the future that were inherent in doing volunteer eye surgery in other needy places of the world. The first consideration was the expense of travel and supplies, even though pharmaceutical and optical houses were generous in providing needed items. Secondly, adjustments had to be made to new time zones, which is enervating and tiring. Weeks are needed to get back to a normal sleep pattern. Thirdly, risks are involved. At a moment's notice the country in which one is serving may develop political instability with its inherent dangers. There are tropical diseases to consider, chief among them malaria, which is still the world's greatest killer. And finally the world's AIDS epidemic is a constant threat. In Africa there are more than twenty-two million people with HIV, the virus that leads to AIDS, compared to 1.5 million Americans with HIV. AIDS deaths have orphaned 13.5 million African children, as noted in *World Magazine*, September 9, 2000.

Suffering tugged at the heart of Jesus. He healed all manner of diseases and disabilities. My commitment to Jesus Christ prompts me to walk in his steps, to do the things that he did, and to teach the things that he taught. The plight of a blind person was of great concern, rousing a compassion ("sorry heart") that energized me to ask, "Need this be?" To be blind, when prevention or cure existed, was unthinkable.

Recent statistics number seven billion people in the world today of whom forty million are blind. Eighty percent of these live in poverty-stricken areas of Africa, Asia and Latin America. Christian Blind Mission indicates that seventy-five percent of these could have been rescued with preventive and curative care. It is hard to believe many millions suffer from trachoma, the "Egyptian eye disease." Twenty million are infected with onchocerciasis, known as "river blindness." One hundred thousand small children lose their eyesight each year because of Vitamin A deficiency. Measles takes a dreadful toll.

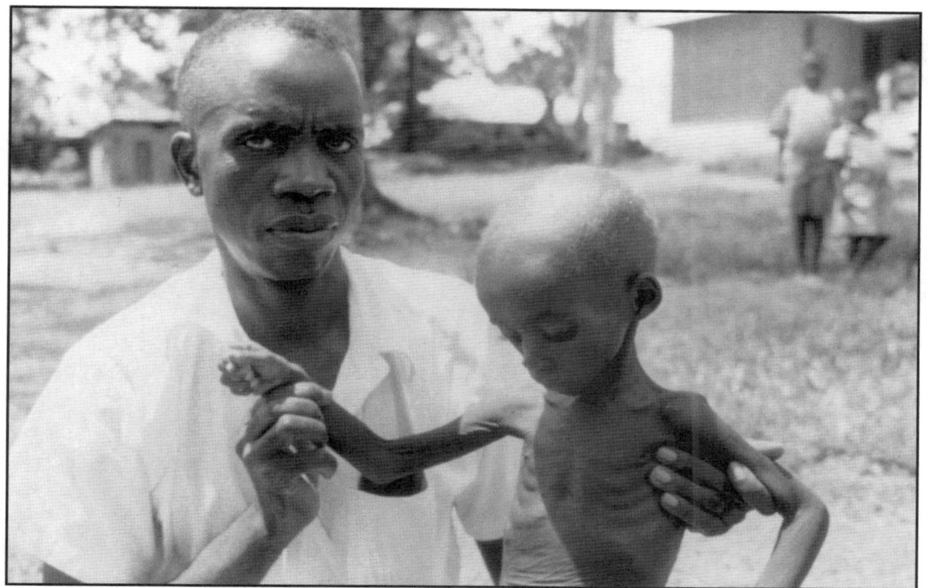

Taiama senior dispensing nurse, Abraham Lavaly, with a child afflicted with kwashiorkor.

We ask about the causes. Malnutrition and poor hygiene aggravated by lack of clean water stand at the top of the list. There is insufficient education and lack of medication. And finally there are shortages of eye doctors, eye hospitals and instrumentation. Consequently, there are vast areas in Asia where one out of four people is blind and one out of two people suffer from an eye disease. There are many villages in West Africa where up to fifty percent of the adults are blind because of the complications of onchocerciasis. The happy ending to this story is that a cure has been found. The pharmaceutical company, Merck, Sharp and Dohme has made available ivermectin, also known as mectizan, to the World Health Organization for free distribution to countries needing it. This wonder drug has protected millions of people from the threat of blindness.

Africa's size, which is two and a half times larger than the United States and has one billion people speaking more than 1,000 different languages, has special difficulties in reaching the curably blind. Only one in ten people in Africa who are blind from cataracts ever undergo corrective surgery. Africa has only five hundred ophthalmologists in fifty-six countries. In contrast, the U.S. has 15,000 ophthalmologists for an area less than half the size of Africa.

It is understandable, then, that a retired ophthalmologist still healthy and willing to serve should seize the opportunity to be a blessing. No other answer would do than – "Here I am, Lord, send me."

Chapter Sixty-Seven

1990: Medical "Retirement"

January 1, 1990, was like any other winter day except that I did not need to go to the office. Official retirement had taken place at midnight December 31, 1989. By January 11, Ruth and I were back in our beloved Sierra Leone. One of the first persons we met was Mr. Joe Skasko, a policeman from Pennsylvania. He had a love and concern for orphans and their care at Pa Loko. His interest in Sierra Leone continued to grow over the years. He became a personal friend of the Sierra Leonean ambassador to the United States, Mr. John Leigh. He went so far as to make a special trip to Sierra Leone to bring back a young person needing advanced surgery, and while there made arrangements for arrival of a forty-foot container he had packed at the St. James Presbyterian Church in Mechanicsburg, Pennsylvania. It contained a wealth of supplies for the care of orphans, as well as medicines and surgical equipment for the Kissy Health and Maternity Centre and Kissy UMC Eye Hospital.

Following the cataract extraction and intraocular lens implantation of Mrs. Regina Bangura, wife of Bishop T. S. Bangura, I will always remember the statement she made as she left the hospital. It was "'Fraid for nothing," as she strode out the clinic door.

Memorable also was the audience with President Momoh that Rev. Eustace Renner arranged for Ruth and me. It was a friendly visit during which he expressed an appreciation for the Kissy UMC Eye Hospital. It was apparent his brother had undergone a cataract operation with IOL implantation a short time before and had briefed him on the hospital's ministry.

The most memorable occasion was attending the Rev. Angie Myles' church in Kossoh Town. She had invited the Rev. Moses Massaquoi to preach. He used Luke 18 and the account of the blind man. I was given the privilege of conducting the baptismal service. A fifteen-year-old young lady presented herself after accepting Jesus Christ as her Lord and Savior. Some consternation had been involved in this because all her people were Muslim. Yet, her decision was final. At the baptismal service she was asked to give a testimony. It consisted of her singing, beautifully, "I Have Decided to Follow Jesus."

Angie Myles with family members.

Angie Myles was always helpful to people in difficult situations and at one time was in charge of a large group of orphans cared for by the Swedish United Methodist Church working at Pa Loko in Sierra Leone. Presently, she is country director in Sierra Leone for Children of the Nations, which provides responsible care to orphaned and destitute children. This is done by equipping the nationals and giving the children every possible advantage available to grow in a stable, Christ-centered environment, empowering them to be the leaders of tomorrow.

Chapter Sixty-Eight

A World to Serve

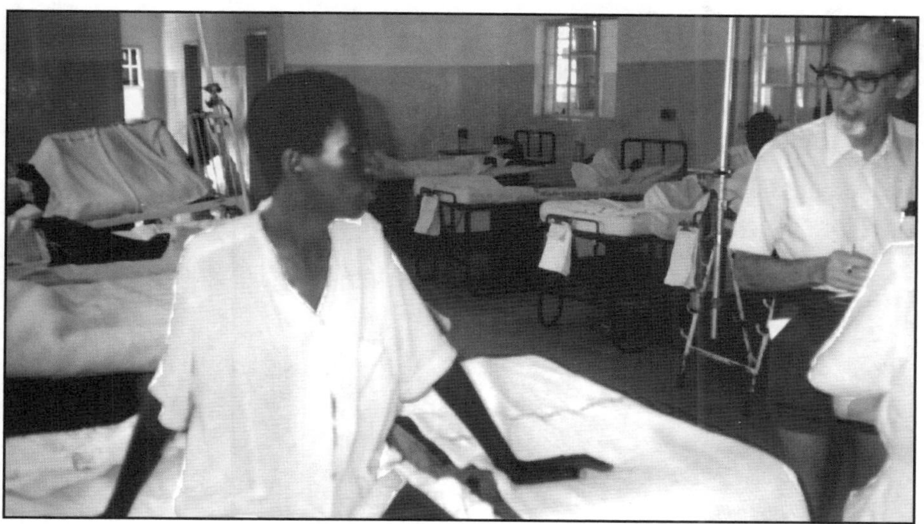

Dr. James Foulkes (far right) giving compassionate care to an AIDS patient in Zambia.

While we were performing eye surgeries at Kissy in January of 1990, we had important visitors, Jim and Martha Foulkes. Jim was an old friend from general surgery residency days. He went to Zambia while we went to Nigeria and then Sierra Leone. The visit in 1990 was for him to learn how to do some eye procedures. His work at Mukinge Mission Hospital in Zambia had blind patients and no one to care for them. During the two weeks he was at Kissy, he took careful notes, performed some minor procedures and then returned to Zambia. There, he had further training and eventually established an eye ministry. During his visit, he invited me to come and help him. Being free, I took him up on the invitation while Ruth decided to return home to Alexandria. It was a very fruitful time at Mukinge and before I left Jim was doing very well at the slit lamp and with some eye procedures.

Later on in 1990, I was invited to come to the Maua Methodist Hospital in Kenya. They had volunteer ophthalmologists coming from time to time and were always inviting whoever might be available. Ruth joined me in this visit and it was a very fruitful one of two weeks. We had to cross the equator in order to get to the Maua Hospital, and on occasion we had to stop our car to let elephants or other wild animals cross the road in front of us. A plus to the visit to Maua was visiting the Maru National Park. We couldn't believe the wild life that we saw.

Almost immediately upon entering the park, we came upon a group of cheetah, which are very rare to see. Other animals included zebra, waterbucks, giraffes, wart hogs, gazelles, ostriches, kudu, impala and more than one buffalo in one menacing herd.

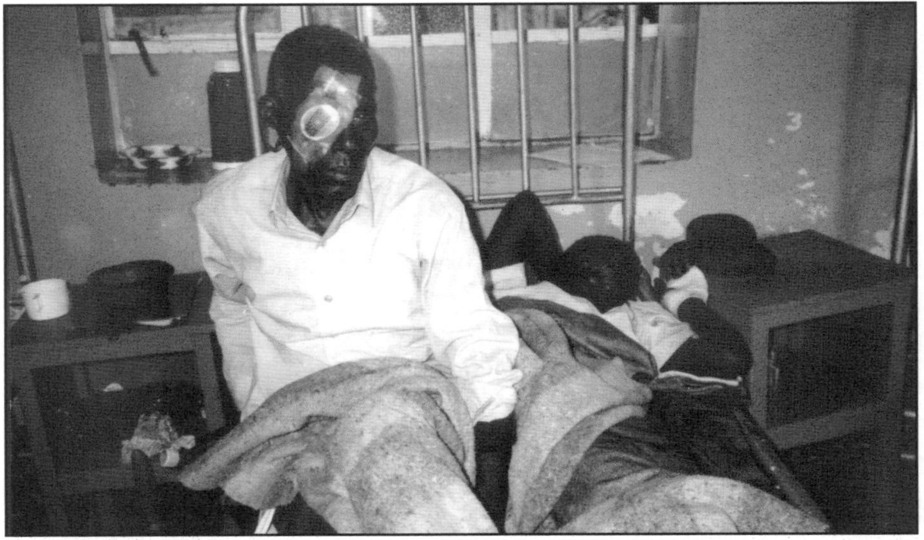

Two patients – one bed. Maua, Kenya.

An unusual feature of conducting eye surgery at Maua in Kenya was its cool weather due to elevation. On visiting the wards, we often saw two people in one single bed, not only because they were so filled up, but also because the patients felt warmer with a partner.

Before leaving Kenya, we also visited the Lighthouse for Christ in Mombasa. Dr. Dean Larson and his wife Carol were there at the time. We stayed several days, impressed by the surgery that Dr. Larson performed.

Medical missionaries meeting at the Lighthouse for Christ in Mombasa, Kenya.

In 1991, I was invited to Cairo to present a paper on "Trabeculectomy with Iridencleisis." This was to be done at the International Eye Foundation, Society of Eye Surgeons, Fifth World Congress. Ruth did not accompany me, so I resolved not to go sightseeing to see the pyramids without my wife. Some years later it was possible for us to make the trip together, at which time we did see the wonderful archeological sites of Egypt.

Dr. Richard Lockwood with his wife, Lucinda, and their children.

Dr. Richard L. Lockwood arrived at Kissy with his family in January 1992. Christian Blind Mission generously underwrote their support. He was an excellent surgeon and Christian witness.

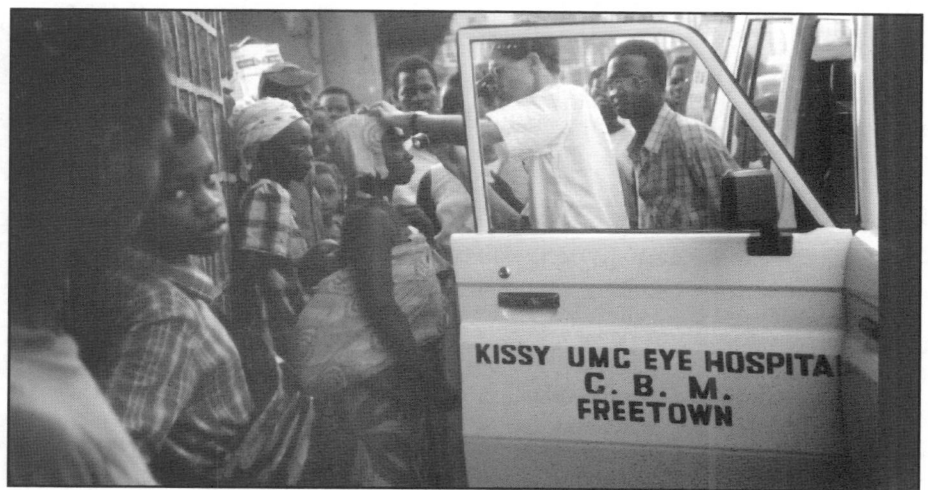

Dr. Cook examining a queue of beggars on Siaka Stevens Street.

Dr. Richard Cook and his family, also supported by Christian Blind Mission, served the two following years, doing a wonderful work. In spite of a heavy load of surgery and clinical duties, he completed projects such as examining the beggar population in Freetown. During this time, Sierra Leone was undergoing great political instability. Years later, Dr. Cook returned to do volunteer surgery at Kissy. With these two doctors at Kissy, I was able to respond to an invitation by Dr. Herb and Ruth Billman to help for several weeks at the Cape Coast Clinic in Ghana. They had the clinic well set up to include surgery. It was an enjoyable time of Christian fellowship.

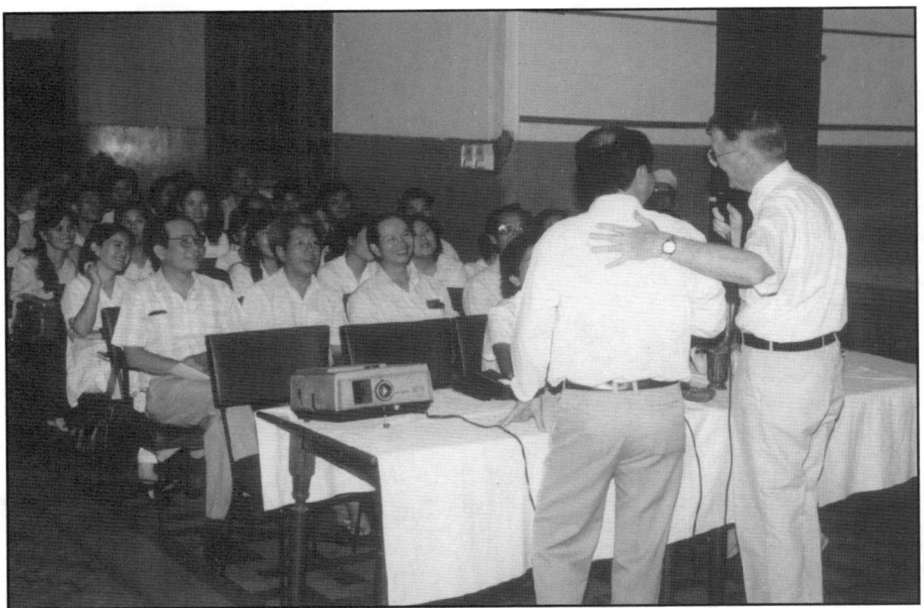

Sharing ophthalmological expertise in Ho Chi Minh City, Vietnam.

In 1993 the trip was to Vietnam, specifically to Ho Chi Minh City. Dr. Harry Brown of Surgical Eye Expeditions International had arranged the trip. My co-volunteer was Dr. George Biernbaum. Although this trip to Vietnam was brief compared to other trips I made, it was very productive as the twenty-seven ophthalmologists we were there to train were intent and learned almost immediately the various steps needed for intraocular lens implantation. Before we left, three of the doctors implanted their first intraocular lens.

Later in July, I received a invitation to help the eye surgery in Cape Haitian, Haiti. Dr. Hollis Clark and his wife, Wanda, had started the work at Cape Haitian. It was a very enjoyable time, although I felt my surgery was not as precise as I would have wished. I questioned whether or not the patients Dr. Clark had to deal with were more difficult than other patients in the world.

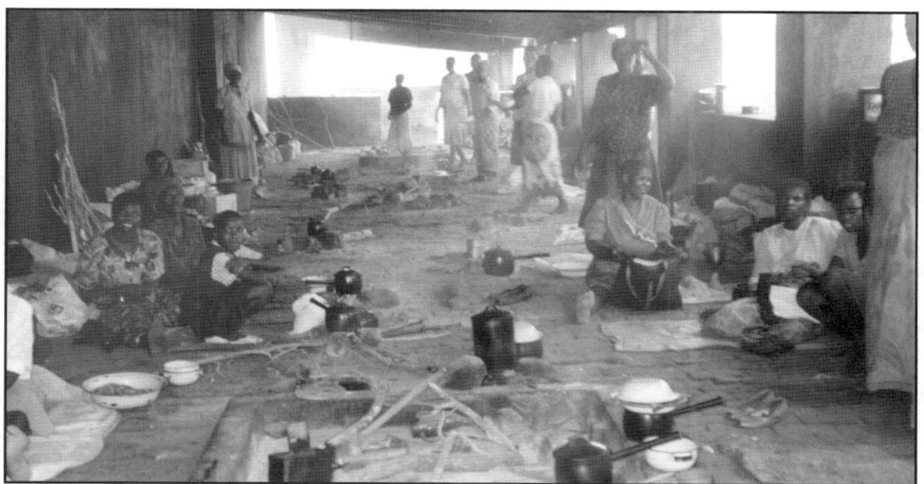

One of the African post-op wards.

In November, Ruth and I responded to an invitation to do eye surgery in Karande, Zimbabwe. It was here that Dr. Dan Stevens had a general surgery practice, but like our experience in Sierra Leone, he felt medical help should be given to the many blind in prison. Dr. Stevens was especially adept as a general surgeon, and within a week was able to perform eye surgery. It gave me great satisfaction to know yet again that a doctor would be able to help the blind – the totally blind – to see. An interesting note: Dr. Stevens' father was an ophthalmologist but did not do surgery. On subsequent visits to Karande, the son was able to teach the father how to do cataract extractions and implantation of intraocular lens.

Dr. J. Baasanhuu (in white) of Mongolia with S.E.E. team: (from left) Dr. Harry Brown, Mr. Wilfred Kline, Dr. James Standefer and Mr. Kelly Brown.

In 1994, the trip planned was a challenging one. Along with personnel from Surgical Eye Expedition International, we traveled to Outer Mongolia. The surgery we performed was at Ulaanbaatar, the capital of Mongolia that had a population of 500,000. The other 1.5 million in the country were scattered throughout, ranging from the lake country in the north to the Gobi Desert in the south. We were very warmly received in Mongolia and again taught a class of ophthalmologists how to implant intraocular lenses.

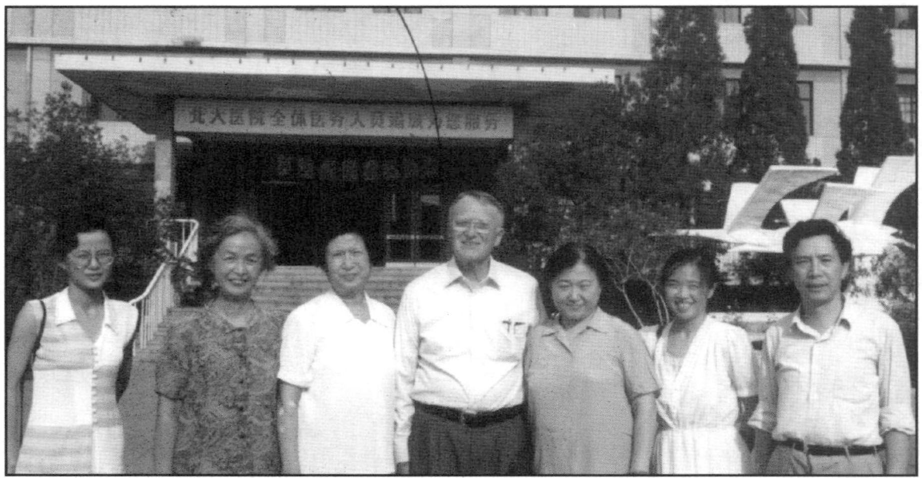

Flanked by six ophthalmologists from Beijing, China, in front of a large eye hospital.

Before returning home, we made a side trip to China. In Beijing, I had a wonderful experience of instructing and demonstrating the surgery and seeing the Great Wall of China.

Dr. and Mrs. Tendai Munyeza, Old Mutare Hospital, Zimbabwe.

In 1995, we made a trip to Zimbabwe where the United Methodist Church was involved in many ministries. Ruth and I were taken to the Old Mutare Hospital under the direction of Dr. and Mrs. Tendai Munyeza. It was very gratifying to help the many blind people in their area. Across the road from the hospital was the twenty million dollar Africa University. Today the university is serving the United Methodist Church by providing a full complement of university studies to those from many countries.

In 1995, we made a volunteer eye surgery to Abak, Nigeria. When we arrived, we were overwhelmed with the number of people in need there. (This experienced is elaborated upon in Chapter 77, "A Rugged Constitution.")

We also went to Chicuque, Mozambique in late 1995. The hospital was large, with only five doctors and a great need for ophthalmological services. There were so many people in need of eye surgery, we couldn't fit them all into our surgical schedule. I was determined then and there to return. I did return and was delighted my son Tim accompanied me on the second visit.

We visited Zing, Nigeria in 1996. Zing was dear to our hearts because we had visited this area more than forty years earlier.

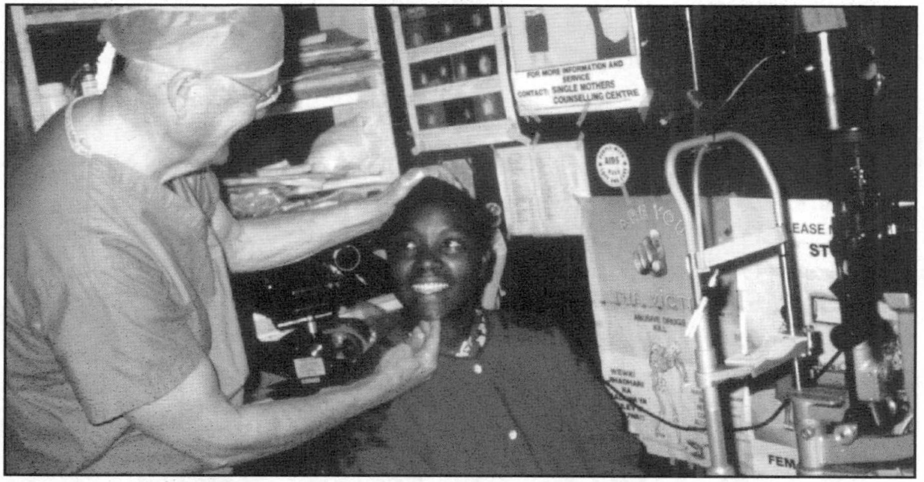

A sixteen-year-old girl who could finally go to school after cataract extraction and intraocular lens implantation.

In October 1996, I returned to Maua. They had more than thirty patients waiting for surgery, eight of whom were bilaterally blind, or totally blind. By the time our volunteer surgical ministry was completed, all thirty patients had intraocular lenses implanted. Especially noteworthy was one sixteen-year-old girl who had never been able to see to learn to read, but after the operation was gleeful and looking forward to attending school.

In 1997 another trip was made to Maua. On this visit, we delivered 210 pounds of medicines and supplies for their eye program. Again, more than thirty patients were operated on in a two-week period. On the first day of surgery, four totally blind patients were served; afterwards they were delighted to see, be productive and obtain a measure of dignity.

One of our surgical patients in Bolivia.

Later in 1997, I was invited to go to Cochabamba in Anzaldo, Bolivia. The cataract surgery at Kissy in Freetown was done at sea level; however, in Bolivia we conducted surgery at 8,000 feet. The elevation was apparent, as we walked more slowly on the way to the hospital each morning. Larry Acton, associated with the Oklahoma Conference, had arranged the trip. In the large group of twenty-eight volunteers were several nurses; the one assigned to me was so extremely efficient, she made my work such a pleasure. The purpose of this trip was to be God's special servants, to share Christ's love in ways that made a difference.

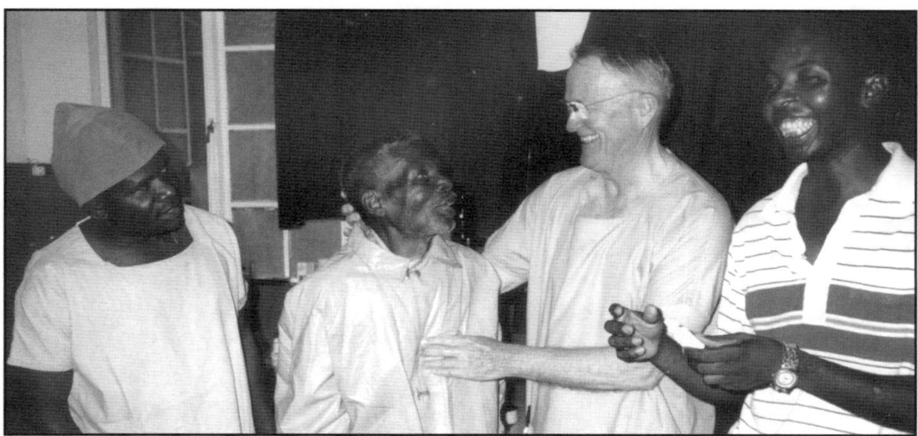

This dear man was surprised to see that his surgeon was a white man. Chicuque, Mozambique.

Three years earlier in September 1995, Ruth and I had made a trip to Mozambique. Now in 1998, I was accompanied by my ophthalmologist son, Tim. We arrived in Maputo and realized that we were in the midst of a very wet season. El Nino had struck. Cholera was rearing its ugly head in Maputo. We made arrangements to be transported to Chicuque Hospital. The patient load was overwhelming, and with sadness we had to ultimately leave after two weeks without doing all of the cataract patients needing surgery.

In 1998, an invitation was extended to do eye surgery in Honduras where Dr. Henry Gibson had worked. A clinic had been established at Limon. The Carolina Honduras Health Foundation made a volunteer trip annually and in 1998 wanted to have some help with blind patients. We were unable to perform a large number of surgeries because of some religious celebrations. In addition, a patient who had received a trabeculectomy procedure for glaucoma at a previous eye camp had told people the surgery had taken away some of his vision. We explained that successful glaucoma procedures sometimes do affect vision, but that the procedure was designed to keep him from going completely blind. For this reason, the rumor grew that anyone submitting to eye surgery would be blinded.

In preparation for this volunteer eye surgery program, Ruth and I had packed four large boxes, each weighing seventy pounds that contained medicines and supplies. Also in the boxed were sophisticated instruments, including a Haag Streit slit lamp, Zeiss OPMI-I operating microscope, keratometer, A-scan and representative intraocular lenses. Our spiritual team counselor advised us to try to understand and accept the situation. It was with heavy hearts that we ultimately left Limon for our return to the U.S. after only performing a total of two eye surgical procedures. As Jesus said, "How often I have longed to gather your children together, but you are not willing." (Mathew 23:37)

More than one hundred eye operations were performed in Lilongwe, Malawi in 1998.

We also visited Lilongwe, Malawi in 1998. The International Surgical Eye Expedition headed this project. A number of eye surgeons were brought together, two from the United States and four from Central Africa. It was an impressive project where more than one hundred cataract operations with implantations were done. Plans were made for a similar project the following year.

In March 1999, a return trip was made to Zing. Because we had such an overwhelming response our previous visit, I was happy to have the help of Dr. Iorav James of Mkar Hospital, which was some distance away. His willingness to come to Zing to help was really appreciated. The crowd of blind patients was overwhelming. We each handled forty cases. His were intracapsular cataract extractions and mine were extracapsular cataract extractions with intraocular lens implantations. More significant was the fact that I was able to meet some of the people whom we had known forty-four years earlier. Some of them needed cataract surgery. I also was able to greet an old friend of mine, an old hunting companion. He was now quite blind. We had the joy of restoring his sight, which thrilled his soul.

Some months later I returned to Kenya and did more eye surgery at Maua. On the way to Maua from Nairobi, we again had to stop the car to allow elephants to cross the road. Some dramatic surgeries were done, especially on a nine-year-old girl who wanted to go to school but could not see. We were able to help her with an intraocular lens. Unbelievably, I suffered an injury to my leg in the operating theater and was unable to move about to work up patients, let alone do surgery. After being confined for two days I realized I would not be able to resume surgery, so made plans to return home. Fortunately, the injury healed itself in a matter of several weeks.

Later on in September 1999, I made a trip to Ghana. I had been to Ghana before and knew their need. This time I was willing to go far up country from the Cape Coast headquarters. At the completion of this trip, I realized I had been privileged to do volunteer eye surgery in fourteen different countries ranging from Africa, Haiti and Bolivia to Vietnam, China and Mongolia. The Lord used this ministry in a wonderful way, not only for the restoration of physical sight, but also for the sharing of spiritual insight into the love of God as revealed in Jesus Christ. I was most grateful to be a part of this ministry.

Chapter Sixty-Nine

Ten Years: 2002 to 2011

Ruth and I often wondered: "Will we make it to the turn of the century when we will be 83 and 79?" How has our family survived so many years, almost daily ministering in diseased environments and treating patients with deadly illnesses? How could 182 crossings of the ocean have been without mishap? We survived travel on unpredictable roads while a number of our missionary friends perished. None of our six children was left with a life-long problem or illness. They literally skirted snake pits during their childhood. On occasion we had to deal with a poisonous snake that had invaded our home. We constantly thanked God for our good health and spiritual blessings. When illnesses came, as they did, death did not supervene. How wonderful to face the twenty-first century!

This mamba snake was more than six feet long and was found in our childrens' play area at Rotifunk.

Ruth and I visited Kissy in 2000 and 2001 during the dangerous times of civil war. We only could go in, do our work and then leave. But on these visits we did as many as seventy eye operations, which meant a great deal to the waiting blind.

In February 2002, we had the opportunity to return to Sierra Leone. During a church service at Boughman Memorial United Methodist Church, we were honored to have in attendance the President of Sierra Leone, Alhaji Ahmad Tejen Kabbah. The President's entourage was seated at the right front of the church.

Ruth and I had been directed to the first pew on the left. Accompanying us was serviceman Peter Gilgen from Haag Streit Corporation. We wondered how he and President Kabbah would manage the service, which usually lasted more than three hours. Despite the heat everything went well and all had a truly spiritual experience.

At the close of the service I received a note from one the president's assistants asking me to remain in my pew. President Kabbah came over and shook hands with Ruth and me. After formalities, I shared with him my pleasure of being able to shake hands with all the past presidents of Sierra Leone: Sir Milton Margai, Sika Stevens and Joseph Momoh. During our visit, I mentioned we included him in our prayers. I also told him that if we could be of service to him, we would be happy to do so. He took us up on the offer and requested an eye examination.

There was intense scurrying by the Kissy Eye Hospital staff to prepare for the arrival of the president. His examination went well. He was concerned about some of the other patients, especially a little girl who needed to have an eye operation. He offered to underwrite the expense of her operation. He was unable to accept Ruth's invitation to have tea with us in our apartment as President Joseph Momoh had done several years earlier. Ultimately, he and his party left with the flurry an important visit like this entailed. We breathed much easier after he left.

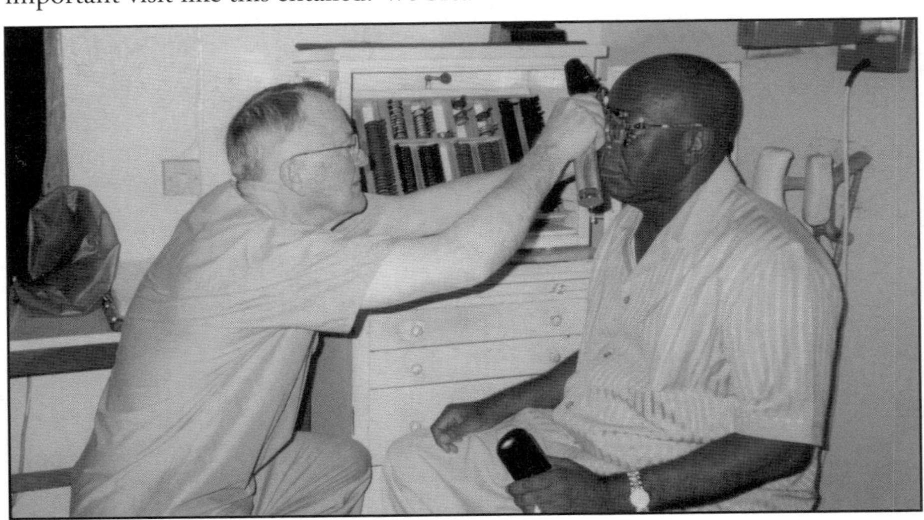

President Kabbah being examined at Kissy UMC Eye Hospital.

Several days later, we received a note of thanks from President Kabbah. Included in the note was an invitation to attend his upcoming birthday party. We were pleased to go, but felt a bit out of place, being the only white people present. It was a time of political uncertainty; warring factions limited road travel. However, we went to the birthday party and enjoyed visiting with other attendees. When the food was brought in, a messenger came to Ruth, asking if she and I would come to greet the President. He had decided to have Ruth start the line of filling plates for the feast. We were then given seats next to the President and his party. A delightful, but rather nervous, time was had.

During out trip to Zing in April 2002, the highlight was seeing Malam Baba Jatau of Bambur. He had been our dispensing nurse at Bambur in 1952, fifty years earlier. After we left Nigeria in 1955, he continued to be a respected medical worker as well as church leader. He had been elected the tenth Tallah (Chief) of Bambur but because he was a Christian he was not allowed to take the position. He would not relent his Christian faith for the role of chief. However, in succeeding years this injustice was overturned and he was sworn in as the peoples' choice, the chief. (For those who have access to my second book, *Glorious Witnesses for Africa*, there are more details of Babba on page 44.) During this visit to Zing, we were impressed that Dr. Thomas Kemper, who presently is the Executive Secretary of the General Board of Global Ministries, would call all the way from Germany to inquire how the work was going.

Dr. Thomas G. Kemper, Executive Secretary of the General Board of Global Ministries of the United Methodist Church.

2003. In 2003, we had the opportunity of returning to Kissy at the end of January and were pleased with the work the staff was doing. We were especially thrilled in February when we became aware of an estate gift being given by Mr. Reuben Schneider of Paynesville, Minnesota. This gift ultimately was used in part to build the Zing Eye Centre in Nigeria.

Initially, most patients slept under the trees. Now post-op patients enjoy a ward bed at Zing Eye Centre.

In March of 2003, the prospect of a war with Iraq loomed. I remember writing a personal letter to President Bush advising him not to become involved in any war with Muslims. Our experience living and working with those who followed the Koran gave us an understanding of their unrelenting stance. There would be great difficulty establishing peace when Muslims' rules were not the same as the "Christian West." Unhappily, war was declared and the United States was involved in this conflict for nearly a decade.

During our visit in May that year, I began treating little Augusta Conteh's glaucoma. Her father is Bob Conteh, our chief dispensing nurse, who also has glaucoma. Ultimately, arrangements were made for Augusta to come to the United States. She was given first class treatment for her eye problem. In June 2011, eight years later, I received an e-mail from her with the news that she was enjoying good vision and was preparing to enter college. In June of 2003, I had the honor of baptizing Ezri Sabrina Farnum in the Koronis chapel. On that trip to Koronis, Ruth and I were rear-ended by a speeding pickup. Our Subaru was "totaled." We escaped with bumps and bruises. The Lord is kind. The following day we returned to Alexandria with a new car, which is being driven to the present day.

In July, we volunteered again to perform surgery at Zing. On returning to the U.S., Ruth and I enjoyed a reunion with former missionaries to Nigeria that was held at Lake Junaluska in North Carolina.

Tim literally walked into the lake to beach the boat.

A week later, while fishing for muskie on Lake Miltona, my boat motor stopped. I was on the south side of the lake. The fuel gauge had broken and I was out of gas. It was 2:00 p.m. There was a breeze from the south. I realized I was drifting out toward the middle of the lake – northward in the direction of our cabin. The sky began to darken with gusts of wind tossing my boat. Unbelievably, by 4:00 p.m. I had been driven entirely across the lake and now was hung up in rushes. Even though the water was only chest deep and I could have made my way to shore less than a quarter mile away, as a loyal captain I stayed with my ship, swallowed my embarrassment and used my cell phone to call Tim. He was just completing his last patient and assured me the "coast guard" was on the way.

Still in his suit, he motored out in our smaller aluminum boat, delivering gas in an extra container. The amount of gas in the container turned out to be disappointingly meager but was sufficient for me to plough through the rushes and head for our dock. By now the waves were eight feet tall (a fishermen is telling this tale). Again, the motor choked and died. Tim threw a rope and with the tiny 9 hp outboard on his boat, pulled my larger craft with its 115 hp motor. The wind was now so bad and waves so high we knew we would not be able to safely land at our dock, so we kept going across the bay and succeeded in reaching the public access where there was some measure of protection. To get the large boat on the trailer was a struggle; Tim was finally able to maneuver it by working in thigh deep water. Those were the days when Tim could move anything to which he put his shoulder – even mountains. At the end of it all, we had a giggling session.

Ruth's and my visit to Kissy in October 2003 was a bit more exciting than we had wanted it to be. One night, I was awakened and thought I heard some tampering of the downstairs doors. Four thieves had accosted and tied up our two watchmen, and were breaking into not only the main building but also the surgery. I decided I would turn on the generator lights. The noise of the generator starting and the flooding of lights frightened the thieves away – in fact, they left a goodly number of things they had intended to take. However, they must have been embarrassed because they tried to rob us again three nights later. This time, they were met by lots of patients, as well as guards, who drove them off.

2004. Our January and February eye surgery was done at Zing. The new Zing Eye Centre was being completed. On the return flight, we were delayed in Kono because of the severity of the harmatan (dust storm). The dust was so thick planes could not fly.

In April, Ruth was admitted to Douglas County Hospital with a severe urinary tract infection. A few weeks later, of her own choice, Ruth decided to give up driving her car. She had experienced a humbling incident while shopping at Pete's County Market. When she placed the groceries in the car and attempted to start it, she could not remember how to do it. After an extended time, she was able to work things out but realized her driving days were over. She gave her precious Honda to the Kissy UMC Eye Hospital. It was transported to Freetown in a container secured by Art Jacobson and others, and filled by Roger and Melanie

Ruth enjoyed her blue Honda but ultimately we shipped it to Kissy UMC Eye Hospital in one of Roger Reiners' containers.

Reiners. To unload it, dockhands ignored using the key and pulled wires to cross them for starting. All these repairs had to be done later by Roger. It is now a favorite means of transport for Dr. and Mrs. Buchan and the hospital staff.

In the latter part of May, I returned to Kissy several days ahead of Tim, Becky and Debby who joined me. It was good I had arrived first, as I had enough time to catch a large rat that had taken up residence in our apartment. The girls would not have been comfortable sharing the facilities with a rodent. Tim and family did a wonderful service. The staff will never forget the "Gess girls."

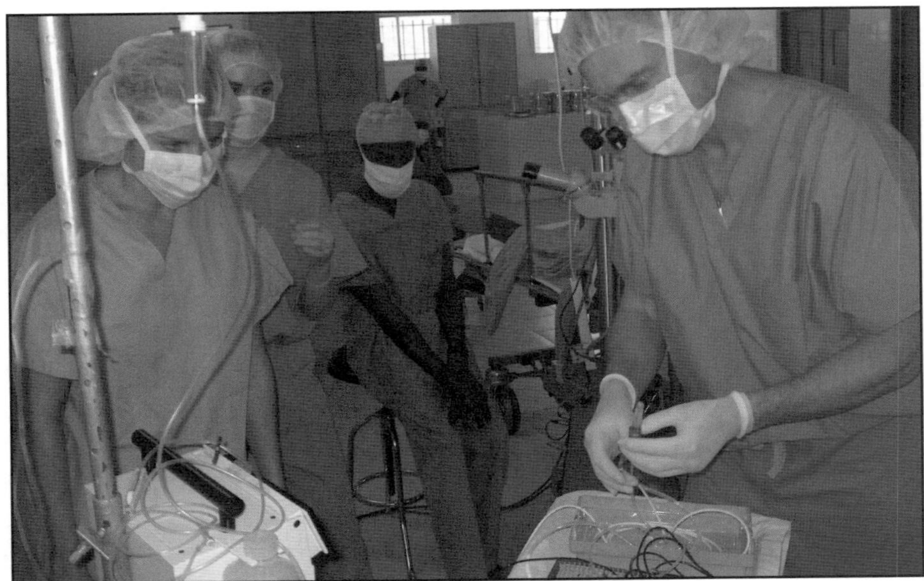

Debby, Becky and Tim in Kissy surgery. Debby is now doing cataract surgery by phacoemulsification in Alexandria.

Several weeks after returning from Africa, Debby set about painting our house with help from future husband Eric. Ruth had finally been able to leave the Lake Burgen house and move into town. She was quite willing to have a single-floor dwelling. The front window at the new home played an important role as she lost mobility. She watched patients come and go from Tim's clinic across the street and John's clinic next door. She was always interested when she saw a man or woman who was being attentive to his or her spouse.

Ruth enjoyed looking out our front window and watching the goings on at both the Gess Eye Clinic and Alexandria Eye Clinic.

In July, Ruth was able to travel to Vancouver to attend the Christian Ophthalmology Society meeting, the last meeting she ever attended. During the meeting, we had a partial family union with Tim and Joanne, Irene Blair (Ruth's sister who lived in Vancouver) and Paul and Arlet who spun up from Seattle in their open Miata convertible.

A visit to Kissy in September gave me much satisfaction when I examined a patient with good vision on whom I had done a trabeculectomy twenty-two years earlier. Back in the U.S., I attended my first Christian Blind Mission meeting at which I was made a board member. The scope of Christian Blind Mission is awesome, with outreach in more than one hundred countries and more than a thousand projects. The years with Christian Blind Mission were challenging and filled with great responsibility. I felt this especially during a trip in 2005 to Bensheim, Germany, where I represented the U.S. contingent.

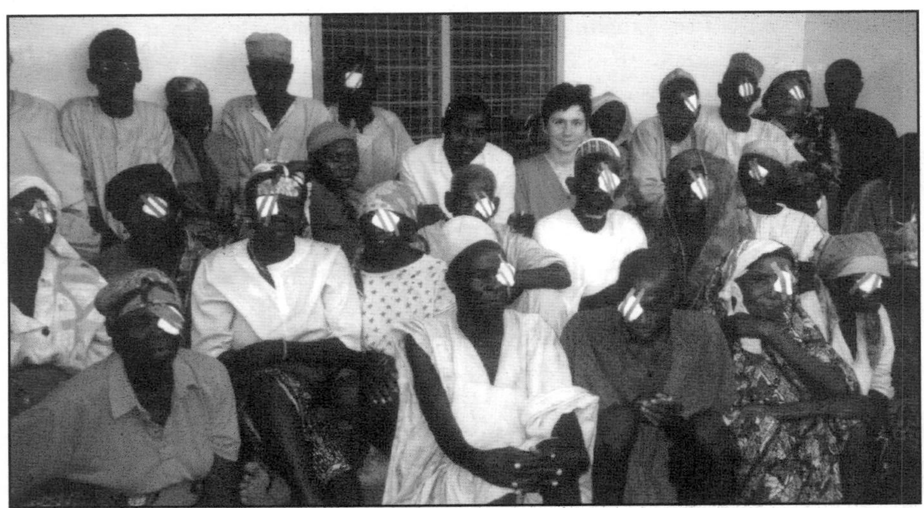

Zing Eye Centre under the direction of Ina Schoenfeld Dabale.

2005. On January 20, 2005, the Zing Eye Centre was dedicated. During the celebration and activities, I came to know the government intern who was working at the Zing Maternity Centre. His name was Dr. Gideon Avar. He was planning to go into OB/GYN, but during my stay at Zing, he came over to the eye hospital to see how we handled eye patients and conducted eye surgery. He became interested in the specialty of ophthalmology, and when we suggested Christian Blind Mission might give him a scholarship for two years of surgical preparation, he accepted their offer and subsequently became the outstanding ophthalmologist at the Zing Eye Centre.

Dr. Gideon Avar.

Instead of returning to the U.S., I took a flight to Freetown where I met Tim. We made plans to do some outreach surgery at Jaiama Nimi Koro. We were concerned about not having electricity at Jaiama, as the rebels had used the mission house as their headquarters and when they left, tore out the wiring from the compound. Providentially, the Rev. Don Eslinger and a party of volunteers were passing through Freetown on their way to Makeni country. He asked if we had any particular needs at Kissy. I mentioned that a portable Honda generator would be a great blessing for our trip to Jaiama. He reached into his pocket and handed me an envelope. It contained $1,000 in cash. That afternoon we purchased the generator and had the radio station in Freetown (which broadcasted throughout Sierra Leone) announce our coming visit to Jaiama the next day. Nurse Alice Maturi and a host of patients met us. Twelve cataract extractions with IOL implantations were done in the two days we were there before we had to return to Kissy for another overwhelming load of surgeries.

The Milbank shipping container, which had been packed by Roger Reiners and his crew, had been languishing in customs for nearly two months. I mustered my courage and visited the President's compound to consult with his assistant. Special permission was given for clearance. The night before we left Kissy, the container was delivered to the hospital compound and unloaded. Custom fees were unduly high. Two custom officials accompanied the container. When they were assured with their own eyes that only medicine and surgical supplies were unpacked, they relented and allowed the shipment to enter duty free.

By July of 2005, Ruth was no longer able to accompany me on my visits to Africa. She began to have some difficulties with speech and walking, and had bouts of confusion. Episodes of unsteadiness resulted in some falls, but in spite of falling nineteen times over the next few years, Ruth never fractured any bones, for which we thanked God. I slipped away for one day that month to attend the 67th reunion of the Central High School class of 1938. Less than twenty former students came from a class that had originally numbered a thousand.

During 2005, I became especially active as a board member of the U.S. division of Christian Blind Mission. It gave me an opportunity to travel, and on one such trip I was led to the National Advising Council meeting in New York. Present at the meeting was Rudy Giuliani who was running for President. While visiting with him, a press agent took our picture. Also at the meeting was Miss America, Heather Whitehouse. All the activities were under the leadership of Alan Harkey, the secretary for the U.S. branch of the Christian Blind Mission. I had great admiration for his commitment to world eye care. It was he who began the movement to cure the blind of the world by 2020. Following that meeting I went on to Lake Junaluska for an Operation Classroom meeting.

Later that year, Tim and I made a trip to Kissy where Tim did as many as eight phacoemulsifications a day. It was impressive to see how Tim was able to do these procedures without the staff support he was accustomed to in Alexandria.

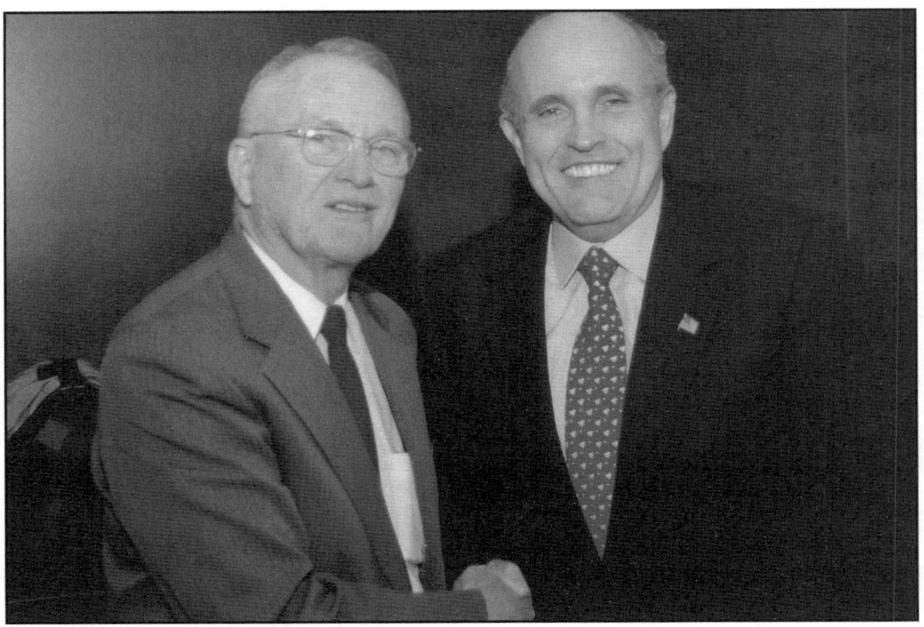

I had the opportunity to meet Mayor Giuliani while in New York attending a Christian Blind Mission National Advising Council meeting.

The staff was in awe. Peter Gilgen, who did a beautiful job of servicing our Haag Streit slit lamps, had also joined us.

We had a nice visit from Beth for several days during the early part of December. On December 31, the five other children celebrated our 60th wedding anniversary. Mary directed a hilarious skit of our original wedding in Winnipeg. Ruth and I enjoyed the evening so much. Several weeks later, we received a DVD from Paul of the pictures that had been taken. For the accompanying music, he had created a "quartet" by singing all four parts himself of the song "My New Life," Ruth's and my favorite song sung originally by our four sons.

2006. On our February trip to Kissy in 2006, Tim and I were accompanied by Michael Bynum. He was an employee of Ziess Optical Company who volunteered to service our Ziess operating microscopes. He found the people delightful and continued friendships years later with some of the people he had met on this visit. Shortly after our trip to Sierra Leone, Beth, Bob and daughters Becky and Christy did volunteer missionary service in Botswana. The Hopkins family made a number of trips to southern Africa.

In March, Ruth required hospitalization and was then transferred to Knute Nelson Nursing Home. It was now apparent she was dependent on a walker, but still had several falls in our home. One occurred just after I had left for church. She spent the entire time on the kitchen floor until I returned. Fortunately the sermon was not too long.

In May of 2006, Ruth spent some time at Clearwater Suites while I had meetings with Christian Blind Mission in Greenville, South Carolina. Later on in June, I flew to Frankfurt on my way to Bensheim for Christian Blind Mission's annual meeting. Sometime later, the members of the U.S. contingent of Christian Blind Mission met in Colorado Springs for a meeting. It was then I realized I had a conflict of interest and would not be able to continue indefinitely with Christian Blind Mission, as much of my fundraising was for Kissy, Zing and Mutumbara.

In August of 2006, it was a thrill to be able to participate in Lake Koronis Assembly Grounds' 85th anniversary. Ruth and I were able to stay in a very comfortable motel. Several weeks later, at Glen Eyrie in Colorado, I had the privilege of attending the reunion of former missionaries to Nigeria with whom Ruth and I had the pleasure of working with so many years before. During the month of November, Ruth stayed with Sharon's Senior Care Service while Roger Reiners and I made a trip to Kissy.

Our cabin on Lake Miltona near Alexandria.

2007. In 2007, I attended the Macalester College class of 1942 reunion. It was a joy to fellowship with old friends. In September, we had the opportunity to purchase a cabin on north Lake Miltona. This has proved to be a real blessing. Later in September, Michael Bynum made it possible for Malcolm Albert and his daughter to come to the States. In fact, the stay was prolonged and Melanie and Roger Reiners helped house him. He spoke at the United Methodist Church in Alexandria. He also sang a solo with his beautiful base voice.

In the middle of the night on September 2, 2007, Ruth experienced extreme, frightening and disabling vertigo and was unable to rise from her bed. I called Tim and John who managed to place Ruth in a wheel chair. We used our aluminum ramps to exit the house and Tim pushed Ruth a block to the emergency room. (We always wondered what it must have looked like on the hospital's surveillance camera. There was Tim, a respected ophthalmologist, wheeling his gray-haired mother down the street in the dead of night.) The reason we decided to get

Ruth to the emergency room in this manner was based on a previous experience when an ambulance had been called. Police had arrived first on the scene and the ensuing protocols had caused delays in getting her prompt care. Once Ruth was finally loaded into the ambulance, it traveled the one block to the emergency room. The ensuing bill was shocking.

In November of 2007, I attended the American Academy of Ophthalmology meeting in New Orleans. At the end of the month, I made a trip to Freetown and then to Mutumbara, Zimbabwe, where Doctor and Mrs. Emmanuel Mefor are ministering. It was exciting to see the new eye clinic being erected. A Kipor generator was secured for the eye program, assuring an electrical supply for the surgeries.

2008. By 2008, Ruth had been in nursing homes on and off for two and a half years. The caregivers at Knute Nelson felt caring for her at home would be extremely difficult. However, she was adamant in coming home so we made arrangements for professional care to come in several days a week. Despite the doubts of the professional staff at Knute Nelson, Ruth managed for the next two and a half years because of her "true grit." She only wanted to be with me and became anxious if I wasn't present.

April 3 was a sinister date. A new toilet was installed under the steps in the basement. It had a slow leak that was not discovered for TWO YEARS when the surrounding sheet rock grew mold halfway to the ceiling.

July 24 was a happy day. I caught my first muskie, a 40-inch lunker. The guide submitted the story to the Sauk Center newspaper.

Guide Lee Olmschenk holding the forty-inch muskie I landed several hundred yards from our Lake Miltona dock. Later, I caught a four-foot, thirty-pound monster.

PAGE 2B Sept 9, 2008

Sauk Valley **Herald**

Muskie memory

Dr. Lowell Gess waited a lifetime to land a muskie and thanks to Sauk Centre's Lee Olmschenk, he did, landing this 40-incher. PHOTO SUBMITTED

Sauk Centre guide helps 87-year-old retired doctor fulfill one final wish

The newspaper article that chronicles my fishing triumph.

In August, we had the pleasure of Beth and her entire family visiting us. They stayed at the Lake Miltona cabin. Beth's children and in-laws enjoyed the Monarch boat we had, even though I was never happy with it. It was too much of a boat, the one with a 115 hp motor. Eventually, I donated it to the Lake Geneva camping program.

It always was a pleasure to attend Salem Evangelical Church's "Salem Fest" the second Sunday of August. My roots, of course, are there. My parents and relatives are buried across the road in the cemetery. A few old friends were still able to attend the event. I had the privilege of addressing the congregation.

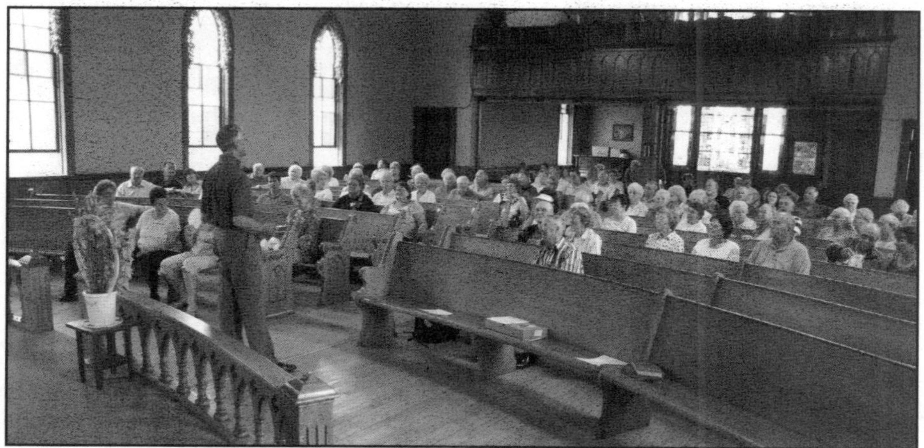

Enjoying the annual Salem Fest from the second pew.

The following week, Tim and I took a trip to Nerstrand. We got gas at Nerstrand and supplied ourselves with sausages from the Nerstrand Meat Market. The owners remembered us and gave us meat for our sandwiches, which we ate on the old home site and birthplace of my mother. The land, now owned by Tim and Beth, is fertile; crops are assured each year. More than two hundred black walnut trees grow along the fence lines.

In September 2008, Dr. Ainor Fergusson suffered a fatal heart attack. The program at Kissy was in serious doubt.

Then the stock market collapsed. In spite of the cataclysmic happenings going on around the world, our portfolio was in good shape after I rectified an "unauthorized" transaction our broker had made.

On October 3, I was thrilled to land a four-foot muskie monster. Then the old Sea King outboard motor Edward Fischer had loaned us sixty-five years earlier (and was later given to me by his widow) suffered a cracked crankcase and was no longer usable. I put it up in the garage for sentiment, a symbol of bygone days.

2009. The year 2009 proved to be one of the most surprising of my life. It started out by my being locked out of the car – while it was still running at the main door to Bayfields, a store at the local mall. On three other occasions, Ruth's arm had touched the automatic lock as she got out of the car. When the door shut behind her, there was no way to get back in. I had to hire a taxi to get back home to get another key and then go back to Bayfields to move the car.

In March, my cystoscopic examination led to surgery. The pathology report had revealed a highly differentiated transitional cell carcinoma. The day following the surgery, Ruth and I were interviewed for a TV report that was on people who received Meals on Wheels. It was not apparent I was in distress. A trip to Kissy was made in April with Roger Reiners. A new water line was connected to the Gumma Valley line. We hoped this took care of our Kissy water problems. A month or two later I was locked out of the car again when Ruth's arm touched the lock, but I learned my lesson. I began to carry an extra key.

May 10th was memorable. Andrew and I attended a Gaither concert at the Target Center in Minneapolis. The Gaither Trio and Vocal Band was a favorite over the years. The harmony and message substance of their Saturday evening FamilyNet TV show has been a blessing, which I enjoyed at least weekly for the past twenty years.

In June of 2009, Garrett-Evangelical Theological Seminary established a scholarship in my name. I was embarrassed to let this be known, but the scholarship was substantially underwritten. In July, another surgery removed more bladder tumors. (Within the following twenty-two months, I faced six major surgeries, all involving general anesthesia.)

While I was falling apart Ruth was renewed – on August 15th she made both her bridge bids in a game with Mary and Steve Boehlke. Sadly, her sister Beverly

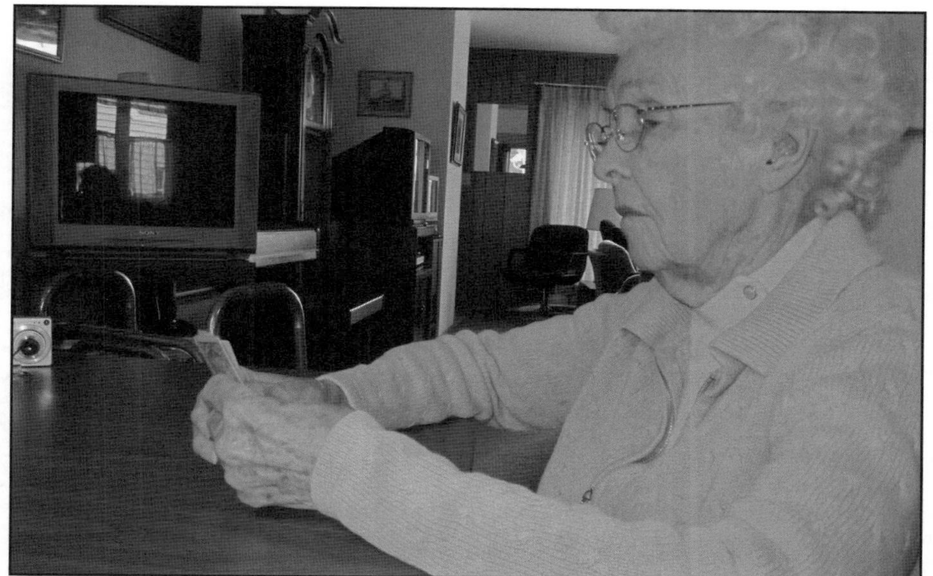

Ruth playing bridge at age ninety-three and making her bid.

died on August 23rd. I had the opportunity to attend the Nigerian missionary reunion in Oklahoma City in September and then had a third surgery on November 19th. BCG treatment made life miserable for four months. My spirits were lifted, however, by the visit of Dr. and Mrs. Kiru, dear friends who had ministered at the ECWA Eye Hospital in Kano, Nigeria for fifteen years. They spent extended time with Melanie and Roger Reiners at Milbank, South Dakota.

We received an exciting communication in December 2009 from the UMC Sierra Leone conference, which reported Rotifunk was considered the best outlying hospital in Sierra Leone in the 1950s and 60s. I shared this information with the staff who was there at the time, for truly we had everything we needed to do a good job at Rotifunk.

2010. On January 13th following devotions with Ruth, we began to reminisce. Especially foremost was the topic of the church's growth in Africa since we first arrived in 1952. I decided that this fact should be recorded. I determined to write a book called *Glorious Witnesses for Africa*, which was published in 2011.

Ruth went through a period of panic when she "lost" (misplaced) her diamond ring on February 19th and didn't know how she could live without it. Happily, it was found in a dresser drawer on July 17th.

A cystoscopy in February revealed no new growths, which was cause for joy. *Glorious Witnesses for Africa* was being written and our household was a busy as I cared for Ruth. The pain from the effect of the BCG treatment was unrelenting – for month after month. A cystoscopy in June was more painful than one can describe.

A confirming cystoscopy was done in July. By July 17th Ruth had weakened to the point where she was not able to get out of bed. We had her checked at the hospital and she insisted on being returned home; however, she still could not manage and we realized she needed professional care. Arrangements were made for her at Diamond Willow where a compassionate staff cared for her. At first she managed with her food and moving about a little bit with assistance, but by October she had suffered several transient ischemic attacks that compromised her swallowing.

During my October 15th visit to the doctor, a resurgence of the bladder cancer was noted. A biopsy later revealed an invasive high grade urothelial carcinoma with angio lymphatic and muscularis propria invasion. A urostomy was the only remaining option. On October 25th Ruth stopped breathing. She had been able to communicate with us until the last two weeks, but eventually was unable to take food or fluids. A memorial service took place on October 30th with the beautiful participation of all of our children. Pastor Jeff Hansen officiated. Pastor John Praetorius was the special speaker. The committal service was at the Salem cemetery near Paynesville. In order to attend the funeral, I had to get discharge clearance from the hospital due to another surgery. It was not an easy day to "lay to rest" the love of my life, my beloved of nearly sixty-five years.

On December the 2nd, a radical urostomy was performed by Dr. Kurt L. Hansberry and Dr. Gary L. Paulson at Douglas County Hospital. Unfortunately, three weeks later a raging pyelonephritis required a readmission. Physiotherapy at Bethany Home for a month restored me, enabling me to walk again. I thank God for renewal at the end of a "challenging" year.

2011. Early in 2011, an allergy that had irritated my eyes for several years was eradicated by removing the ancient carpets in my bedroom and study and replacing them with vinyl flooring. Also included was the kitchen rug. The relief was dramatic. No medications have been needed since.

In February, I had recovered sufficiently from my December 2010 operation and ensuing infection to attend the reunion of former Evangelical Theological Seminary students at Naperville. I represented my class of 1945, the oldest class present. The next class represented was five years behind me. It was a pleasure to visit with Bishop Wayne Clymer who was the keynote speaker.

At one evening meal I was a bit tardy. Every one was seated at the tables. I found one that had an available place. To my right was Dr. Howard E. Mueller and his wife, Mary. We had been missionaries together in Sierra Leone in the 1960s. To my left was a former president of ETS, Dr. James Stein, along with his wife. I did not know the couple across the table.

Following grace, our table was the first served. Small talk ensued with the delicious meal. While waiting for the desert, Dr. Mueller announced to the members of our table that our friendship extended over almost 50 years, as they had come to Taiama where Ruth and I were conducting an eye and a general clinic program. Since Mary was in her first pregnancy, they wanted to be near a surgeon who could intervene surgically should it be necessary. The delivery was normal and a beautiful little girl was brought into the world.

The man across the table said, "So you are Dr. Lowell Gess. I have ministered with the General Board of Global Ministries for forty years. Your name has frequently been brought before us in our meetings. How nice to meet you personally."

Following this, President Stein spoke up: "When my mother reached her eighties, she moved from North Dakota to assisted living accommodations in Alexandria, Minnesota. Her eye surgeon was Dr. Lowell Gess to whom she was referred because he was placing intraocular lenses within the eyes following cataract extractions at a time when this procedure was not available at the Mayo Clinic or the University of Minnesota's Department of Ophthalmology. She obtained excellent vision."

All this was overwhelming for me. Finally, finding some words I said, "I thank God for the call to medical missions and the training and skills afforded me to appropriately minister in the name of Jesus."

On April 29th I attended the 60th anniversary of graduating from the Washington University School of Medicine in St. Louis, Missouri. Only Marvin Levin and Wendell Kirkpatrick were able to join me in representing the class of 1951. On May 8th in Memphis, Tennessee I attended the Southern Eye Institute's celebration, arranged by Dr. Cathy Schanzer and Tom Lewis, where I received their 2011 Humanitarian Award for "outstanding missionary service." It was startling to see the flooding from the Mississippi River that surrounded Memphis. On June 4th Andrew and I set off for Bismark, North Dakota – a sentimental journey we truly enjoyed. Bill and Marilyn Strutz were perfect hosts and had arranged for us to have a walk-through of our house that we built way back in 1968. Al Brady had been our architect and builder. It was a wonderful day. On June 6th I passed my driver's license. What could be more perfect for someone living alone cherishing independence and freedom?

Now, on July 13, 2011, my 90th birthday, I am submitting the last of the material that makes up this autobiography. I am opening a new chapter of living, but I still am very much aware of the Lord's clear words: "Be a Medical Missionary" spoken 79 years ago. I look forward to glorious things yet to come.

"For I know the plans I have for you," declares the Lord, "plans to give you hope and a future." Jeremiah 29:11

Part IV: Ruth

Place me like a seal over your heart,
like a seal on your arm;
for love is as strong as death,
its jealousy unyielding as the grave.
It burns like blazing fire,
like a mighty flame.
Many waters cannot quench love;
rivers cannot wash it away.

– Song of Solomon 8:6-7a

Chapter Seventy

Ruth Writes: A Brief Autobiography

I, Ruth Adabelle Bradley Gess was born April 5, 1917, in my grandparents' house in Brookdale, Manitoba, Canada. I was the first child of George Ray Bradley and Myrtle Esther Clegg Bradley. My father was president of the local bank; the Royal Bank of Canada had transferred him there. He began his career in banking in Merriton and St. Catherine's, Ontario, Canada, where his large family of six brothers and two sisters originally lived. My father made only one trip back to Ontario after his marriage, and my mother never did meet any of his family, although she corresponded with one of his sisters for some time.

Ruth held by her father, George Ray Bradley, who went by the name "Brad."

My mother was the youngest child of Angus Campbell Clegg and Catherine Kennedy Clegg. Family genealogical records trace her ancestry back to Ireland and Scotland. Her father had at one time assisted in the Riel Rebellion (which occurred in North Central Canada when the Indians fought against the government) by taking supplies to the soldiers. My grandfather later became a butcher in Brookdale, Manitoba, where they were early pioneers when the railroad was built. His parents eventually retired to Tacoma, Washington.

After working in the Brookdale bank, my father was transferred to the bank in Gilbert Plains, Manitoba. While there, my next youngest sister, Irene, was born. My father was then transferred to manage the bank in Regina, the capitol city of Saskatchewan. Beverly was born in Regina and was several months old when we returned to Brookdale where we lived with my mother's parents and brother until my father started working in Winnipeg.

I began school in Brookdale at the age of seven. The school had burned down and was rebuilt, so starting school earlier wasn't possible. I was, however, allowed to skip second grade. When our family was reunited in Winnipeg, I entered the fourth grade. There we lived in light housekeeping rooms, apartments and finally a house. My father was out of work for long periods of time, so these were hard years. Finally when I was in the eighth grade, North Star Oil Company hired my father to be an accountant and travel throughout Saskatchewan Province as an auditor.

Ruth as a young scholar.

When I was sixteen, my father suddenly died of a heart attack in Saskatchewan. My mother received some life insurance money, so our family moved to an apartment where we stayed until Irene's marriage to Nat Blair. I had finished business college and was working in an office. I supported our family until I entered nurses' training at Winnipeg General Hospital in 1942. My youngest sister, Beverly, had graduated from high school and business college, worked for a while and then married Ervin Petznik at Elim Chapel in 1944. Beverly accompanied Erv to Naperville, Illinois, where Erv was a seminary student. When Nat and Irene were married, they helped our family out financially for some time. When Nat was posted overseas, Irene returned to Winnipeg with her daughter, Judy. My mother lived with her until Nat's return.

On visiting Bev and Erv in Naperville, I met Lowell Gess, a seminary student who had roomed with Erv and whose great desire was to become a medical missionary. I also was considering missionary service, following my exposure to the world's needs as presented in both Elim Chapel and Bethesda Church in Winnipeg. I was planning on enrolling in nurses' training at the Winnipeg General Hospital. Our courtship was carried on by correspondence and short visits in Naperville, St. Cloud or Winnipeg.

Lowell graduated from the seminary and I from nurses' training in 1945. We were married in Winnipeg on December 29, 1945.

Thus began our journey of faith in world service.

Chapter Seventy-One

Ruth's Background

Ruth's parents were married in 1915. Her banker father was posted to several different locations. The end of his work and their move from Regina, Saskatchewan was prompted by a life-shattering incident when a lawyer was allowed to temporarily overdraw his account. The entire bank staff was dismissed. The family returned to Brookdale where Ruth lived with her grandparents and attended school from age seven to nine. Her father was unable to find a job commensurate with his skills and resorted to rural odd jobs in Saskatchewan. At age nine, the move was made back to Winnipeg when Mr. McPhee, a dear friend of Brad's, helped arrange for work for Brad as an accountant at a flour company. They lived in a small, furnished room while Beverly was a baby. Uncle Jack, Myrtle's brother, helped secure an apartment that accommodated Ruth and Irene as well as Bob Clegg, Jack's son, who was studying to become a certified accountant.

Brad could not endure his job, which he felt insulted his abilities. After three years, he resigned. This decision proved to be disastrous as he wasn't able to then find a position where he could utilize his skills. By now Ruth was in the fourth grade. Her father continued to do odd jobs, even selling ice cream sandwiches while living in rural St. Boniface. Ruth remembered that as a child she walked along the railroad tracks searching for coal for the stove.

When Ruth turned fourteen, Brad secured a job with North Star Oil auditing business and corporate books. This took him back to Saskatchewan where many of these businesses were located, but North Star assured him he would be transferred back to Winnipeg in the future. Ruth's mother would accompany him during the summers while the three girls lived in Brookdale with Grandpa and Grandma Clegg. These summers were wonderful.

After two years in this job, on one of his trips Brad picked up a hitchhiker and drove him to Alameda, Saskatchewan, where the hitchhiker's mother-in-law lived. He was invited to an evening meal. While visiting before supper, a dog came up to Brad. He patted the dog and slipped out of his chair with a fatal heart attack. A week or two earlier he had been examined at a hospital and admitted for pleurisy, but asked to be discharged early. He was anxious to get out, complete his trip and transfer back to Winnipeg. The year was 1933. Brad was forty-eight years old.

At Brad's death, the family's only asset was an insurance policy of $5,000. One thousand dollars of it was used for burial and other expenses. The remaining $4,000 helped support Myrtle and the three girls for the next two and a half years. The Vimborg apartment in Winnipeg served as home. A cousin, Elsie, was taken in as a paid boarder while she attended business college. Ruth's mother slept on a front room couch. Their downstairs neighbors repeatedly played "There's an Old Spinning Wheel in the Parlor" on their record player, serenading the Bradley family for months. In succeeding years, Ruth finished high school and a six-month business college course.

Ruth, second from left, with a number of the secretarial staff at Midwest Paper Products.

At eighteen, Ruth landed her first job as a secretary. She was skilled in typing and Greg shorthand. Her first job was at a bridge company. About a month later, her lung collapsed without warning and she was consigned to a bed for more than a month. She was not taken back at the bridge company, but landed another job at Midwest Paper Products. She was part of a large work force. After working for five years at a salary of $45 a month, she asked for a raise as she was the sole support for her mother and two sisters. The request was denied. She walked out the door – and down to the business college from which she had graduated.

Mr. Angus, the principal, had just received an application from a grain exchange company for a secretary. The next day, she was engaged at her new job, which paid $90 a month. In two years she saved enough money to enter nursing school at age twenty-five. She roomed with Eileen McKibben for the entire three years. During that time she served as president of the Christian Nurse's Association. She graduated from the Winnipeg General Hospital Nursing Program as a registered nurse on May 23, 1945. On December 29, 1945, Ruth married Lowell Gess, a marriage that lasted for more than sixty-four years.

Roses are appropriate at graduation time.

Along with her husband she was commissioned as a medical missionary at Calvary Evangelical Church in St. Paul, Minnesota on November 9, 1952. Official commissioned medical service continued until 1975 (except for a five-year leave of absence in Bismarck, North Dakota from 1967 to 1972). Upon retiring from the General Board of Global Ministries of the United Methodist Church, the family lived in Alexandria. Volunteer visits were made back to Sierra Leone for three-month periods during the succeeding years.

Following her husband's retirement from ophthalmology in Alexandria in 1990, as much as six months of the year would be spent in volunteer missionary service to countries such as Sierra Leone, Nigeria, Kenya, Zimbabwe and Honduras. Visits would be made two or three times a year to the Kissy UMC Eye Hospital. She experienced a severe stroke in 1993, which slowed her overseas work. Her last trip to Sierra Leone was in the fall of 2004 – her 162nd ocean crossing.

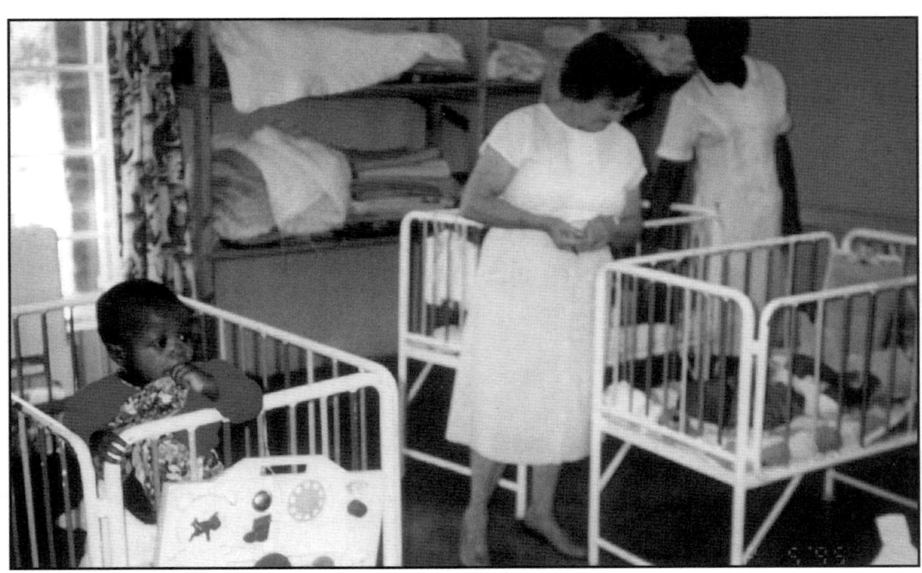
Ruth assisting with pediatric care at Old Mutare, Zimbabwe.

Her service, besides these countries, was that of being a loving mother to six children – Timothy, Mary, Elizabeth, John, Paul and Andrew. Her conversion and commitment to the Lord Jesus Christ, as well as the call to medical missions, happened during the long and tedious five years at the paper products company and during the Elim Chapel pastorate of Mr. Turnbull. Looking back, she graciously accepted that five year long sojourn of pounding the same typewriter for $45 a month as it was during that time her life was being molded by Jesus.

Jesus is all the world to me,
My life, my joy, my all;
He is my strength from day to day,
Without Him I would fall.

When I am sad, to Him I go,
No other one can cheer me so;
When I am sad, He makes me glad,
He's my friend.

– Will L. Thompson, 1904

Additional information: Angus and Catherine Clegg (parents of Ruth's mother, Myrtle). Ruth lived with them in Brookdale from age six to nine. Grandpa Clegg developed oral cancer from his constant companion – his pipe. Grandma Clegg was diabetic.

John (Jack) and Mary Lawrie (Mary was Myrtle's sister with whom Myrtle lived for a number of years after their daughters had left home following their marriages). Mary suffered from severe arthritis. Their sons were Angus and Robert.

George Ray Bradley (Ruth's father) 1885 - 1933

Myrtle Esther Clegg Bradley (Ruth's mother) 1892 - 1970

Chapter Seventy-Two

Memories of My Friend Brad

by R. G. McPhee

(This letter was written to Ruth by Mr. R. G. McPhee, a man who knew Ruth's father, Brad, as a young man. It provides additional details of Brad's life and Ruth's family.)

Myrtle and Brad in their younger years.

February 1981

I first met Brad when Mom, Gordon and I moved to Gilbert Plains (Manitoba) in September 1919. He was manager of the Sterling Bank and we became good friends.

I found out that he liked to play hockey, and as that was one of my favorite sports, we lined up as the "Stonewall Defense." I will always remember his expression: "You take the man – I'll take the puck," and they had to be good to get past us.

We were badly in need of hockey equipment and decided to canvas the merchants. Brad started off with a donation of twenty dollars from the bank; I followed with the same from Western Canada Flour Mills for whom I worked.

Each storekeeper felt obligated to match our contribution and we wound up with over $150, and we were able to beat every team we played, except Dauphin. Bus Best and "Cherk" Fraser were our best forwards, and Nels McGregor was our goaltender.

I remember the Bradleys had two girls, Ruth and Irene. Mom said Irene was just learning to walk. In 1922, I was made travelling superintendent in charge of country elevators and we moved to Winnipeg. The same year Brad was moved (transferred) to Winnipeg, and later that year he was moved to Regina as manager of the bank and "Beverly Regina" was born there.

Irene, Beverly and Ruth in Regina.

Later, he became friendly with a lawyer there who asked for a loan that was higher than the bank allowed (without authority from the head office), and when the man failed to pay back the loan the bank clamped down on Brad and he was out of a job (along with the rest of the bank staff). I knew Mr. Potter, Western Bank superintendent, and I went to see him, but he told me there was nothing he could do as that was one law the bank would not allow any branch manager to break, and said it was one of the hardest things he had every done as he admired Brad very much. Myrtle and the three girls came to live at Brookdale with the Cleggs and Brad got a job as a helper in a grain elevator for that fall.

The next spring, 1924, he came into Winnipeg and sold stocks and bonds on a commission basis, which was very small. That summer I was doing considerable repair work on our elevators and had a big job at Togo, Saskatchewan, installing a new leg bolt and buckets, also a new Gerber distributor spout which weighed about 300 lbs., so I persuaded Brad to go with me. Employment was very poor and good mechanics were working for as low as $.25 per hour; however, my company allowed me to pay (him) as high as $.50 and board. So I had the material shipped and Brad and I set off in my car. We boarded with Mrs. Charlie McGregor who had about eight other boarders.

Brad and I worked ten hours a day and usually went a little late for supper. This particular night I have in mind we were the last two to come to supper, and there was T-bone steak on the menu. We both ordered T-bones and the waitress, who was a Ukranian girl and had an eye for Brad (who was always kidding her), said to me, "I am sorry, but we only have one steak left – what will you have?" Of course I raised the roof and Mrs. McGregor came in to see what was the matter. The result was she sent Charlie (her husband) out to get another steak.

We spent about a month at Togo and I sent Brad's pay to Myrtle each week.

We had no rope and tackle to get this Gerber up to the top floor of the elevator and I could not find one in Togo, so thought I would have to send to Winnipeg for one.

I have to tell this, as it became a big topic in town. One of the elevator men next to ours used to spend a lot of time watching our work and wondering how we were going to get this 300 pounder up to the cupola. Well, one night I had a brain wave that we could tie the Gerber onto the transmission rope and then take the igniter out of the end of the engine and Brad could turn the engine and I could guide it up as I climbed the ladder to the top. I had a small rope as a signal to Brad. One pull meant "Stop" and two pulls "Go Ahead." Well it worked like a charm and when our man came around the Gerber was upstairs. Naturally, he wanted to know how we got it up and I said, "You are not going to believe this, but Brad pulled it up by himself." He asked where Brad got his strength and I told him Brad was a "wrestler" and just worked to keep in shape. He told it all over town that McPhee had one of the strongest men he had ever seen.

When we got back to Winnipeg I still had a few jobs to do, so he got about another month's work. That fall I asked Donald Grant, our office manager, if he could give Brad a job, so Brad got a job in our office and Myrtle and Bev came to Winnipeg and lived in part of Harold Taylor's house near Central Park. Harold was our printer. Later, Brad rented a house in Norwood and walked to work. Bob Lawrie came and stayed with them and went to school. The next year Brad moved the family to Banning St. and he was offered a job and travelled with the North Star Oil Company as auditor, covering Manitoba and part of Saskatchewan, which he held until his sudden death from heart trouble.

He was on his way home and was giving an agent, whose house was in Alameda, Saskatchewan, a ride. They had intended to spend the night in Alameda. Brad was sitting in a chair when he suddenly fell over.

Brad's only finances amounted to $4,000 insurance with North Star. Myrtle asked my advice on how she should handle this money. I advised her to figure the least amount she could get by on, and ask the insurance company to pay her this amount per month, which she did and managed to get you girls through school. I always thought she did a wonderful job.

I hope these few lines will give you some idea of the years you spent in Winnipeg. Brad was everybody's friend. There will never be another like him.

Chapter Seventy-Three

A Thumbnail Sketch

by Ruth

(Found in a private folder of Ruth's after her death and not dated. Except for a few items, most things are left as she originally wrote them – some in complete sentences and some in fragments – just as she prepared her talks when presenting to groups.)

Heirs Together of the Grace of Life – 1 Peter 3:7

Neither Lowell Gess nor Ruth Bradley could have imagined the path they were destined to follow together. In spite of seeming insurmountable difficulties, they sought the leading of the Lord that he would confirm and make possible their dream of serving him in Africa.

There were many difficulties:

1. The possibility of entering medical school, after a delay to serve as pastor in an emergency situation in Minnesota
2. The influx of returning GIs into medical schools – a miracle of acceptance
3. The problem of support for family – three children
4. Two years preaching
5. Aid from Board of Missions

The joy of packing for Nigeria in 1952, the year of John's birth – Guinter Memorial Hospital! Lowell was known as the "doctor with the Bible," and he shared the Good News in surrounding villages.

This is a story of a young seminary student who was a former farm boy, and a young nursing student, a city girl, who met and shared dreams of serving the Lord in far-off lands, especially Africa.

Upon Lowell's graduation from seminary and ordination as a pastor, he was called to a church in Minnesota. I obtained a registered nursing degree in Winnipeg and I was married December 29, 1945, in my hometown of Winnipeg, Canada. Lowell served as a pastor in Minnesota for two years at the St. Cloud and Graham churches and later at Mayer, Minnesota, keeping his dream of Africa alive by taking pre-medical courses at the University of Minnesota and St. John's University. We became the proud parents of Timothy during the time of waiting for acceptance into medical school. When acceptance came from Washington University School of Medicine in St. Louis, Missouri, we felt this affirmed the call we believed we had to serve the Lord as missionaries of the Gospel through medicine.

By Tim's first birthday, Lowell was in medical school in St. Louis and Tim and I were with Lowell's parents in Nerstrand, Minnesota. Lowell promised to send for us as soon as possible. This happened by the end of October. For the first few weeks we lived in two small rooms where we had to get water downstairs. This was a trying time for Lowell when many accepted students were falling out. Lowell took time to find another room nearer the medical school. He made friends with the pastor of a Presbyterian church, who offered him an opening in East St. Louis as pastor to a small congregation there for a salary of $100 a month, with the use of the parsonage. We shared the parsonage with another medical student. They also had a baby boy.

Ruth and Tim joined me in medical school after I had found housing.

Our family in front of our St. Louis house at the beginning of the third year of medical school.

During this time we welcomed our daughter Mary into our family. For two years the men commuted to St. Louis to medical school, and Jane and I shared a 7:00 to 11:00 p.m. nursing position at a local hospital. In the third year of medical school we were forced to move back into St. Louis, as the demands of the school program were increasing. Back to rooming houses, and finally a third floor apartment with a private bathroom. Luxury! Lowell studied at the medical school library each evening.

By the second year in the apartment we welcomed Beth, so you can understand that my nursing experience was used to care for our own family. When we left St. Louis, our Board of Missions put us on a salary of $100 per month with the promise that we would repay this if we didn't go to the foreign field.

The summers were so terribly hot in St. Louis that we only spent one summer there and spent the others in Nerstrand so we could be with Lowell's parents. He painted houses with his father and was a famous softball fast pitcher for the local team. During all of these years we managed to attend Lake Koronis Assembly Grounds for their annual meeting. In later years, five of our six children would work as lifeguards or a pastry cook. It was at Koronis where Mary and Steve fell in love. While life guarding at Koronis, Andrew, our youngest, met a high school "sweetheart," Carrie Weiss. In the providence of time they were married.

The years in St. Louis were happy ones, with Lowell concentrating on studying and my caring for the children, after our return to St. Louis from East St. Louis, where he had served the small church. We have happy memories of wonderful friends – the Dales, Craigs, Pastor and Mrs. McIntyre, etc. Upon Lowell's graduation from medical school, we moved to St. Paul where he interned at Ancker Hospital. Some friends from Calvary Church helped us financially so we could buy a little old house within walking distance of the hospital. We were

Beth and John had joined our family by the time we boarded the *S.S. America* for our trip to Nigeria.

happy there with Tim attending kindergarten. At the end of his internship our assignment to Nigeria had to be delayed, as John was born in Kentucky where Lowell was relieving a doctor who was on vacation for one month. The next months, until our sailing in December, were busy with preaching assignments for Lowell, purchasing supplies for shipment to Nigeria, selling our house and returning the loan, and spending the last short time in Nerstrand with Lowell's parents. We sailed on the *S.S. American* from New York for England where we transferred to the *Accra* for the journey to Nigeria.

We had a wonderful trip to Nigeria with weather gradually becoming tropical. Arrived in Lagos without proper papers so we were delayed in leaving the ship, with a little lecture from the English office. Train trip to Jos and further preparations for the trip to Bambur. Lovely house and much help in hospital and house. I taught the children with Calvert Course until Tim was admitted to boarding school.

These memorable years in Nigeria, with joys and sorrows, Paul's birth and his serious illness and wonderful restoration. Tim and Mary in boarding school.

Return to U.S.A. for two years of residency for Lowell in general surgery at Akron General Hospital. Dr. Heinmiller visiting and urging us to return to Africa – to Sierra Leone. Again much planning and packing and arranging for schooling for children. The next three years were at Rotifunk Hospital, where Lowell started a surgical program. Children eventually went to Rupp Memorial School at Kabala, and Andrew was born. Pleasant times working with Harrises and others.

In 1960, we returned to Akron for Lowell's third year of surgical residency. He surprisingly received acceptance from University of Minnesota Ophthalmology Department for entrance into the program in June of 1961. Lowell spent that

Our house in Minneapolis during the ophthalmology residency.

year doing deputation for the Board, and the children completed the school year before moving to Minnesota.

Lowell bought a house on Oakland Avenue in Minneapolis, and we moved in early summer. Three years of study for Lowell, some deputation, good fellowship at Oakland Ave. E.U.B. Church, progress of children through school, resulting in Tim's graduation from high school, Mary and Beth planning to return to school in Africa – Nigeria, and the rest to Rupp Memorial School in Sierra Leone. In 1964 our deputation trip on the way to New York, and the World's Fair, and then the Pan Am flight to Sierra Leone. Tim was left behind at Lake Koronis to attend Westmar College.

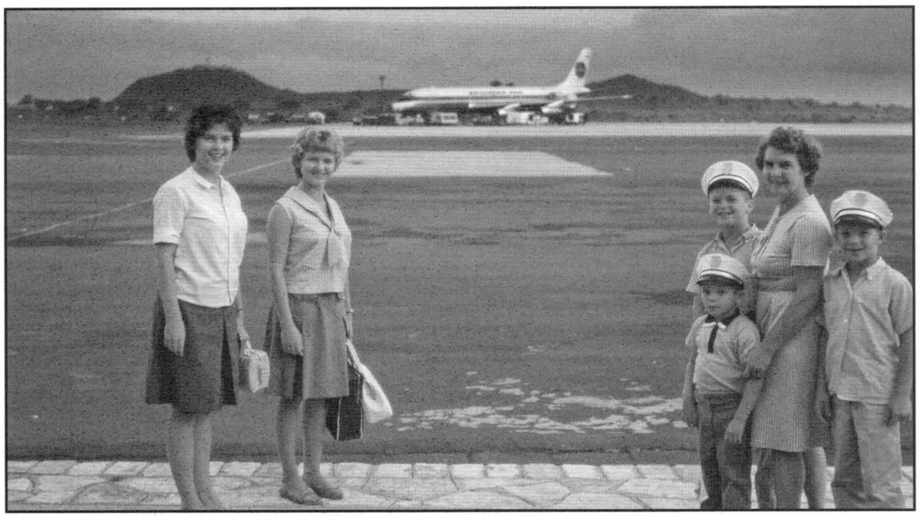

At Dakar airport where Mary and Beth transferred to a plane going to Nigeria, while the rest of us headed to Sierra Leone.

In between our African tours, we made some sentimental trips. I had happy days, wonderful times, in my youth at Clear Lake in Manitoba, Canada. One visit there was on July 21, 1969, when Neil Armstrong stepped onto the moon declaring "One small step for man, one giant step for mankind." We sneaked our children into a private gathering to witness this historic event on television.

Clear Lake! Happy memories of childhood and young womanhood – spruce trees and chewing gum, birch trees for making crafts, clear cold water fed by mountain springs.

My first visit as a nine year old was in 1926. Uncle Angus and Auntie Mary's family and the Davidson neighbors – fifteen in all – spent two weeks at the cottage. There we had a log raft and wore brilliant American Beauty colored bathing suits made from someone's castoff underwear and had then been dyed. We had a grand first of July Dominion Day picnic, even though rain left mud deep on the steep hill behind the cottages.

This was the beginning of the love story with this beautiful little lake in northern Manitoba. At a later time, cousin Elsie and I attended the CGIT (Canadian Girls in Training) on its shores. Wonderful friendships, sleeping in tents, lots of rain and depleted groceries necessitating several meals of pea and lettuce salad – all made for a memorable time.

The year Dad died, 1933, my cousin Angus brought a large tent to the campground and pitched it on a wooden floor. Camping became all the more exciting. The Administration Office and Jamboree hall were built of logs. Scattered throughout the grounds were shelters and huge cook stoves, wooden tables and benches. A large refrigeration building was filled with blocks of ice. Each group of campers had their own locker and padlock. Even so, things occasionally were missed. An enterprising lady put hard-boiled eggs in her locker, which caused a hilarious time when some caddies from the golf course tried to break the eggs into the frying pan in full view of their camping neighbors!

At Clear Lake, hours were spent in the sun and water, bicycling, roller skating and attending the nightly talent shows in the Jamboree Hall. Our tent was left there all summer with young people coming and going and relatives visiting on Sundays who brought food, supplies and spending money. What fun around the camp stoves, where at one time there might be eight kettles boiling, bacon and eggs frying, porridge and pancakes cooking. The open-air fellowship was wonderful. One evening a friendly woman cooked pancakes for all the campers!

Later when I was working in an office and in nurses training, short vacations took me back to my favorite lake. The years passed, I married, and we were blessed with six children. When my husband took me up to Clear Lake – my expectations were great. But alas, all had changed – not the lake, campground or shopping area – but those friends of other days were not there. I sat on a bench by the pier and reminisced with a lady from the area who also had memories of another time, sharing our nostalgia for friendships' past. Soon I was ready to leave and return home and to Africa with that hope that the life I am now living will also have wonderful memories.

Africa is the land of my calling. Africa is where my last two babies were born. Africa is where I am needed as a registered nurse and Christian witness. It is not a matter of "if" I will return to Africa or when I will return to Africa – I am ready NOW! Perhaps some day some of my children may have a nostalgic place of their own.

Chapter Seventy-Four

Ruth's Statement of Faith

(Written in 1972)

I believe in God as the creator and sustainer of the universe. I believe in Him as a personal, loving Father, forgiving, healing and reconciling. I believe His plan is for a full and abundant life for all of His creatures, and I believe that people are continually being brought into a new relationship with Him through Jesus Christ. I believe Christ showed us by His life and teachings what God was really like, and taught us how God wanted us to live. I believe that His life and His death on the cross reconciles us to God. My response to Christ has been, and is constantly, an inviting of Him into my heart and life, that He may live in and through me.

Prayer is an exciting and living experience to me. I am always anxious to be a part of small prayer groups, which are a blessing to me. I treasure the Bible, because in it I learn of God's ways and of His promises and demands upon us. Only through this book do I have contact with the earthly life of Jesus, His followers and the early church. I believe God speaks to us through the Bible.

I believe that the community of believers, the church, is Christ at work in the world today. We are "ambassadors for Christ" in seeking to bring people back into friendship with God. However, I do feel that as times and cultures and customs change we must adapt our methods and ways of expressing the unchanging love of God.

In person-to-person relationships I feel called to love and to care, and to have honesty and integrity in all my living. I feel we are called as Christians to fight intolerance, injustice, racism, indifference, and violence itself, by being actively involved in the political and public structures of our society, that all may have equal opportunity to enjoy and benefit from the plenty that is available.

Ruth as a young woman.

I honestly believe that Jesus taught – and God expects – nonviolence from His children. The very fact of nonviolence often causes violence on the part of others, and this is what I believe Jesus meant when He said that He came "not to bring peace, but a sword." I know that my nature often reacts violently, but I do not believe that He intends for us to willfully harm any person, physically or otherwise.

I feel called to this type of ministry, feeling perhaps that I might help to be a bridge of understanding between the two emphases. The things that unite us are much greater than those that divide.

I believe physical health is one of God's intentions for humanity, and I believe this includes the ability to see. I enjoy working with my husband in eye care. We intend to be an arm of the local church, reaching out in concern to those in need. I try to identify myself with them as with brothers and sisters in Christ, being helpful wherever and whenever I can. To those outside of the church relationship I want to be friendly, concerned about their needs, and willing to share what I have.

I respect others of non-Christian faiths. However, I believe that Christ was unique, and the most complete expression of God that man can know. I would seek to understand their faith and way of life, that I might confirm them in the truth they understand and help them to enlarge their understanding of God.

I will be constantly mindful that I am a guest in the country, and the guest of those with whom and under whom I work. I will try to be helpful without being dogmatic or overbearing. Authors who have impacted my life are: Dr. Ralph G. Turnbull, pastor; Elton Trueblood, writer; Dietrich Bonhoeffer, theologian; and Keith Miller, writer.

I believe I have an outgoing personality. I am friendly and meet people easily. I believe my greatest strength lies in the fact that I realize that I can't "go it alone," either without the help of others or of God. I tend to have an aggressive nature, and at times I am impatient. I feel that my recognition of these traits makes it possible for the grace of God to help me.

Ruth and Andrew "doctoring" one of our dogs in Sierra Leone.

I believe that God's intention for humanity is that a full, creative, meaningful, and abundant life may be experienced, and I feel that this life is possible for every person, especially as they come to know God's forgiveness and love, which He revealed to us in Jesus Christ.

I feel humanity is most in jeopardy today, by a feeling of self-sufficiency. There is a feeling that the physical world is all there is, and the spiritual or supernatural is just the figment of someone's imagination. I feel, too, that life is becoming so mechanized and computerized that somehow we are losing touch with one another as persons and feel little responsibility for the many who do not experience a meaningful life.

In relation to my last statement above, I feel that even the church stands in jeopardy today either through carelessness, indifference or even willfulness by failing to be what she is called to be as the Body of Christ in the world. That body is to be given "for others," and as it fails to enter into the needs of others, it fails to be the Church.

I believe that the Christian's response should be one of concern for all the needs of people today, whether it be physical, emotional, mental or spiritual. I believe that the Christian should begin as a listener but then address himself to whatever is within his power to remedy. Caring and active concern on the part of Christians today would go a long way to relieving the alienation and hopelessness many people feel.

I believe that "word" and "deed" are inseparable in God's intention. I believe we are called as Christians to good works, but then to be ready always to tell of the "hope that is within you" (1 Peter 3:15), that the thanks and glory may be God's.

Ruth's mother, Myrtle, Ruth and Irene.

I believe, however, that we are justified before God by faith, and that our deeds are the outcome of a love relationship that exists between God and us, which can only find expression in our love and concern for others, as so beautifully expressed in Matthew 25:40 (NEB) "Anything you did for one of my brothers here, however humble, you did for me."

I was born in Brookdale, a small village in Manitoba, Canada, and although I started there, I spent from fourth grade on in city schools in Winnipeg. I have a background of church and Sunday school involvement, as well as youth activities related to the church. The death of my father when I was sixteen years of age made me suddenly aware of a need to know some of the answers to life and death, and I found myself praying, "Lord, give me understanding."

During my teen years, I felt a growing awareness of God, through Christ, and gradually a sense of wanting to commit my ways to Him, that I could be useful. Upon graduation from high school, I attended business college and then worked in an office for several years. Finally, I felt that nurses' training would help me qualify for some particular service, perhaps on the mission field. The year I graduated from nurses' training, Lowell and I were married and I then concentrated on raising a young family. Even during our early years on the field in West Africa, I spent most of my time caring for our family, and on two different periods taught them with the Calvert Course until the boarding school opened. During this time I was actively involved in women's meetings and Sunday school classes. Throughout the last term in Sierra Leone with all of the children in boarding school, I was able to work in the clinic full time with my husband. This was a meaningful and rewarding experience for me. I treasure the love and friendship of many of our Sierra Leone friends.

Our family in 1960.

With our return to the U.S. in 1967, I became a homemaker, active in WSCS Church Women United, taught a Sunday school class, and had a considerable amount of speaking engagements in relation to our mission service. I was also active in the local Medical Auxillary and a study club. I have served as Chairman of Commission on Ecumenical Affairs, as well as being a member of the Pastor Parish relations committee.

A very meaningful experience for me was being at the Regional School of Missions in Bloomington, Minnesota, and then teaching "The New Generation in Africa" at Wesley Acres in North Dakota. The background reading was a great joy to me.

My marriage and family have brought me a great sense of fulfillment, but not to the exclusion of others. Perhaps our very real concern for others has helped to bind us together as a family.

In the last few years, I have read a lot and many of the books have resulted in a deepening of my devotional and prayer life. It is an exciting experience to be a Christian today, but even in my gratitude to God, I am made deeply aware of those in need and long – somehow – to share with them as I am able.

I am a registered nurse and hope to continue to use these skills in our Kissy UMC Eye Hospital. I also hope to help build bridges of understanding between the people from different backgrounds. I hope to be a link between the church in the U.S. and the church in Africa. During our married life we have lived in rural areas, in urban ghettos, in suburbia and on the mission field in Africa. I believe I can continue to work in each area, but in view of our years in West Africa, I feel drawn to continue our involvement there.

Ruth at home in her later years, her faith strong and ever growing.

Chapter Seventy-Five

"A Tribute to My Mother"

by Beth
(Written at age 14)

Mom is a wonder woman. Standing 5' 1 ½" in her stocking feet with her dark hair and blue eyes, people would never guess all she does and all she means to our family.

Ruth was an accomplished seamstress.

She is a nurse, cook, seamstress, counselor, and walking dictionary and encyclopedia all in one. We would be lost without her. If a member of our family can't find something, all we do is yell "Mom," and before long that which was lost is found.

Because my mother is a registered nurse, she has the chance to use her knowledge with all the minor accidents that happen around our home.

When I grow up I hope to be as good a cook as my mother. Not only is our food delicious, but we get a nice variety of food.

Since my mother sews, we can have a larger wardrobe. I was reminded of this more back in the States because of the comment of one of my friends. She said she wished her mother could sew.

Mom is very intelligent. She seems to have an endless amount of information. I love to get her opinion on subjects because they seem the best.

I think the characteristic I appreciate most about my mother is that she is a wonderful counselor and guide. I may go to her at any time, and talk to her about anything, and I can be sure of an answer. I think she uses more psychology on us than we realize. She is quite liberal in letting us do things. She lets us think things out for ourselves, which is often much harder than doing something just because she said to do it. Of course, if we did go ahead and do something wrong, she would let us know we weren't supposed to do it.

I think mothers are taken too much for granted these days. I know without my mom our family would be lost.

Beth continued her tribute to Ruth up until her last days with us.

Years later, when Beth was asked to give a Mother's Day tribute at a church occasion, she added the following: Mothers, we thank you for your faith in us, for your example, for preparing us to live in this world, and for leading us to a commitment to our Lord and Savior, Jesus Christ.

Chapter Seventy-Six

"This Is Home"

by Mary
(Written at age 17)

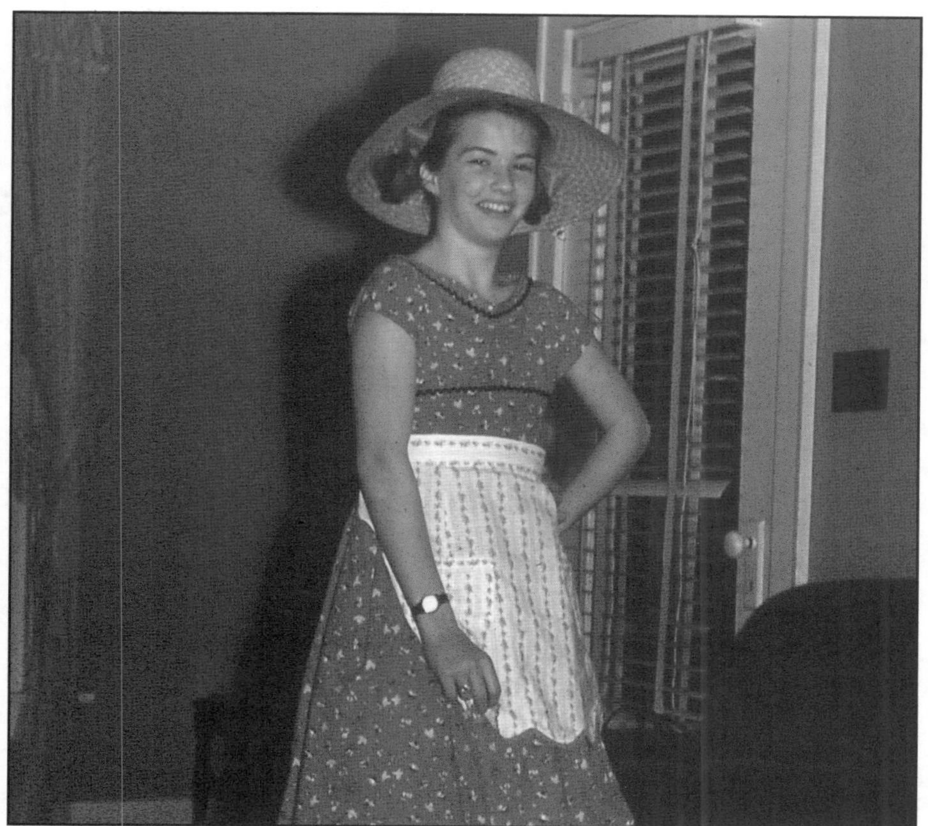

Mary as a high school senior when she wrote "This is Home." Mary could cut a caper as well as do serious writing.

Most people have at least one place that they can call home. This consists of more than merely a building; home is the composite of a multitude of little things that each person has experienced and loved there.

Home, to me, is a sunny, dew-drenched morning before the sun is hot; awakening to the singing from hospital staff prayers; the chirp of myriads of birds; the aroma of frying bacon; a multicolored and mismatched table service; a dog and cat vying for bits of waste from a slab of freshly killed beef; highly peppered rice dishes; the crackling sound of an expanding thin roof that breaks the heavy silence of noon; a tall glass of cold lemonade or iced tea after resting; a kerosene refrigerator wick that doesn't burn properly – hence, a defrosting ice-box that won't gel gelatin or freeze ice cubes; Campbell's soup for supper; a small child's prayer at family worship; a brilliant sunset over the swamp; the roar of the electric generator that comes on at dusk; swarming, buzzing bugs around each light; a lively game of "Rook"; the cozy atmosphere of soft music or children's records; warm, buttered popcorn; the dim of light bulbs when the electric water heater for baths is turned on; perpetually balmy nights; closely packed stars; a moon that one can just about read by; thousands of fireflies sparkling in the grass; the scurry for kerosene lamps when the generator blinks its going-off warning and the sudden stillness as it ceases; taut, crisp sheets; the security of a mosquito net; the stray firefly that finds its way into the darkened bedroom; an occasional cough of the night watchman; and the distant beating of drums.

Yes, this is my African home, and I love it.

Chapter Seventy-Seven

A Rugged Constitution

Ruth was an avid camper.

When Ruth and I had our physicals in Midway Clinic in St. Paul prior to our going to the mission field in 1952, the doctor told Ruth that she had a rugged constitution and would do well as a missionary. The children and I could not remember Ruth ever becoming ill. There were many times when she would be nursing members of the family but would not contract the disease herself. At one time in Africa the entire family contracted hepatitis, all seven of us, but not Ruth.

That ultimately changed. In 1973 while we were serving in Bo, she told me at breakfast on a Friday she was not coming down to the clinic for prayers. When she did not arrive at the clinic in the next hour or so, I wondered what might be troubling her, so I went back to the house. She was lying in bed ashen and in great pain. An examination suggested a gallbladder attack. It had been ten years since I had done my last gallbladder surgery and our instruments were largely eye instruments. I gave her a Demerol injection and then we discussed pain management.

I then informed the staff and the mission superintendent that Ruth needed surgery. We made a hurried trip from Bo to Freetown, a distance of approximately

160 miles. We knew that KLM had a flight Friday evenings from Freetown to Amsterdam. We could get help in the Netherlands or in Germany. While securing tickets, I found out that the cost was as much to fly to Amsterdam as it was to fly to New York City. We decided that it would be more appropriate to go to our own country where English was spoken. We boarded a plane, transferred in Amsterdam and arrived in New York late Saturday afternoon.

Ruth's trip for gallbladder surgery – from Freetown, to Amsterdam, to JFK airport in New York to the Mayo Clinic in Rochester, Minnesota.

Being a Saturday, we were unable to contact anyone from the Board of Missions. A sudden inspiration prompted me to inquire about a flight from New York to Rochester, Minnesota, where the Mayo Clinic is located. We learned that there was a direct flight leaving within two hours. We arrived in Rochester Saturday evening and went directly to the Mayo Clinic's emergency room. The doctor admitted Ruth to the hospital. On Sunday, blood work was done and on Monday morning her gallbladder operation was performed. They used subcutaneous sutures and said that they didn't need to see her again. We were free to fly back to Sierra Leone after being absent for only ten days and resumed our work at the Bo Eye Clinic.

This was the first problem that Ruth had experienced since her lung collapsed at age eighteen. However in 1993, twenty years after her gallbladder surgery, when we were on the way back from doing volunteer eye surgery in Zimbabwe, Ruth suffered a stroke on the flight from Hawaii to Los Angeles. Her vitals signs were normal, but she appeared tired and was reluctant to talk. I made arrangements with the stewardess to have an ambulance meet the plane upon arrival and requested that everyone remain seated while Ruth and I were escorted off the plane.

On debarking the plane we were met by paramedics. They insisted they needed to examine the patient before the ambulance could take her to the hospital. I tried to reason with them that I was a doctor and that she was in immediate need of medical treatment. This made no impression upon them and insisted that since I was her husband, I was not in a position to make medical decisions objectively. I finally said, "If you don't want to take her to the hospital promptly, I'll hire a taxi." At this point they decided they would take her and while I gathered the suitcases, Ruth was put on a cart and the two men wheeled her from the plane to the airport terminal.

On arriving at the airport building there were steps to climb. I was about halfway between the plane and Ruth when I saw them ask Ruth to get off the gurney while they lifted the gurney up the steps and Ruth climbed the stairs behind them. When I finally caught up to them, Ruth was placed in the ambulance. They were about to start their examination routine and start IV fluids. I tried to reason with them that since the hospital was only five minutes from the airport, it would be wiser to wait with the IV. With all the bouncing and the moving of the ambulance it would be difficult to get a needle in a vein. Again there was an altercation, but I prevailed.

On arriving at the hospital, I secured a cart, placed Ruth on it and took her in because I was no longer willing to be delayed by this emergency crew. On coming to the registration desk, they took our information and I was shown into a room. Ruth was nowhere to be seen. As I inquired about her whereabouts, they said that the emergency doctor was examining her but that I was to remain in the waiting room. With all that had happened prior to this, without another a word I went through the doors and searched until I found where Ruth was being examined.

I spoke with the emergency doctor and explained Ruth had experienced a stroke on the left side of the brain near the visual area. On the plane when I checked Ruth's fields, she evidenced a complete bilateral right lateral hemianopsia. The young doctor looked at me with surprise, but said, "Come along and we'll do a scan." The lesion was found exactly as described. The doctor then called the attending physician who arrived in about fifteen minutes. When he came in the room, he had a broad smile on his face for apparently he had been told about some of the trials I had endured. He checked the scan, confirmed the field changes and sent Ruth up to the floor where she was immediately treated with heparin. He asked if I had a place to stay and offered to take me to a nearby motel.

I visited Ruth the first thing in the morning. She had already regained some speech with the prompt treatment she had received. However, when examined by the doctors she had difficulty answering some of the questions and was coy about it. One question was: "Do you know where you live?" Ruth answered with a little chuckle: "Of course I know where I live." "Would you tell us the name of the city?" Ruth's reply: "Everybody knows where I live." Ruth had anomia, an inability to use proper names.

In succeeding days she markedly improved. Within four days we were able to take a flight to Minneapolis and were met by Steve and Mary. We stopped at the emergency room of the Douglas County Hospital for blood clotting time, and then whisked her to our home on Lake Burgen. Dr. McCrery took over and Ruth did extremely well except for the loss of vision to the right side in both eyes. This made it difficult for her to read because she could not see the letter until she had focused on it. Within a few months she learned to look ahead and was able to read once more.

Ruth steadily recovered from her stroke so that she was able to accompany me two years later on a voluntary eye surgery trip to Abak, Nigeria, in 1995. At the hospital in Abak we were met with more than one hundred patients who needed eye surgery. I selected forty patients who were bilaterally blind and did their cataract extractions with intraocular implants first. Later, we performed surgeries on those who had just one cataract eye. We were very comfortable with the guesthouse where we had the luxury of having someone do the housekeeping and having a cook who prepared meals for us. In the tropics where it is so hot, each of us was given a bed in which to spread out. We used the mosquito nets but after a number of days Ruth began to complain of "chigger bites" on her feet and ankles. We didn't think anything of it at the time and ultimately arrived home to our house on Lake Burgen.

Several days later when I came home for lunch Ruth was still sitting in her favorite chair. It was apparent she was ill. I immediately took her to the hospital. The doctor did a thorough examination and decided Ruth had the flu. We returned home. Ruth took some aspirin and felt better. The next day she became extremely ill. We took her back to the hospital and this time I requested a giemsa

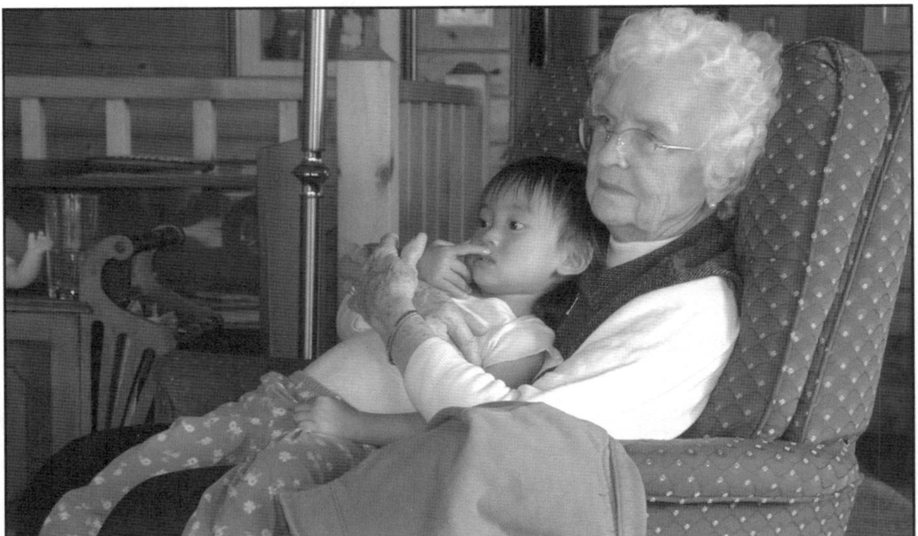

Ruth in her better days holding Anna, Andrew's oldest daughter, in her favorite chair.

blood smear to rule out malaria. The smear showed many falciparum parasites – the deadly type of malaria. The problem was where in Alexandria would we find proper medication for a critically ill patient who was in the throes of a possible chloroquine-resistent type of malaria? As it turned out, the daughter of the Trumm Drug owner had made a trip to Africa just several months earlier and had purchased the new medication that controlled malaria even though chloroquine did not. With the proper medication, Ruth steadily improved and within several days was herself again.

After this experience, several times a urinary tract infection supervened and she needed to be hospitalized. But it wasn't until 2005 when Ruth began to have transient ischemic attacks (TIAs) that she showed signs of failing. After hospitalizations she needed nursing care at Knute Nelson Nursing Home. On her third admission to Knute Nelson, the care became very restrictive. She was not allowed to walk by herself or even try to get out of the wheelchair without automatic sensors setting of an alarm that brought nurses running. Ruth could not live in this restricted way. We signed a legal policy freeing the nursing home from any responsibility if she had a fall. During her problems and ill health, Ruth did fall seventeen times but never fractured any bones.

After being at Knute Nelson for several months, Ruth insisted on coming home. All the department heads were in agreement that she could not manage at home. Ruth, with her aggressive nature, tried to escape the hospital one night. This prompted a new discussion with the department heads and they agreed to allow her to come home in my care as long as they would be able to participate with home nursing care. On February 1, 2007, Ruth came home. Twice a week she had a bath by a visiting nurse and physical therapy once a week. Ultimately she began to get weaker, but we managed for two and a half years before her weakness overwhelmed her and I was unable to lift her.

Ruth showed dramatic improvement during the last two and a half years she was at home.

She agreed in July 2010 to enter Diamond Willow, a nursing facility. Ruth was pleased with the compassionate care of the staff, but some weeks later in October she had another stroke, which made it difficult for her to swallow. She had difficulty speaking but prayers came spontaneously. She denied having any pain. On October 25, 2010 at the age of ninety-three, Ruth passed away. In December we would have celebrated sixty-five years of marriage. I thank God that out of all the people in the world, Ruth and I found each other. Our lives were filled with joy, serving God by serving others.

Chapter Seventy-Eight

"Let Not Your Heart Be Troubled"

Following one of our daily devotional periods, four or five years before Ruth's death (on October 25, 2010) when her health was slipping, she said: "I don't fear death, I am concerned (anxious) about the events leading to death." Ruth's father had died suddenly while on a business trip. Her mother was struck by an errant automobile while she in a crosswalk in 1970. She was admitted to the hospital semi-comatose, but lived through the night.

Ruth's mother, Myrtle, participating in a Christmas cookie-decorating contest surrounded by Mary, Andrew, Lowell and John.

In the morning, Beverly, Ruth's sister from Fort Wayne, Indiana, and Ruth found each other in the Seattle airport while transferring to Vancouver. They immediately taxied to the hospital and were directed to their mother's room by the nurse who cheerfully informed them that "Myrtle" was conscious but found it an effort to speak. Their other sister, Irene, had been with their mother earlier in the day. Now Ruth and Bev were by their mother's bedside. She could not open her eyes, but her face lit up when they spoke to her. She could not answer back. While Ruth held one hand and Bev the other, Ruth was led to pray a few sentences which included Psalms 91: "The Lord shall give his angels charge over you, to keep you in all your ways." Each of the girls expressed their love and thanked their mother for being so good to them and making provision in difficult times. It was then that Myrtle spoke, "I have tried."

Ruth and her mother a few years before her fatal accident.

At that moment, the nurse came in and asked if Ruth and Bev would step outside for a moment while some attention was given to the patient. Less than a minute later, they were called back into the room. Their mother was no longer breathing, having passed into the presence of Jesus, her redeemer and Lord.

Dying was not the concern with Ruth. It was not death that she thought about. It was in the panic and possible pain of dying that occupied her mind. How does one endure the dying process? I would assure Ruth that medicines help if any pain is involved, but with firmness I would emphasize "Remember the promises of Jesus in the Gospel of John, chapter 14":

- Verse 1 "Let not your heart be troubled; you believe in God, believe also in me."
- Verse 2 "I go to prepare a place for you."
- Verse 3 "Where I am, there you may be also."
- Verse 18 "I will not leave you comfortless."
- Verse 19 "Because I live you will live also."
- Verse 27 "Peace I leave with you."

As Ruth weakened and needed professional care at Diamond Willow, she suffered another stroke in early October 2010. Ultimately, she was unable to swallow food or drink, including tea, which she dearly appreciated every day in her final years. She denied any discomfort or pain. Even when she was unable to speak, her response to our questioning about discomfort or pain would be met with denial by moving her head from side to side and not up and down. She died in her sleep, spared the question of "Will dying be difficult?"

Married nearly sixty-five years.

Chapter Seventy-Nine

Farewell, My Love

(Written for Ruth's funeral, October 30, 2010)

I thank God that out of all the people in the world, Ruth and I found each other to become "heirs of the grace of life" (1 Peter 3:7). Love at first sight became real for us. We became husband and wife a year later.

Ruth, the love of my life.

Not only was I drawn to Ruth by her beauty and character, I rejoiced to learn she had received a call to missions. I had often wondered who would go with me to some place of service half a world away. Ruth already had instructions from the Lord like those given to Abraham: "Leave your country, your people and your father's household and go to the land I will show you, and all [those] people will be blessed through you!" (Genesis 12:1-2). In preparation, she attained a registered nursing degree.

While brought up in a nominally Christian home, it wasn't until she was in her early twenties that in her words she was "converted" and took hold of the new life offered by Jesus. During work breaks for seven years she would steal away and read her Bible. Half of her Bible was underlined with black or red markings. At this time she felt a call to Christian missions as a nurse. A salary of $90 a month during the last two of the seven years enabled her to save enough to train for her registered nursing degree.

Her prayer life and her revered love for the Bible continued throughout her lifetime unknown to her children as they were tucked away in their beds during these vigils. However, as a family while the children were growing up we read through Hurlbut's *Story of the Bible* a number of times. Wherever she went, she always wanted to be involved in a Bible study. If there wasn't one, she would start one.

Ruth loved music and enjoyed participating in her high school production of Gilbert and Sullivan's *HMS Pinafore.* **Rush is in the center of the second full row.**

Ruth intensely loved music. She sang in groups and choirs from youth on. She never considered her voice as being gifted but she stated that heaven would take care of that. Each day for years it had been Ruth's and my practice to read the Bible, pray and sing a hymn. It was during one such time on January 13, 2010 that the inspiration was born from the scripture reading (Acts 10:39-43) that a book could be written about the glorious growth of the Church in Sub-Saharan Africa during our lifetime. *Glorious Witnesses for Africa* resulted.

In recent years our singing has been from Kenneth Osbeck's *Amazing Grace*, which gives background about hymns and their authors. Inside a Hersey's chocolate kiss I once gave Ruth we were amused to read this message "Sing! No matter how bad it sounds." Coming up the stairs from our basement bedroom one morning, our son-in-law, Steve, remarked that our singing didn't sound so bad and complemented Ruth on her alto.

Together we served congregations at St. Cloud-Graham and Mayer churches. Our four years of medical school and one year of internship were managed on a meager income. Some of our living quarters had no wallpaper and no running water. In spite of demanding studies we were sublimely happy for we were following the Lord's call and direction for our lives.

We lived a mobile life. On short notice Ruth could successfully organize a move. She managed long-term planning for our children as they grew up in Africa. Clothing sizes had to be adjusted for the passing of three years. One time, we had twenty-seven pairs of shoes of various sizes in our luggage. Ruth was called upon to do some home schooling. Tim, Mary, Beth and John travelled with us on our first trip to Nigeria. Paul was born there. Andrew was born in Sierra Leone where the mission board next transferred us. How Ruth managed our household is awesome to me to this very day.

Ruth was a devoted wife, supportive in all the trials and tribulations of a mission doctor. She was a loving mother – the children really had a full time mother. Ruth always assured me that with her background she didn't need or expect much of the fineries of life. Even with our little or no financial resources, it is unlikely that any of our children ever realized how grim things were at times. I never heard our children say that they went to bed hungry. They had a mother's love and she was there for them. She managed to care for their every need.

Ruth made it possible for me to practice medicine. She organized everything else, including the clinics and travel arrangements, freeing me to diagnose and treat patients' ailments.

I know of no greater human love that is possible than that with Ruth, my dear wife. In these moments I release her into the care of our loving Lord and Savior, Jesus, whom we loved, honored, shared and followed all our days together.

Farewell, my love.

Part V: Our Children

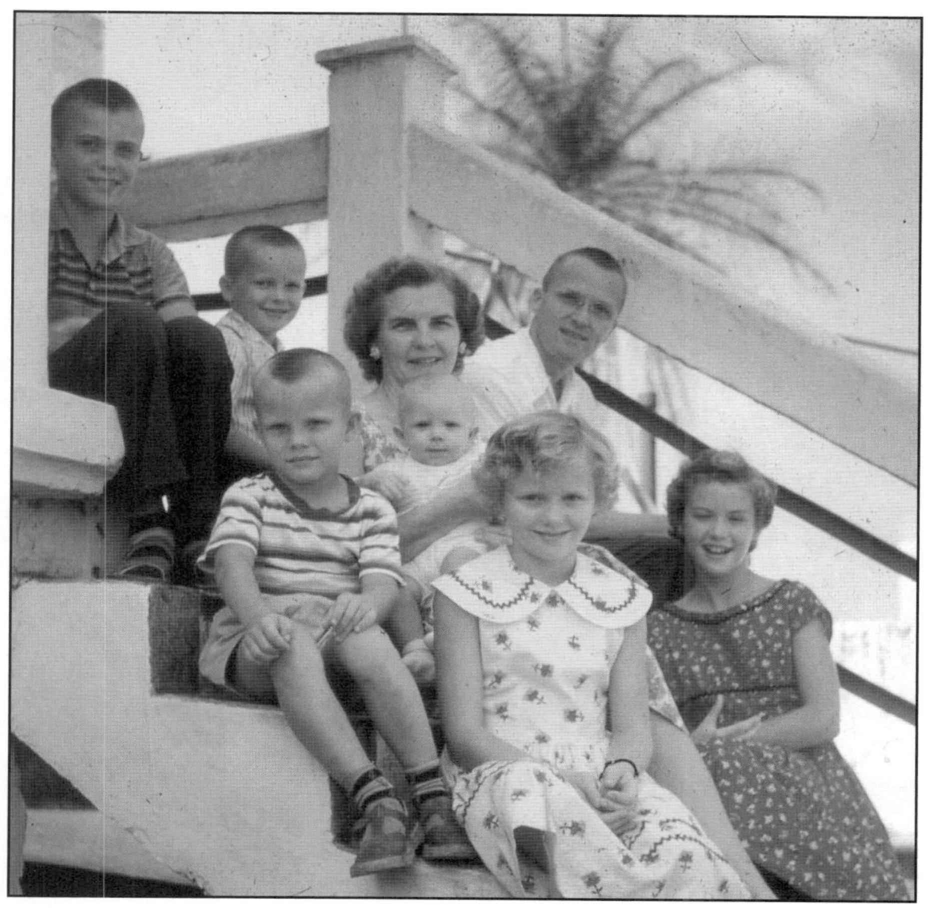

Like arrows in the hands of a warrior are children born in one's youth.
Blessed is the man whose quiver is full.... – Psalm 127:4-5a

Chapter Eighty

Timothy

For this reason I am sending to you ***Timothy****, my son whom I love, who is faithful in the Lord. He will remind you of my way of life in Christ Jesus, which agrees with what I teach everywhere in every church. – 1 Corinthians 4:17*

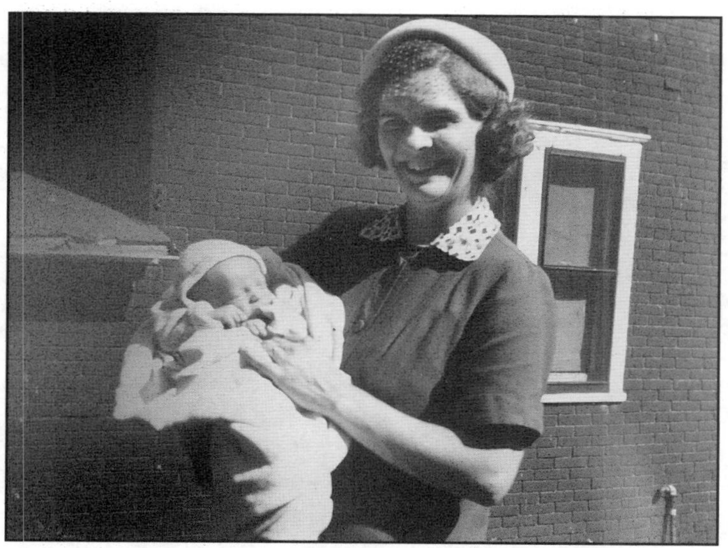

We prayed that Tim would not be an only child. Our prayers were answered bountifully.

Our first child, Tim, was born in Minneapolis while Ruth and I served the Mayer Evangelical United Brethren Church and I was finishing up pre-medical courses at the University of Minnesota. He was a very active youngster. When he found a way to climb out of his crib, I threatened I would do something about it. With a radiant face he said, "Ice cream?"

In St. Louis during my medical school training, Tim grew up watching "Howdy Doody" on our neighbor's TV. One day during the show's intermission, Tim went outside to play and discovered a batch of eggs. Before intermission ended, all of the eggs had been smashed on the side of the garage. A serious discussion followed.

While living in our St. Clair house during my internship at Ancker Hospital, Tim began school. The following year he was home schooled for a while in Nigeria at our mission house in Bambur but then attended Hillcrest School in Jos.

While Tim was active and headstrong as a child, he was also dependable. On our trips in and out of Africa, he had the responsibility of carrying our cameras in a metal ammunition box. With a stable oldest child, Ruth and I were blessed as his sisters and brothers joined our family.

Tim had paper routes in Akron, where I was in a general surgical residency, as well as in Minneapolis while I was in ophthalmology residency. In high school he excelled in swimming and track. His four-mile relay team holds the cinder track record to this day. I had the joy of being present during the event. Tim began the first four laps of his mile run and provided a lead for the next runner. The third trackster also lengthened that lead, but it was the final lap that was dramatic. At the beginning of the last 440 run around the track, the public address system came on. The announcer excitedly said: "Ladies and gentlemen, it is obvious that a new track record is being set today. Why don't you bring him in?" The crowd began to cheer and then erupted as Bill Bernard crossed the finish line.

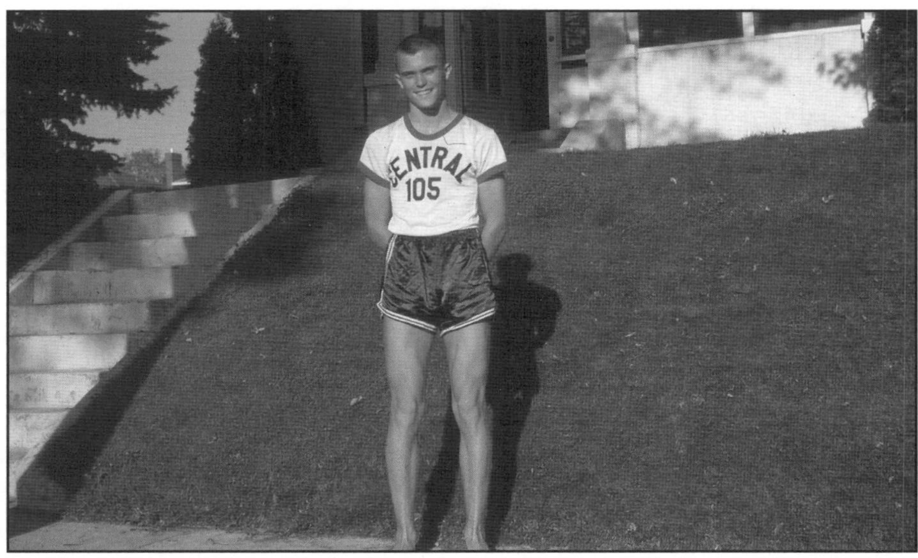

Tim (along with his teammates) still hold the record for the four-mile cinder relay at Central High School in Minneapolis.

It was hard to leave Tim in the U.S. at Westmar College when we returned to Sierra Leone in 1964. He graduated with a B.A. and then obtained a B.S. of Medicine at the University of North Dakota. He then earned his M.D. from the University of Minnesota.

After his internship at St. Paul Ramsey Hospital (formerly Ancker Hospital), he served at the Indian reservation at Fort Yates, North Dakota.

During a three-month visit with us at Bo in 1975, he learned many ophthalmic procedures – including performing cataract and glaucoma surgery – that put him in an advanced residency position at the Ophthalmology Department of the University of Minnesota.

When the time came to decide on a place to practice, he asked Ruth and me if he and his wife Joanne could come to Alexandria. We were delighted beyond measure, but I feared what could occur in a father-son combined practice, as fathers never stop being fathers. From the first day, he was his own boss and soon eclipsed his father with his new techniques. During our three-month forays to Africa and other places in the world, Tim covered for us. None of our patients was left without a careful follow-up.

Tim became the first ophthalmologist north of the Twin Cities to utilize phacoemulsification for cataract removal prior to the implantation of intraocular lenses. Other doctors began using phaco about a decade after Tim had started using it in Alexandria.

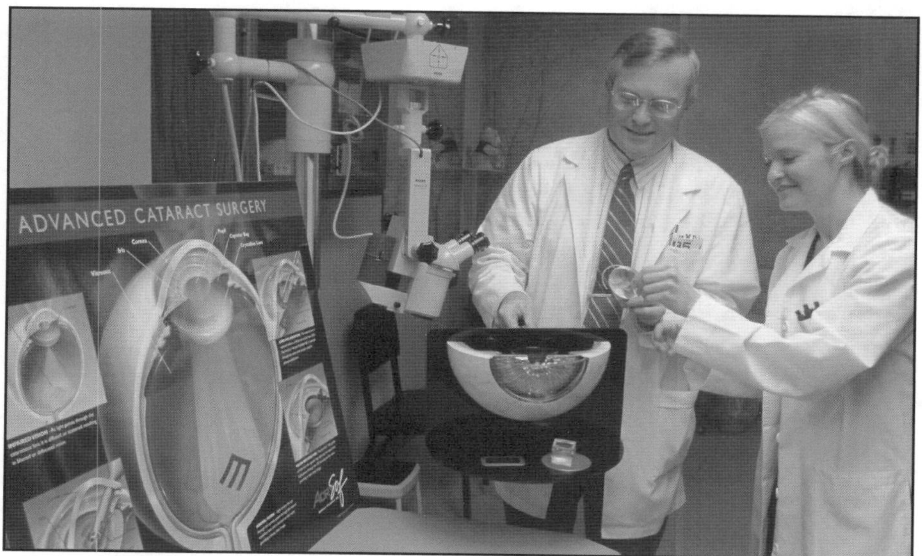

Ophthalmologist, Dr. Tim Gess with ophthalmologist daughter, Deborah Gess Ristvedt, discussing intraocular lens features.

Tim continues as a skilled eye surgeon. His wife, Joanne, ably manages the practice. He has the help of his four beautiful daughters from time to time. His second daughter, Deborah Ristvedt, is also an ophthalmologist and joined his practice in July 2011. She and her husband, Eric, welcomed daughter Sophie in July 2011. The eldest daughter, Rebecca (Becky) Walsh, is married to Matt and is an R.N. They have sons Miles and Mason. Beautiful Sarah Gess has a son, Landon, and Elizabeth (Elly) Gess graduated with a B.A. from Westmont College in California in the spring of 2011. Elly married Brett Hayes, a catcher for the Florida Marlins in the National Baseball League, on November 4, 2011.

Tim's family. Front row (from left): Elly, Debby with daughter Sophie, Sarah with son Landon, Becky with sons Miles and Mason. Back row (from left): Brett, Eric, Tim, Joanne and Matt.

Tim suffered a neck injury in 2009, which required surgery. During his pre-surgical treatment, a palliative injection resulted in neurologic signs and symptoms. Thankfully, he is able to see patients and has a full surgical load.

Tim frequently checks up on his father. His visits are appreciated beyond measure. Tim is a loving son.

Chapter Eighty-One

Mary

*And **Mary** said: "My soul glorifies the Lord and my spirit rejoices in God my Savior." – Luke 1:46-47*

Mary was born in St. Louis during our medical training. When I first saw her, she had a ribbon in her hair that the nurses had given her. She always seemed to do things early. She began walking at eleven months. The first day she walked was when we carried her into our little federated church in St. Louis and set her down on the floor; she spied a favorite friend and walked into his extended arms. She continued to walk the entire day after realizing that she had balance. Words came early, and she prayed in sentences before the age of three. (My parents worried because I didn't begin to talk or say words *until* three.)

Mary as a small girl in Nigeria watching a road grader. Ruth made her dress.

In grade school, Mary always needed extra work to keep her busy. She was very energetic and willing to take on new things. On her first day of school in Akron, Ohio, after we had returned from Africa and I began a general surgery residency at the Akron General Hospital, she attempted to walk home from school by herself. She missed a turn and kept walking into unknown territory. Eventually, the police officer we had called brought her home.

During the time of our ophthalmology residency in Minneapolis, she had the thrill of being a cheerleader at Central High School and joined the National Honor Society as a junior. However, when we returned to Taiama, Mary decided to go back to Africa for her last year of high school and attended Hillcrest School in Jos, Nigeria, along with her younger sister Beth.

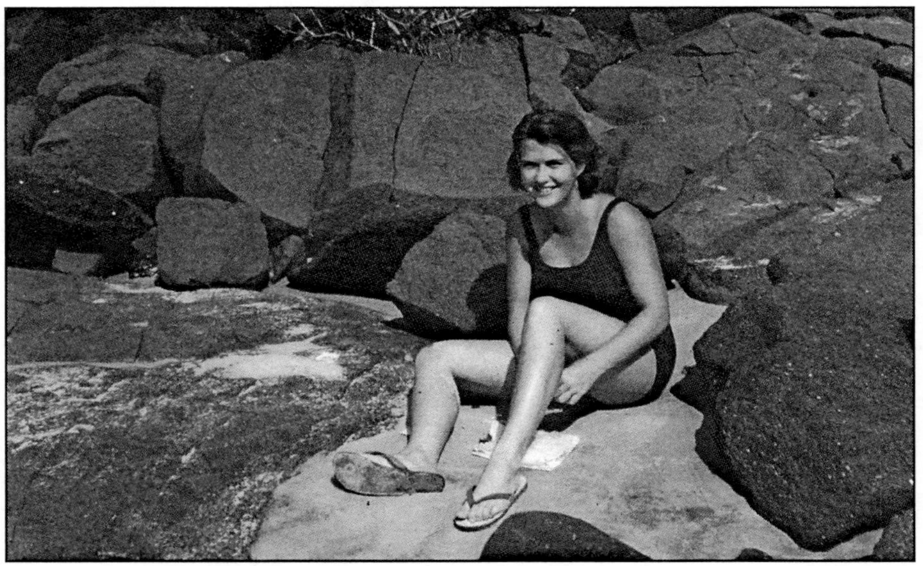

Mary when she was a high school senior at Hillcrest in Jos, Nigeria, holidaying on Hamilton Beach with the family near Freetown.

She attended Westmar College for only a year while Tim was still there. She wanted to pursue nursing, so it was necessary for her to transfer to a qualified program; she attended the University of Minnesota and earned a degree in nursing.

Like all the other Gess children, Mary worked summers at the Lake Koronis Assembly Grounds. All four boys served as lifeguards, but Mary became a cook. A friendship with Steve Boehlke at Koronis led to wedding bells and a move to Princeton, New Jersey, where Steve was in youth ministry following seminary graduation. Mary received a Master's Degree in Maternal-Child Health from the University of Pennsylvania and a Doctorate Degree in Clinical Psychology from Yeshiva University and postgraduate certification in psychoanalysis. Her office is in St. Louis Park, Minnesota, where she sees adults and couples. Her husband Steve is in leadership training for corporations, which include Exxon, Merck, Sharp and Dohme and others. I shall forever have a deep respect for Merck in that they made available at no charge their discovery of mectizan, which has cured 20 million people afflicted with onchocerciasis known as "river blindness."

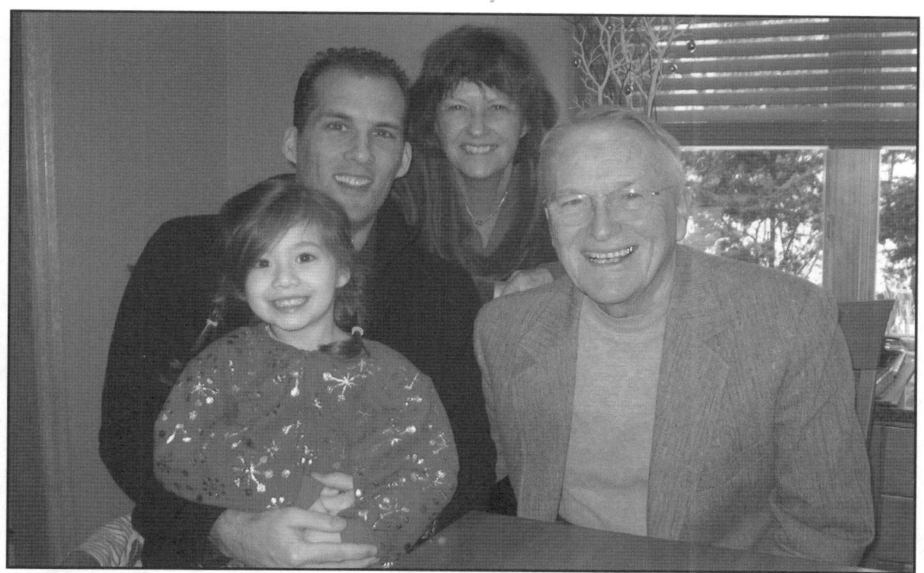

Four generations of "Gesses." From left: Eva Luna Boehlke; Dr. Christopher Boehlke, opthamologist; Dr. Mary Boehlke, clinical psychologist; Dr. Lowell Gess.

Mary has fond memories that include cooking, reading, being at the ocean and enjoying music in Africa as well as the U.S. "Cooking with Mom was great fun. She was patient as well as encouraging in the midst of the mess and 'experiments.' Dad and Mom brought the classics to Africa in packing barrels, so we enjoyed these. The Freetown library carried the whole 'Tarzan' series in paperback! We

Mary with husband Steve, daughter Jennifer, and son Christopher with wife Gabby.

spent memorable vacations at beautiful Hamilton Beach, swimming and chasing hermit crabs. Dad always had a variety of records playing. We would run and sing to the music. With basic support from Mom and Dad as well as from Beth and my four brothers, there was always plenty of fun."

Mary and Steve have a son, Christopher, who is also an ophthalmologist; he is married to Gabby and has two children, Eva and Noah. Their daughter, Jennifer, is a specialist in advertizing.

Mary often points her car northward to visit Alexandria. Ruth especially anticipated these visits and Mary's nursing care. She still faithfully visits and calls several times a week. Mary is a loving daughter.

Chapter Eighty-Two

Elizabeth

When Elizabeth heard Mary's greeting, the baby leaped in her womb, and ***Elizabeth*** *was filled with the Holy Spirit. – Luke 1:41*

Beth, like Mary, was born in St. Louis during our four years of medical school. Just as she was beginning to enjoy Forest Park and her friends, we moved to St. Paul for my internship at Ancker General Hospital, now called Regional Hospital.

Beth (under two years of age) discovered applying lipstick was not as easy as it looked.

I have fond memories of Beth as a little girl. She was into everything. One day she "borrowed" Ruth's lipstick and applied the lipstick with youthful inaccuracy. She also found coins in Ruth's purse to buy candy. "When I was about six years old, I began to steal money from my mother's purse to buy candy at a nearby store. One day I hid orange 'peanuts' up in a tree in a vacant lot. Some neighborhood girls came to our door with the candies, asking if they were mine. I remember Mom taking me up to my bedroom. She didn't discipline me, but talked about Jesus. Then she asked me if I wanted to accept Jesus as my Savior. I said yes. I never stole again."

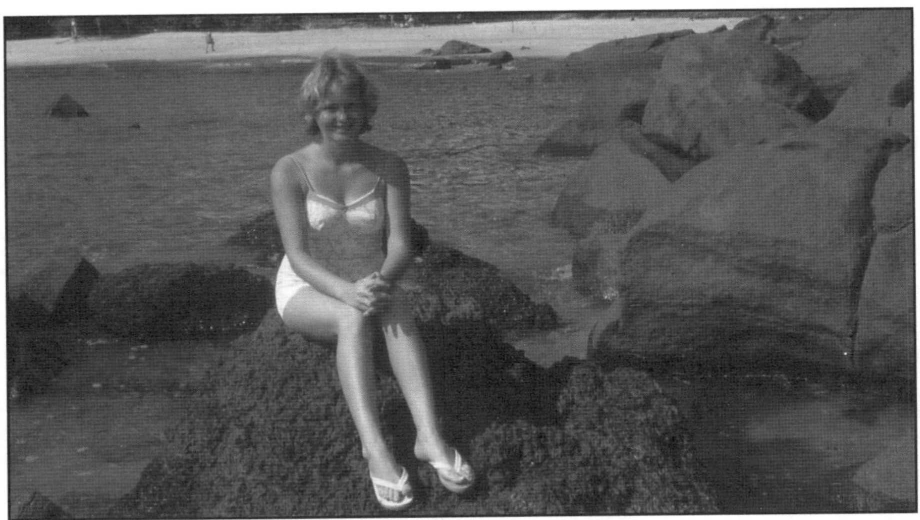

High school student Beth sun bathing at Hamilton Beach.

Beth also had some home school training at Rotifunk for a short period before joining Tim and Mary at the Kabala Rupp Memorial School. She also attended Hillcrest in Jos and had some exciting trips between Nigeria and Sierra Leone when she came to visit us at Taiama. She spent her senior year in high school in Bismarck, North Dakota, where her brother John was her escort for the graduation ball. At Seattle Pacific University, she earned her B.A., majoring in speech. An M.A. was granted in Professional Counseling from Liberty University. She is trained in EMOR (Eye Movement Desensitization and Reprocessing).

Beth married her classmate, Bob Hopkins, following graduation from college. Together they set out in a little Colt Dodge sedan for Anchorage, Alaska, where Bob serves as a meteorologist. Over the years he has worked his way into a top managerial position. Beth and Bob have raised two sons, John and David (recently married to Stephanie), who are computer software engineers. Daughter Rebecca (Becky) Glosser is married to Jesse, an R.F. engineer. Becky is a certified teacher in the state of Alaska. Her gift for teaching harkens all the way back to her childhood as she played "teacher"

Beth on her way to the Bismarck High School prom.

Beth's family. Back row: Christy, Beth, Bob, Becky. Front row: John Robert, David and Becky's husband, Jesse.

with the other children. Christine (Christy), the youngest Hopkins, attained her registered nursing degree in 2012.

With Bob and occasionally other members of her family, Beth has taken volunteer trips to Africa. During these trips she lectured in schools on topics such as family ethics. It was on one of these trips that Becky and Jesse fell in love.

Beth joined Anchorage's Cornerstone Clinic in November 2007. She provides therapy for most mental health issues, such as anxiety and depression. She works with individuals, couples, families and adolescents. Her special interests include relationship issues (premarital, marital, friends, family, etc), weight loss, anger management, trauma, grief and loss, addictions, and faith-based concerns.

It is a joy to hear Beth's voice on the telephone, to learn of her news and of her family. It is a tender moment when she signs off. It is always: "I love you."

Chapter Eighty-Three

John

***John** replied in the words of Isaiah the prophet, "I am the voice of one calling in the desert, 'Make straight the way for the Lord.'" – John 1:23*

The arrival of John in August of 1952 delayed our departure for Africa for several months. He was born at Redbird Mission near Pineville, Kentucky, and was delivered by Dr. John Shafer just after he and his family had returned from a vacation.

Prior to our North Atlantic rough ocean crossing, I had considered seasickness mostly psychological. When our entire family, including four-month old John, all experienced seasickness on that crossing my opinion changed. Motion illness is real.

During the meningitis outbreak at Bambur in Nigeria, John became alarmingly ill. We had to know if he had contracted meningitis. I performed a spinal tap on him on the dining room table and our fears were relieved. John survived a viral infection.

John had a passion for toy cars. He pushed them around with appropriate car sounds. On one trip into Jos for supplies, we suddenly realized a member of our family was missing. We scurried to the last place where we had shopped for supplies and found John, still directing his car, on the floor.

Even at age four, motorcars were important to John. Later on he rebuilt a Volkswagen engine.

As a child, John was indestructible. A run-a-way Land Rover stopped just a split second before going over a ledge – John was playing in the road directly below. Once, when Ruth accelerated turning left at a stoplight, John, sitting on the front seat, was hurled out into the street. Ruth slammed on the breaks and instructed him to get BACK INTO THE CAR! He did.

One of the wild boars shot by John on Mount Bintumani.

Hunting held a great attraction for John in Africa. He was allowed to have a firearm at KRMS (Kabala Rupp Memorial School). With John around, no monkey was safe at Taiama. Monkey burgers are quite tasty. However, Surry, our African cook, would not eat them with us because monkeys "too much favored mortal man." Along with Paul and me, John also made the trek up 6,930-foot Mount Bintumani.

Ruth insisted every child should be able to swim. A life saving course enabled John to be a lifeguard at Koronis like his three brothers. Adept at water as well as snow skiing, he could "barefoot." His real love was soccer. On a visit to Seattle Pacific University, Ruth and I were able to watch John compete. He turned out to be the hero by scoring the winning goal three minutes before the game ended. Ruth's comment: "My, that is really a strenuous game with all that running."

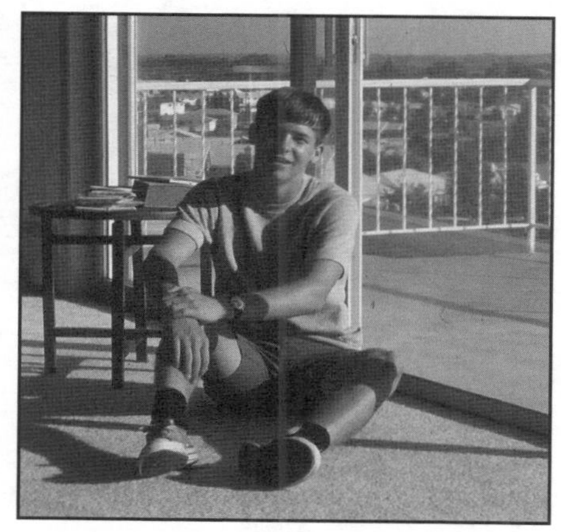

John was a sports enthusiast in high school.

John graduated from Seattle Pacific University with a B.S. in Biology. He then went on to a M.S. in Visual Science and an O.D. in Optometry. John has carved out a successful optometric practice in Alexandria, with offices next door to our house.

John married his college sweetheart, Ruth Cederborg, who has degrees in clothing and textiles as well as a J.D. in law. Son Adam is an ophthalmologist (married to Rena a psychiatrist), daughter Britta is in Hamlin University law school, and Peter just graduated from Northwestern College in St. Paul with degrees in history and psychology. He is a soccer coach and family care coordinator.

Optometrist, Dr. John Gess, with son Adam, an ophthalmologist who will start a cornea fellowship in 2012.

Little known hobbies of John's are cooking and gardening. His gardens are precisely laid out according to his attention for detail. I have been told by patients that they consider John the best eye doctor they ever had. I am proud he is my son.

John's family, from left: Peter, Britta Lisa, daughter-in-law Rena, Adam, Ruth and John.

Chapter Eighty-Four

Paul

***Paul** entered the synagogue and spoke boldly there for three months, arguing persuasively about the kingdom of God. – Acts 19:8*

Paul was born in Bambur, Nigeria. He got off to a rough start, as noted in Chapter 27, "Beyond the Help of Human Hands." After weathering this serious illness early in life, he became a very active boy. One time he wandered away from home; ultimately he was returned by two policemen who asked if he belonged to us. His clothes looked as if he had been in a mud bath and his face was streaked with dirt. He was happily licking an ice cream cone. Yes, we received back our ragamuffin.

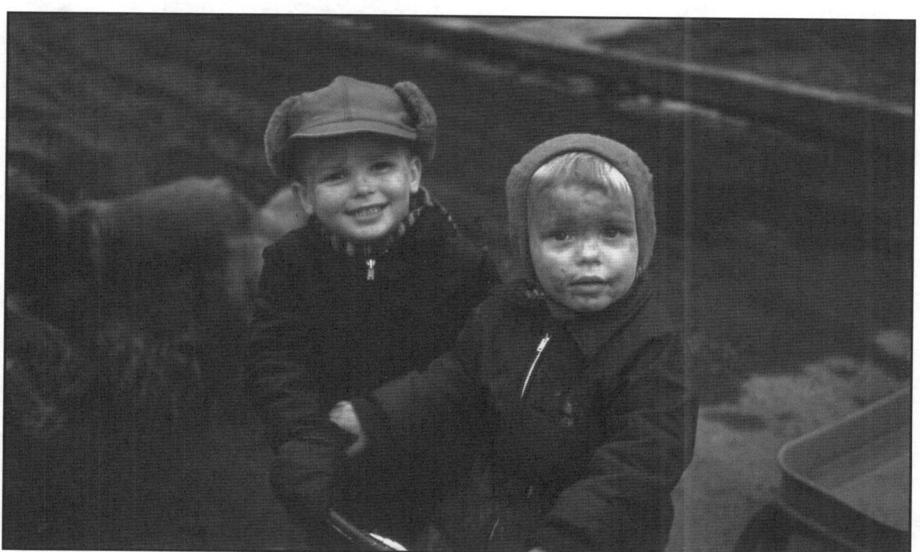

As an extrovert, Paul (right) was at the center of most activities, willing to take on any challenger.

Paul was our "Nick Nutzen" (nutzen is a German term for mischief maker) whether innocently or not. He always seemed to be getting into trouble. School buses were his nemesis. I suppose we could blame the "other fellow," but at one time he was banned from the school bus for a week. John saw to it that he got home and took care of the situation so that Ruth and I were never aware of the incident.

Paul was a gifted speedster on the track and football field.

Spending much of his young life in Africa, Paul could play soccer but he didn't know the rules of football when he arrived at Hughes Junior High School in Bismarck, North Dakota. He excelled as a speedster in track events, which was noted by the football coach. At one track meet I was sitting in the stands unknown to anyone beside me. I heard someone say during the 440 event, "Watch that Paul Gess on the third turn. That's where he always overtakes the lead." Suddenly a man came up, sat down and remarked: "They tell me you are Paul's father. With such speed we would like to have him as the ball carrier on our football team. Would you give your permission even though he is not heavily built? He would need to take a lot of hits in spite of the good-sized fellows we will have around him."

This was the forewarning Ruth and I received prior to Paul telling us he had decided to go out for the Bismarck High School football team. True to the coach's words, Paul took relentless beatings as he was tackled on average twenty times a game (without fumbling) and ended up always at the bottom of the heap. He could hardly get out of bed Saturday mornings after the Friday night games. However, he would make it to church on Sunday and by Monday he was willing to go through it all over again. During his last game he suffered a "cracked rib" but still played the entire game. He was voted "Athlete of the Month" by the Quarterback Club of Bismarck and made All State. When college football scholarships were offered, he politely turned them down.

Paul's memories of Africa include playing Shanghai and singing along with Andy Williams; the expedition up Mount Bintumani where he was almost eaten by a wild boar – and then eating boar meat after John and I dispatched one with my 300 H&H magnum bored by Weatherby; hunting in the Kasewe Hills; meals of leaf stew, jollof rice or curry; the white, sandy, beautiful beaches in Sierra Leone; later vacations and life guarding at Lake Koronis Assembly Camp, and singing with the entire family in John Peterson's "Night of Miracles."

Lake Koronis lifeguards, John and Paul. Tim and Andrew were also lifeguards at Koronis.

Paul graduated from Seattle Pacific University with a B.A. in Sociology/Social Welfare. He obtained a Masters of Divinity from Fuller Theological Seminary and a Masters in Marriage, Family and Child Therapy from California Family Study Center. Presently he is in private practice as a licensed mental health counselor as well as Director of Treatment Programs of Northwest Family Life with lead groups for State Certified Domestic Violence Treatment Program. Paul's wife, Arlet, is the office coordinator for the Edmonds School District Transportation Division, son Aaron is a student at the Art Institute, stepsons Joshua is a CAD specialist and Jason is a calibration technician.

Paul's family, from left: Jason, Joshua, Aaron, Arlet and Paul.

With his lifelong interest in meteorology, he is aware of the conditions in Alexandria, but his calls are not only about the weather. He continues to surprise with his ingenuity. Singing all four parts of "My New Life" recorded on the DVD of Ruth's and my 60th wedding anniversary was true artistry. I always have to smile while visiting with Paul. Thank God that his life didn't end following the more than twenty-four hours of convulsions that occurred two weeks after his birth. Ruth and I always knew that Paul's life was spared because he would be special.

Chapter Eighty-Five

Andrew

***Andrew**, Simon Peter's brother, was one of the two who heard what John had said and who had followed Jesus. The first thing Andrew did was to find his brother Simon and tell him, "We have found the Messiah" (that is, the Christ). And he brought him to Jesus. – John 1:40-42a*

The baptism of Andrew in Africa by Mission General Secretary, Dr. Carl Heinmiller (right) who was assisted by Pastor J. K. Fergusson (left) and Rev. Clyde Galow (back).

Andrew was born in Rotifunk and spent more years in Africa than his brothers or sisters. In his preschool years, Andrew developed Henock-Schonlein's Disease and was confined to bed rest for a month. The entire family tried to be creative to make his compliance possible. Thankfully, the purpura of the skin was the main manifestation with no lasting effects on the kidney or joints. We thanked God for a full recovery.

Some of Andrew's schooling was home based with Ruth and Norma Harris as teachers. He then joined John and Paul at Kabala Rupp Memorial School and later attended Hillcrest School in Jos. During our leave of absence in Bismarck from the mission field, he developed a love for a most unlikely sport, hockey. When we returned to Sierra Leone in 1972, his hockey "career" sadly ended. He graduated from Alexandria High School where he wrote and sang the graduation school song. A standing ovation followed.

Andrew became a hockey enthusiast when we lived in Bismarck, North Dakota.

The last two years of high school and the first year at Hamline University were prodigal. He then recommitted his life to the Lord and changed his perilous course to one of purpose while attending a Fellowship of Christian Artists event in Estes Park, Colorado. He then transferred to Azusa Pacific University in California and earned a B.A. degree in communications. A Master of Divinity was obtained at Fuller Theological Seminary in 1985. Work in a series of Christian ministries followed, including radio program development and announcement, award winning multimedia slide shows and Sonshine Company outreach to disadvantaged children.

Advanced education resulted in a M.Ed. in Adult Education/ Training & Development from Oregon State University (1989) and ultimately a Ph.D. in Communication from Regent University in 1999.

He then spent nine years at George Fox College in Oregon in management studies and has taught for the past ten years as Associate Professor of Communication Studies and Director of Communication Internships at Bethel University.

Andrew (top) took after Ruth with his love for music and drama.

Andrew is skilled in the arts. I have some of his paintings on the wall. His photography is of the highest grade. The cover pages of *Glorious Witnesses for Africa* and the present *Be a Medical Missionary* demonstrate this artistry. His DVD of Ruth's life shown at her funeral is well done and moving. I often play it at those times when my longing for her overwhelms me.

The love story that resulted in his marriage to Carrie Weiss is tender. They had met at Koronis while he was a tanned lifeguard and she was a high school student. More than a decade later, a spur of the moment telephone call reunited them. Significantly, they were married at the Koronis chapel. Two trips to China resulted in the adoption of babies Anna and Aimee, who bring grace to their busy household. The girls enjoy swimming at Lake Milton beach no matter what the temperature of the water.

Andrew keeps in constant touch with Alexandria. It is always a joy to welcome him and his family. Carrie, like Mary, often whips up mashed potatoes with meat and gravy. Of course, Andrew tops it off with his specialty, root beer floats. Carrie is a true homemaker but is also a piano teacher to ten or twelve students.

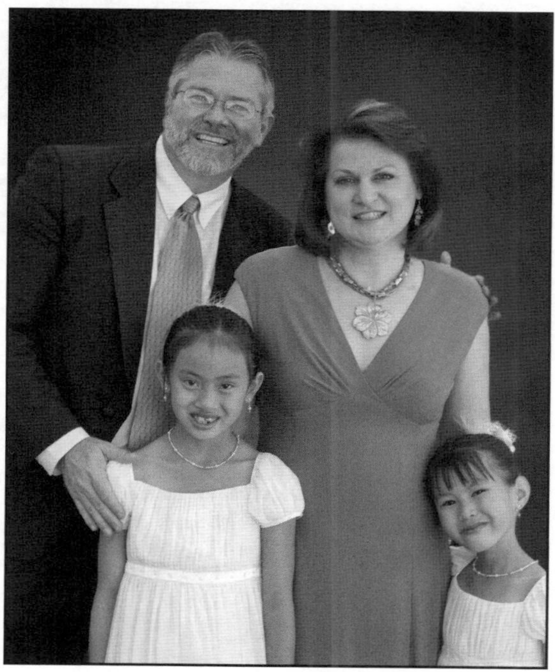

Andrew, his wife Carrie, and daughters Anna (left) and Aimee.

Andrew more than anyone has encouraged my literary attempts with skillful suggestions as well as the handling of pictures. Over the years Andrew cost Ruth and me many extra prayers, but they were well worth it as our hearts gladdened when he turned back to the ways of the Lord. I love him and all my children.

Our Family: Epilogue

For years, people questioned us about removing our children from the U.S. school system. Would it make it harder for them to pursue future studies? Mary chose to complete her high school senior year at Hillcrest in Jos, Nigeria, to be with Beth and visit us in Sierra Leone during holidays. The children did well with home schooling and missionary schools. Today, three are counselors with multiple postgraduate degrees; two are eye doctors; one is a university professor. Thank God for their successes.

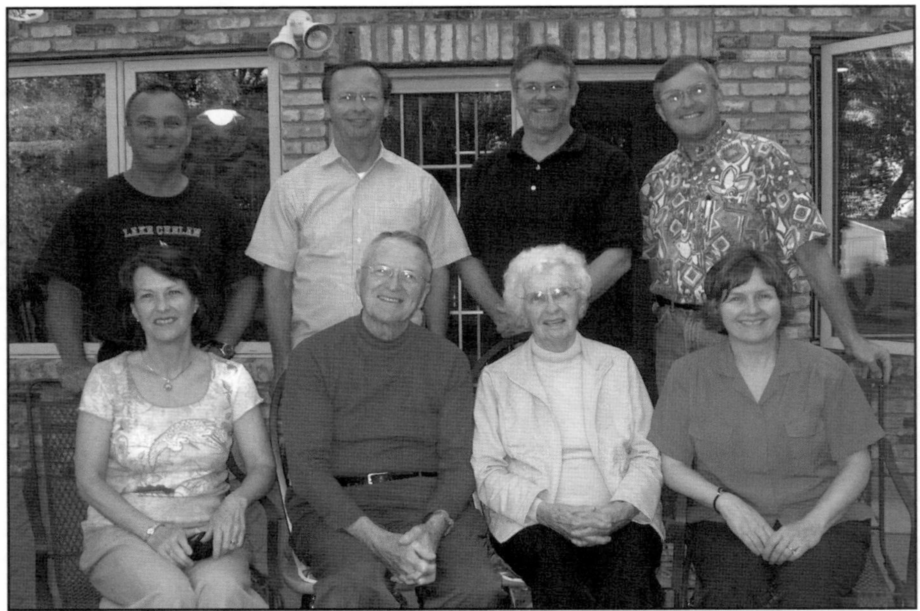

Our last family photo, taken in 2009. Back row: Paul, John, Andrew and Tim. Front row: Mary, Lowell, Ruth and Beth.

Part VI: Favorite Stories

My mustachio period didn't last long. Ruth was neutral. Since they were away at school, not one of my children has any memory of their father as Omar Sharif.

"All work and no play makes Jack a dull boy."

Chapter Eighty-Six

An Unbelievable Happening

In our early days in Sierra Leone while serving at Rotifunk Hospital, I met Siaka Stevens, a labor union official of Sierra Leone. The meeting took place in Moyamba, which is only about ten miles from Rotifunk. He was cordial and interested in the program that the mission was conducting at the Rotifunk Hospital. In those days the Rotifunk Hospital was one of three premier hospitals serving Sierra Leone's population of five million.

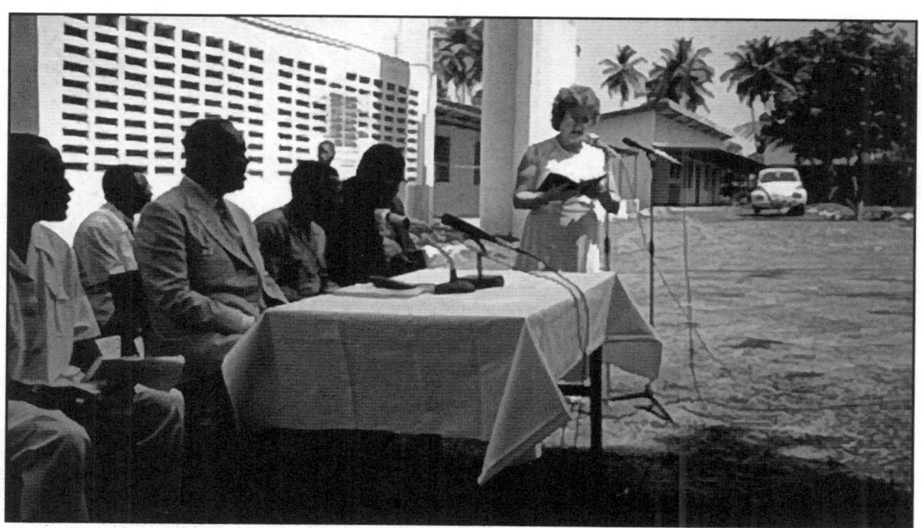

President Siaka Stevens listens attentively while Ruth reads Scripture at the eye hospital dedication.

Eventually Mr. Siaka Stevens became nationally known for his groundwork in labor unions. In fact, he became popular, especially among the taxi drivers in Freetown the capital. With their enthusiastic support during the presidential election, Siaka Stevens was elected president of Sierra Leone.

During the time of President Stevens' presidency, he would occasionally retreat to a hideaway or vacation home far up country in Sierra Leone known as Yifin. Doctor and Mrs. McClure manned this station resting at the base of

Mount Bintumani. In 1974 when the Mission Board sponsored a visit of our four sons to Sierra Leone, Dr. and Mrs. McClure invited our family to spend some time with them at Yifin during the Christmas season. It so happened that President Siaka Stevens also planned a holiday at Yifin at the same time. We were aware of one another's presence and during our visit we were invited to the President's compound to celebrate his birthday. Mrs. McClure thoughtfully baked a birthday cake for him. We were royally treated and assured we would not be offered alcoholic beverages during the celebration. A good time was had by all, especially our four sons, as they still were recovering from an unbelievable happening that occurred two days prior to the party.

Our four sons with Dr. and Mrs. McClure (and Ruth far right) at Yifin.

While I was helping Dr. McClure in the clinic and Ruth and Mrs. McClure were having good visits, our four boys decided they would go hunting. The Bintumani area was flush with game. They geared up for their little trek and with their rifles and shot guns slung over their shoulders, they set out. Whether or not they realized it until it happened (not one of them will admit to it), their path took them past the gate of the president's compound. Here they were, heavily armed, walking past the gate of the president of Sierra Leone. When they could no longer retrace their steps, they kept moving forward and with smiling faces, greeted the heavily armed guards at the gate. They used the native expressions of "Chu show," "How de body," and " I tank God" as they passed by. Smiles from the guards were returned and our boys continued on their way, happy to be alive.

Chapter Eighty-Seven

Wristwatches

At the age of twelve I was promised a gold Bulova wristwatch if I did not smoke by age twenty-one. My parents wanted to ensure I would not develop the addiction. I accepted the agreement with enthusiasm and was rewarded with the watch at my college graduation.

My father smoked as a teenager and continued until he was nearly seventy years old. He stopped "cold turkey" when he and a friend one day were having coffee and cigarettes. My father commented: "This cigarette doesn't taste good."

His friend replied: "Why don't you quit?"

Mutually they resolved not to light up again unless the other did so. Neither smoked another cigarette for the rest of their lives, which for my father was the last twenty-two years of his life – and yet the cause of his death at age ninety-two was carcinoma of the lungs.

The Bulova gold wristwatch given to me on my twenty-first birthday by my parents for not smoking still runs – if you wind it.

Ruth had never had the privilege of owning a good wristwatch. Her "cheapie" stopped during the last trimester of her pregnancy with Mary. She commented at the time she had hoped to be able to time contractions with Mary's delivery.

Our finances barely put food on the table, but I determined that she would have a watch some how.

At Barnes Hospital where I was in my second year of medicine, an emergency announcement came for type O blood. I inquired if a remuneration were involved. In their desperation for a unit, I was offered TWENTY DOLLARS! The next day I was in a jewelry shop purchasing a gold Bulova lady's wristwatch with a gold band just like mine. Twenty dollars in 1948 was big money.

Ruth wore that Bulova more than twenty years before replacing it with a battery operated quartz watch that did not need winding. The Bulova still runs accurately today – when wound.

The day came in Africa when I desired a watch that did not need to be wound. It was always easy to forget that mundane matter. On my birthday, Ruth presented me with a beautiful quartz Omega. In 1975 in Freetown it was deftly stripped from my arm when I was surrounded by a group of young thieves. Feeling my disappointment, Ruth presented me with another birthday present several years later while I was in practice in Alexandria – a Rolex Oyster Perpetual wristwatch that needed neither winding nor a battery. It was a thing of beauty. However, thieves had taken to stripping Rolex watches from people on crowed streets. For a time I substituted my genuine Rolex with a "Rolex" wristwatch bought off the street for seven dollars. Eventually it died. In retirement and with little travel, my genuine Rolex is on my wrist today – no batteries, no winding.

My replacement Rolex from thirty years ago has been faithful to the present moment.

That was my SECOND Rolex Oyster Perpetual. When planning an assault on Mount Bintumani in 1960, I noticed an advertisement in *Time* magazine touting Rolex watches that had accompanied mountain climbing teams. The thought came to me that perhaps the Rolex Watch Company in Switzerland might be interested in knowing that following a period of surgery in the Kurubunla area, a team of missionaries was intending to scale Mount Bintumani, the tallest peak in that part of West Africa. Their advertising often mentioned that their watches have been to the top of places like Mount Everest, L-2 and other noted peaks. In the letter I asked them if they wanted a Rolex to accompany us in the climbing of Mount Bintumani. They generously sent a Rolex Oyster Perpetual Explorer automatic watch officially certified as a chronometer. They mentioned that the watch would not need to be returned. Perhaps they had decided this when they learned Mount Bintumani was only 6,390 feet in elevation. Compared to Mt. Everest's more than 29,000 feet, it would not make for dramatic advertising. I passed the watch on to our oldest son, Tim, as I already was enjoying an Omega. Perpetual motion is of great advantage but expensive, hardly able to compete with reasonably priced battery operated quartz watches.

Chapter Eighty-Eight

Hunting

In 1952 when we arrived in Nigeria to work at the Guinter Memorial Hospital, a side activity was hunting on Saturday afternoons to secure meat for the staff and missionaries. In Africa, where there were few firearms, game was abundant. I remember being able to capture seven ducks with one shot on a small lake near our hospital. At other times we secured spur-wing geese, which were huge and weighed up to twenty pounds. However, it was more exciting hunting for antelope and other large game such as wild boar and buffalo. Whenever I would ask the staff what they would like to do for fun on a Saturday afternoon, the request was always the same – "Let's go hunting." Hardly ever did we return without one or two antelope to share with the staff and the missionaries. Also along the way there were many bush fowl and guinea fowl, which were delicious birds.

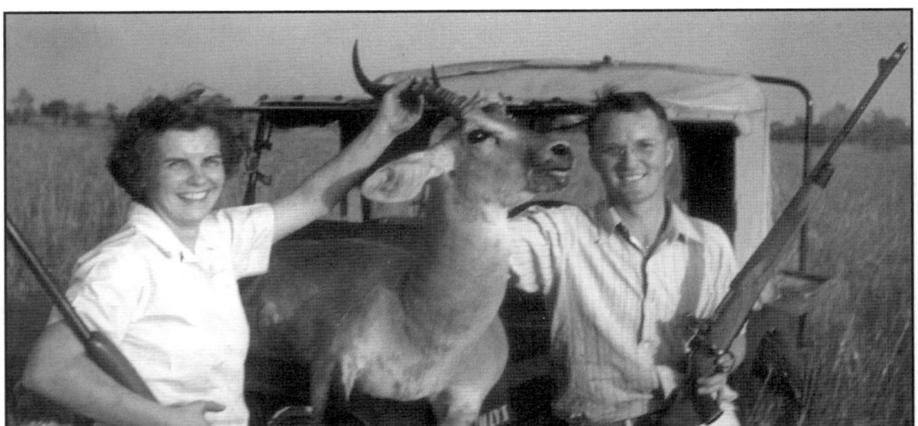

A 170-pound kob (mariya) antelope Ruth and I brought down nine miles from the hospital in the Lau Swamp in 1954.

On one occasion I decided to take a trip up the Benue River for large game. I took along a tent and our cook, Mai Doki. After going up the river hardly half a day's journey, we came to an area of expanded water. We were told there were hippopotamuses in the area. We decided it would be a challenge to capture one. We set up camp and then hired a canoe and crew from the local indigenous people. They took us to the area where the hippopotamuses were known to be. And, as they had reported, we soon came upon a group of hippo in the water.

I was not an experienced hunter and I did not know that more lives are lost from hippopotamuses as compared with lion, elephant and other large animals. With abandon I encouraged them to get close to the hippo for me to fire my 30-06 rifle. The native hunters and guides hesitated, which I didn't understand at the time. However, they did move closer and when a large bull surfaced exposing his nose, eyes and ears, I understood the anatomy enough to place a shot between his eye and ear. After firing one shot there was pandemonium and all the hippopotamuses disappeared under the water. The men with the paddles furiously headed for the shore. I learned later that the hippo with its large jaw was able to actually and literally chop a canoe in half; indigenous people occasionally drowned when their canoes swamped as many of them did not know how to swim.

After getting to the shore they all indicated we were to go back to base camp. I said "Well, why don't we wait and see if we have captured our hippo?" but they were insistent and so we went back to camp for the night. The next morning they took me out again in the canoe and went along the shore. At one point there was excited talking and they pointed out a little rise in the bog on the shore of the lake. They worked the canoe to that area and then with their machetes they began to cut through the thick weeds. Suddenly, up popped the huge body of a hippopotamus. They then cleared a path to the open lake and towed the hippopotamus to our base camp.

Butchering so large an animal was a formidable task. Custom had it that the quarters of the captured animal were shared with the chiefs of the area. However, we were in an area in which there were five chiefs – and the hippo had only four quarters. The least ranking of the chiefs was given his choice of other parts and he selected the neck of the hippopotamus, which had a great deal of meat on it.

While the butchering was going on, I took my leave and went to the camp where our tent was about fifty yards away. I was sitting on a portable chair with my rifle propped up against it enjoying the surroundings when suddenly my cook came running. He spoke in Hausa but I understood exactly what he was saying. "Likita, ka zo!" ("Doctor, come!") The terror in his eyes made me pay attention. As I sprang up, I grabbed the rifle and ran toward the group of men who were butchering the animal.

I couldn't believe my eyes. An altercation had occurred and they had suddenly divided into tribal groups, Hausa and Ibo. They were threatening to go after each other with their machetes. Diffusing a situation like that without somebody being killed demanded action. Without hesitation I slipped a cartridge into the gun's chamber and fired just over their heads. The concussion of the missile paralyzed everyone where they stood, with machetes upraised. I leveled the gun at the group and made a very effective speech in Hausa that came easily: "If anyone lifts his machete to harm another man I will use this firearm." Everyone froze.

Mai Doki, a wonder diplomat, gained their attention and explained the details as to how the meat was to be divided. Mai Doki made sure that we got some choice steaks from the hippo. I was surprised it was delicious, tasting just like ordinary fish. It brought to mind the northerns, walleyes, sunnies and croppies we had enjoyed in Minnesota. I was also surprised to see how thick the hide of the animal was. It measured up to several inches. From the hide they made whips to drive their herds of cows and goats.

I decided to keep the skull of the hippo, and brought it back to Rotifunk. I buried it in the ground and after a period of time dug it up, and it was nice and white and shiny because ants had removed all flesh tags. It was so attractive that I placed the skull in a large trunk and brought it back to my home in Minnesota, the skull of a hippopotamus. This is quite a centerpiece of conversation because the teeth and tusks can be more than a foot in length.

Flanked by replicas of the twenty-five pound northern (left) and the thirty-pound muskie (right) rests the skull of the 4,000 pound hippopotamus. Its meat tasted like fish.

Surprised by Danger. The first hunting trip to Mount Bintumani was made in 1960 with five other adult missionaries. In 1966 while we were stationed at Taiama, I made the trip to Kabala Rupp Memorial School to bring John, Paul and Andrew home for the Christmas holidays. Before returning to Taiama, John, Paul and I climbed Mount Bintumani along with eight carriers for our supplies. One of the eight was a renowned guide and hunter, Mr. Lansana, who would carry only one item – my 300 H&H high-powered Model 70 Winchester bored by Weatherby. Fourteen-year-old John carried our Model 12 Winchester pump shot gun loaded with buck shot and rifled slugs intended for game. Paul had a rifle with a clip of .22 shells.

With this arsenal we began our trek, reaching Sukarela at the base of Mount Bintumani just before sundown. The daylight made pitching our tent easier. At 6:00 a.m. the next morning we began our slow and cautious climb. Paul captured a monkey that was the protein for our meal at base camp, which was about a thousand feet lower than the peak of this 6,390-foot mountain, the highest peak in West Africa.

The following day we climbed to the top and viewed the world from this awesome height. Like the trip six years earlier, we had a worship service. Coming down crossing a draw, I was able to add venison to our menu with the most astounding shot of my life – I downed a large male harnessed antelope at sixty paced yards away while he was on a dead run. I simply aimed at the place where he would land from his bound and discharged the heart shot.

The third full day on the mountaintop, which was to be our last, remains very vivid these forty-six years later. Lansana, our respected guide, suggested that only he with John, Paul and myself do the hunt, without additional carriers spooking the game. In a short time his keen eye found a herd of pigs a considerable distance away. He led us in a circle downwind with the intention of having the herd of twelve come to our concealed lair. While he was checking the lay of the land, John, Paul and I pressed on slowly.

Suddenly, only several yards beyond my feet, a red boar sprang up from a concealed ledge. I fired from my hip, as there was no time for a placed shoulder-aimed shot. Though it was not a fatal blow, it turned the pig. Before I could shove another shell into the chamber, all eleven other pigs rose up out of the thick thigh-high grass with the largest boar making his charge. At that moment I heard the boom of John's 12-gauge, not once, but three or four times to stop the enraged animal. Another shot from him also downed my wounded one. As fast as he could pump, he fired five shots while I reloaded one shot into my bolt-action rifle. Paul, with his "pea-shooter" .22 gauge rifle, and Lansana had wisely jumped to a high boulder. Pork never tasted so good.

On our return trip we shared some of the meat with villagers in the area, but the carriers were careful to keep their share for their own people.

The next day we picked up Andrew, our second-grader, from Kabala and returned to Taiama and Ruth, our dear wife and mother, who successfully pretended to enjoy our exciting tales. Even during our sojourn in Bismarck, North Dakota, hunting with the boys was always a great event.

Each of the four Gess hunters captured a deer in the North Dakota Badlands.

Chapter Eighty-Nine

The One That Got Away

The *Star Tribune* on April 6, 2011, ran a full-page article in their Outdoors section on "Muskie Mecca." Lake Vermillion, Lake Mille Lacs, Lake of the Woods, Leech and Cass lakes were highlighted with no mention of Miltona where in the last two years I had landed four muskies, the largest measuring four feet long. A replica hangs on my wall – a true trophy!

Our wooden boat at Crane Lake where we were being hosted in Dr. Jack Bonner's cabin.

The state record muskie, weighing fifty-four pounds, was caught at Lake Winnibigoshish in 1957. Our family had been living in Akron, Ohio, where I took a two-year residency in general surgery. Before returning to Sierra Leone, we returned to Minnesota to buy provisions and pack. During this flurry of activity, I slipped away one evening with my wooden boat and drove up to Lake Winnibigoshish, sleeping part of the night in the car. In the morning I shoved my frail craft into the lake and journeyed up the river that connects Big Winnie with Little Winnie. Near the mouth of the river where it empties into Little Winnie on its way to connect to the Mississippi River, I saw a disturbance a few feet from the shore. Rough carp fish usually makes such disturbances, so I did not bother to cast. About thirty seconds later, one of the two men in a boat following me DID CAST and a fish slammed his lure.

The struggle of the angler's life began. He did not have a heavy line. The man manning the motor followed the rushes of the fish, which torpedoed in every direction. The fish tired after about twenty minutes and was maneuvered near the boat. The configuration of vertical blotches of the fish confirmed a huge muskie on a tenuous line. An inadequate net was slipped over the head and the body of the fish was pulled into the boat by the skipper.

On returning to the dock, a large plank was secured on which the fish was placed. The men each carried an end of the board. An official scale read the weight of the muskie at fifty-four pounds – a record that stands today in 2012 fifty-five years later.

I watched the entire drama unfold before my eyes, repenting that it was not my line that was playing with the monster. The saying goes that it takes a thousand casts to catch a muskie – I could have at least made one cast. He might have been "the one that didn't get away."

In 2009 fifty-two years later, I lazily was trolling a surface bait several hundred yards away from our dock on Lake Miltona. The rod suddenly bent over. It couldn't have snagged a rock or clump of weeds as the bait had a little propeller churning on top of the water. When the line went out a different direction, I knew I had a fish. He objected to being brought in and came out of the water to shake off the hook. My eyes widened and my mouth dropped open as I realized I was having a tug of war with a huge muskie. The battle between man and beast took about fifteen minutes before the fish could be inched to the boat for netting.

Once the fish was in the net, I experienced some difficulty with it being hung up on something, as I couldn't lift him into the boat. When I realized that it was only the weight of the fish that prevented me from getting it into the boat, I knew I had a problem and began to ponder my predicament. All at once the fish came up, attempting to clear the water again. I quickly tipped him into the boat, sped for our home dock, asked a neighbor to take a picture and then put the fish back into the water to rejoin his family. A replica adorns a wall in the Miltona cabin.

The muskie measured four feet long (actually it was forty-seven inches) – but this is a fish story and is "mostly" true.

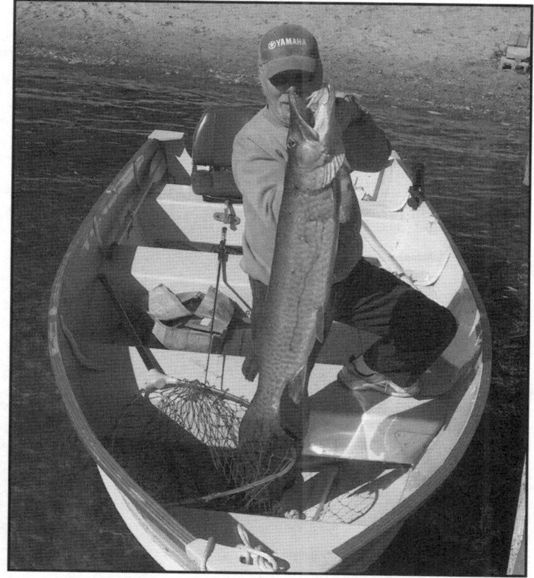

My four-foot muskie being held by neighbor Pete Anderson.

Chapter Ninety

Cutthroat

In 1956, during my general surgical residency at the Akron General Hospital, one evening at mealtime I was on my way to the cafeteria and passed through the medical ward. A student nurse rushed out of a patient's room crying, "Somebody help!" With a short sprint, I was at the bedside of a handsome young man who had been thrashing and flailing in his bed. He had upset his food tray, but I noticed a small piece of steak still on it. Apparently he had tried to swallow a large piece, which had gotten stuck.

He was unresponsive. I found nothing in his mouth. I called for an emergency surgical set. None was available on this medical floor. Moments were fleeting. He was not breathing. His color was gone. His pulse was feeble. Cardiac arrest was imminent. I stuffed my right hand into my pocket and grabbed my Swiss army knife, which has been my constant companion over the years. Without site preparation, I steadied the trachea in the sternal notch with my left hand and plunged the small sharp blade through the skin into the trachea and spread the incision. His cough sprayed us but he was able to breathe!

I stayed with him for over an hour and explained over and over what had happened, and what needed to be done. I knew he understood when he grasped my hand and continued to hold it and just look into my face.

In subsequent days, he broached spiritual topics. He was grateful to God for a new chance to live a "gifted" life. One phrase that I never forgot was: "What would have happened if you had not been here?"

I have had a number of Swiss army knives over the years. The smaller blade is never used and is always available with its original keen sharpness if another such emergency should arise.

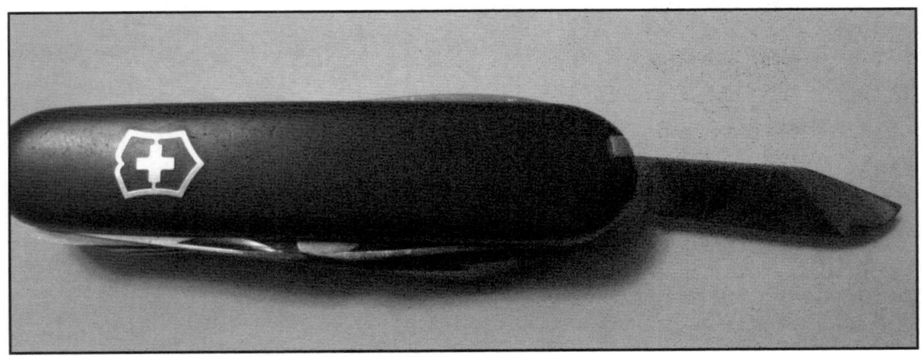

A Swiss army knife has accompanied me every day for the last seventy years.

Part VII: Faith

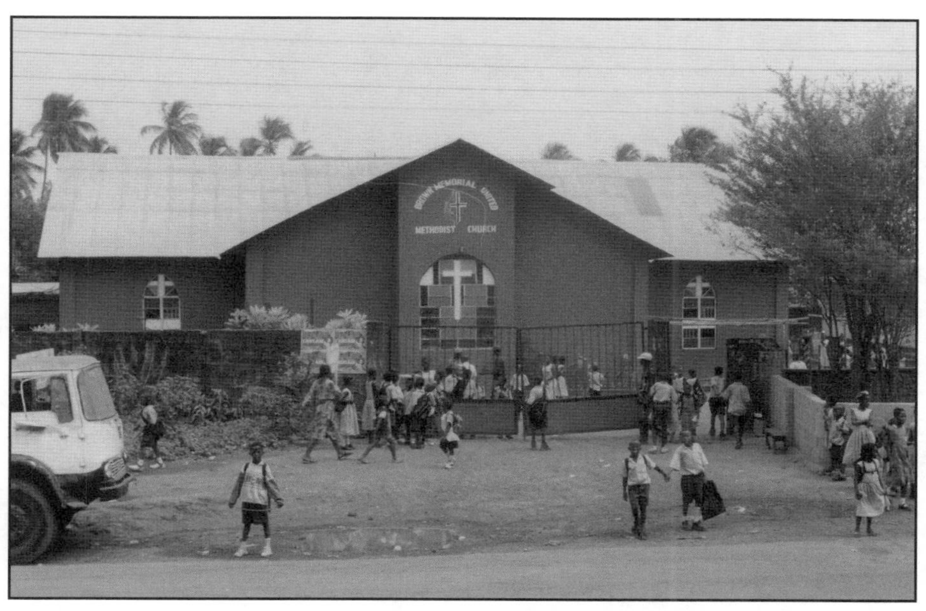

Brown Memorial United Methodist Church is on the same compound as the Kissy UMC Eye Hospital.

The Spirit of the Lord is on me,
because he has anointed me
to preach good news to the poor.
He has sent me to proclaim freedom for the prisoners
and recovery of sight for the blind,
to release the oppressed.... – Luke 4:18

Chapter Ninety-One

Defining Moments

In front of the Lake Koronis tabernacle at the time of my public declaration to fulltime Christian service.

Everyone has defining moments that shape their lives – standing for the truth; refusing to cheat whether in school or in life; pursuing sports, drama or music; entering the military – all can affect the rest of one's life. Marriage, career and choosing a church home can also be significant defining moments. I had a number of defining moments in my life.

The original defining moment at age nine was my conversion that offered the relief of sins forgiven (I John 1:9). That, together with my "burning bush" call to be a medical missionary at age eleven proved to be the major DEFINING MOMENTS that shaped my life. All subsequent happenings fell into place in relation to the Lord's call. I was confident that God would intervene in each crisis, problem or set back to accomplish His Purpose in my life. I believed Psalm 37:5: "Commit your way to the Lord, trust also in Him, and He shall bring it to pass."

Other defining moments followed:

A bible study at age twelve defined the manner in which I was to live – "For we preach not ourselves, but Christ Jesus the Lord, and ourselves, your servants for Jesus' sake." II Corinthians 4:5

At fourteen an important moment was having all the right moves come into place to be able to underhand pitch a softball fast and accurately.

At Koronis Assembly Grounds at age fifteen it was my response to an altar call for full time Christian service.

Ultimate happenings then burst upon my life:

- Being elected chief honor camper at Koronis
- Being elected president of:
  - o Evangelical Church Conference Youth Fellowship, Koronis, 1938-1940
  - o Minnesota Young Peoples' Conference of the Minnesota Council of Churches, 1941-1942
  - o Interdenominational Central Regional Planning Conference Youth Movement at Lake Geneva, Wisconsin, which included states from Ohio to the Dakotas, 1942
  - o First year class (Juniors) Evangelical Theological Seminary, 1942-1943
  - o Student Body Evangelical Theological Seminary, 1944-1945
- Marriage to Ruth on December 29, 1945
- First child (Timothy) born on the day that a successful examination was written that qualified me for medical school training, 1946
- The commissioning to serve as medical missionaries at Calvary Evangelical Church officiated by Bishop E. W. Praetorius
- The first surgery in Nigeria, January 12, 1953
- Life-saving tracheotomy on a twenty-eight-year-old man during surgical residency (using my Swiss pocket knife), 1956
- Successful assault on Mount Bintumani where we left II Corinthians 4:5 written on a piece of paper sealed in a bottle, April 27, 1960
- Having groups of young people respond to altar invitations while I was a special speaker at Lake Koronis Assembly Grounds Camp
- Changing from general surgery to ophthalmology
- Placement of first intraocular lens following cataract extraction
- Honors granted by Seratoma, Westmar College, Republic of Sierra Leone, Macalester College, University of Minnesota Department of Ophthalmology, the American Academy of Ophthalmology, Washington University School of Medicine, Garrett-Evangelical Theological Seminary, and the Christian Ophthalmology Society

Scrubbing for surgery in Kurabonla at foot of Mount Bintumani, 1966.

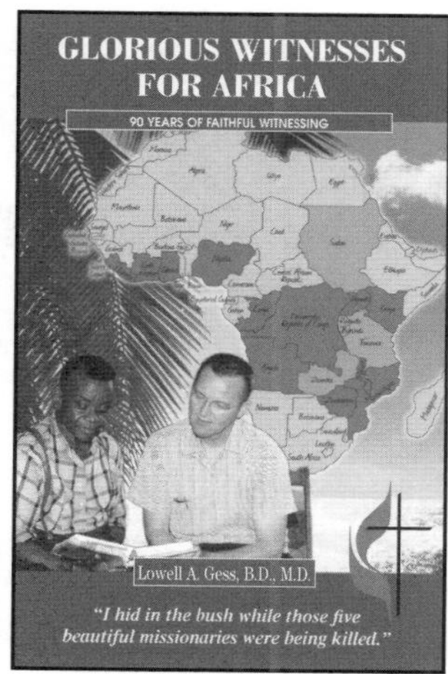

- Overlooking Freetown from Mount Leicester Road in 1976 and feeling the call to continue medical missionary work every year for the rest of my life
- A February 1, 2007, decision to care for Ruth in a home setting thought impossible by professional care givers
- Authorship of *Mine Eyes Have Seen the Glory*, 2002
- Ruth's and my 60th wedding anniversary DVD by Paul
- Andrew's DVD of Ruth's life
- Authorship of *Glorious Witnesses for Africa*, 2011
- Freedom from cancer following six major surgical procedures in a twenty-two month time span allowing a new "window" for living and serving

My "defining moments" may appear trivial as compared with God's:

- The creation of the universe and the human race made in the image of God
- The deliverance of the Ten Commandments to establish the moral and spiritual basis for mankind

- The full revelation of God in Jesus Christ through His person, work and continued intercession
- The establishment of the Church, the body of Christian believers
- The promise of God as stated in John 3:16-17

"For God so loved the world that he gave his one and only Son, that whoever believes in him shall not perish but have eternal life. For God did not send his Son into the world to condemn the world, but to save the world through him." – John 3:16-17

Chapter Ninety-Two

Basis for My Faith

Jesus Christ is Savior and Lord

Down through the years, Ruth and I were often asked about our Christian faith – and only rarely about our registered nurse and medical doctor training. We were asked what we say to people in Africa and whether it is appropriate to expect them to change their beliefs and ways when they have their own culture. My answers contained the following truths.

I come as a Christian, a follower of Jesus Christ, to minister in His name. I feel "called" to provide healing for the sick and sight for the blind. My love for God and my neighbors make my services available to people of all loyalties and faiths.

Through Scripture, I share the truth of the Gospel, which brings hope, strength and transformation of lives. This Christian truth is not one of many truths about God. It is the revelation brought to us by Jesus Christ – who was not one of many teachers, guides or prophets – but the only-begotten Son of God.

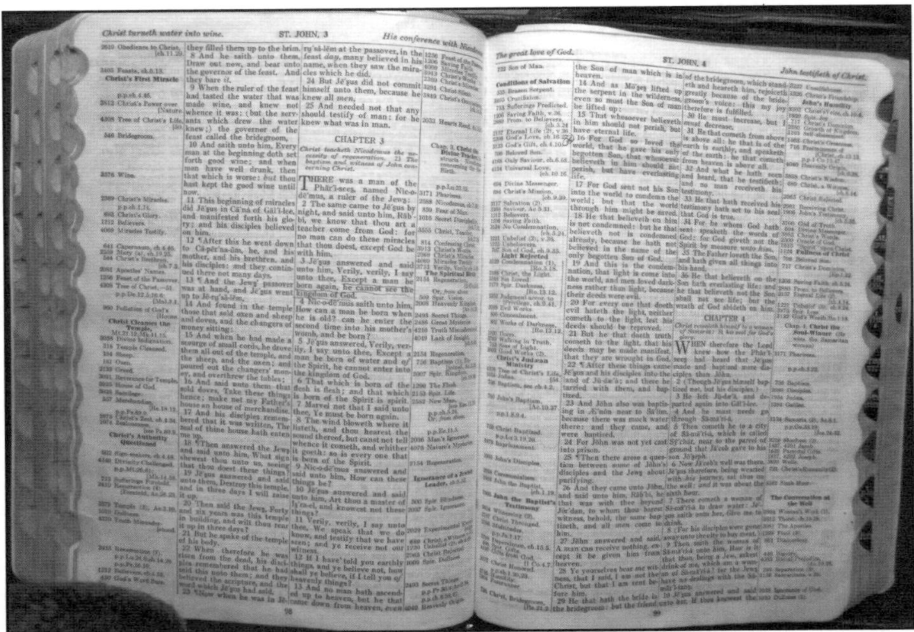
Christ turneth water into wine.
ST. JOHN, 3
The great love of God.
ST. JOHN, 4

The Word of God.

Unfortunately, we are facing today many who may represent the Christian faith who no longer believe that the revelation brought to us by Christ Jesus is THE TRUTH, but a truth. We are called upon to defend the absolute uniqueness of Jesus Christ and the revelation He delivered through His words and deeds, sacrificial death and glorious resurrection. I believe the Bible, which affirms that Jesus Christ is THE SAVIOR of the world. Jesus says, "I am the way, the truth and the life. No one comes to the Father except through me." John 14:6

I tell people that I believe it was God's will for me to make known the Gospel of God's love as revealed in Jesus Christ and to bring people to God through Him, whom knowing is life eternal. I want to share the Lord Jesus Christ as Savior rather than "some" truth or do some healing that is not redemptive. It is important to me to "Go into all the world and preach the good news to all creation." Mark 16:15

For me, being a missionary is being obedient to Christ's command: "You will be witnesses for me…to the ends of the earth." Acts 1:8 (KJV)

It is important not just to read the Word. It is important to preach it, rather than expound on one's own thoughts on the matter. There is to be reason, yes; experience, yes; tradition, yes; Scripture – by all means! Reason can be manipulated. It can be faulty. Experience can be doing the same thing incorrectly over and over again. Tradition can stifle new advances. The church was wrong; Galileo was right. As far as Scripture is concerned this is the authority that is needed to preach the Word. It will inspire even those who are not great preachers by simply letting the words of Scripture be accountable in that hour. Preaching the word in season and out is the mandate of the clergyperson.

The place of prayer in all of this must not be minimized. For four decades before doing any eye procedure I have prayed with the patient, for healing, for the ministry of those caring for the patient's needs. With prayer in one's heart and the Bible in one's hand it is impossible not to succeed to help and bless. It was Jesus who said in Mark 16:15-18: *"Go into all the world and preach the good news to all creation. Whoever believes and is baptized will be saved, but whoever does not believe will be condemned. And these signs will accompany those who believe; in my name they will drive out demons; they will speak in new tongues; they will pick up snakes with their hands; and when they drink deadly poison it will not hurt them at all; they will place their hands on sick people, and they will get well."*

What is prayed for is a conversion experience, enlightenment, a sudden awareness of the majesty of God. We can be impressed by the extent of the universe. But the only real clue we have to God is in the revelation of His love and person through Jesus Christ. "The Father and I are one," the Scriptures enjoin us. "No one comes to the Father but through me" (John 14:6). A magnificent sunset, beautiful mountains, expanses of grain and corn, the vastness of the sea – these help inspire. However, they certainly did not prompt early Christians to face the wild beasts in the amphitheater. The apostles based everything on Jesus. Paul admitted he knew nothing in his preaching but Christ Jesus. People approach truth in different ways. Pilate uttered the famous question "What is truth?" Philosophers down through the ages have immersed their lives in that pursuit.

I thought it would be a good thing to be knowledgeable about what had been discerned by the best minds. I was anxious to learn from the great philosophers of the past as well as from those of recent times such as Kierkegaard. However, it was during an early morning dawn on Lake Geneva in Wisconsin that all that is relevant finally came down to the Christ of the Scripture. Not Scripture per se. It was the Christ *of* the Scripture. This freed me from seeming inconsistencies so boldly brayed by the doubters and unbelievers. The Bible contains thirty-nine Old Testament books and twenty-seven New Testament books. We cannot be sure how many authors are involved. The theology of some is radical, hard to understand and seemingly inconsistent. Not so with the person and work of Jesus Christ. No one censures Jesus (apart from his contemporaneous scribes and Pharisees). You never hear someone decrying Jesus Christ as a bad person. The Christ of the Scriptures is inviolate.

In my thinking, it is important to stick to essentials. I want to be careful about expositions that are pet subjects. I want to avoid the politically acceptable harangues, the fine points of sexual orientations, the outlines of what will happen and when it will end. We know where things are headed as we see the moral degradation of our country and world. We are not to avoid really important questions such as the one the lawyer asked of Jesus, *"What must I do to inherit eternal life?"* (Luke 10:25) It is important for people to know. They want to know about heaven and how to get there. Jesus threw the question back to the lawyer for the answer and received the correct one when the lawyer said, *"Thou shalt love the Lord thy God with all they heart, soul, mind and strength and thy neighbor as thyself."* And when the lawyer asked who his neighbor might be, Jesus took the occasion to give the parable of the Good Samaritan and the compassion that was evidenced. And so in the final analysis when Jesus asked, "Who now of these three thinkest thou was neighbor to him who fell among thieves?" The lawyer said, "He who showed mercy." The response of Jesus to him was, "Go and do thou likewise."

Christ, the Answer for the World. It is my desire to share Christ as the solution to the world's need. I believe it is altogether proper to challenge beliefs and practices ("culture") that recognize evil spirits as inhabiting the world around us which need to be assuaged. I object when cooked rice is scattered into the bush to appease the spirits while undernourished children are standing by. Cleanliness and providing proper foods and protective nets to ward off disease must be practiced instead of placing amulets around a baby's neck.

The immediate appeal of suffering tugs on my heart. Christ had compassion on those in need, and healed all manner of disease in mind and body. I am constrained to follow Him as best I can.

I believe that we build schools, churches and hospitals not only to make Christians out of non-Christians, but because we cannot be Christian without providing them.

I am persuaded that one does not throw away one's life by losing it in service, but rather finds it in the natural expression of the will of God.

We preach not only to bring people to the Lordship of Jesus Christ, but because we cannot help but share with others the overflow of our own abundant faith for victorious living.

We go to needy places in response to Christ's command, "Heal the sick…say, the Kingdom of God is come near you." Luke 10:9 (KJV) As a missionary, I seek to identify with the needs of the people.

We go to foreign fields, not to be Christian by making Christians, but to make Christians by being Christian.

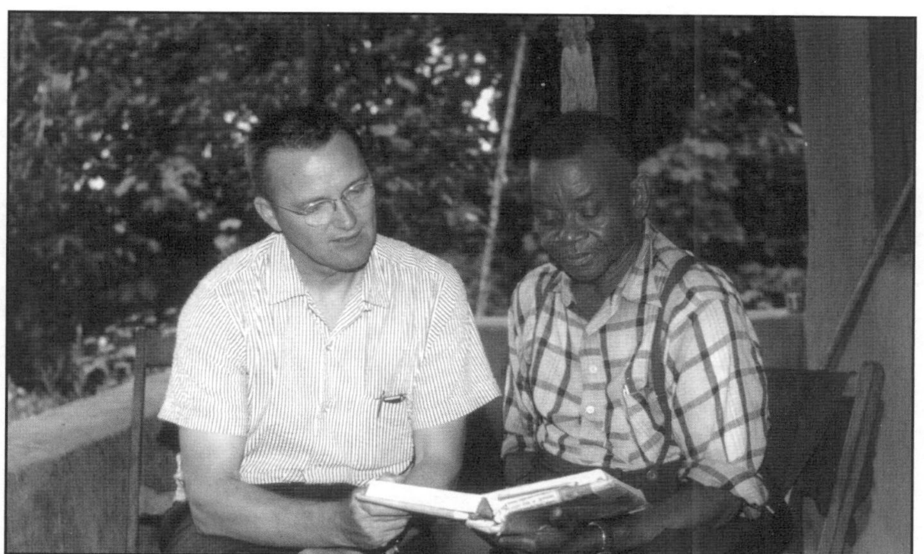

Pastor C. V. Rettew, survivor of the "Hut Tax War" of 1898, and I searching the Scriptures.

I am convinced that merely the maintenance of life is not important. It is important to remain faithful.

Jesus preached as no one else ever has preached. He taught as no one else has ever taught. He healed in miraculous ways. He lived with people. He loved with a matchless love. He shared. That's the Word. He shared all that he had with others. I suppose that if you and I preached, taught, healed, lived, loved, and shared, and if we did this long enough we incorrectly think heaven could be brought to earth. However, we have been trying this for 2,000 years and the world still is unredeemed. This is because the way of love is the way of the cross. There is no other way. When we realize that in spite of all the wonderful preaching and teaching and healing and living and serving and sharing that Jesus did, the way of the cross was the only way he could become the Savior of the world.

Does that mean that we have to physically die? It does for some. A friend of mine in Sierra Leone, a pastor, was killed because he was preaching in an area that was violent and did not accept the challenges of the Christian message. It may not mean that we have to be killed to effectively deliver Christ's message. What it does mean is that we may have to be willing to be humble rather than great, to live in ordinary circumstances rather than in luxury, to be willing to let go being the president of a company, famous, a politician, or one wielding great power and still be willing to serve in the name of Christ in a way that is lowly. I don't mean to infer that all of us have to die, but we are being asked to die to our own needs, our own wants, our own wishes, and to consider God with all our strength, mind, and power, and our neighbors as ourselves.

We face a humanity too precious to neglect.
We know the remedy for the ills of the world too wonderful to withhold.
We have a Savior too glorious to hide.
We have an adventure too thrilling to miss.

I look forward to a safe arrival in the mansion prepared for believers as promised in John 14. I am not troubled because I believe in God and the Lord Jesus Christ. Human and medical "challenges" will no longer be in my hands. To be with Him will complete my journey.

Chapter Ninety-Three

"The Elder Brother"

Cleaning out an old file in early 2011, I came across two yellow-tinged, old pieces of paper with notes scribbled in my handwriting. It was a sermon I preached on March 12, 1959, at Rotifunk several months before the birth of Andrew.

At a 1954 missionary prayer meeting in Bambur, Nigeria, Lois Schmidt reported on an article she had received in a pamphlet from England. It was entitled "The Elder Brother" written by Rev. R. W. Dixon and delivered at Keswick in 1953. It so impressed me that on arriving home I wrote down the central theme. Five years later I developed what I could remember and delivered the sermon at Rotifunk. Down through the years my wife and children have heard me preach repeatedly on "The Prodigal Son" but never on "The Elder Son" except for references while presenting "The Prodigal Son." Here, fifty-three years later with some enhancement, is the sermon "The Elder Brother."

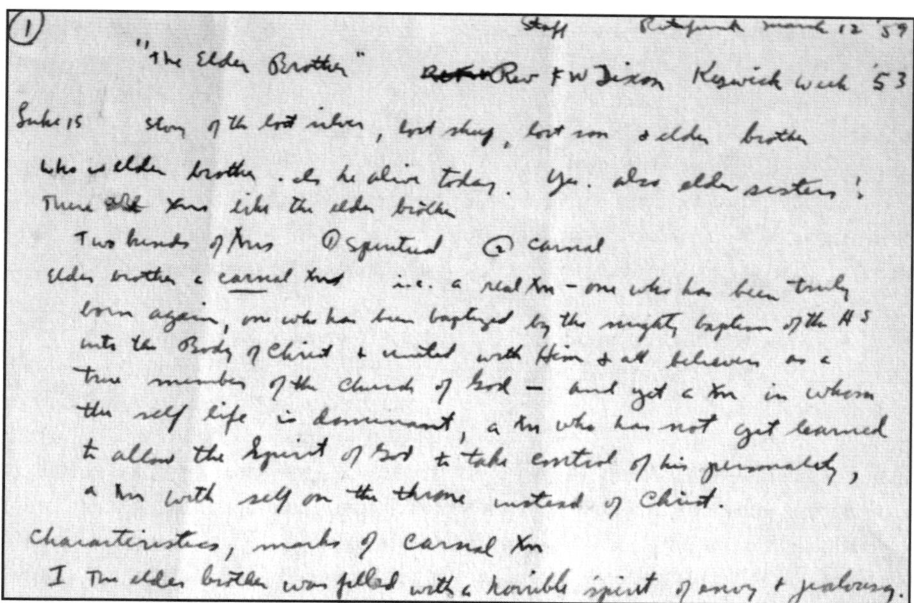

(1) Staff Rotifunk March 12 '59

"The Elder Brother" ~~Rotifunk~~ Rev F W Dixon Keswick week '53

Luke 15 Story of the lost silver, lost sheep, lost son & elder brother

Who is elder brother. Is he alive today. Yes. Also elder sisters!

There are Xns like the elder brother

Two kinds of Xns (1) Spiritual (2) Carnal

Elder brother a carnal Xn i.e. a real Xn – one who has been truly born again, one who has been baptized by the mighty baptism of the H S into the Body of Christ & united with Him & all believers as a true member of the Church of God – and yet a Xn in whom the self life is dominant, a Xn who has not yet learned to allow the Spirit of God to take control of his personality, a Xn with self on the throne instead of Christ.

Characteristics, marks of Carnal Xn

I The elder brother was filled with a horrible spirit of envy & jealousy.

Original notes from "The Elder Brother" sermon.

The Elder Brother

Luke 15: The stories of the lost silver, lost sheep, lost son and elder brother.

Who is the "elder brother?" Is he alive today? How about an elder sister? Are there Christians like the elder brother?

There are two kinds of Christians: 1) spiritual, and 2) carnal.

The elder brother is a carnal Christian, that is, a real Christian – one who has truly been born again, one who has been baptized by the mighty baptism of the Holy Spirit into the body of Christ and united with Him and all believers as a true member of the church of God, and yet a Christian in whom the self life is dominant, a Christian who has not yet learned to allow the spirit of God to take control of his personality, a Christian with self on the throne instead of Christ.

Characteristics, Marks of Carnal Christian:

I: The elder brother was filled with a horrible spirit of envy and jealousy, which can find its way to unsuspecting hearts.

This prompted his reaction to his brother's homecoming.

A real Christian would have said "Wonderful, our prayers are answered, my brother has returned. How glad I am." And then dashing in would have greeted his brother, "My dear brother, I join with my father and everyone in welcoming you home again. Thank God you have returned." What really happened was the elder brother sulked outside. This terrible thing called jealousy causes havoc in our lives and in our service to God. It makes one intolerant, critical, censorious, where people are found saying: "Yes, he's a grand fellow, but…." Jealousy damages spiritually and physically. It is seen in the face and heard in the voice. It starves out joy, peace and power from our lives. Paul spoke to the church at Corinth about being carnal: "You are yet carnal, for there is among you envying (jealousy), and strife, and divisions." Jealousy is the first mark of a carnal Christian.

II: The elder brother found service a drudgery instead of a delight as found in Luke 10:29: "These many years I have been slaving for you." The elder brother was not lazy. Laziness is not necessarily a mark of a carnal Christian. God save us from being spiritually lazy, but also save us from being feverishly active – bristling about, always having to do things, and making a good deal of noise about it. One of the marks of carnality is work, work, bustle, bustle, noise! The spiritual Christian is possessed by a quiet dignity and poise. He has an amazing capacity for work, but there is no fever or bustle or assertiveness or rush, but rather a quiet pursuit of the work of God in which he is engaging, not in the energy of the flesh, but in the power of the spirit. The elder brother was busy, but not out of pleasure or delight because it was God's work, but as a slave. Really, the elder brother was not serving his father at all – he was serving himself. Does the love of Christ constrain us to serve ourselves no longer, but truly to serve him? Do we serve out of a sense of duty or because of the wondrous privilege of serving such a glorious master? If our work has become irksome, drudgery, or without delight, carnality is creeping into our lives.

III: The elder brother was dominated by self instead of by the Holy Spirit.

1. He was self-righteous. How quick he was to tell his father that he had not transgressed his commandments at any time. One really wonders about that. He had a "holier than thou" attitude that he was better than other Christians.
2. He was self-centered (verse 29). The capital "I" appears three times. He wanted to be in the center of the picture, relating every conversation back again to himself, desiring to be made a fuss of and wanting appreciation.
3. He was full of self-pity. He acted like a baby. In I Corinthians 3:1 Paul says "And I, brethren, could not speak to you as unto spiritual, but as unto carnal, even as unto babes." The elder brother could not stand to see his returned brother the center of things – with the calf being killed, a ring placed on his finger, a robe on his shoulders and shoes on his feet.
4. He was self-satisfied. The elder brother was content with his efforts to keep the law, and felt apparent success in doing so.

IV: The elder brother was filled with base ingratitude. "You never gave me a kid, that I might make merry with my friends." One wonders whether he had any friends. The elder son overlooked his privileges, position, and possessions, and did not express appreciation. The least he could have been grateful for the fact that "There go I, but for the grace of God."

V: The elder brother showed a complete lack of sympathy for the lost. He did not rejoice when his brother came home. He even refused to refer to his brother as "brother" but used "thy son." He was so ready to speak about the sins his brother had committed (in verse 30), about harlots, riotous living, squandering of money, and so on. We can ask ourselves, "Do we have a concern for the disenfranchised people without knowledge of Christ or are we unsympathetic, unfeeling, criticizing, condescending? Do we overlook the downtrodden, the oppressed, the starving, and the ill?

VI: The elder brother was out of sympathy with his father. He failed to share his father's concern for his brother, and he even questioned his father's action. He did not agree with what his father had done in receiving the prodigal back. The elder brother was not guilty of the grosser sins of the flesh but of the sins of the spirit. Paul in Galatians 5:19 writes about the works of the flesh: adultery, fornication, uncleanness, lasciviousness, idolatry and witchcraft. The other elder brother was not guilty of any of these, but he was guilty of hatred, strife, envying. He lacked the fruits of the spirit of love, joy, peace, long suffering, gentleness, goodness, faith, meekness or self-control.

This is a very damaging picture. I am unable to end the sermon in this way on the elder brother. Surely, there must be a cure for carnality.

Cure for the Carnal Life

The father said in verse 31, "Son, thou art ever with me, and all that I have is yours." What the father is really saying, 1) Think of your privilege. You are my son! 2) Think of your position. You are ever with me. "Blessed be the God and Father of our Lord Jesus Christ, who has blessed us with all spiritual blessings in heavenly places in Christ." 3) Think of your possessions! All that I have is yours. Here we find God's remedy for the carnal life. "In him Christ dwelleth all the fullness of the Godhead bodily and you are complete in him." "And if children, then heirs; heirs of God, and joint heirs of Christ." The cure for carnality is to become Christ filled, Christ possessed, Christ directed. The good news, the Gospel, is that in spite of our refusing to yield and "Go in," our father comes out to us (verse 28) and then entreats us (John 3:16) through the wooing of the Holy Spirit. We may refuse the Lord, but he does not denounce us. And yet we must remember how early in the Bible (Genesis 6:3) "The Lord said, 'My spirit shall not always strive with men.'" There is a point beyond which the Spirit can reach us. God has so fashioned us that we make our own decisions. Our will is supreme. I implore you, exercise your will for good, for God. Hear again what he says: "Son, thou art ever with me and all that I have is yours." "The earth is the Lord's and the fullness thereof." The Father waits for you. Let Christ change you from being a carnal follower to that of being a spiritual Christian. Let Jesus come into your heart.

Chapter Ninety-Four

Humility

"Have Thine Own Way," a hymn by Adelaide A. Pollard, became a favorite of mine early in life as it expresses in words my feeling and longing for humility. I am very much aware that I am clay only to be molded in the Master's hands. Three times in my life I had heard the oft-requested sermon of Bishop E. W. Praetorius' "The Potter and the Clay."

Have Thine own way, Lord! Have Thine own way!
Thou art the potter, I am the clay.
Mold me and make me after Thy will,
While I am waiting, yielded and still.

Have Thine own way, Lord! Have Thine own way!
Search me and try me, Master, today!
Whiter than snow, Lord, wash me just now,
As in Thy presence humbly I bow.

Have Thine own way, Lord! Have Thine own way!
Wounded and weary, help me I pray!
Power, all power, surely is Thine
Touch me and heal me, Savior divine!

Have Thine own way, Lord! Have Thine own way!
Hold o'er my being absolute sway!
Fill with Thy spirit till all shall see
Christ only, always, living in me.

I remember three occasions when that desire for humility was put to the test.

In Nigeria in the early 1950s we established special clinics and care for patients afflicted with leprosy. In many cases the disfigurement was shocking – absent fingers, toes, hideous changes to the face, foot ulcers. With our modern medicines, restorations were taking place. The populace became aware of these healings.

Entering my office at the hospital, I was surprised to see a strikingly beautiful young woman whom the staff had allowed to sit in the chair beside my desk. As I sat down, she slid off her chair, kneeling in front of me. Her well-rehearsed story poured from her lips.

She had become aware of the telltale lesions of leprosy on a clothed part of her body. She ran away from home before it became known that she was suffering from leprosy and would be branded as a "leper."

She pled for healing but without tears and a composed face.

Nurse Crystal Springborn with the lady who sought help for her leprosy.

I reached out to help her back to the chair and promised to do for her what was being successful for others, reminding her that it was God who heals and renews.

By God's grace she suffered no disfigurement during the course of her treatment.

In Rotifunk, as told in Chapter 31 "From Death to Life," the mother knelt in front of me preventing my walking away from a hopeless situation which ultimately had a beautiful ending.

The third occasion was in the foyer of a church. Ruth and I had just returned from our term at the Bo Eye Clinic. A prominent Christian recognized us and knelt down in front of us explaining that he had been following our medical missionary work and now was honored to meet us. Reflexively we both reached out to assist the man to stand. Remembering Jesus' words in Matthew 10:19: "At that time you will be given what to say, for it will not be you speaking, but the Spirit of your Father speaking through you." I replied, "All praise be to God."

Chapter Ninety-Five

Grandchildren of the Church? Addressing the Skeptics

"How does one get started on this missionary angle?" This was the remark of a fellow student in medical school. "What right have you to go as a missionary and try to change people who likely are getting along all right in their own way?" Stated in such a way, it appears to some that the Christian faith may be intrusive and offensive. Their intimation is that Christians are trying to pawn off an unwanted product on uninformed people.

In answering his first question, "How does one get started?" I tried to put into non-theological language the experience I had of being called of God to serve as a medical missionary. I told him that I felt called to minister to those in mission fields who are in need of medicine and the Gospel. I was aware of areas in our mission where the closest doctor was more than a hundred miles away and who was trying to minister to a half million people. I suggested, furthermore, that a Christian is not always the one making a particular choice. A "call" is often involved, one is chosen: "You did not choose me, but I chose you and appointed you to go and bear fruit – fruit that will last." John 15:16

I would like to have added another suggestion: that Christians must obey the great commission of Christ, "Go into all the world and preach the good news to all creation" (Mark 16:15). A busy bacteriology laboratory is not the most conducive place for a frank discussion of the things of the Spirit. I did add I was being sent by the church and the church had the "say" as to where I would serve.

"I'll wager that eighty percent of our class does not go to church," this friend said. "What contribution has it to make?" At this point another student who had been brought up in India of Christian missionary parents noted the fact that while the Christian population of India is only about two percent, it nevertheless makes up about one-third of the newly-organized Indian government. Time did not permit him to tell of the great ministry that the Christian church offered in the way of educational, medical and agricultural advancement in India.

It was evident that the student who was wondering about the value of the Christian church had forgotten that the United States and Canada were founded by men and women who feared God and had come to these shores because they wanted freedom in their worship. He overlooked the fact that the Church had been the major channel through which the revelation of God in Jesus Christ has been given to men, and this meant more than ritual, history, tradition, and artistic media such as architecture, painting, and music. Wherever the church has gone, it has been a spiritual antiseptic to pagan corruption. In some cultures half of the children die before their second birthday. Religious practices (animism, etc.) on some occasions throw ceremonial rice into the bush to assuage the spirits while undernourished children are standing by.

Where do we find schoolhouses, colleges and hospitals? It is where the light of the Holy Scriptures has been carried and allowed to shine.

Whoever heard of infidels sending out missionaries to enlighten the dark corners of the earth? What apostles of infidelity have left home and loved ones to spend life itself in heathen lands to help savage and barbarian tribes? What hospitals for lepers have they established? Even the questions bring a smile.

As far as infidels' efforts are concerned, the cannibals might continue to eat their fellow men and mothers might continue to sacrifice their children to bloody idols until the end of time. The infidels have confined their efforts largely to finding fault with the Bible, the Church, and those people within the church who are trying to follow Jesus Christ.

It makes a difference when the Church is there. Through its ministry, the saving power of Jesus Christ pulses. It proclaims the timeless message, "If anyone is in Christ, he is a new creation; the old has gone, the new has come." (II Corinthians 5:17)

It was quite shocking finally to point out to my student friend that the very educational institution in which this conversation was going on was, in its inception, a Christian school founded on the faith that in truth there is freedom.

What had happened in this youth to make him question the place of the Church and the validity of the Christian message for every age and clime throughout the whole wide world? I knew him well enough to know that his grandmother was "terribly religious."

In musing over this situation I remembered that God's Word included a somewhat similar circumstance, and as always, it provided the answer – this time in the first verses of chapters 26, 27 and 28 of II Chronicles. Kings Uzziah, Jotham, and Ahaz were father, son, and grandson. Uzziah became king when he was sixteen years old and for fifty-two years he led his nation from glory to glory. He was possessed with a dominant religious passion and his first act was to restore the temple services. Later he enlarged the boundaries of the nation; strengthened its defenses; created a new and unfailing water supply; developed agriculture, and spread the fame of his country beyond Egypt until it was written of him "he was marvelously helped."

All this means that God was his helper. Before one really gets started in the story of Uzziah's life, one comes upon this statement: "He did what was right in the eyes of the Lord" (II Chronicles 26:4). That was his secret.

Uzziah was succeeded by his son, Jotham. Jotham began to reign when he was twenty-five and he reigned sixteen years. The fine record of his father is repeated in the son. Credit is given, too, to his mother Jerusha, the daughter of Zadok the priest. It is written of him, as of his father, "He did that which was right in the sight of the Lord." The record is quite good, quite worthy. He had not the driving personality of his father and had not his passionate religious interest, but everything is quite good and satisfactory.

There is, however, one strange note in the story. We read these arresting words about Jotham. "He did not enter the temple of the Lord." No reason is given for his conduct. Perhaps he had enough of preaching and psalm singing in his early life to last him all his days. We have all known people who have talked that way. Some of them, too, have been justified. The interesting and arresting thing about it is that he got along very well without it and is praised by the historian for doing what was right. In this day and age there are many like Jotham. In going behind their indifference and their nonattendance at church you find that there is always an early church inheritance. A man I knew who had an important position used to teach Sunday school, sing in the choir, and now he never attends a church service. Furthermore, he gets along so well that people who make church sacrifices often wonder.

Although I never liked physics very well, there is a principle in mechanics called momentum. We watch a great throbbing locomotive take a train of cars and transfer to them the impulse of its own power so that when separated from the engine the cars will speed along the rails with apparent purpose. There are plenty of men who are still moving under the momentum of just such a shunting experience inherited from their parents.

These men are still religious. They feel at home in a religious atmosphere. Their friends are churchmen. They are interested in the best things in the community. They salute the church, but they do not enter it. They get along very well on an inherited religion. They have enough of momentum from the original impulse of their life to carry them along down into the future.

BUT what about the next generation? The momentum fades out in the third generation, and Ahaz, Jotham's son, comes to a dead end. The record is reversed. We read the simple story in a clear statement, "He did not do what was right in the eyes of the Lord." He not only did not enter the temple of his fathers, but he turned against it. Read the record.

It is amazing, isn't it, how an Old Testament account helps us to better understand our fellow men and some of their strange attitudes toward worship.

Yet it should not be amazing. If grandparents and parents are diligent in the reading of the Word of God and are faithful to the Church of Jesus Christ, the children and the children's children will be found among those who love the Lord and want to live for him whether at home or in the fields white unto the harvest.

Precious grandchildren.

Bibliography

Adolph, Harold. *Today's Christian Doctor.* Summer 1999.

Alldridge, T. J. *A Transformed Colony: Sierra Leone.* Seeley and Co. Ltd.: London, England, 1910.

Behney, J. and Paul H. Eller. *The History of the Evangelical and United Brethren Church.* Abingdon Press: Nashville, Tennessee, 1979.

Candale, G. S. *West African Snakes.* Longmans, Green and Co. Ltd.: London, England, 1961.

Cox, Emmet D. *The Church of the United Brethren in Christ in Sierra Leone.* William Cary Library: South Pasadena, California, 1970.

Dong, Peter Marubitoba, et.al., *The History of the United Methodist Church in Nigeria.* Abingdon Press: Nashville, Tennessee, 2000.

Eller, Paul H. *History of Evangelical Missions.* The Evangelical Press: Harrisburg, Pennsylvania, 1942.

Faust, Arthur and Aletha. *From Pero Station.*

Fuller, John G. *Fever! The Hunt for a New Killer Virus.* Clarke, Irwin & Company Ltd.: Toronto and Vancouver, Canada, 1974.

Fyfe, Christopher. *A Short History of Sierra Leone.* Longmans, Green and Co. Ltd.: London, England, 1962.

Gess, Lowell A. *Mine Eyes Have Seen the Glory.* RLE Press: Alexandria, Minnesota, 2002.

Gess, Lowell A. *Glorious Witnesses for Africa.* Alexandria, Minnesota, 2011.

Graham, Billy. *Just as I Am.* HarperCollins: Carmel-New York, 1997.

Matchette, Katharine E. "When the Dog Bites," *Good News*, March-April, 1983.

Mills, J. S. *Mission Work in Sierra Leone, West Africa.* United Brethren Publishing House: Dayton, Ohio, 1898.

Moede-Manz. *Herman Ludwig Manz.*

Noll, Mark A. *Turning Points: Decisive Moments in the History of Christianity.* Baker Book House Company: Grand Rapids, Michigan, 2001.

Olewiler, Dean and Lowell Gess. "Uterine Rupture," *West African Medical Journal,* 1954.

Olsen, Lois. *Contentment is Great Gain.* Leone Press: Milwaukee, Wisconsin, 1996.

Olson, Gilbert W. *Church Growth in Sierra Lone.* William E. Eerdman Publishing Co.: Grand Rapids, Michigan, 1969.

O'Malley, J. Steven. *On the Journey Home: The History of Mission of the Evangelical United Brethren Church, 1946-1968.* General Board of Global Ministries UMC: New York, New York, 2003.

Osbeck, Kenneth H. *Amazing Grace.* Kregel Publications: Grand Rapids, Michigan, 2002.

Pierce, Lorraine Esterly. *Marching Through Immanuel's Ground.* RLE Press: Alexandria, Minnesota, 1999.

Qualls, Alyssa. Internet report, 2000.

Sibthorpe, A. B. C. *The History of Sierra Leone.* Elliot Stock: London, England, 1968.

Williams, Henry. *The Gospel and Medicine.* Notes.

Appendix

Preparing for eye surgery at Saiama, more than 250 miles away from our Rotifunk hospital.

We preach not ourselves, but Christ Jesus the Lord;
and ourselves your servants for Jesus' sake.
– II Corinthians 4:5 (KJV)

Fifty-Year Tribute to Lowell

To Lowell, My Dear Husband
(written in 1996)

I was really touched as I read your tribute to me on our 50th wedding anniversary. I feel that my reading of your curriculum vitae and list of professional awards was not sufficient to pay tribute to you as an outstanding example of a Christian husband, lover and companion.

In the early years of our marriage when you were so involved with your medical training, I was happy to devote myself to you and our children, and because I came from a frugal background, I cheerfully accepted our limited resources. (You know that I still find it difficult to spend money.)

I must admit that leaving my country and my people was not easy, but the sense of God's calling was very real. It was a joy to become your partner in many ways – as wife, mother of our children, nurse, teacher, administrator, secretary and partner in sharing the Good News of the Gospel. I was never concerned about our meager income during years of training and serving in West Africa. We often had more than those around us.

I really admire you for your careful, conscientious yet brave ventures in ophthalmology, which have proven beneficial to so many in Africa, Asia and here in the United States.

The Lord knew us better than we knew ourselves, and our being together happily for fifty years is His great gift to us!

I LOVE YOU and I'm grateful for every day He allows us together. *"Heirs together of the grace of life."* 1 Peter 3: 7

Your loving wife, Ruth

Dr. Lowell Gess' Curriculum Vitae

Lowell Gess was born in July 1921, in Paynesville, Minnesota. He attended a country school and the Salem Evangelical Church in rural Paynesville. Throughout his early years, he participated in the camping program at Lake Koronis Assembly Grounds, and was active in the Evangelical Youth Fellowship on a state and national level and in the interdenominational Christian Youth Fellowship.

His family moved to St. Paul, Minnesota, where he graduated from Central High School in 1938. He attended North Central College in Naperville, Illinois, for one year, but completed college at Macalester College in St. Paul, Minnesota. At the age of nineteen, he was licensed to preach by the Minnesota Conference of the Evangelical Church and served a rural church. He graduated from Macalester College in 1942 with a B.A. degree. He attended the Evangelical Theological Seminary at Naperville, graduating with a B.Div. degree in 1945. Shortly thereafter, he and Ruth Bradley, a registered nurse from Winnipeg, Canada, were united in marriage.

Dr. and Mrs. Gess served the St. Cloud-Graham circuit and the Mayer Church while he completed his pre-medical studies. In 1947, he entered Washington University School of Medicine. He received a Jackson Johnson Scholarship and a scholarship from First EUB Church of Naperville. Dr. and Mrs. Gess served a small Federated church in East St. Louis, Illinois, for two years. For the last two years of medical training and internship at Ancker Hospital in St. Paul, the Board of Missions of the Evangelical United Brethren Church placed them under appointment.

In 1952, Dr. and Mrs. Gess and their family were appointed to the Bambur Hospital in Nigeria where they served three years. On their return to the U.S., he entered a surgical residency in Akron, Ohio. The Board of Missions then sent him to Rotifunk, Sierra Leone, to establish a surgical program. During this period, Dr. Gess became aware of the many people who were blind because of cataracts. In 1960, he was accepted into the ophthalmology residency programs at Washington University School of Medicine and the University of Minnesota Department of Ophthalmology. To be near his aging parents, he trained at the University of Minnesota. In 1964, he returned to Sierra Leone and established an eye program at Taiama. In 1967, he went to Bismarck, North Dakota, and worked for the Quain and Ramstad Clinic as an ophthalmologist. Further postgraduate ophthalmological training was done in 1969 at Harvard.

The General Board of Global Ministries of the United Methodist Church renewed Dr. and Mrs. Gess' missionary appointment in 1972. They were assigned to an eye ministry in Bo, Sierra Leone, for a three-year period. He returned to private practice in Alexandria, Minnesota, and since that time has served the church in Sierra Leone as a volunteer medical missionary. During this period, an eye program was established and a new hospital was constructed by the General

Board of Global Ministries – the Kissy UMC Eye Hospital – to serve the eye needs in Sierra Leone.

Dr. Gess has been actively involved in the latest advances in the ophthalmological field, including intraocular lens implantation. He has designed and copyrighted his own intraocular lens. The program at the Kissy UMC Eye Hospital has made available this advanced surgical technology to the people in West Africa.

He has published the following papers:

1. "Onchocerciasis in Sierra Leone, Africa," *The Sierra Leone Medical and Dental Bulletin*, Jan. 1974, Vol. 1 No. 2, pages 57-60.
2. "Granulomatous Dacyoadenitis Caused by Schistosoma Haematobium," *Archives of Ophthalmology*, Feb. 1977, Vol. 95, pages 278-280, Jakobiec, Gess, Zimmerman.
3. "Scleral Fixation for Intraocular Lenses," *American Intraocular Implant Society Journal*, Fall 1983, Vol. 9 No. 4, Pages 453-456.
4. "Trabeculectomy with Iridencleisis," *British Journal of Ophthalmology*, Vol. 69, No. 12, pages 881-885, Dec. 1985.

Dr. Gess delivered the third article listed above at the annual meeting of the American Intraocular Implant Society in New Orleans in 1983. He delivered the fourth article at the annual meeting of the Welsh Cataract Surgical and Intraocular Lens Congress in Houston in 1980, and an updated version at the International Congress of Ophthalmologists in Cairo, Egypt, in February 1984.

Dr. Gess is an honorary member of the Lions and Rotary Clubs. He received the "Service to Mankind Award" from the Alexandria Sertoma Club in 1979, a Doctor of Humane Letters from Westmar College in 1985, the order of the Rokel for Distinguished Service from the Republic of Sierra Leone in 1991, a Distinguished Citizen Award from Macalester College in 1992, the Outstanding Achievement Award from the Vision Foundation of the University of Minnesota's Department of Ophthalmology in 1992, a Distinguished Humanitarian Service Award from the American Academy of Ophthalmology in 1993, the Alumni Achievement Award from Washington University School of Medicine in 1996, the Distinguished Alumni Award in 1999 from Garrett-Evangelical Theological Seminary, and the 2001 Christian Ophthalmology Society J. Lawton Smith Award.

Dr. Gess is an ordained minister and member of the Minnesota Conference of the United Methodist Church. He serves as an interpreter of the mission outreach of the church. He also serves the people of Sierra Leone as a volunteer ophthalmologist at the Kissy UMC Eye Hospital in Freetown. In recent years, he has taught and demonstrated surgery for extracapsular cataract extractions with intraocular lens implantation in Sierra Leone, Ghana, Nigeria, Kenya, Zambia, Zimbabwe, Mozambique, Malawi, Bolivia, Honduras, Haiti, Vietnam, China and Mongolia.

Few joys match those that people experience when they are delivered from blindness.

"Inasmuch as you have done it unto one of the least of these my brethren, you have done it unto me." – Matthew 25:40

Gess Family History

Michael Fredrick Gess was born October 4, 1828, in Sandow (or Sandolo), Germany. He married Johanna Caroline Schultz on April 1, 1854. They came to America on the ship *Gerhardt* sailing from Schonwerder, Prussia, which arrived June 9, 1856. They settled in Juda, Green County, Wisconsin. There were four children in the family: John (June 29, 1856); Ernestine (May 5,1858); Frank (September 28, 1855 – Lowell's grandfather); and Mary (March 22, 1861). Johanna Caroline died during Mary's birth. His subsequent marriage to Ernestine Wilhelmine Strutz (Minnie) produced six more children: Wilhelmine, Rachel, Amelia, Gustav, William and George.

The family moved to a farm north of Paynesville, Minnesota, around 1866. Upon Michael's death on January 20, 1908, a large tombstone was placed in the southwest corner of the Salem cemetery. Individual headstones mark the actual gravesites of Michael and Minnie, and the death of two infants. Alongside are the markers of Lowell and Ruth Gess as well as markers for Ruth's parents, George Ray Bradley and Myrtle Esther Clegg Bradley.

Frank Gess married Mary Knoble, whose parents immigrated to America from Switzerland. Their children were Alma, Arlie, Freda and Arthur.

Arthur Edgar Gess (born September 4, 1895 – died February 15, 1988) took over the farm and on July 11, 1915 married Frances Emma Wolf (born September 1, 1895 – died April 25, 1983). Their children were June Eloise Gess (born June 17, 1919 – died 1999), and Lowell Gess (born July 13, 1921).

On December 29, 1945, Lowell married Ruth Adabelle Bradley, a native of Winnipeg, Canada, whom Lowell had met while in seminary. They were blessed with six children: Timothy, Mary, Elizabeth, John, Paul and Andrew.

All six of our children were present for Ruth's committal service at the Salem cemetary.

Wolf Family History

Paul George Wolf was born in Kitzinger, Bavaria, Germany, in 1815. He married Elizabeth Vogel of Markstaft, Bavaria, Germany. They immigrated to the United States by way of Quebec and the Great Lakes, and settled in Wheeling, Lake County, Illinois, with their three oldest children.

Eight years later, with their then seven children, they joined two other families in making the trip to Minnesota. These were the Adam Knopf Sr. and the Christian Erb families. These three families named the township Wheeling, as it was still unnamed when they arrived. They brought with them seventy-five head of cattle. These were made to ford the Mississippi River while their wagons and other supplies crossed on a ferry near Winona.

They all took homesteads in Rice County. The Wolf family put up a corral in what is now the Nerstrand State Park to hold their share of the cattle. Their cabin was erected west of Waterfall Road.

It is of interest to know that this wooded area stayed in the family until it was sold back to the Federal Government. A change was later made whereby the state took this in exchange for other wooded areas in the northern part of the state.

The next year they settled on the farm. (It was still in the family and operated by Dewey Wolf, a great-grandson at the time my mother wrote some genealogical notes in 1955. It was then owned by Lowell Gess until it was passed on to Timothy Gess around 2000.) Paul G. Wolf, however, did not live long at this new home. Like the other pioneers he also had to clear the land. In doing this, at the age of forty-one, he was fatally injured when a falling tree hit a branch that snapped back, killing him as the blow hit his head. At the time of his death, Elizabeth, the youngest child, was only two years old. Since there were no cemeteries at that time burial was made in the grove near their home. It now has a head stone.

The task of helping care for the family fell to fifteen-year-old John B. It was with him and his family that his wife, Elizabeth, continued to make her home until her death in 1893.

Other members of the family were Barbara (Mrs. George Knopf); Mike, who died in the Civil War; Conrad; Sally (Mrs. John Bosshardt); Mary (Mrs. Martin Gagststetter); and Elizabeth (Mrs. Emil Rehnke). At the time (1955) of this article about a century after the arrival of the Paul Wolfs, there are thirteen surviving grandchildren of the original thirty-two. There are about seventy great-grandchildren, over one hundred great-great-grandchildren, and about sixty great-great-great- grandchildren among the descendents.

Index

(c) Refers to photos within the color section of book.

H

Repeat Surgery After Thirty-Seven Years

Fatu after her cataract operation and IOL implantation.

While I was changing the dressing of an elderly patient who had undergone a cataract extraction with intraocular lens implantation the day before, the patient turned her head and looked into my eyes with the joy of newly restored sight. "You don't recognize me," she said demurely with a winsome smile. "Thirty-seven years ago when I could not deliver my baby, you helped with an operation."

In the following moments the events were reconstructed. It was in the middle of the night in 1957 that I attended the patient who was now sitting before me. Following a prolonged labor in a nearby village she was brought to Rotifunk hospital to have a Caesarean section.

"That baby boy you delivered had the opportunity to go to school and presently is a professor at Fourah Bay College. His name is Lowell," she said.

That I had been involved in two such different operations begs explanation.

Following the four years at Washington University School of Medicine and a year's rotating internship at Ancker Hospital in St. Paul, Minnesota, Ruth, a registered nurse, and I were appointed as medical missionaries to Bambur, Nigeria.

Surgical procedures were done almost daily during those first three years of our missionary service. On an extended furlough of two years, I took a surgical residency at Akron General Hospital. Knowing a little more about general surgery, I returned to West Africa, this time to Rotifunk, Sierra Leone. It was then that this patient had been assisted in the birth of her baby.

During the three years at Rotifunk, the number of blind people in need of care overwhelmed us. An ophthalmologist could not be found. The General Board of Global Ministries of the United Methodist Church inquired if I would be interested in addressing this need. Following a three year residency in ophthalmology at the University of Minnesota, we were back in Rotifunk providing eye care but also performing occasional surgical procedures such as incarcerated herniorrhaphies and Caesarean sections.

It had been thirty-seven years between these two operations. During those years, tens of thousands of people had been served, representing meningitis epidemics, the cruel curse of malaria, parasitic diseases, overwhelming infections, malnutrition and countless surgical emergencies and elective procedures. Of the 30,000 surgeries performed, more than half were on the eye.

In times of reflection, Ruth and I realized that many of these people may not have survived had we not responded to the missionary call to serve in that needy part of the world. We were always grateful for our health and counted it a privilege to be able to minister to others in their time of need, for we held in our hands the wonderful remedy for their illness and blindness. We praise God for allowing us to share these earthly blessings and ultimately the spiritual blessings of a new life in Jesus Christ, the author and finisher of our faith, who admonishes us in the Beatitudes (Matthew 5:16) to "Let your light shine before men, that they may see your good deeds and praise your Father in heaven."